3rd (Auckland) Mounted Rifles

4th (Waikato) Mounted Rifles

7th (Southland) Mounted Rifles

8th (South Canterbury) Mounted Rifles

11th (North Auckland) Mounted Rifles

12th (Otago) Mounted Rifles

ECHOES OF GALLIPOLI

ECHOES OF GALLIPOLI

IN THE WORDS OF NEW ZEALAND'S MOUNTED RIFLEMEN

TERRY KINLOCH

Foreword by the Rt Hon. Helen Clark

EXISLE
PUBLISHING

First published 2005

Exisle Publishing Limited,
P.O. Box 60-490, Titirangi, Auckland 1230.
www.exisle.co.nz

National Library of New Zealand Cataloguing-in-Publication Data
Kinloch, Terry, 1958-
Echoes of Gallipoli : In the words of New Zealand's
Mounted Riflemen / by Terry Kinloch.
Includes bibliographical references and index.
ISBN 0-908988-60-5
1. New Zealand. Army. New Zealand Mounted Rifles.
2. World War, 1914-1918—Campaigns—Turkey—Gallipoli Peninsula.
I. Title.
940.41293—dc 22

This book is published with the assistance of a grant from the History Group of the Ministry for Culture and Heritage.

Text design and production by *BookNZ*
Cover design by Dexter Fry
Printed in China through Colorcraft Ltd., H.K.

Dedicated to
New Zealand's mounted riflemen

Contents

Acknowledgements

I would like to thank the following people: Chris Pugsley, Glyn Harper and Ian McGibbon, ONZM, for their advice and guidance, and for reviewing the draft manuscript; Colonel Mark Wheeler and Lieutenant Colonel Paul van den Broek (New Zealand Army) for reviewing the draft manuscript; the late Bill Meldrum for his support and for granting me permission to quote from his father's records; the Chief of Army, Major General Jerry Mateparae, ONZM, for funding the maps and the photographs; Ian Watt at Exisle Publishing for taking a chance with an unknown author; Douglas Thwaites of the Australian War Memorial, Blair Gatehouse of Oxford University Press (Australia) and Andrew Caldwell of 'New Zealand Geographic' for permission to publish maps; Dolores Ho at the Kippenberger Military Archive, Army Memorial Museum in Waiouru; Bruce Ralston and Diane Gordon at the Auckland War Memorial Museum Library; Gillian Tasker at the Wanganui District Library; Jocelyn Chalmers at the Alexander Turnbull Library; Carolyn Carr and her patient staff at the Defence Library, Wellington; Ann Edmonds and Julie Molina at the Trentham Camp Library; Greg Bradley; Walter Guttery at Personnel Archives, Headquarters New Zealand Defence Force; the staff of the Commonwealth War Graves Commission, especially Alex Sutherland, Ilhan Bettemir and Maureen Annetts; and lastly, my wife Carol, for reviewing the manuscript, collating the casualty database, accompanying me to Gallipoli and to the Commonwealth War Graves Commission cemeteries in Egypt and Turkey, and for accepting the many long hours at the computer that this task has demanded of me. I would also like to thank everyone who granted me permission to publish photographs and excerpts from diaries, letters and interview transcripts. For those copyright holders I was unable to locate, I trust that the material quoted meets with your approval.

Foreword

The New Zealand Mounted Rifles Brigade

This book tells the story of the New Zealand Mounted Rifles Brigade and its service in the Gallipoli campaign. As we look back, almost 90 years later, we reflect on what was a terrible but hugely significant episode in our history. The service and the immense sacrifice of the brigade along with the rest of the New Zealanders in that campaign has developed a special meaning. It was at Gallipoli that we New Zealanders began to develop our own unique identity.

I visited Gallipoli in both 1995 and 2000 for significant anniversaries of the Anzac landings. I toured the battlefields and in 2000 saw the grave of my great-uncle, Frank Clark, a trooper in the New Zealand Mounted Rifles Brigade, who was killed at Hill 60 in August 1915.

My great-uncle and his colleagues came ashore into a war few of them could have ever imagined before they left New Zealand. One New Zealand soldier wounded at Chunuk Bair described it as 'hell'. He said it was 'utterly lonely and hopeless. Bursting shells all around, confusion all around too. War at its worst!' This was the everyday experience of ordinary soldiers at Gallipoli.

My great-uncle wrote home from Hill 60 on 21 August that: 'there are stray bullets flying everywhere and one stands a chance of "stopping one" at any time. Our sergeant was standing in our trench yesterday and he got one in the right breast.' He wrote further: 'the big guns from land and sea make an awful row and this is accompanied always with machine guns and rifle fire. We can hear the shells screaming overhead and the shrapnel bursting all day long.' He died seven days later.

Of 8556 New Zealand soldiers who served on the Gallipoli peninsula, 2721 died and 4752 were wounded. The suffering of their families was great too. For a small country, with a population in 1915 of only some one million people, this was a human tragedy on an unprecedented scale which affected almost every New Zealand family.

The men of the New Zealand Mounted Rifles Brigade played an important role and this book tells their tale. It will help to preserve their experiences for generations of future New Zealanders. Lest we forget.

Helen Clark
Prime Minister

Introduction

These New Zealanders and Australians and, best of all, the Australian Light Horse and the New Zealand Mounted Rifles, and above all the last named, are the flower of our troops or of any other troops in the world.

General Sir Ian Hamilton

The magnificent brigade of New Zealand Mounted Rifles … had been worked until it was almost entirely consumed.

Charles Bean

ON THE HOT AND sunny afternoon of Sunday 8 August 1915, 248 men belonging to the Auckland regiment of the New Zealand Mounted Rifles (NZMR) Brigade crept up Rhododendron Ridge and joined the survivors of the Wellington Infantry Battalion on Chunuk Bair, a hilltop on the Gallipoli peninsula in Turkey. On the way up the ridge they passed the scattered bodies of many dead and dying New Zealanders, victims of Turkish artillery and machine gun fire. The Aucklanders barely had time to clear the shallow trenches of the many dead and wounded Wellington infantrymen before they faced the first of many fierce Turkish bayonet attacks. For the rest of the day they were subjected to showers of hand grenades and relentless artillery, rifle and machine gun fire. They gave as good as they got, catching and throwing back live grenades (they had few of their own), shooting down charging Turks at ranges of a few metres and climbing out of their trenches to conduct their own desperate bayonet charges whenever the Turks got too close. When there were no grenades to throw back, they dug stones out of the trench wall with their bayonets and threw them at the Turks. What little water they had soon ran out, and the sun beat down on them mercilessly. Men were killed and wounded with every passing minute.

The fighting eased off a little at sunset, and at 10.30 that night the New Zealanders on Chunuk Bair were reinforced again. Among the new arrivals this time were 173 more mounted riflemen, this time belonging to the Wellington regiment of the NZMR Brigade.

When the sun rose the next morning the ferocious battle picked up where it had left off the night before. On 9 August the New Zealanders on Chunuk Bair suffered what Cecil Malthus described as 'an ordeal even more intense and dreadful than Malone's men had endured [the day before]. Bombed, shelled, sniped, raked with machine-gun fire, suffering extremely from thirst, they utterly refused to be dislodged, but they could only get some relief from time to time by getting out and charging with the bayonet, or catching the Turkish bombs [grenades] and hurling them back. And all day the sun blazed down on their agony.'[1] Many of the wounded men who crawled out of the front line died before they could reach the medical stations in the valleys. Stretcher bearers and medics could not help because many of them were dead or wounded themselves.

A few more reinforcements and a little ammunition reached the front line during the day, while the Turkish attacks diminished gradually. During the night of 8–9 August the exhausted New Zealanders were relieved by two British infantry battalions. Only 22 Auckland and 73 Wellington mounted riflemen walked off the hill unaided. The next morning an unstoppable Turkish attack overwhelmed the newly arrived British defenders and took back Chunuk Bair.

The capture of Chunuk Bair and its adjacent hilltops by the MEF (Mediterranean Expeditionary Force, an Allied coalition of British, Australian, New Zealand, Indian and French troops) in August 1915 was supposed to break the back of the Turkish defence on Gallipoli and force the Turks to withdraw from the peninsula. This would allow the ships of the Royal Navy to sail through the Dardanelles without interference and threaten Turkey's capital city of Constantinople (modern Istanbul). It was confidently expected that this would be enough to force Turkey out of the First World War. None of these glorious goals came close to being achieved. Nonetheless, its part in the fight to hold Chunuk Bair on 8 and 9 August 1915 is one of the great achievements of the New Zealand Mounted Rifles Brigade. It came at a terrible cost. The NZMR Brigade was 1900 strong on 5 August 1915.[2] During the fighting, 500 reinforcements arrived, bringing the total strength of the brigade to 2400 men. Six days later, the brigade had lost nearly 700 men, 200 of whom were dead.

New Zealand's mounted riflemen had one more ordeal to endure in late August. While the other exhausted survivors of Chunuk Bair were rested, the NZMR Brigade lost another 236 men, killed in two futile attempts to capture an insignificant knoll called Hill 60. When the brigade was finally pulled out of the firing line in September and sent away from Gallipoli for two months' rest, fewer than 250 men paraded. The others were dead, missing, in hospital to recover from wounds or sickness, or already on their way home, unfit for further service.

Heavily reinforced, the brigade returned to the peninsula in early November, but six weeks later it was evacuated along with everyone else in December 1915, when the MEF finally admitted defeat.

When nearly 2500 New Zealand mounted riflemen signed up to serve King and Country in August 1914, at the start of what became the First World War, the only fight going was that against the Imperial German Army in France and Belgium. Turkey was not in the war at all, and none of the New Zealanders had ever heard of a place called Gallipoli. Nine weeks later, these men and their horses, together forming the New Zealand Mounted Rifles Brigade and the separate Otago Mounted Rifles Regiment, left New Zealand as part of the Main Body of the New Zealand Expeditionary Force (NZEF). The NZEF was supposed to sail to England, where it would be incorporated into the British Army and finish its training. After that the New Zealanders would go to France and Belgium to fight the Germans on the Western Front. This was confidently expected to be a short, sharp scrap, with British victory as the inevitable outcome. Instead, seven months after leaving New Zealand, the volunteer horsemen would be fighting for their lives, without their horses, against the Turkish Army at Gallipoli.[3]

In November 1914, while the convoy carrying the NZEF (and the Australian Imperial Force, or AIF) was crossing the Indian Ocean, Turkey joined the war on Germany's side. The Australians and New Zealanders disembarked in Egypt in early December to help defend the Suez Canal against Turkish attack. After three months of boring training, most of the NZEF and the AIF (together known by now as the Anzacs) were earmarked for combat, but not on the Western Front. Instead they were allocated to the MEF, whose task it was to invade the Gallipoli peninsula in Turkey.

The horsemen of the NZMR Brigade were left behind when the initial landings took place at Gallipoli on 25 April 1915. Three weeks later, with the invasion stalled and casualties soaring, three of New Zealand's four mounted rifles regiments were called forward to Gallipoli as infantry, leaving their precious horses behind in Egypt. It was not the kind of fighting the mounted men had expected or trained for, but they were willing to do their bit in the trenches for a few months until the Turks on Gallipoli were beaten, as they surely would be. After that, they confidently expected to return to their horses and finish the war on horseback.

Fifteen hundred New Zealand mounted riflemen landed at Anzac Cove after dark on 12 May 1915. The next day Trooper William Hay became the first battle casualty in the brigade, when he was mistakenly killed by a nervous New Zealand sentry. Most of the mounted riflemen took over front-line trenches on Walker's Top, where they were surrounded by the decomposing corpses of Anzacs and Turks killed since the initial landings on 25 April.

After just one week ashore, many of the mounted riflemen had their first taste of full-scale trench warfare when 40,000 Turks attacked all along the Anzac front line on 19 May. The New Zealanders played a key role in fighting off the attack at Walker's Top. Thousands of brave Turkish infantrymen were killed by Anzac machine gun and artillery fire. One hundred and sixty Anzacs, including 27 mounted riflemen, also lost their lives. Five days later, 3000 dead Turks and a few hundred Anzacs were buried in the only armistice to take place on Gallipoli.

Late in May the Otago regiment arrived at Gallipoli and was attached to the NZMR Brigade, where it remained for the rest of the campaign.

On 28 May a squadron of the Canterbury regiment captured a new Turkish trench a few hundred metres inland from No. 2 Outpost. The Turks counter-attacked fiercely, and the entire brigade was called upon to rescue the besieged defenders. This ill-conceived attack cost the lives of another 23 mounted riflemen.

By the end of May, General Sir Ian Hamilton, the MEF commander, realised that his force was still stuck and going nowhere fast. A new plan was needed to break the deadlock on Gallipoli. A series of bold reconnaissance patrols by New Zealand mounted riflemen in the Sari Bair hills to the north of the Anzac position showed that this lightly defended area offered potential for a breakout. Hamilton's new offensive duly took place here in August 1915. It would be his last chance to secure victory on Gallipoli.

June and July were relatively quiet months, as the necessary reinforcements made their way to Gallipoli from England. While they watched and waited for something to happen, the Anzacs gradually grew weak and dispirited as disease, poor food, ceaseless work and constant stress sapped their strength and their morale. By August many of the Main Body men were gone – dead, or evacuated sick or wounded.

On the night of 6 August the men of the NZMR Brigade successfully carried out the opening moves of the breakout. In a series of well-planned silent attacks, made without any covering fire and with unloaded rifles, they captured six Turkish positions in the foothills of the Sari Bair range and helped to clear the way for Australian, Indian and New Zealand infantry brigades to climb up to Chunuk Bair and the other hilltops of the Sari Bair hills. These follow-on attacks were largely unsuccessful, but Lieutenant Colonel William Malone's Wellington Infantry Battalion did gain a foothold on Chunuk Bair before dawn on 8 August. The Turks attacked ferociously, and reinforcements were needed almost immediately. The Auckland and Wellington mounted rifles regiments answered the call.

The Gallipoli campaign destroyed the original New Zealand Mounted Rifles Brigade and the Otago Mounted Rifles Regiment. Half of the 4000 mounted riflemen who served on Gallipoli died or were wounded (727 and 1239 respectively).[4] Before September, almost everyone was also sick at some stage. The mounted riflemen who fought the rest of the war on horseback from 1916 until late in 1918 were, in most cases, not the same men who landed on Gallipoli in May 1915.

Gallipoli is the most famous First World War battlefield outside the Western Front. It was an expensive failure. Half of the nearly one million men who fought there on both sides were killed or wounded. It is not my intention, in this book, to address the full scope of the Gallipoli campaign, or to comment on the reasons for its ultimate failure. Both subjects have been covered many times (perhaps too many times) already. Nor is it my intention to retell the story of all of the New Zealanders who fought on Gallipoli. Dr Chris Pugsley has already done us that service with his *Gallipoli: The New Zealand Story*. This book will tell the story of the men of the New Zealand Mounted Rifles Brigade, from their mobilisation in New Zealand in August 1914 until their evacuation from Gallipoli in December of the following year. In doing so, I do not seek to diminish the contributions and losses of the other New Zealanders and the other nationalities that fought on Gallipoli. Their stories have been told, or will be, by others.

The narrative is built around the regimental war diaries and the letters, diaries and interview transcripts of more than 40 mounted riflemen who were there. Many of these personal recollections have not been published before now.

As the opening quote exemplifies, the New Zealand Mounted Rifles Brigade was considered by many to be one of the best, if not the best, brigade on the peninsula.[5] More recently, Pugsley described it as 'one of the finest fighting bodies that New Zealand has ever raised'.[6] Despite this praise, and the fact that over 17,700 New Zealanders served in the ranks of the NZMR Brigade during the First World War, its story is almost entirely unknown today. Dr Glyn Harper, another eminent New Zealand military historian, stated recently that the history of New Zealand's involvement in the First World War has not yet been given the coverage that it deserves.[7] The aim of this book, and the one that will follow it, is to correct that deficiency for the men of the New Zealand Mounted Rifles Brigade.

Originally this book was to be part of a larger work covering the entire First World War, but so much material was available that the decision was made to split the subject into two parts. This book will therefore be followed by another telling the story of New Zealand's mounted riflemen from 1916 until their return home in mid-1919.

The telling of their story comes too late for the men of our First World War mounted rifles regiments, for they are all gone now. Most of those who lost their lives during or immediately after the Gallipoli campaign lie in Turkey or Egypt. Some are buried in neat Commonwealth War Graves Commission (CWGC) cemeteries in Turkey, but many more are commemorated on memorial walls, for their bodies were buried at sea, lost or never identified. Others are buried on Lemnos Island and Malta, or in Gibraltar, England or New Zealand. This book contains no 'Roll of Honour', listing all those men who died or were wounded. To my mind, such casualty lists imply that those men who were neither killed nor wounded are somehow less deserving of honourable mention. Ideally, a 'Roll of Honour' should list the names of every one of the New Zealanders who served in Egypt or at Gallipoli. Such a list is impracticable, yet anything less is inadequate.

It is difficult to really understand the Gallipoli campaign without visiting the peninsula. If you ever have the chance, visit the battlefield and the little cemeteries all over it. You will be made welcome by our former enemies, and the New Zealanders whose bones lie there would thank you, if they could.

Prologue

*It cannot be too frequently impressed upon all ranks of mounted rifles
that they are in no sense cavalry. They are only intended to fight on
foot; their horses enabling them to make longer and more rapid movements
than the infantry soldier.*

NEW ZEALAND VOLUNTEER FORCE MANUAL FOR MOUNTED RIFLES, 1895

*I have served in war already with New Zealand Mounted Rifles …
and I should esteem myself lucky indeed if ever I had the good
fortune to encounter Continental Cavalry in reasonably broken ground
with them at my right hand.*

GENERAL IAN HAMILTON, 1914

THE NEW ZEALAND MOUNTED Rifles Brigade was both the biggest and the last horse-mounted fighting force to be sent to war by the New Zealand Government. Its genesis was in the colonial cavalry troops of the New Zealand Wars (1845–72), which evolved into the mounted rifles contingents that served with distinction in the Boer War between 1899 and 1902. Between that war and the First World War, New Zealand refined the concept of an expeditionary force of troops that would be available to serve overseas in the defence of the British Empire. The first test of the government's plans came in 1914, when New Zealand went to war against Germany, Austria-Hungary and Turkey.

No British cavalry units took part in the New Zealand Wars, but dozens of cavalry units raised by settlers did. Their weapon of choice was the sword, followed by the revolver and carbine, and their preferred tactical role was shock action – charging on horseback into enemy cavalry, destroying them with swords. Colonial cavalry units were active in all but the earliest campaigns of the wars, but it was almost always in the secondary and rather demeaning roles of reconnaissance, liaison and convoy escort. Opportunities for mounted shock action were few and far between.

The colonial cavalrymen longed to catch an enemy force on open and reasonably flat ground. With no cavalry of their own, Maori sensibly avoided such terrain. They stood a much better chance against the British and their colonial allies by fighting from prepared defensive positions that were inaccessible to cavalry. Against such tactics, the colonial cavalry could do little more than provide early warning for the infantry, scout the enemy positions and be prepared to pursue a retreating Maori force if the opportunity arose. Withdrawing defenders, fleeing on foot across open or even moderately difficult ground, were easy prey for cavalry. Maori leaving a battlefield usually chose routes that were too rough for mounted pursuit, but not always. Cavalry units conducted small-scale cavalry charges against fleeing Maori on foot at Rangiaowhia, Orakau, Te Rangi and Opotiki, in each case inflicting casualties with their swords. European accounts of these actions claim that they engendered in the Maori 'a wholesome dread of the Cavalry'.[1] New Zealand's colonial cavalrymen did not always confine their attention to armed opponents. On several occasions unarmed, wounded or surrendering men, women and children were cut down by sword-wielding troopers, leading to well-founded allegations that atrocities were being committed by cavalrymen.[2]

In 1885 all of New Zealand's Volunteer Force cavalry units were turned into mounted rifles units. This was much more than just a name change, as the New Zealand Volunteer Force Manual for Mounted Rifles makes clear. 'It cannot be too frequently impressed upon all ranks of mounted rifles that they are in no sense cavalry. They are only intended to fight on foot; their horses enabling them to make longer and more rapid movements than the infantry soldier.'[3] Because mounted charges into enemy cavalry were no longer required of them, the horsemen did not need swords or lances. Mounted riflemen had the same mobility as cavalry, but, because they dismounted out of direct fire range, they were much less vulnerable. New Zealand's mounted troops still required 'all the *élan*, dash and spirit of Cavalry, but [they] trained to fight dismounted'.[4]

The 1895 manual listed the duties of mounted rifles units as the provision of picquets, patrols and scouts; the capturing and holding of advanced positions until infantry could arrive; the rapid reinforcement of infantry; and rapid movements against the flanks or lines of communication of an enemy force.[5] Clearly, mounted riflemen were no longer considered to be 'real' cavalry. Equally clear, though, was the distinction between mounted rifles and mounted infantry. A mounted rifleman was a horseman who was trained to fight on foot, but also to carry out some of the other cavalry functions, such as reconnaissance and screening. A mounted infantryman was no horseman. He rode a horse when he had to, but he fought on foot, and did not undertake reconnaissance or any other cavalry role. Mounted riflemen thus fitted in between cavalry and mounted infantry, performing some of the secondary roles of cavalry, but fighting on foot.

As the nineteenth century ended, the primary duty of New Zealand's Volunteer Force was the protection of the country from invasion. At the same time, there was a growing belief in government circles that New Zealand, as a colony reaping the benefits of belonging to the British Empire, should be prepared to repay that debt by assisting the Empire militarily whenever and wherever its interests were threatened. New Zealand's commitment of troops to the Boer War (referred to hereafter as the South African War) just before the turn of the century was the first demonstration of this new trend in foreign policy.

In 1899 New Zealand sent its first troops overseas in the name of Imperial solidarity, when it despatched the first of 10 Volunteer Force mounted rifles contingents to South Africa. This war was the culmination of years of increasing tension between the British and the Boer descendants of the first Dutch settlers in South Africa. In 1877 the British in South Africa annexed the adjacent Boer republic of Transvaal. Nine years later, the discovery of gold in the Transvaal led to a large influx of mainly British immigrants, who were discriminated against by the Boers. Negotiation achieved nothing, and in October 1899 the British went to war with the Boers in Transvaal and the neighbouring Orange Free State.

Mounted troops were needed to keep up with the mobile and elusive Boers, and New Zealand sent 6500 mounted riflemen and 8000 horses to southern Africa. Most of the men, especially in the early contingents, came from Volunteer Force mounted rifles units. Two hundred and thirty New Zealanders died from wounds or disease during the war. Many horses also died from sickness, and only one New Zealand horse returned home from South Africa. The mismanagement of horses by the British Army in South Africa was a scandal: 400,000 horses, mules and donkeys died needlessly from malnutrition, disease and overwork.[6] New Zealand's horses were similarly affected, but not because their riders were negligent. The New Zealanders did have a lot to learn about how to keep their horses fit and healthy, but the major causes of the high losses were the lack of time for newly arrived horses to acclimatise before they were committed to long treks, not enough good food and water, punishing work rates with inadequate rest and the poor performance of the British veterinary service, upon which the New Zealanders also relied.

The employment of New Zealand's mounted rifles contingents in South Africa differed markedly from that laid down in pre-war doctrine. The conflict was largely one of movement across large distances. The Boers rode their tough little horses everywhere, and British infantrymen on foot could not catch them, or even keep up with them. Before long, instead of supporting them, British and colonial mounted troops replaced the infantry as the major combat force.

Despite very limited training and inadequate equipment, the New Zealanders performed creditably in their first foray into Imperial warfare. Senior British commanders described the New Zealand rank and file in glowing terms, emphasising their good horsemanship, use of ground and native cunning. They were also noted for their ability to look after themselves, with little guidance required from their superior officers, and for their discipline. Some New Zealand officers were less well regarded, and it was generally held that New Zealand troopers under British commanders performed the best. Field Marshal Lord Wolseley, the Commander-in-Chief of the British Army, went so far as to rate the New Zealanders ahead of any mounted troops in Europe, including those of his own army.[7]

Before the South African War, the Volunteer Force mounted units considered themselves to be a cut above the rest of the force and this self-confidence grew during the conflict. The New Zealand public was also impressed by the performance of the mounted riflemen in South Africa. The 'belief that the colonial fighting man was adaptable, good on a horse and adept with a rifle had been inculcated in the national psyche by the exploits of New Zealand's contingents'.[8]

Many of the older men who served in the ranks of the NZMR Brigade in the First World War first gained operational experience in South Africa. Friendships, based on mutual professional respect, that were formed with British and Australian commanders would pay rich dividends 15 years later.

British Imperial defence policy in the years before the First World War was based on three principles. The first line of defence for the Empire as a whole was provided by the Royal Navy. In return for its protection, the countries of the Empire were responsible for the defence of their own shores, and they also had to be prepared to contribute fighting forces for Imperial service overseas.[9] Their impressive performance in South Africa secured mounted riflemen a place in any future New Zealand contribution to

Imperial fights. When New Zealand passed legislation in 1900 to establish an 'Imperial and Colonial Reserve Force' from the Volunteer Force, available for deployment anywhere in the world, it consisted of artillerymen and 1000 mounted riflemen. A later British suggestion for a permanent deployable colonial force recommended that the force should be made up of mounted riflemen.[10]

The Volunteer Force was the only resource from which to draw a New Zealand expeditionary force for service overseas. Unfortunately, however, it was no longer a credible military force by anyone's standards. After a brief surge of enthusiasm during and after the South African War, numbers in the Volunteer Force were in steady decline by 1910. Personnel turnover was very high, and the attendance at training of those still in the force was unsatisfactory.[11] Many of the officers and non-commissioned officers (NCOs) were elected to office, often on the basis of their popularity and local standing rather than their military knowledge or experience. Units were sometimes commanded (and outfitted) by local worthies with little military background but a fine eye for what constituted an impressive uniform. Discipline was often lax, and decisions were usually reached by democratic consensus. The Volunteer Force was equipped with a hotchpotch of old-fashioned and worn-out weapons. Most Volunteers served in the glamorous combat units (infantry, mounted rifles and artillery), while the less popular but vital supporting units (supply, engineers, signallers, transport and medical) were poorly manned and badly equipped. There was no consistent structure: units were often organised and trained according to the whims of local commanders. Most seriously, there was no systematic training to establish and maintain standards across the force. With various small Volunteer Force units scattered across the country, there was a need for large-scale exercises to bring them together for combined training, but this rarely happened. 'Squadrons, about sixty strong, as a rule went to camp separately, and it was the exception for two or three of them to assemble at a so-called regimental camp.'[12] This meant that officers seldom had the opportunity to practise commanding their units in combination with the other arms and services.

As long as the Volunteer Force was not expected to front up and fight in a 'serious' overseas war, many of these problems did not matter too much. New Zealand's success in South Africa appeared to prove that the lightly trained and part-time Volunteer Force was quite good enough to fight alongside British Imperial forces overseas, but more thoughtful New Zealand and British leaders saw the South African War as an anomaly, fought against an amateur, irregular and third-rate enemy that did not play by the rules. The 'dangers of pitting inadequately trained amateurs against the regular forces of a major power were fully recognised'.[13] A war against a major Continental power such as Germany would certainly be a much more serious proposition, and to take part in it Imperial forces would need to be highly capable. That demanded compatible doctrine, training, equipment and structures, and high professional standards across the Empire. In 1909, New Zealand, Canada and Australia agreed to develop and maintain expeditionary forces for use in overseas Imperial emergencies if required. Implicit in this decision for New Zealand was the abolition of the Volunteer Force, which had come to the end of the road. In 1911, at British suggestion, it was replaced by the new Territorial Force.

The Territorial Force was regionally based. Military Districts based on Auckland, Wellington, Canterbury and Otago were formed, each with an 'establishment' of 7500 men. A total of 12 standardised mounted rifles regiments, 16 infantry battalions, eight artillery batteries and support units in proportion were formed from the confusing and scattered collection of Volunteer Force units. Most of the Volunteer Force officers, a 'fair proportion' of NCOs and 2000 other ranks transferred to the Territorial Force. Each new unit had a small permanent staff of instructors and administrators. New equipment scales and unit structures, based on the 'War Establishments' of the British Army, were introduced. A major re-equipment programme began, focusing first on modern artillery, machine guns and rifles. British Army training manuals were adopted. Mandatory annual training requirements were laid down, and men who failed to fulfil their duties were threatened with removal from the Territorial Force rolls. Democracy was banished, and the election of officers was replaced with a competitive commissioning process, based upon superior performance and examination results.[14]

The Territorial Force needed 30,000 men if it was to be strong enough to defend New Zealand and to play a useful part overseas. At its formation, the new force could muster only 11,000 men, so compulsory military training was introduced in order to reach and maintain the required strength. All fit European men in New Zealand were required to serve in the Territorial Force between the ages of 18 and 25, after which they were transferred to the Reserve for another five years.

In the unlikely event of an invasion force appearing offshore, the North Island of New Zealand would have been defended by a Territorial Force division based on the Manawatu Plains, with the Auckland Mounted Rifles Brigade covering Auckland from Hamilton. The South Island would have been defended by a division on the

Canterbury Plains near Christchurch, with the Otago Mounted Rifles Brigade covering Dunedin from the Taieri Plain.[15] The role of the mounted riflemen was 'to anticipate and locate any raiding party landing on our coasts, and engage it until the arrival of the less mobile troops. With this object in view every squadron in New Zealand is made acquainted with its own terrain, especially the sea front and the most direct routes to it.'[16]

Men enrolled in the Territorial Force could not be compelled to fight overseas. This meant that any expeditionary force would have to be manned by volunteers, and a clause permitting this was added to the legislation. Given the level of patriotic fervour and Imperial support that characterised New Zealand society in those innocent times, finding enough volunteers was not expected to be a problem – and it was not, at least for the first years of the First World War.

The British Army lent New Zealand Colonel Alexander Godley and a number of other British officers, warrant officers and senior NCOs to help build the Territorial Force. Godley was a keen horseman with a lot of experience commanding

and training mounted forces. He had served as Adjutant of the British Mounted Infantry before gaining operational experience with mounted troops in Africa before and during the South African War. He was offered the post of Commandant of the New Zealand Military Forces in the rank of major general. General Sir Ian Hamilton encouraged him to go to New Zealand in order to be able to work with the 'magnificent material' of New Zealand's mounted troops.[17] Godley accepted the post and quickly established the New Zealand Staff Corps and the New Zealand Permanent Staff. These professional cadres of Imperial

Alexander Godley.

23

and New Zealand officers, warrant officers and senior NCOs were distributed among the units of the Territorial Force to train and administer them.

Under Godley's vigorous leadership training began in earnest in 1911, with a rapid and ambitious progression to brigade-level camps in the summer of 1914. His aim was for 'all ranks [to] have realized … that there is more to soldiering than merely learning to drill and shoot in small bodies at local village camps'.[18] Andrew Russell, then the commander of the Wellington Mounted Rifles Brigade, was unimpressed with the 1913 camp. 'We had 1,100 mounted men in all, and except for the weather which was atrocious, all went well. The training was ludicrously inadequate. Fancy trying to go through squadron, regimental, and brigade training in ten days … I do not say we are as loosely knit as Home [British] Territorials, but we have no real cohesion. No deep-founded sense of instinctive discipline.'[19]

Godley identified three useful roles for a New Zealand expeditionary force in the event of a European war between the British Empire and Germany: they could attack Germany's colonial possessions in the Pacific, help defend the Suez Canal in Egypt from a Turkish attack (assuming that Turkey would fight the Empire at Germany's side) or fight alongside the British Army in Europe.[20] The last option was Godley's first choice, but he recommended that, in any event, New Zealand's expeditionary force should first go to Egypt, from where it could be sent to wherever the situation demanded.

In 1912 Australia and New Zealand agreed to contribute a combined force of nearly 18,000 men (11,400 Australians and 6050 New Zealanders) to the Empire if needed. New Zealand's contribution was to be based on an infantry brigade and a mounted rifles brigade. British war planners wanted to be able to slot the Australian and New Zealand forces into their own divisions under British command. The governments of Australia and New Zealand were worried about their contingents' loss of national identity under such an arrangement. Australia insisted on its men fighting together in an Australian division under Australian command. New Zealand could not and did not impose such a requirement, and agreed that its expeditionary force could fight as part of either a British or an Australian division. By the outbreak of the war, New Zealand's contribution had grown to 7500 men. Australia's contribution was to be 20,000 men in an infantry division and a light horse brigade. The plan was for New Zealand's contribution to come from the Territorial Force, with each battalion, regiment or battery providing about a quarter of its manpower initially, and sustaining this contribution for the duration of the emergency.

In 1913 there was a dress-rehearsal mobilisation for some of New Zealand's mounted riflemen. In December of that year, striking wharf workers became too much for the police to handle, and Prime Minister William Massey enrolled 200 'special constables' to guard and work the wharves and to deal with trade union demonstrations. Most of the constables were Territorial Force mounted riflemen from the country districts of New Zealand. Known as 'Massey's Cossacks', they dealt with the strikers quite brutally: 'at Wellington the Mounted Rifles ... made short work of the strikers. Mounted, and armed with stock whips, they rode through the town and not only effectively dispersed riotous gatherings but pursued the rioters into the houses, and then dealt with them in such a manner that they had little stomach for a continuance of law-breaking.'[21]

In 1914, Godley provided a good summary of the state of New Zealand's mounted riflemen immediately before the war.

With time, and more training of the commissioned and non-commissioned ranks, who are at present the weak spot in the organisation, the existing mounted rifles regiments of New Zealand will be in no way second to the first and best of the New Zealand contingents which did such good service in South Africa. ... The men are practically all drawn from country districts; few come from the towns. A large proportion of them are either shepherds or farm-hands, or are engaged in some country pursuit for which the ubiquitous motor-car or bicycle has not yet replaced the horse. Consequently ... they practically all can ride and find their way about. ... The quality of the horse-flesh varies very much in different localities, and the horses are of course in all sorts and sizes – from the racehorse brought by the jockey-boy down to the pony which, when not employed as a troop-horse, carries the children (two or three together) to and from school. But they are all handy and can get around the country, and, when not too big, are on the whole well suited for the work of mounted riflemen. ... The collection of saddles brought to camp, with a bit of sacking or a saddle-cloth put under them to take the place of stuffing, would not be an ideal equipment with which to take the field. ...[22]

A British commentator noted that New Zealand's mounted riflemen had ridden and worked with horses nearly all their lives, and were 'accustomed to hard work, and ... having had to think and act for themselves, have acquired that intelligence which, when intelligently dealt with, produces the most valuable fighting-man'.[23] According to New Zealand colonel Arthur Bauchop, 'The mounted branch of the Military Service in New Zealand is composed almost entirely of the farmer, a dweller out of towns, who owns his horse. ... The men who form this branch have, as a rule, been working and riding horses all their lives, and live with their horses quite as much as [British] Cavalry of the Line. Their methods in regard to the care of their horses in many ways are original, but the result quite justifies the means. ... Men are always found in the islands who will ride seventy to eighty miles to one of these training camps, which usually last seven to eight days.'[24]

General Ian Hamilton, the British Army's Inspector-General of the Overseas Forces, who visited New Zealand in May 1914 to assess the country's armed forces, wrote:

New Zealand is fortunate in being able to muster at a very moderate expense such a fine body of men as the Mounted Rifles. The higher commands are in capable hands, the instructors are able, and all ranks are animated with a keenness and initiative that deserve high praise. ... The squadrons move at a good pace, and come into action quickly; and they possess in a wonderful degree (considering the want of practice) that cohesion without which it is impossible to handle any considerable body of horsemen. The horses are up to weight, show some quality, and look to be in good condition; some of the units are quite remarkably well mounted ... The activity of the horses and the nerve of their riders were brought forcibly home to me by two little incidents in my inspection. On one occasion the scouts of a brigade were sent out to a flank to reconnoitre; they popped over a five-strand barbed-wire fence as if it had been a two-foot drain. Another time a troop about to advance had to be specially ordered to go through a gate instead of jumping the wire fence in front of them. ... Finally, I can only say I have served in war already with New Zealand Mounted Rifles [in the South African War], and I should esteem myself lucky indeed if ever I had the good fortune to encounter Continental [German] Cavalry in reasonably broken ground with them at my right hand.[25]

Less than a year after this report was written, New Zealand's mounted riflemen were put to the 'war test' on the hills of Gallipoli. Ironically, they would be under General Hamilton's command, but without their horses, and with not a single German cavalryman in sight.

The story of the build-up to the First World War is complex, and a detailed understanding of it is not necessary. A brief summary should give the reader an understanding of how New Zealand came to be at war with Germany, Austria-Hungary and Turkey (collectively known as the Central Powers) in 1914.

In the early years of the twentieth century, Germany was increasingly seen by statesmen in France, Russia and Great Britain as a threat to European stability and security. Germany was becoming more powerful economically and militarily, and its erratic leader, Kaiser Wilhelm II, dreamt of creating a global empire to rival that of Great Britain. The ambitious naval expansion programme the Germans launched to further this aim alarmed the British in particular. Sooner or later, they decided, the upstart German Kaiser would have to be put in his place. As the years passed it became increasingly likely that this would have to be done on European soil, not at sea, which was Britain's preference.

The leaders of Germany and its major ally Austria-Hungary knew that their military strength was at its peak in 1914. They also knew that Russia and France were catching up. If war had to come, they reasoned, better sooner rather than later. Germany was also worried that its position in central Europe made it vulnerable to attacks from France to its west and from Russia to its east. These two countries were allies, and this fuelled Germany's greatest fear, of a war on two fronts at once.

The Austro-Hungarians were concerned that the independent state of Serbia would stir up trouble in their Slav-dominated southern provinces, and they looked for an excuse to deal with the Serbs militarily before this could happen. Serbia could not defeat an Austro-Hungarian attack alone, but Russia stepped up as Serbia's guarantor.

All these factors set the stage for a major European conflict. The only thing missing was a half-decent reason for the war to begin. The trigger for the First World War was the assassination of the heir to the Austro-Hungarian throne by Bosnian extremists in Sarajevo on 28 June 1914. This gave the Austro-Hungarians the excuse they wanted to declare war on Serbia, which they accused of supporting the assassins. Russia duly mobilised its army in support of Serbia, and Germany honoured its 'blank cheque' promise by doing the same for Austria-Hungary. Once the mobilisation of these mass conscript armies had started, it proved difficult to stop. A major European conflict was in the making and, at the end of July, the British government secretly warned the governments of the Empire to expect war with Germany in the near future.[26]

On 1 August, Germany declared war on Russia, and, two days later, on France. The British initially stayed on the sidelines, but were drawn into the war when the German Army invaded Belgium (whose neutrality was guaranteed by the British) on its way to France. On 4 August 1914 Great Britain and its Empire declared war on Germany and, a week later, on Austria-Hungary as well.

On 2 August the Turks signed a Secret Treaty of Alliance with Germany. Turkey mobilised immediately 'as a precaution' but delayed making a formal declaration of war for nearly three months. The delay was due partly to the unreadiness of Turkey's army, but mostly because its leaders were not all in favour of war. The alliances linking Russia to France and Great Britain meant that when Turkey finally did declare war on Russia at the end of October, it was automatically at war with all the Allies, including the British Empire.

These distant events would have been of no more than academic interest in New Zealand, half a world away, were it not for New Zealand's loyal membership of the British Empire. This was fundamental to New Zealanders in 1914, far more so than their Commonwealth membership is today. Most white New Zealanders still considered Great Britain to be 'Home', even though only a quarter of them had been born there. In 1912 the British Foreign Secretary warned the nations of the Empire that their security would be threatened if Germany were allowed to dominate Europe. The governments in Pretoria, Canberra, Ottawa and Wellington did not dispute this assessment. Across the Empire it was agreed that Great Britain spoke for all, so when Britain declared war on Germany and Austria-Hungary, it did so with the full support of New Zealand and the rest of the Empire. 'Like most of the participants, New Zealand went to war in 1914 with immense enthusiasm. Conceived in terms of supporting the Empire, its participation was wholehearted and substantial.'[27]

1

War with Germany

One of the comic opera instructions issued ... was that all troops were to grow
moustaches to make them look older, or more ferocious, and it was difficult to keep
a straight face on parade when one of the finished products was on show.

EDWIN MCKAY

... many people had a vague idea only of what a troop horse should be.
The remount portion of the camp could show anything from a draught horse
to an unbroken outlaw.

CHARLES POWLES

ON 4 AUGUST 1914, King George V declared that a state of war existed between the British Empire and Germany. This legally committed New Zealand and the other countries of the Empire to the fight alongside Great Britain, but did not oblige them to actually send troops. That technicality did not matter in New Zealand, where the government had no intention of shirking what it saw as its Imperial duty. A military contribution was readily available from the new Territorial Force, and the population expected full support for the 'Old Country'. This enthusiasm was shaped by the New Zealand experience in the South African War (1899–1902), the only conflict most people could remember. This was recalled fondly as a great Imperial adventure, concluded successfully and at little cost in casualties. Few people yet realised that a war against massed European conscript armies equipped with machine guns and modern artillery would be a far more lethal affair.

New Zealand Prime Minister William Massey offered troops for Imperial service on 6 August. The Cabinet in London accepted the offer and asked New Zealand to send, as quickly as possible, an expeditionary force of one infantry brigade, a mounted rifles brigade, an artillery brigade and support units, totalling nearly 8500 men and 3800 horses.[1] Major General Alexander Godley was appointed to command the force. The pace of events then picked up dramatically, as the government had promised to have the entire expeditionary force on its way to Europe in the breathtakingly short time of three weeks. New Zealand did not want to miss the war, which was forecast by most commentators to be a short, sharp affair, lasting for only six months or so, 'by which time the allies would be across the Rhine'.[2]

As New Zealand prepared its forces, London decided the use to which they would be put. British Regular Army garrisons in Great Britain, India, Ireland and elsewhere were urgently required for the Western Front, but they could not be moved until they had been replaced. Also, German colonies in the Pacific and in Africa needed to be captured. Most of the members of the British Cabinet thought that the relatively untrained and inexperienced colonial forces would be suitable for either of these secondary roles, but not for the 'main event' against the German Army in France and Belgium. Herbert Asquith, the British Prime Minister, overruled them and decided that the Australian and New Zealand contingents would be brought to Europe to fight the Germans alongside the British Expeditionary Force (BEF).[3]

New Zealand's major contribution to the Imperial war effort was called the New Zealand Expeditionary Force (1914), quickly abbreviated to the NZEF. In order to keep the NZEF up to strength throughout the war, the initial deployment of a large Main Body was to be followed by the regular dispatch of reinforcements to replace casualties. The NZEF Main Body and the First Reinforcements, which were to sail together, totalled 8427 men and 3815 horses.[4] 1940 of the Main Body men and 2032 of the horses belonged to the New Zealand Mounted Rifles (NZMR) Brigade.

The NZMR Brigade consisted of the following units:

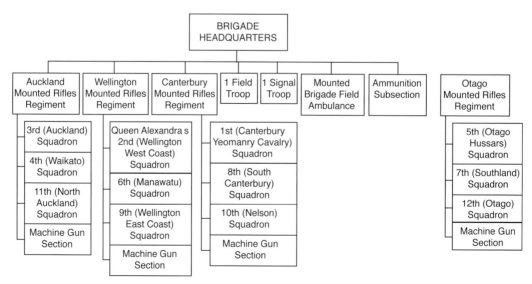

A fourth regiment, the Otago Mounted Rifles Regiment, was also part of the NZEF. It was identical in structure and manning to the other three regiments, but it was designated as a divisional cavalry regiment and it was not a part of the NZMR Brigade.[5] When it reached Gallipoli the Otago regiment was attached to the NZMR Brigade, so its story will also be told in this book.

Each mounted rifles regiment numbered 549 men and 608 horses organised as a headquarters, three squadrons and a machine gun section.[6]

A squadron of 158 men and 169 horses comprised a headquarters and four troops. Each troop consisted of eight four-man sections. The section was the fundamental building block of the mounted rifles regiment. In combat, one man in each section was responsible for holding the horses when the other three men fought on foot. The four men lived, worked, fought and sometimes died together, and they usually became close friends. Camp duties were shared: one man was responsible for cooking, another for looking after the horses, the third for keeping the campsite clean and tidy, while the fourth took care of the section's share of guards and fatigues.

In addition to its mounted riflemen, each regiment also had a veterinary officer, a doctor, a chaplain, and a number of signallers, cooks, medical orderlies, farriers, saddlers, trumpeters, clerks, batmen, drivers and sanitary staff. The mounted regiments had no motorised transport. Instead they used bicycles, packhorses and horse-drawn wagons.

Mobile 'horse artillery' for the brigade was to be provided by the British Army once the NZEF reached England.[7] Medical support was provided by a Mounted Brigade Field Ambulance, staffed by 126 men (including a dentist) and equipped with 80 horses. The field ambulance could treat up to 50 wounded men at a time. Badly injured or seriously ill men would be stabilised there before being sent further back to military hospitals, while less serious cases would be treated at the field ambulance and returned to their units. The New Zealand Engineers provided a field engineering troop of 77 men and 75 horses, and a signals troop of 33 men and 17 horses. The brigade was completed by an Ammunition Sub-Section, a supply unit that could be integrated into whatever division the brigade was attached to.

Although its men rode horses, the NZMR Brigade was not a cavalry formation. Mounted riflemen rode their horses to a battle, where they dismounted under cover to fight on foot as infantry, with rifles and bayonets. Cavalry and mounted rifles units did, however, share some roles, such as scouting and providing security for the infantry.

31

The entire mounted rifles brigade could put only as many riflemen in a firing line as a single infantry battalion. This meant that the brigade could not fight prolonged actions on its own against large or entrenched groups of enemy infantry. Its job was to deal with small or isolated enemy outposts and patrols, and to engage and delay larger enemy forces until supporting infantry brigades caught up and took over the fight. Unlike the other elements of the NZEF, the NZMR Brigade was not intended to fight as part of a British infantry division. Had it got to the Western Front, its role would have been as corps troops or army troops, supporting several infantry and cavalry divisions.

The men in the mounted rifles regiments were known informally as 'the Aucklands', 'the Wellingtons', 'the Canterburys' and 'the Otagos', and mounted riflemen as a whole were often referred to as 'the mounteds'. These terms will appear throughout this book, as will the abbreviations AMR, WMR, CMR and OMR for the Auckland, Wellington, Canterbury and Otago mounted rifles regiments respectively.

Each mounted rifles squadron in the NZEF was maintained throughout the war by one of the 12 Territorial Force mounted rifles regiments. The squadrons were named after these parent regiments, and the men wore their badges throughout the war. For example, in the CMR, the squadron provided from the 1st Mounted Rifles (Canterbury Yeomanry Cavalry) Regiment was known as the 1st (CYC) Squadron, and those from the 8th (South Canterbury) and the 10th (Nelson) regiments were known as the 8th (South Canterbury) and 10th (Nelson) squadrons respectively.

The Territorial Force regiments enrolled, medically examined and equipped the mounted volunteers. Serving Territorial Force soldiers or Territorial Reserves were the first choice to fill the ranks of the NZEF. When these sources provided less than half the numbers required, because many volunteers were too young or medically unfit, untrained civilians had to be accepted as well. Volunteers had to be between the ages of 20 and 35 and single men were preferred to married men. The minimum height was 162 centimetres (5 foot 4 inches) and the maximum weight allowed was 76 kilograms (11 stone 9 pounds) 'except in special cases'.[8] The men signed up for the duration of the war, plus any additional demobilisation period. With daily rates of pay ranging from 30 shillings for colonels to five shillings for troopers, the men of the NZEF were relatively well paid. Only the Australians received more.

Major General Godley had little trouble finding suitable commanders for the mounted rifles brigade. Colonel Andrew Russell, a 46-year-old farmer from Hawke's Bay, was selected to lead the brigade. Russell had received formal military training in the British Army in the late nineteenth century and served for three years with British regiments in India and Burma before returning to New Zealand in 1892. In 1900 Russell had formed and trained the Hawke's Bay Mounted Rifles Volunteers. He did not serve in the South African War. By 1911, he was the commander of the 2nd (Wellington) Mounted Rifles Brigade. When Godley offered him the command of the NZMR Brigade on 10 August 1914, Russell accepted, commenting that 'It is a great compliment, must do my best. … It is quite the best command, and many there are to envy me.'[9]

Russell's only serious competitor for the job had been 43-year-old Arthur Bauchop, the commander of the Otago Military District in 1914. Despite the fact that Bauchop

Andrew Russell.

William Meldrum.

John Findlay.

Charles Mackesy.

Arthur Bauchop.

was a professional officer and Russell was not, Godley gave the command of the brigade to Russell. Bauchop was not pleased. 'I have had it out with him,' wrote Godley, 'and said to him distinctly that I did not think his qualifications were as good as Russell's and he now quite understands the position.'[10] Bauchop received the command of the Otago Mounted Rifles Regiment instead.

Lieutenant Colonel Charles Mackesy, a 53-year-old farmer from Whangarei, was appointed to command the AMR. Despite his nickname of 'German Joe' (soon changed to 'Old Joe' for obvious reasons), Mackesy was an Irishman who had moved to New Zealand from the United States in the 1890s. He joined the Marsden Mounted Rifles as a trooper in 1900, and by 1911 he was commanding the Territorial Force 11th (North Auckland) Mounted Rifles Regiment. Well-educated and fluent in several languages, Mackesy was outspoken and religious: he often lectured his men on his biblical interpretation of current events. Mackesy had a large extended family, and when several near relatives enlisted into the North Auckland squadron, someone renamed the squadron, which was drawn from the North Auckland Mounted Rifles, or NAMR, 'Nearly All Mackesy's Relations'.[11]

Lieutenant Colonel William Meldrum, a 49-year-old farmer and retired solicitor from Hunterville, commanded the WMR. In 1900 Meldrum had formed and served in the Hunterville Mounted Rifles Volunteers and 14 years later he was commanding the 6th (Manawatu) Mounted Rifles Regiment. Meldrum was a good cricketer and rugby player at provincial level, and he had been the New Zealand chess champion in 1896. Despite these successes, he was a modest man. He took great interest in the welfare of his men, but he was also a strict disciplinarian who expected his orders to be obeyed without question.[12]

Lieutenant Colonel John Findlay was the only regimental commander in the brigade who had fought in South Africa. A 45-year-old Ashburton farmer in civilian life, he was brought out of semi-retirement in the Territorial Reserve of Officers to command the CMR. He is described by the regimental historian as a 'leader [who] is at once beloved and respected by his subordinates, wise in his dealings, and a very capable soldier'.[13]

Recruiting for the NZEF began on 8 August. All over New Zealand, eager horsemen quit their jobs, said goodbye to their families, caught the horse in the front paddock and rode off to join up. The CMR was quickly over strength, with a waiting list big enough to have formed another regiment. The other regiments and battalions were the same. Within a week more than 14,000 volunteers had stepped forward to serve in the NZEF.

By and large, they joined up for the adventure. Some had vague ideas of Imperial duty, and others talked of avenging 'poor little Belgium', but most of them wanted to see the world, and this was their only chance. Most of the volunteers had been born in New Zealand, and they did not want to end their lives here without having been overseas. Few of them thought much about death. The South African War had seemed to show that modern warfare was a relatively safe occupation for all but an unlucky minority.

Ken Stevens rode into Whangarei on the day that war was declared and put his name down for the North Auckland squadron of the AMR. On his way home afterwards, he met a German, Friedrich Petersen, who had served in the German Army before migrating to New Zealand. Petersen told him 'I fink the Ghermans vill vin', but Stevens was unconcerned. Like most of the volunteers, he saw the war as a wonderful chance to see something of the world 'on the cheap'.[14]

William Peed left his Taihape farm and rode to the WMR mobilisation camp in Palmerston North on his horse Jock. He was sworn in and appointed Troop Sergeant of 3 Troop, 6th Manawatu Squadron. After spending the first week of September in hospital with influenza, he had his fortune told.[15] The results are not recorded, but it must have been good news, because he survived the war.

Some men who were rejected resorted to ingenious methods to get away with the NZEF. After he was turned down Len Wales thought things over in the Hawera pub. He read in the evening newspaper that deserters from His Majesty's Forces were being granted a pardon if they immediately enlisted with the NZEF, so he 'confessed' to being a deserter from the Royal Navy. 'Considering I had never been in it, I reckon I answered all questions very well.' Given the choice of 'returning' to the navy or joining the NZEF, he chose the latter, and was duly enrolled into the WMR.[16]

Most of the early volunteers for the mounted rifles regiments came from rural New Zealand. In the CMR, for instance, '24 of the officers listed their occupations as farmers, six were accountants and in banking, 11 were lawyers, two were regular officers, as well as a warehouse manager, a land agent and a merchant'. Sixty per cent were from farming occupations, six per cent were clerical, four per cent were professional, 'and the remaining 30 per cent were unidentified labourers, transport workers and tradesmen mostly from the smaller centres of inland Canterbury'.[17] The AMR was more urban in its make-up than the other regiments. 'There were lawyers and schoolmasters and students; there were bushmen and farmers and stockmen; there were tradesmen and labourers and clerks; one single tent in the Epsom camp included a schoolmaster, a barber, a coach driver, an accountant, a carpenter, a farm labourer, a commercial traveller, a farmer and a lawyer.'[18]

Riding instructors on loan from British Army cavalry regiments assessed the horsemanship of the mounted rifles volunteers. These old-school cavalrymen were unimpressed with the rough and ready colonial riding style. ' "You might be able to stick on," remarked one of the instructors, "but I wouldn't say you could ride".'[19] The troopers took the criticism with a pinch of salt, noting that the cavalry style of riding was 'pretty', if nothing else. According to Lieutenant Colonel Bauchop, the average mounted rifleman was a competent horseman, but 'cannot be considered a good horsemaster'.[20] Neither their peacetime Territorial Force training nor their civilian occupations had exposed the men to the necessity of preserving the health and fitness of their horses under prolonged operational conditions, though this potential problem was corrected during the war.

Ralph and Arnie Sparrow. The Sparrow brothers sailed with the Main Body in 1914 and served in the Nelson squadron of the CMR throughout the war.

The uniforms worn by the men of the NZEF in 1914 were locally manufactured copies of British Army patterns. The mounteds did not wear the distinctive peaked 'lemon-squeezer' hat.[21] Instead they wore a felt slouch hat with a wide brim and a fore-and-aft crease in the crown. Around the crown of the hat was a khaki puggaree with a dark green stripe running through it. The badge of the parent Territorial Force regiment was usually, but not always, worn on the front.[22] The uniform worn by troopers, non-commissioned officers and warrant officers was made of a coarse, heavy greenish-brown woollen serge material. The tunic had a high collar, on which brass regimental badges were usually worn. Brass 'NZMR' badges were worn on the shoulder epaulettes, and embroidered badges of rank on the sleeves. A grey cotton flannel collarless shirt was worn beneath the tunic. The mounteds wore baggy woollen riding pantaloons with laces at the knee, with woollen puttees from below the knee to the ankle and black leather ankle boots with steel spurs. Over the tunic the men wore a New Zealand-designed leather ammunition bandolier and a belt. Five pouches on the bandolier and up to four on the belt allowed a total of 90 rounds of .303 inch rifle ammunition in five-round clips to be carried.

The officers' uniforms were of a different pattern and of better quality. They wore a single-breasted tunic with an open collar over a khaki cotton shirt and tie. Embroidered rank was worn on the cuffs of the sleeves. Riding breeches of khaki Bedford cord material were worn with brown leather riding boots, or with leather leggings or woollen puttees above brown boots and spurs. A leather Sam Browne belt was worn over the tunic, with a pistol holster and ammunition pouch attached.

The mounted rifle volunteers who cleared the entry hurdles assembled at district mobilisation camps on city racecourses: Alexandra Park in Auckland, Awapuni Racecourse in Palmerston North, Addington Showgrounds in Christchurch and Tahuna Park in Dunedin. Volunteers for the other units of the mounted rifles brigade assembled at Awapuni and the brigade headquarters staff concentrated in Wellington.

As the men poured in, so did the horses needed to carry them into battle. Nearly 4000 animals were needed immediately for the NZEF Main Body and First Reinforcements, and a steady flow of replacement horses, or remounts, was also required for the duration of the war. Fortunately, with 400,000 horses in New Zealand in 1914, there were plenty to choose from. 'The horse played a vital part in everyday life in New Zealand, especially in the country areas. Cars were not common, and the farm tractor was very rare. Draught horses were essential on farms, and some large stations had six or even more six-horse teams. In the towns, the horse-drawn hansom cab was the taxi of the time. Commercial stables hired out riding horses, gigs and coaches.'[23] Forty thousand horses were considered to be suitable for military riding purposes and 10,000 others were suitable for draught (pulling guns or wagons in artillery, supply, transport and ambulance units) and packhorse work. The cruel lessons of the South African War, during which many thousands of horses died unnecessarily, had resulted in the establishment of the New Zealand Veterinary Corps and Remount Branch in 1907. These units proved to be invaluable in providing sound horses for the NZEF throughout the war.

The Defence Department had a clear picture of what constituted a suitable horse for military purposes. 'Light and weedy animals that will not stand the strain of prolonged work in the field, vicious horses, kickers, and unbroken mounts are useless … the stamp to be aimed at is a small, active, short-legged, short-backed animal … as well bred as possible consistent with strength'.[24] Mounted rifles horses had to be 'from four to seven years of age, practically sound, from 14.2 to 15.2 hands in height …No greys, duns or light chestnuts will be taken. Geldings are preferable to mares!'[25] Many of the horses used by the peacetime Territorial Force mounted rifles regiments did not match these descriptions, but as far as Godley was concerned, they were usually good enough.

Each volunteering mounted rifleman was supposed to bring a horse with him. If the horse was suitable the government bought it and issued it back to him. However, not everyone turned up with a good horse, so the Defence Department asked the general public to donate horses to the war effort. The response was immediate. For example, the Lake County provided 61 horses, and the Eltham Patriotic Committee donated nine to its local squadron. Racing clubs, schools and farmers' unions also donated horses, as did many individuals. Mr A. F. Roberts of Roxburgh offered nine unbroken four-year-olds, commenting that 'they are small horses but as tough and as hard as nails'.[26]

Some donors stipulated that the horses were for the use of particular soldiers, but these wishes were not always respected. William East 'had a black hunter horse, called Killarney, a beautiful beast. It was given to me by a farmer with a big estate. The first thing that happened was an officer coming along, and deciding he liked it. He took it and I was given a dud.'[27] Donors were not allowed to impose any other conditions, such as demanding the return of the horses after the war.

The final shortfall in horses for the NZEF was made up by the purchase of horses from breeders and private owners. The average cost of a riding hack was between £15 and £30, and each packhorse and draught horse cost the Government up to £40.[28]

The details of each horse (number, colour, height, sex and distinguishing marks) were entered in regimental ledgers. **N↑Z** was branded on one fore-hoof, and the horse's military number was branded on the other. Donated and purchased horses were sent to Remount Depots near the district mobilisation camps, where they were allocated to riders without horses. The officers selected their mounts first, and the rest of the horses were issued to mounted riflemen. Typically, the horses were paraded around a ring, and troop leaders picked horses in turn. Some old hands had secretly marked the best horses with inconspicuous pieces of string the night before. When their hopes were dashed by this selection process, 'loud were the lamentations'.[29]

First impressions of the horses were not always favourable: 'many people had a vague idea only of what a troop horse should be. The remount portion of the camp could show anything from a draught horse to an unbroken outlaw.'[30] The animals from the lower South Island had just come through a particularly harsh winter, but even taking this into account 'there was still a look of roughness about the horses, and they were anything but uniform in stamp. Quite a number of the animals seemed to have been badly broken, if broken at all, and generally there was not the appearance of quality one would expect to see in a collection of remounts purchased for war service.'[31]

Volunteering mounted riflemen were also supposed to bring along their own riding equipment, including the 'strongest, largest and best saddle obtainable'. Unfortunately, Territorial Force horsemen had been allowed to turn up at pre-war training camps for years with any old saddle and bridle. This did not matter too much for weekend parades and short annual camps, but such shoddy equipment would not last long under wartime conditions, and would inevitably cause sore backs for the horses, and pressure sores. Defence Department plans to re-equip the Territorial Force mounted units with modern British 'Universal Pattern' military riding equipment were interrupted by the coming of the war. In the WMR, most of the saddles that arrived with volunteers were immediately condemned as unserviceable, and the story was the same in the other regiments.[32]

The Military Districts were authorised to purchase suitable saddles locally, but little was available or affordable at such short notice. Some cheeky volunteers ordered saddles from gullible suppliers, promising them that the Defence Department would pay the bill. By the time the unauthorised invoices were received in Wellington, the offenders were on their way to Europe and nothing could be done to recover the money from them.[33]

After all avenues had been investigated, a serious shortfall of riding equipment remained. Urgent orders were telegraphed to the Imperial authorities for additional equipment to meet the NZEF when it reached England. The shopping list included 4000 horse blankets, 2000 sets of mounted rifles saddlery, 1000 pairs of 'large pantaloons for mounted riflemen', 230 horseshoe cases and 2000 hoof-picks.[34] At the same time, local contracts were awarded for 750 sets of riding equipment.

A fully equipped New Zealand mounted rifleman on horseback.

The importance of a well-designed saddle becomes apparent when one considers the weight that a troop horse had to carry. Each mounted rifleman carried a .303 inch Short Magazine Lee Enfield (SMLE) rifle on his back, a leather bandolier full of ammunition around his body, a bayonet, water bottle, haversack and sometimes a pair of wire-cutters. Officers did not carry most of this equipment, but they were weighed down, nonetheless, with a compass, telescope or pair of binoculars, clasp knife, Field Service Pocketbook, watch, whistle, Sam Browne belt and pistol. Everyone carried bread, cheese, and an iron ration (usually biscuits and a can or two of bully beef). In addition to the rider, saddle and bridle, each horse carried two blankets (one for the horse, one for the rider) folded under the saddle, a horse-brush, a folded greatcoat, a mess tin, a shoe case containing two horseshoes and nails, a second bandolier containing 90 rounds of ammunition (worn around the horse's neck), a nose bag containing one day's ration of grain, a peg and heel rope, a picketing peg, a head rope attached to the bridle, a waterproof sheet and a mallet or axe. Including the rider, the total weight carried by a troop horse could easily reach 130 kilograms.

Such a heavy weight needed to be carefully distributed on the horse to avoid causing problems. The modern British Universal Pattern (UP) saddle was designed to carry this weight evenly; the various New Zealand-manufactured saddles were less able to do so. Fortunately, this hotchpotch of saddlery was replaced in Egypt in early 1915 with UP saddles.

While men, animals and equipment were assembling across New Zealand, 10 cargo and passenger ships in New Zealand waters were taken into government service and converted into His Majesty's New Zealand Transports Nos 3 to 12. Bunks with straw mattresses were fitted for the men, and narrow stalls were built for the horses, which were to be spread across all ships. Seventy days' supplies for men and horses were purchased and loaded aboard, along with nearly 11,000,000 rounds of .303 inch ammunition. Fresh water for the horses would have to be replenished at each port of call.

The NZEF would not be trained to an operational standard in New Zealand. As soon as it could be assembled and equipped, the New Zealand convoy was to sail to Australia, where it would join the Australian Imperial Force (AIF) and accompany it to England via the Suez Canal and the Mediterranean Sea. Advanced training would be conducted once the NZEF disembarked in England, after it was integrated into British or Australian formations. In New Zealand, equipment was distributed and basic drill, rifle shooting and fitness training were carried out. There was no time allocated for collective training above regimental level, and precious little even for that.

Russell was disappointed that he could not assemble his brigade for training before it left New Zealand. He did inspect it, regiment by regiment, and he did not always like what he found. On 3 September Russell wrote that the WMR was 'being badly organised and doing little work'. A week later, he noted that the same regiment had 'no discipline'. Of his brigade as a whole, he wrote: 'Only 1/2 the men are territorials; the balance are ex-South African contingents and civilians, consequently they are by no means up to the standard of the ordinary territorial regt. However peg away is the only game. I hope to be tolerably unpopular with some of them before I am done.'[35]

One WMR mounted rifleman remembers the six weeks he spent at Awapuni Racecourse 'because of the wonderful hospitality of the people of Palmerston North, and the shocking weather. It rained and blew, often levelling the tents, and at night it froze. Manoeuvres over the flat country, mainly covered in rushes almost horsehigh, were also soggy affairs and few were sorry when the regiment entrained for Wellington for overseas service.'[36] Clutha Mackenzie, a 19-year-old farm worker from Balclutha who served in the WMR, wrote of this period:

> *Usually, during the day, in independent troops of thirty to forty men, they wandered about the district, among the pleasant suburban homes of Palmerston [North], along shady country roads or up into the hills. They walked or cantered for an hour or so, and then, selecting a likely-looking homestead, they would unsaddle and unbridle their mounts and leave them to graze the succulent grass at the sides of the road, or roll if they wished, while a man was put at both ends of that road to prevent their straying. Then the others would lie in the shade or sun themselves on the bank opposite the homestead, sleeping, smoking, reading or playing cards. Scarcely ever did the oracle fail to work. The door of the house would open and a fair maid appear, anon, a mother and a sister. The first would come tripping down the path to the soldiers and enquire: 'Mother says would you like some tea?' 'Well,' they would reply, 'it wouldn't be a bad idea, would it? But, I say, wouldn't it be a lot of trouble?' 'Oh, not at all.' And she would skip away back to the house … A brief interval was followed by the appearance of large trays of cups, the whole of the household crockery from the drawing-room, breakfast-room and kitchen, with scones and cakes, and all the luxuries of the storeroom, and, perhaps, apples from the barn. The good family, as is only in keeping with proper hospitality, would join in the feast; and the disappearance of two or three cheery troopers into the house to assist in washing up would end one of those irresponsible, warm-hearted little scenes which were so many in those far-away days of August 1914.*

According to Mackenzie, military life was simple and satisfying. Palmerston North was usually 'a quiet country town of sober habits and eminent respectability', but now 'the echoing emptiness of her streets was gone, the lights shone brilliantly across the Square, the air was full of the murmur of the crowd, the tread of heavy boots, the tinkling of spurs and glasses and the laughter of merry parties. Perspiring waiters and flustered waitresses fed the hordes in the hotels, while the [swimming] baths worked overtime. The road to the camp lay like a searchlight beam across the landscape – the cloud of never-resting dust lit by the strong headlights of a thousand taxis which

'Mother says would you like some tea?' Refreshments for mounted riflemen in Lower Hutt.

careered along the rough road … Happy and weary, the men came streaming back to camp, entering by the front if before "Lights Out", through the pine plantations if after.'[37] The public of New Zealand took considerable pride in entertaining the troops. 'Khaki was found to have a very potent influence over the youth and beauty of Auckland town, which was very satisfying, and just as it should be.'[38]

Volunteers with no previous military experience often found service life to be frustrating and demanding, and occasionally downright hilarious. 'There were times,' wrote Edwin McKay, 'when I felt tempted to walk between two officers and try a double-handed salute, but I smothered the temptation. … One of the comic opera instructions issued to officers and O/R (other ranks) was that all troops were to grow moustaches to make them look older, or more ferocious, and it was difficult to keep a straight face on parade when one of the finished products was on show.'[39]

The friendly rivalry between the infantry battalions and the mounted regiments in the Territorial Force was encouraged during the mobilisation period to foster regimental *esprit de corps*. Lieutenant Colonel William Malone, the commanding officer of the Wellington Infantry Battalion, thought that he had scored a point one night on the subject of haircuts. He got one of his officers, hair cut to the roots, to stand up, and called on all present to note the perfection of the 'Infantry cut'. Not to be outdone, Lieutenant Colonel Meldrum, the commanding officer of the

WMR, ordered one of his officers to stand up. When Captain Hastings, who was completely bald, did so, Meldrum could say; 'Gentlemen, this is how we do it in the Mounteds!'[40]

Discipline was strict, but there was little offending. The risk of being left behind was sufficient to deter all but the most hardened criminal. As the sailing date neared training became tedious and the men longed to go. Russell wrote on 15 September: 'We are beginning to wonder if and when we shall get away … naturally we are all feeling very impatient. Training in the meantime goes on. But I find some of it very desultory and inefficient.'[41]

Inevitably, in the absence of facts, rumours took their place. The men did not yet know that they were to fight with the BEF on the Western Front, so the destination and employment of the NZEF were the subjects of much speculation. Garrison duty in Great Britain or at some Imperial outpost was an early and very unpopular favourite. 'Fits of depression occasionally swept over the A.M.R. owing to fears that colonial troops would not be considered efficient for modern war, that the war would be over before the New Zealand Force could get anywhere, that garrison duty in some inglorious spot would be their portion, and so on.'[42]

The official line was that the Main Body men were transformed from a 'disorderly mob' into 'a fairly efficient machine' by the time they left New Zealand. In fact, they were nothing of the sort, as many of the volunteers realised. According to Jim McMillan, 'by the end of September, having been knocked into some sort of shape, but by no means expert in the art of soldiering, the recruits were ready to embark for overseas'.[43]

The NZEF was supposed to sail by the end of August, but its departure was postponed by the New Zealand government because of worries about the Imperial German Navy's East Asiatic Squadron. This powerful enemy force, which included the fast and well-armed armoured cruisers *Scharnhorst* and *Gneisenau* and the light cruiser *Emden*, was on the loose somewhere in the Pacific Ocean. Under British pressure, the government reluctantly agreed to allow the NZEF to be escorted as far as Australia by one small and unreliable cruiser, departing from New Zealand on 25 September. This delay changed the course of the war for the NZEF. Had the force sailed in August or early September 1914, it would probably have reached England before Turkey entered the war. Most likely, after a period of unemployment on the Western Front, the mounteds would have been relieved of their horses and converted to infantry or pioneers, and the NZEF and the AIF would probably not have gone to Gallipoli.

Major Peter Wain (left) leads the South Canterbury squadron of the CMR through Christchurch.

A few days before the new sailing date, the NZEF Main Body and First Reinforcements were brought to the ports of Auckland, Wellington, Lyttelton and Port Chalmers. The ships carrying the CMR and the other Canterbury units sailed from Lyttelton after memorable farewells. 'Pretty girls were wildly enthusiastic and were not particular as to how many troopers they fondly took farewell of, women smiled and laughed, though there were often tears in their eyes, and the men were laboriously humorous. A band played airs … the troops, swarming on the railings and the rigging, sang lustily snatches of song; and finally, amidst the fortissimo strains of the National Anthem, a wild holloing from every one, and a bellowing of fog-horns, the ships drew slowly away from the wharf.'[44] The Canterbury ships joined the Otago transports off Banks Peninsula and sailed north to Cook Strait, where they were supposed to rendezvous with the Wellington ships.

The Auckland transports *Waimana* and *Star of India,* escorted by the little cruiser HMS *Philomel,* sailed from Queen's Wharf on 24 September in very rough weather, intending to meet the rest of the convoy in the Tasman Sea. Meanwhile, the WMR loaded its horses onto trains in Palmerston North and headed south to Wellington.

Clutha Mackenzie described the scene:

> *The camp buzzed with excitement, and, when night came, all were busy getting the gear ready. No one slept, and, in the dark, silent hours before the dawn, the camp was struck. The neat lines of tents became merely small bundles and odd poles, while hundreds of figures passed hither and thither amid blazing fires of straw. In the early light the Regiment moved away from the pleasant camp of Awapuni ... In the middle of the morning, struggling engines creaked away with the long lines of horse-trucks and carriages of rowdy troopers who cheered wildly as they set out at last upon their adventures. They crawled along the low country of the Manawatu, then along the rough cliffs above the sea, over the hills, and at length down the rocky gorge to Wellington. The troops detrained, watered and fed the horses, hung about for a while, and eventually led the horses to the wharves. Four great grey transports lay alongside, and the sun shone down hotly on a scene of seething activity, a crowd of troops working with the energy of enthusiasm, long strings of horses filing up huge gangways and disappearing into lines of horse-boxes around the bulwarks, or swinging aloft singly by cranes to be lowered swiftly into the black depths of holds.[45]*

While they waited for the rest of the NZEF to arrive, the Wellington units had a dismounted parade for the Governor and 15,000 spectators at Newtown Park on 24 September. They then joined their horses on board *Maunganui*, *Orari*, *Arawa* and *Limerick*. The ships left the wharves and anchored in Wellington Harbour, expecting to sail the next day.

Instead of receiving sailing orders, the men of the NZEF were told that 'Owing to unforeseen circumstances, the transports will not at present sail, and orders for disembarkation will be issued in due course'.[46] Prime Minister Massey had decided the previous evening to postpone the convoy's departure again after the Australian Governor General had warned him that the convoy would be in great danger if it attempted to cross the Tasman Sea without a stronger escort.[47] Massey would not allow the NZEF, New Zealand's pride and joy, to sail until its safety at sea could be guaranteed by a more powerful escort. He knew 'that the enemy, if he met ships full of troops, had the right to sink them and drown the men'.[48]

The Auckland ships were recalled to harbour, to the disgust of the troops aboard. Walter Carruthers wrote, 'You should have seen the look on the chaps faces in the morning when they came up on deck & found that we were back in the harbour & just about to drop anchor. A lot of them are talking of deserting if we have to go into camp again. You don't know how disappointed we were to come back after going out like we did'.[49] Ominously, the seas had been so rough in the 24 hours that the Auckland ships were at sea that 12 horses had died. The South Island transports *Ruapehu*, *Hawke's Bay*, *Athenic* and *Tahiti,* which were waiting in Cook Strait, were summoned into the harbour. The ships tied up at the wharves at Wellington and unloaded many of the men and all of the horses. 'Dawn broke grey and drear, and the troops were in the depths of depression'.[50]

The CMR went to Lyall Bay, while the other mounted regiments 'mournfully' rode north to Trentham Racecourse. The NZEF spent the next three weeks conducting apparently aimless and leisurely training. 'The Wellington Mounteds … passed a fortnight there, riding along the valley roads and manoeuvring over the steep hills. It was not so bad either, for day after day passed with glorious sunshine and cooling breeze, and the city was within reach by a weary train'.[51] The people of Wellington put on balls and sports meetings to entertain the men while they were there. Russell was unhappy about this latest delay, writing to his father on 4 October: 'Everyone very low. … I believe we should have started. Risks must be taken'. In the same letter, he described his brigade as 'A magnificent lot of men, with ill-trained officers. Not their fault, but their misfortune'. Russell also commented on the chances of the NZEF seeing any fighting at all. 'I do not suppose we shall do much more than drive the Germans across the border this winter – then it will remain to be seen if internal dissension does not lead to the break up of the German Empire. If it does not, the war will last into June or July. In this case we shall get a chance of getting to the front. Do hope we do.'[52]

In early October, Massey was finally satisfied that most of the German raiders were operating well away from the convoy route. As soon as a stronger naval escort force comprising HMS *Minotaur* and the Japanese battle cruiser *Ibuki,* 'a huge black three-funnelled monster',[53] arrived in New Zealand waters, the transports were allowed to sail. The Auckland ships sailed south, their bands appropriately playing 'It's a Long Way to Tipperary', and berthed in Wellington on 15 October. On the same day the rest of the force was brought back to the Wellington wharves and embarkation began. 'Once again, the bright stars long before dawn looked down upon the bustle of a breaking camp, looked down upon the flaring piles of burning straw, the collapsing tents and the happy laughing throng of happy troopers. Early in the dewy morning they clattered out of the [Trentham] race-course gates and away

'The great day at last'. Waikato mounted riflemen and horses embarking on His Majesty's New Zealand Transport No. 12 Waimana *in Auckland.*

down the winding road in the [Hutt] valley bottom. Afternoon found them skirting the harbour beneath the great rocky escarpments of Wellington's hills.'[54] Percy Doherty wrote in his diary: 'As the minutes crept on to 2 o'clock, the boys began rolling in both literally and figuratively speaking, as some of them had been imbibing rather freely. Some of them cut it rather fine too, and nearly missed the bus; two in particular…fell asleep in a hotel, they woke up to find they had 10 minutes to catch the boat, so dashing outside they saw an empty handsome [*sic*] cab; needless to say this was right into their hands. One fellow got up into the driver's seat and drove his mate to the wharf, where they jumped out leaving the cab standing – but they caught the boat.'[55] The ships left the wharves one by one that afternoon, each cheered by large crowds.

The men and horses of the NZEF spent their last night in New Zealand on board the ships moored in Wellington Harbour. Finally, at 6 a.m. on the morning of Thursday 16 October 1914, the convoy weighed anchor and set sail for Europe, led by its escort of four warships. It was a fine and breezy day, with mist lying across the water. Thousands of eager men lined the rails, waving to passing ships and to distant spectators on land. At the forts near Pencarrow Head, the New Zealand flag was dipped in salute as each ship passed in the channel. 'In single line-ahead, the fourteen great grey ships, their smoke trailing away over the port quarter before a fresh wind, passed down the wild rocky gap of the [harbour] entrance. The grey seas rolled in a long swell, grey, flying clouds hid the eastern mountain tops. The passengers of an in-bound steamer had hurried on deck, clad lightly against the chill wind, [and] sent a faint cheer to each passing ship.'[56] Once the transports left Cook Strait and reached open water beyond Cape Farewell, they took up their convoy formation of two five-ship columns, with the naval cruisers ahead, behind and to either side. The ships then steamed westwards into the rolling swells of the Tasman Sea.

As they finally got away, New Zealand's mounted riflemen recorded mixed feelings in letters and diaries. 'The great day at last,' wrote William Pyle. 'We are really off.

The NZEF convoy sails from Wellington, 16 October 1914.

49

A splendid sight.' For Percy Doherty 'It was a grand sight and awe-inspiring to see these grey battleships with their guns poking their noses out along the sides and their decks practically cleared for action, ready to settle accounts with any one that dared interfere with us.' Chaplain William Grant felt 'a certain degree of sadness' but 'the feeling of satisfaction predominated – satisfaction that after a long and vexatious delay and a false start, we were at last actually on the way to try conclusions with the enemy … All the boys were in the best of spirits, and speculation was rife as to our route and ultimate destination. One who is cursed with a too vivid imagination could not help wondering … how many of these fine, strapping fellows would return to their native shores!'[57]

That evening, as the sun set ahead of the ships, a last few reminders of home were seen. 'Suddenly a rush is made to the after deck, for far away to the north-east, with its snow-capped peak almost golden with the reflection of the setting sun, can be seen Mt. Egmont … Wistful and sad were the faces of many that evening, as they took a last look at their homeland, and many were the silent messages sent to that distant mountain.' Seeing the Cape Farewell lighthouse 'flashing quite plainly,' Percy Doherty knew it was 'the last glimpse of dear old New Zealand for many days to come, but, nevertheless, we are not downhearted'.[58]

With nearly 8500 troops and over 3800 horses aboard, the convoy carried the largest single body of men and animals ever to leave New Zealand at one time. It was the first great adventure for most of the New Zealanders aboard, and they were full of optimism.[59]

2

We might be a long time getting home

*I thought of the Mounteds and the poor horses and
I am glad I am an infantry man.*

EDWARD BAIGENT

We are looking forward to a good Xmas dinner in England.

GORDON HARPER

THE FIRST FEW DAYS at sea on the 'great adventure' were a miserable experience for men and horses alike as the ships, in Clutha Mackenzie's words, 'rolled and creaked and swayed up the grey, lumpy swell, lurched over the crests and plunged away down into the troughs. The spray lifted over the bows and swept along the decks, the wind howled dismally through the rigging, and the ship was wet and comfortless. All was grey – the ships, the sky, the sea and the long trails of smoke fleeing away to starboard.' Dejected men lay in rows 'like corpses in their blankets, with pinched white faces peeping out … others moped about searching for the drier, warmer corners'.[1] Some men tried to eat, but few of them could keep anything down. 'Rations were very plentiful for those who had any desire for them.'[2] 'Three quarters of us are sick,' wrote Edward Baigent. 'It would take a super human man to be otherwise, stuck down in the hold with tin baths in every alleyway and all hands doing their best to fill them. None of us would worry if the German Fleet were to attack us today.' The horses also suffered until they found their sea legs, as Gordon Harper recorded. 'The horses are feeling it a good deal and are looking very droopy & tired. Ours are in rather a bad place as the sea breaks over them when it is rough.'[3]

Conditions varied from ship to ship. Those men lucky enough to be travelling on passenger liners had a few more comforts than those aboard cargo ships, but there was precious little room on any of the vessels. On one a space the size of two average three-bedroom houses served as the sleeping quarters for 600 men.[4] The portholes were sealed at night to stop lights from showing, and this made the areas below deck very stuffy. No alcohol was allowed on the New Zealand ships (unlike the Australian ships), but dry canteens sold toiletries, soft drinks and food for a few weeks until their stocks ran out. Fresh water was used only for drinking and cooking, but a vessel still went through 26 tonnes of it every day. On each ship there was one big canvas bath full of salt water for every 50 men. Salt-water soap was issued for washing, but it was not very effective, leaving the men feeling sticky afterwards. Censorship was imposed as soon as the troops sailed, and letters home were not allowed to contain references to ships, convoy routes or details of units.[5]

All ranks were briefed by medical officers on a wide variety of topics, including diseases and their prevention, care of the body, marching, frostbite and sunstroke. They were encouraged to 'keep fit for the honour of their Empire' and told that looking after their health was 'a sacred duty'.[6] The doctors began an inoculation programme – some men refused and 35 were sent home from Egypt – and enthusiastic dentists got busy pulling out teeth. Some men were encouraged to have all their teeth removed and replaced with dentures, in the belief that this would avoid dental problems later on. William Lynch wrote: 'I have decided to have all my teeth out on board ship, the Dentist and Lieut. Davis says that I will be able to have a week off and get a new set in. I will be able to get plenty of soft food on ship.'[7] Lynch finally got his new dentures five months later. Claude Pocock noted in his diary that the 'Dentist and Doctor have been busy all day, some chaps having as many as eleven teeth out, and in spite of my having six out some months ago I had to get as many more out today and a nice condition some of us are in now for eating tough beef'.[8] Ship's biscuit softened in water was often the only food these men could eat.

For most men in the NZEF the daily ship's routine began with 'Reveille' at 6 a.m. This was followed by physical training until the hoisting of the colours at the stern of each transport at 8 a.m., after which breakfast was served. The average 'working day' was filled in with drill parades, kit inspections, lunch, shooting practice and lectures, until the colours were lowered at sunset to the sound of 'Retreat'. Evening lectures for officers and non-commissioned officers (NCOs) ended most days. Soldiers were also used as guards and to assist the ships' crews in the galleys, bakeries, butchers' shops, and in the carpentry and plumbing departments. After a while most of the officers ran out of enthusiasm and good ideas, and the amount of free time for the men increased – for everyone, that is, except the mounteds.

The men in the mounted units were exempted from most training and other duties, but only because their responsibilities for the thousands of horses took up all their waking hours. All 3815 horses had to be exercised regularly and groomed several times a day. Their legs needed to be rubbed and hosed down with salt water every day to stop them from swelling. Their stalls had to be cleaned out, and saddlery had to be checked and cleaned, every day. It was tedious, laborious and unrelenting work, as Clutha Mackenzie recorded. 'From 5 a.m. till 9 p.m. it had been groom, clean decks, feed, water, and exercise; and then, more often than not, it was horse-picket for part of the night. The temperature of the horse-holes had for a long space never fallen below 110°F [43°C].' William Lynch grumbled about having to look after other people's horses: 'I think it is rotten coming down to look after someone else's horses'. The 285 mounted riflemen aboard *Orari*, who had 728 horses to look after between them, had the busiest time of all, as William Grant explained. 'After allowing for orderlies and others on various duties, one man had an average of five horses to look after, and when you consider the work he had to do, getting the forage to the various horse decks, watering, feeding, grooming and "stables," you may be sure that the *Orari* was a very busy ship, and that the men were not troubled with time hanging on their hands.'[9] The *Orari* had a ramp around the deck for exercising the horses, but even so 'the amount of daily exercise that one horse received was not much more than sufficient to keep a certain amount of circulation going in their legs which were at this time getting very "puffy"'.[10] On other large transports, horses were walked around the decks on coconut matting. 'We can walk them around a good sized circle,' wrote Percy Doherty, 'each horse getting about 20 minutes exercise, which they seem to enjoy, and no doubt does them a lot of good. It works out that each horse gets about a mile walk.' On the smaller ships, horses could only be exercised in the aisles between their stalls. As Edward Baigent noted, 'I thought of the Mounteds and the poor horses and I am glad I am an infantry man.'[11]

The horses were accommodated in rows of stalls, usually facing inwards towards the centre-line of the ship. Some stalls were on the upper 'weather' decks, but most were in the holds. They were all very narrow, so that 'to get at [a horse] with a grooming brush is quite a gymnastic performance'.[12] Clutha Mackenzie was entertained by looking along the lines of horse stalls on his ship as it rolled. 'With an even keel only the noses of the horses showed beyond the stalls; but, when the vessel rolled heavily to a beam swell, their heads swung in and out like the cuckoos of cuckoo clocks. One moment, as the ship lay well over into a trough, Mac could see nothing but a long line of posts; the next, as she lifted to a sea, out shot those eighty heads. They trod backwards and forwards in regular step, and were cursed constantly by the men whose bunks were immediately below the trampling hoofs.'[13] The smell of hundreds of horses 'soon reached to every corner of the ship, and seemed to taint the very food', but everyone soon got used to it.[14]

As Mackenzie observed, 'Least of all to appreciate the presence of horses in the vessels were the officers of the ships accustomed to Royal Mails and jolly passengers.' Clad in 'all the immaculate glory of white ducks [uniforms] ... they would frequently be bitten at, or else when one of them was standing comfortably on deck smoking, a horse would give a violent sneeze behind him, and he would disappear into his cabin, muttering wrathfully as he changed into a clean suit'. The captain was not amused by 'the constant trampling of the horses [which] was wearing ugly tracks in his best teak decks'.[15]

As the convoy sailed on, there was a steady but very low incidence of deaths among the horses from such causes as gastritis and pneumonia. Between Wellington

NZEF horses on a troopship at feeding time.

and Hobart, four horses died, and they were thrown overboard after dark so that their floating bodies would not give away the location of the convoy. Horses that were too sick or too badly injured to survive the voyage were shot before being thrown over the side, but this did not always go according to plan. 'Another horse bad today. Our veterinary luminaries engaged it with a revolver & left it for dead with a sack over it. Shortly after they came to heave it overboard and the poor brute was standing up.'[16]

The horses were fed on chaff, bran and hay, occasionally supplemented by linseed oil and salt. They quickly learnt to recognise the bugle call that announced feeding time: 'the chorus of neighs which greeted this bugle was one of the happiest sounds of the ship'.[17] There was 'an excited whinnying, snorting and trampling', as the men attached the feed boxes. 'Comparative silence followed, while the horses in deep content poked their muzzles down into the feed and blew showers of chaff into the air. For a time the satisfied munching went on quietly; but at length the horses which had finished first stamped their feet, and tugged at their halter chains, in attempts to get at their neighbours' feeds.'[18] All things considered, the horses put up with the strange and cramped conditions at sea very well. On a later voyage, Frank Hobson wrote of them: 'The poor horses are having a bad time, but seem to put up with it patiently and resignedly'.[19]

Many of the men were unwilling to be as patient as the horses. The quality of the food was the first cause of friction. Initially, William Lynch was satisfied. 'We have porridge, stew or chops and bread and butter with coffee for breakfast. For dinner we have roast meat with potatoes, turnip, carrots or parsnip with either tea or soup to drink. And for tea we have bread and butter and jam for two nights a week, cold meat three times and cheese and pickles and tea twice'. Benjamin Colbran was content too: 'We had a good dinner of mutton & rice & peaches. Every day we get lime juice for dinner.'[20] After a while, however, the novelty wore off and complaints increased as boredom and the monotony of the menus took a toll. As Claude Pocock wrote, 'it is so seldom we sit down to anything but our beloved stew which is chiefly composed of ragged ends of meat water potatoes and several mysteries we do not understand'. On Pocock's ship matters came to a head after a particularly bad meal, and the angry men sent a deputation to complain to the officers. 'Our spokesman said that our stew was not fit for dogs and its appearance on our tables was far too frequent and the dinner today was not eatable and that it must be remedied for the men would not stand such treatment. At this plain spoken statement we received definite word that our food would improve so all hands dispersed to their various duties.' The protest apparently achieved results. 'There was a marked improvement in the food today. Roast mutton peas potatoes bread butter and limejuice all being good and well cooked so our rumpus yesterday has done some good.' According to Leslie Smith, some men got better food by bribing stewards to give them some of the officers' fare.[21]

Smoking on board was prohibited, as it was 'considered injurious to the men & their marching powers'. Of course this did not stop men smoking, and 'in the most remote and un-thought of places is to be found someone smoking the forbidden cigarette'.[22] There were no laundry services aboard the ships, at least for the enlisted ranks, so they had to wash their own clothes. According to Edwin McKay, 'We did our own washing, and that meant that each man had to sit beside his gear while it dried, to see that no one pinched it'. The 'gentle art' of theft applied to more than just clothes, as Claude Pocock recorded. 'It is common to see a man come up on deck to sleep and have no bedding whatever all the same in five minutes he may be curled up in a complete outfit and walk off with it in the morning consequently some other person has to perform the same sleight of hand trick the next [night] and so the entertainment is kept up.'[23]

On Wednesday 21 October, after six weary days at sea, the NZEF convoy made landfall at Hobart, Tasmania. Fresh water was brought aboard for the horses, and the

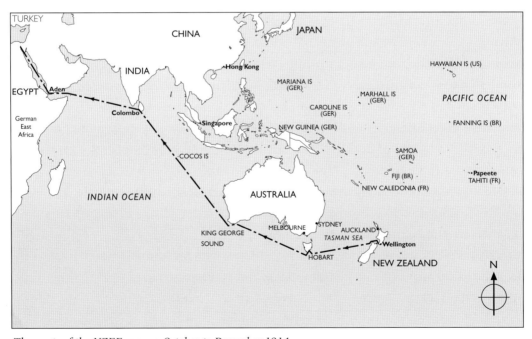

The route of the NZEF convoy, October to December 1914.

men disembarked for a three-hour route march. They appreciated both the exercise and the reception they received. Ormond Burton recalled that the population of Hobart 'thronged around the marching men, walking beside them, breaking into the ranks, and pressing on everyone gifts of the famous Tasmanian apples, cigarettes, and bunches of flowers. It was the greatest burst of spontaneous welcome the New Zealanders ever received.' One proud mounted rifleman, William Ricketts, wrote: 'On the route march the mounted men were put in the lead of the column and at the end of the seven-mile march the infantry were not in sight'. Russell was more critical of the mounteds: 'march discipline indifferent chief fault leaving ranks, loss of intervals, Otago Regt. especially bad'.[24] Shore leave was not allowed, but this did not stop a few men from taking a quick unauthorised trip ashore. 'Some of the boys, keen on adventure, slipped quietly out of the ranks and down side streets, and in the evening other hard cases garbed themselves as stokers, walked boldly past the guard and spent the merriest of evenings in Hobart, to return, perhaps, to a term of C.B. [confinement to barracks] which the holiday was well worth.'[25] The convoy was seen off by a large and enthusiastic crowd on 22 October. Three NZMR troopers were left behind in Hobart hospitals, suffering from pleurisy and pneumonia.

The next port of call was King George Sound, near Albany on the south-western tip of Australia, where the Australian and New Zealand convoys were to rendezvous. Some ill-informed optimists looked forward to a decent break there: 'I think we are staying for a week or two in Fremantle to give the horses exercise'.[26] On the way across the South Australian Basin, as the ships battled rough seas and fog, an ominous wireless message was received. The German raider *Emden*, which had been on the prowl in the Indian Ocean since August, had sunk seven merchant ships in the last few weeks. Several powerful Royal Navy ships were hunting for the enemy vessel, but its exact whereabouts was still not known. Russell commented wryly that *Emden* was 'more than earning her tucker'.[27]

Meanwhile, in South Africa, several retired Boer generals rebelled against the South African government's plans to invade German South West Africa. A few days before the New Zealand convoy reached King George Sound, the British War Council ordered the New Zealand and Australian forces assembling there to proceed to South Africa to assist in the quelling of the mutiny. On 28 October, 13 days out from Wellington, the New Zealand convoy arrived at King George Sound, where they joined the 20,000 men and 7800 horses of the Australian Imperial Force (AIF). While the ships rode at anchor in the sound, taking on water and coal, the Boer rebels were

The convoy sails from King George Sound, Australia, 1 November 1914.

defeated in South Africa, and the combined convoy's destination was confirmed as England via the Suez Canal. In the words of Australian war correspondent Charles Bean, 'This decision, made at the eleventh hour, determined the subsequent history of the Australian and New Zealand Forces'.[28]

The convoy of 36 transports (10 from New Zealand and 26 from Australia) and four warships sailed into the Indian Ocean on 1 November, a 'beautiful summer's morning with a calm sea'. Two mounted riflemen missed the boat. One was ill with a gastric ulcer, while the other, described in the NZEF War Diary as 'an undesirable character, suspected of being a German', apparently had venereal disease.[29] The convoy's route now took it northwest across the Indian Ocean, towards the isolated Cocos Islands. Colombo, the capital of Ceylon (modern Sri Lanka), was the next port of call. The convoy was spread out over 12 kilometres of ocean. From Australia onwards its speed, determined by that of the slowest ship, averaged 10 knots.

During the passage to Colombo, Major General Godley addressed the contentious issue of rifles versus swords for the mounted rifles brigade. Lieutenant Colonel Meldrum did not favour swords. 'To arm Mounted Riflemen at the eleventh hour with swords with the object of testing their strength in shock tactics with German Cavalry, specially trained with the sword and in shock tactics would be to tempt them to their certain destruction.' Godley agreed: 'I am entirely against anything that would lead our Mounted Rifles to in any way place dependence on any arm except the rifle, and I am setting my face entirely against these cavalry ideas … neither they, nor their horses, can be properly trained for shock action or cavalry work in the time at our disposal'.[30]

On 5 November Turkey declared war on the British Empire and its allies. The news quickly filtered down to the men. William Peed wrote: 'Had news that Turkey had joined the Triple Alliance. We might be a long time getting home.'[31] Rumours multiplied about the likely final destination of the convoy, and bets were placed on the most likely contenders. Egypt, India, Zanzibar and South Africa were popular alternatives to the still favourite destination of England.

Not long after the ships left Australian waters, the men were ordered not to throw rubbish overboard, because of the danger that it would be seen by enemy ships such as the elusive *Emden*. Lights showing at night were prohibited for the same reason. The prudence of these orders quickly became apparent. On the morning of 9 November the Australian escort warship HMAS *Sydney* suddenly left the convoy at high speed to take on the *Emden*, which had turned up less than 80 kilometres away at the Cocos Islands. Ken Stevens recalled that some ships handed out 'press releases' as the battle was fought almost within earshot of the transports. The lightly armed *Emden* stood no chance against the *Sydney*. 'Cheer after cheer went up from ship to ship' when it was reported that the *Sydney* had damaged the German ship to such an extent that her captain had beached her on North Cocos Island and surrendered her surviving crew; 134 had been killed.[32] Everyone was excused drill for the rest of the day in celebration, but of course the mounteds still had the horses to look after.

The wreck of the Emden *on the reef at North Cocos Island.*

A captured German officer from the *Emden* told Godley later that 'if they had had the slightest idea that they were so close to us, they would have made a dash into the middle of our convoy and sunk as many ships as possible'. *Emden*'s captain, Karl von Müller, believed that, if he had attacked at night, he would have sunk half of the transports with torpedoes before his own ship was destroyed by their naval escorts.[33] Earlier in the voyage Godley had complained about the 'hopeless slowness' of the Australian ships, but he admitted afterwards that this had probably saved the convoy. Had radio silence and light discipline been less strict, or had the convoy been a little quicker, the lives of thousands of Australians and New Zealanders could have ended in the Indian Ocean instead of at Gallipoli or on the Western Front.

After the excitement of the *Emden*'s destruction, life resumed its lethargic course. Shipboard temperatures soared as the convoy entered the tropics, averaging 26°C and peaking at 38°C in the Red Sea. 'Very hot day,' wrote William Peed. 'We can do nothing but perspire and drink. We paraded to church with shirt & riding pants & shoes & puttees of course. Lolled about.' The men discarded more and more clothes, until it was necessary to issue an order forbidding men to be on deck in 'a nude state'.

One man took exception to this, and wrote to his ship's newspaper complaining about the ship's hose being left uncovered on the deck in full view.[34] Extra efforts had to be made to keep the perspiring horses cool. 'Men spread awnings from the front of the boxes, and watered them steadily from above, so that the horses might be as cool as possible.' More grooming was ordered, with each horse getting two hours' worth every day. Despite these measures, many of the horses became grumpy in the heat, and a man 'passing along the front of a line of boxes, had to be prepared for a horse occasionally making a grab at him'.[35] The heat was not the only problem. 'Last night … we ran into a tropical storm and the thunder and lightning and rain … was new to some of our boys and I think some of them thought their end had come for they up and fled to their bunks below, leaving their bedding and clothes out in the rain.'[36]

The crossing of the equator on 13 November was marked by the traditional King Neptune ceremonies, during which most of the officers and some of the men were 'dipped'. The celebrations were marred when a New Zealand doctor was paralysed after diving into a shallow pool on the deck of one of the transports. He subsequently died at Colombo.

Wrestling and boxing tournaments were popular shipboard events, taken very seriously by competitors and spectators alike. 'Our boxing commenced today and a great slogging match some of them have no science but go for their lives you would think some of them were fighting for a sheep station.'[37]

On 15 November the New Zealand ships arrived at Colombo to take on more coal and water. While the ships were there, HMAS *Sydney* came into the harbour, carrying 190 survivors from the *Emden*. Cheering was forbidden. For most of the men, Colombo was the first sight of a different culture. Ken Stevens 'looked with a strange feeling of wonder at the domes, minarets and other buildings of strange design. … The elephants, camels, bullock drays and rickshaws as forms of transport, completed a scene that made me feel as though I had been lifted into another world.' The local work ethic did not impress Alfred Cameron. 'Took on board 300 tons of coal – very slow process, natives very lazy.' Traders flocked to the ships, as Percy Doherty noted in his diary. 'In no time there was a regular swarm of blacks in their canoes hanging around us…. the coolies scrambled up the gangway like bees waving cards that they had in their hands, which were evidently passes, or such like, to allow them on board; but absolutely no one was allowed on, and it took more than persuasion to get them off – they had to be pushed off.'[38]

The shopkeepers got their opportunity to fleece the visitors when leave parties

Greasy pole competition.

were allowed ashore. 'Two days at Colombo passed merrily enough with forty-five shipfuls of light-hearted troops exploring that Oriental city for the first time; and at the end of it the Cingalese were left in a dazed condition,' wrote Clutha Mackenzie. 'The [Otago] Regiment left quite a respectable amount of cash in Colombo in exchange for some truly magnificent looking articles of jewellery of which the precious ? stones had a truly disconcerting habit of falling out, and the gold thereof of turning green.' Despite these new and wondrous experiences, men like Ken Stevens had a nagging worry that it was all taking too long: 'the press reports convinced me that the allies were having victories on all fronts and we would never see any fighting'.[39]

Leslie Smith wrote, 'BEER very good here (first taste for three weeks)'. Charles Bean noted that 'Several local people spoke rather feelingly about the behaviour of the New Zealanders in town last night and we certainly saw numbers of them laid out [drunk] in all directions on the landing stage. They have only dry canteens and they are liable to break out at every port they come to.' As Claude Pocock explained, men who were caught ashore without permission paid for their crimes with 'fourteen days firing in the stokehole, others two hours [a day] standing to attention … for fourteen days dressed in full marching order, no easy thing I can tell you, others have to scrub out our feed boxes every day for ten days, clean our stables, draw the feed and distribute same … All these fatigues are done between parades when they would otherwise be idle so they get no rest at all now.'[40]

With the destruction of the *Emden* and the locating of another German raider far away on the coast of Africa, the last known threats to the convoy vanished, and most of its naval escorts were reassigned to other duties. The ships sailed on towards Aden in three separate packets according to their speed. For nearly two weeks after leaving Colombo, the seas remained very calm. Cecil Malthus wrote: 'A rowing boat could have come all the way from Albany. A number of us slept on deck, laying out our straw mattresses under the open sky. There was a swift dusk, then starry darkness. But there were heavy showers nearly every night, and it was amusing to see the sleepers awake and break for cover.' For Charles Nicol, 'The chief memories of that run to Aden are those of a sunrise on a perfectly glassy sea, of the fins of hundreds of flying fish flashing in the sun, and of hundreds and thousands of porpoises.' He also recorded that 'an A.M.R. mare on the *Star of India*, in defiance of army regulations, gave birth to a foal … but a foal cannot be kept … even as a mascot, and it had to be destroyed'.[41]

On 20 November, 20-year-old Private Harold Lewis, of the Mounted Brigade Field Ambulance, became the first fatal casualty in the NZMR Brigade when he died of double pneumonia. He was buried at sea the next day.

The NZEF ships reached Aden on 24 November, nine days out from Colombo. It was an uninspiring sight from the ships, nothing 'but a huge mass of yellow rock and sand shimmering in the intense heat'.[42] After coaling and watering the ships, the convoy steamed on into the Red Sea. Rumours grew about what the Turks were up to, fuelled by information gleaned in Aden from British Territorial Army soldiers who had just passed through the Suez Canal en route for India. According to Percy Doherty, 'All sorts of rumours are flying about that the Turks have blocked the Suez Canal'. However, most of the men of the NZEF still expected to land in England. 'Our scrappy wireless service on board almost certainly made mention of Turkey's entry into the war at the end of October, but we failed entirely to realise its significance in our personal fortunes. We were quite sure we were bound for England, as indeed we were – so far.' Gordon Harper was 'looking forward to a good Xmas dinner in England'.[43]

A few men thought that they would be used instead to garrison Egypt, so that British professional soldiers there could be sent to the Western Front, and they were right on the money. On 20 November, Field Marshal Lord Kitchener, Great Britain's Secretary of State for War, cabled Lieutenant General Sir John Maxwell, the commander of the Imperial forces in Egypt, to tell him that 'owing to the Turkish threat [to the Suez Canal], the Australian and New Zealand contingents would disembark and train in Egypt'.[44] The day after the convoy left Aden, a cable from London advised Godley of the decision, about which the New Zealand government was not consulted.

The new plan was for the Australians and New Zealanders to disembark and travel to Cairo, where they would train before going on to the Western Front in the spring of 1915. This made a lot of sense. Strategically, the presence of the colonial troops in Egypt would help to protect the Suez Canal after the British peacetime garrison there left for France. It was thought that the troops would also discourage other hostile action by either the Turks or the restless Egyptians. The mounted regiments of the NZEF and the AIF would be a useful mobile reserve force to respond to any Turkish attacks against the static defences along the Suez Canal.

There were also other, more practical, reasons for the decision. England was just beginning a particularly grim winter, and the training grounds on the Salisbury Plain were overcrowded, cold, wet, muddy and unhealthy. Accommodation was rudimentary, little equipment was available and the training areas were in such demand that each unit could use them for only one or two days a week, weather permitting. The Canadian troops already there were suffering severely in these conditions, and they were venting their frustrations in the nearby cathedral town of Salisbury.[45] It was obvious that the warm, empty spaces of Egypt would be a much better temporary training ground for the Australians and New Zealanders. The men were not told of the change in plans for a few days, but speculation continued: 'Plenty of rumours that we are going to Egypt & will land about Wednesday'; 'Rumoured at lunch time that disembarkation orders are called off, and that we proceed straight to the Old Country'.[46]

The first ships of the convoy reached Suez, at the entrance to the Suez Canal, on 30 November. Percy Doherty wrote: 'There weren't many people about and the few white people that we saw, especially the girls, got a great hearing from

Local traders alongside a troopship at Suez, 30 November 1914.

the boys'. For many men, their first impressions of Egypt were 'decidedly unfavourable, and later it was agreed that on a closer acquaintance there was no improvement'. Leslie Smith observed that 'Niggers came off to us in all kinds of queer boats. Sold us all sorts of fruit & other rubbish.'[47] Both Suez and Port Said lacked the wharf space and the facilities to unload the convoy quickly, so the ships were ordered to sail through the canal and on to the large, modern Mediterranean port of Alexandria. Before the vessels left Suez, staff officers disembarked and travelled to Cairo by rail to identify and mark out camping grounds for the NZEF and the AIF.

Turks were rumoured to be in the vicinity of the Suez Canal, so machine guns and searchlights were mounted on each ship before it entered the 160-kilometre-long waterway. Twenty-five men on each ship were issued with live rifle ammunition and stationed along the starboard decks. 'All on board were hoping that the enemy would be polite and put himself up as a target.'[48] The Turks did not oblige. Each ship was greeted enthusiastically by Indian and British infantrymen on the banks of the canal as it passed them in the bright moonlight. Percy Doherty wrote, 'it looks very funny to see the boat in front if she is round a bend – she looks as if she is steaming over the sand'.[49]

As the ships sailed on, final preparations for disembarkation began. 'Everything being prepared for disembarkation,' recorded Doherty, 'as it is stated that we may get off at Port Said to meet the Turks, who are said to be marching on the Canal, so we may be in action sooner than anticipated.' According to Ken Stevens, 'Grindstones

Troopships in Port Said, 1 December 1914.

were produced and we all sharpened our bayonets'. Alfred Cameron noted: 'Yesterday had identity discs, or cold meat medals, issued to hang around neck'.[50]

The New Zealand ships reached Port Said, 'said to be one of the four wickedest cities of the modern world',[51] on 1 December. William Peed wrote that the soldiers 'were all awakened with the noise of the niggers who were coaling us. We were not allowed to go ashore. … We could buy plenty of cigarettes from Egyptians & Turkish delight & oranges and figs & dates. There was a party in a boat with instruments & they were playing & singing for money of which they got plenty. They had a girl with them who could sing very nicely.'[52]

The convoy bearing the Main Body and First Reinforcements of the NZEF sailed into the Mediterranean Sea on its last voyage on the afternoon of Wednesday 2 December 1914. It berthed at Alexandria early the next morning. That day, Major General Godley officially confirmed what most of the men already knew or suspected: after a period of rest, training and re-equipment in Egypt, and once further Indian and Territorial Army units arrived to replace them, they would continue on to the Western Front. He encouraged the men to behave themselves in Egypt, and to train hard so as to minimise the time required to 'qualify' the NZEF to go to the front.

Various responses to the news are recorded in letters and diaries. 'I think a lot were disappointed that we didn't go to England,' wrote D. McGregor, 'but I reckon we are jolly lucky wintering here, as in England I hear that the troops are up to their necks in mud.' In Clutha Mackenzie's opinion, 'The troops were undecided whether or not to be pleased. Most of them had hoped to see the Old Country and their relatives there. Mac did not care a straw, for he saw no delights in an English winter camp, and Egypt was said to be a fine interesting country. Every one set about telling wild tales of Egypt.... [For some] there was an uneasy feeling that, should they once land in Egypt, they would be left there for the duration of the war.'[53]

Godley quickly laid down the law about the behaviour he expected from the NZEF while it was in Egypt. 'The natives in Egypt have nothing in common with the Maoris. They belong to races lower in the human scale, and cannot be treated in the same manner … Every member of the Force in Egypt is charged with the enormous responsibility of maintaining the prestige of the British race … the extreme danger of having any intercourse with native women is brought to the notice of the men. Syphilis in a most virulent form is rampant in Cairo, and men having connection with prostitutes are running the gravest possible risks … The native drinks are generally the vilest concoctions possible … an almost certain cause of illness.'[54] Inevitably, much of Godley's rather pompous rhetoric fell on deaf ears.

HMNZT No. 10 Arawa *anchored at Alexandria, 3 December 1914.*

Seventy-seven horses had died during the seven-week voyage, less than two per cent of the number embarked in New Zealand in October. Losses of up to a third of the horses had been anticipated, so this very low casualty rate was a great achievement, testament to the meticulous care the mounteds lavished on the horses, and to the fine weather and calm seas encountered for most of the voyage.[55] For the men, 'The days of decks, bare feet and semi-nakedness were at an end, and to-morrow would start again the life of boots and puttees, saddles and tents'.[56]

3

Egypt

It beats me why anyone would want to fight for a place like Egypt. It is nearly all sand & heat.

WALTER CARRUTHERS

To deny the existence of unspeakable vice and grossly open immorality in Cairo is unhappily impossible.

GUY THORNTON

IN 1914 EGYPT WAS a province of the Turkish Empire, but it had been under British rule in all but name for more than 30 years. The country's only real importance to the British and the Germans was the Suez Canal. Once described by the Germans as the British Empire's 'jugular vein', the canal was the favoured route for the movement of troops and trade between England and India, Australia and New Zealand. (The alternative was the long, dangerous Cape of Good Hope route.) Imperial troops had been stationed in Egypt to guard it for decades.

Islam was the predominant religion in Egypt. Turkey's declaration of war on the British Empire in November was followed a month later by the announcement of a *jihad* (holy war) by the Turkish Sultan, the leader of the Islamic faith, calling on Moslems throughout the world to fight the Allies. It seemed that the British presence in Egypt might be short-lived. Fortunately the Egyptians declined to answer the summons, choosing instead to see which way the war went before declaring themselves in support of either side.

The sea approaches to the Suez Canal were quickly secured by Royal Navy warships, but the land routes from the east were not so easily denied. The low-lying desert to the northeast of the waterway between Kantara and Port Said was flooded, and warships were stationed in the canal itself. General Maxwell relied on the Sinai desert as the major obstacle to Turkish forces advancing out of Syria (modern Israel).[1]

He planned to use the Australian and New Zealand force as his reserve while it trained around Cairo. It could be quickly moved by rail to bolster the defences of the Suez Canal when the expected Turkish attack took place.

This was the strategic situation in Egypt when the Australians and New Zealanders began disembarking at Alexandria on the morning of 3 December 1914. Russell wrote: 'Very indifferent arrangements had been made for our reception and despatch, owing to inadequacy of staff in Egypt to deal with so large a body of troops'.[2] According to Charles Nicol, a delay occurred when the Alexandrian harbour pilot who tried to board the *Star of India* was turned back by an overzealous New Zealand sentry, whose orders were to let no one aboard. '"But I'm the pilot," exclaimed that official, as he attempted to push by. "I don't care a damn if you are Pontius Pilate," calmly returned the trooper, as he held his rifle horizontally across the gangway.'[3]

The unloading of the horses was carefully planned. It was expected that many would collapse when they tried to walk after seven weeks of near-immobility, so straw or sand was placed on the docks to provide them with a soft landing. Quite a few *were*

Disembarking the horses at Alexandria, 3 December 1914.

70

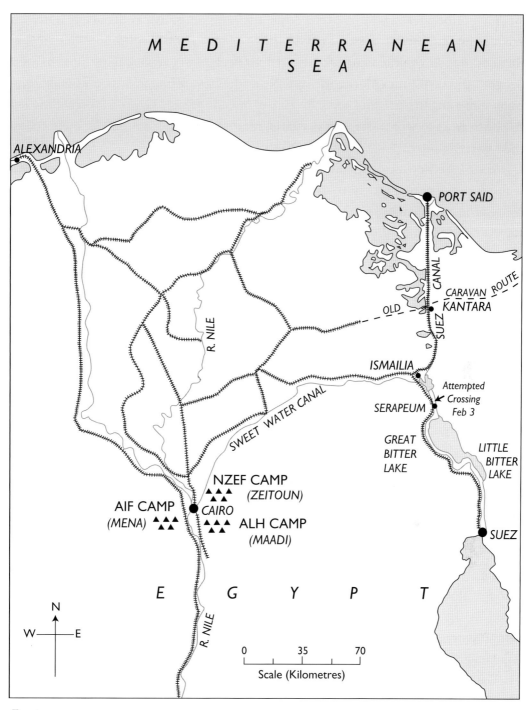

Egypt.

wobbly on their feet as they walked down the long gangways to the dock, 'but their relief at finding themselves on land again was plain to all; it was impossible to stop them from rolling in the sand, kicking up their heels, and even breaking loose in their delight'. But, as Clutha Mackenzie observed, 'they overestimated their strength and came sprawling to earth and soon, for lack of breath, quieted down. The squadron led its horses to a piece of waste sandy ground, removed their covers, and let them roll to their hearts' content.'[4]

Most of the New Zealand horses 'came ashore in remarkable condition. They were well-conditioned and glossy coated, and were quite ready to display their colonial conceits to the smaller-framed Arab horses about the wharves.' It was a different story, however, when they encountered camels, mules and donkeys for the first time. 'Often a stampede was averted only by the men hanging on to their horses for dear life.'[5]

The camping grounds around Cairo were a 200-kilometre train journey from Alexandria. The first NZEF train left Alexandria in the late afternoon, and they continued to depart all that night and into the next day. Clutha Mackenzie and his fellow mounteds 'rugged the horses, and at six o'clock entrained them, packing them tightly in the trucks. The men had a bit of a meal then themselves, bought oranges from the natives, and settled down in third-class carriages of a filthy and uncomfortable kind. Each horse truck bore a chalked date of when it had last been disinfected, but the carriages had no such reassuring legend. As darkness fell, the train started with a series of crashes, and clanked unpromisingly away into the gloom. It was a weary journey, and bitterly cold.' One unimpressed trooper described his berth on the train as a 'vile smelling third-class carriage'.[6]

Despite the lack of comforts, the journey south was full of interest. Guy Thornton wrote of the 'palm groves, fields of maize, cotton, millet, and berseem (a species of clover). We noted with interest the primitive method of cultivating the land with wooden ploughs drawn by buffaloes, horses, mules and sometimes camels. The vivid green of the fields, the feathery date palms, the picturesque (though appallingly filthy) native villages, the silver threads which revealed a network of canals, combined in presenting to our view a strange and beautiful scene.' Ormond Burton's eye was caught by the animals. 'Strings of loaded camels passed in stately fashion with contemptuous jerkings of their heads, little donkeys ambled along quite happily under appalling loads, goats and geese were driven here and there, the quaint oxen marched steadily round and round, turning the waterwheels, and yoked up with the heavy wooden yokes drawing the ploughs and the rough native carts.… Here and there the train would stop at some palm-fringed station, and at once the carriages were besieged by an eager throng selling tomatoes, "orangies," and "eggs-a-cook".'[7]

It took the heavily laden troop trains up to eight hours to reach Cairo. The New Zealanders were unloaded at a station near the eastern suburbs of Heliopolis and Zeitoun.[8] Another hour on foot brought the tired men and horses to their assigned campsite on the edge of the open desert. The first of them arrived about 4 a.m. and in the darkness 'all that could be found was sand and more sand, and, after much wandering, an iron fence [at the Heliopolis Racecourse] to which the horses were tied'.[9] Claude Pocock was disappointed with what he found. 'Now all the way out in the train we were talking of the horses enjoying a bite of grass when they got on land and guess our surprise when we tied our horses to the rails of a race course pegged out in the barren sandy desert with absolutely no sign of a green leaf of any description.' The weary mounteds looked around for something to eat and a place to sleep for a few hours. Some of the horses did not stay tied up for long: when a string of camels came by 'they simply went mad tore up the rails and almost stampeded'.[10]

According to Godley, the ill-preparedness first seen at Alexandria continued at the new campsite. 'The trains have been arriving all day and night, and the men have been dumped down in the desert without food or shelter, as we were not expected so soon, and the staff and labour was quite inadequate to get things ready.' There was little food until the nearby East Lancashire Territorial Division came to the rescue with hot tea and 'summat t'eat'. For a price, men could also have 'a cup of cocoa and a very small French roll from a Greek canteen keeper'.[11] There were no tents and few blankets, and the night was very cold, as Alfred Cameron recorded. 'It is mid-winter here, although quite as hot as the N.Z. summer in the day-time [but] it gets very cold at night. The sand soon got like ice.' That night 'produced a mild epidemic of influenza colds, and some twenty men were ordered off to hospital the first day.… Those who were privileged to experience that first night's bivouac on the sands of the Egyptian desert will long remember it as one of the coldest of their lives.' Many men soon gave up trying to sleep under the unfamiliar northern stars and walked around trying to keep warm. Finally, 'morning dawned upon many very bad-tempered and hungry men'.[12]

The rising sun burnt off the clinging mist, revealing 'a scene as inspiring to an untravelled New Zealander as America to Columbus. Close at hand stood an oriental city of splendid architecture, the early light touching with romance its minarets and pillared galleries. Spread before him, and stretching away into the distance until lost in a soft blue mistiness, lay Cairo, its forest of minarets, its domes and its square-topped houses. Beyond, unmistakable in the blue distance, were the old familiar outlines of the great pyramids.' William Pyle found it all very odd. 'Its strange to watch the new life here. It will take a bit of getting used to. Nothing but donkeys, mules & niggers so far. Haven't seen any dusky maidens yet.'[13]

No one knew how long the NZEF would be stuck in Egypt, but a betting man would have wagered that they would be there until the end of the winter. The first job was to get the campsite ready for a prolonged stay, and work started immediately. After a few days the part of the camp nearest to the Heliopolis racecourse was abandoned when it was discovered that there had been a recent outbreak of ringworm there. Despite the impressions of the new arrivals, a lot of work had actually been done by the advance parties sent ahead from Suez. Water pipes had been laid, horse troughs erected, and camping grounds were allotted to each unit. Showers and dining halls were under construction. Of course there was much still to be done, and the New Zealanders were quick to employ Egyptians for the more mundane and dirty tasks. Benjamin Colbran wrote: 'At daylight we had hot chocolate & a bun & cheese then started to get the horse lines up... We got a mob of niggers to do all the digging while we had a spell.' Another trooper recorded the menial work done by 'the natives' in exchange for 'the scraps and swill from the cookhouses and supplement this by hawking fruit, cigarettes and gazooza (lemonade). ... They do the washing at rates that would make the people at home envious. They sew, make clothes, drive the mules, donkeys, horses, camels, motor-cars, trams and trains, build huts, shave and cut hair and all manner of work at the cheapest rates imaginable.' Claude Pocock noted in his diary: 'We never moved out of camp today being too busy getting every thing in order and by tea time with all our tents erected and the horses picketed out in lines, stacks of fodder stacked up at the ends, shoeing forges, water pipes and troughs erected and the same old calls pealing from the trumpets we felt very much at home and again the familiar ditties of 'It's a Long Way to Tipperary', 'Sons of New Zealand', and 'Home Sweet Home' were coming through the air as the boys busied themselves in making their beds and procuring what articles they could to make their tents look like home.'[14] As Colbran noted on 12 December, men even had to help the weak little Egyptian donkeys to pull the heavily laden transport wagons until the New Zealand draught horses were strong enough to take over – 20 men to a wagon.

Inside an outer perimeter of trenches, huge piles of horse feed grew as the ships at

Part of the NZMR Brigade camp at Zeitoun.

Alexandria were emptied. Claude Pocock watched 'The great piles of hay, chaff etc …
grow higher and longer. It is being built in the form of a blockade round our camp and
when finished will be encircled with barbed wire entanglements and guards mounted
on the top.' According to William Lynch, 'We have got almost everything one could
desire in camp. Cook house, Saddlers shop, Blacksmith's shop, Mess room, pics show,
several canteens, motor garage and so on.'[15] The New Zealand Field Ambulance
established a medical treatment centre in the camp with room for 200 patients.
The nearby Egyptian Army hospital at Abbassia was used for more serious cases.[16]
A post office and veterinary hospital were also built. Over 10 million rounds of rifle
and machine gun ammunition, and nearly 6000 rounds for the 18-pounder artillery
pieces, were stored at the Cairo Citadel or in the camp.

The first horse stables consisted of rush matting on wooden frames, but they did
keep the sun off the animals. The horse stalls in the transport ships were pulled apart
and sent to Zeitoun for use there, as wood was very scarce in Egypt.

The sleeping arrangements for the men were equally rudimentary. 'We all have
mats made out of date palm leaves to sleep on & these are just laid on top of the sand
& I can tell you make a mighty hard bed.'[17] Men applied their artistic talents by using
coloured stones to depict regimental crests and mottoes, and tents were surrounded
by pot plants and pretty patterns of pebbles. Oats for the horses were planted

A home away from home. Three New Zealanders in their bell tent at Zeitoun.

among the tents of the mounted regiments, and flower beds were planted around the various officers' messes. Many tents were decorated inside with framed photographs of sweethearts, wives, or parents.

The local secretary of the Young Men's Christian Association (YMCA) warned anyone who would listen that Cairo was full of 'terrible temptations'. Regimental chaplains set up a large YMCA tent as a hopeful counter-attraction to the 'evils' of the nearby city. Writing materials were provided free of charge, and church services and weekly concerts were held there. 'A post box was kept in the tent, and sometimes no fewer than a thousand letters were posted in a day.' Other 'drawcards' included lectures on aspects of Egyptian archaeology given by local scholars.[18]

Wet canteens (bars) were established in the camp. 'A pint of beer costs one piastre (2½d) and it is good beer too,' wrote Percy Doherty. 'What will the N.Z. wowsers think when they hear, I wonder.'[19] The laws of supply and demand came into effect in a slightly different form: 'as the hot weather came and the temperatures rose the price of drink rose accordingly, until obvious discontent was manifested with the management. Forcible protests had their effect, and the price dropped again.' The wet canteens served another useful purpose, according to Godley, by 'keeping the men in Camp, drinking the wholesome beer provided, instead of going out, and drinking the appalling filth provided in all the drinking shops round about'.[20]

Outside the camp, Greek and Egyptian merchants set up stalls and shops of all descriptions, and they were soon busy selling 'Orangies', 'eggs-a-cook' and postcards, 'dirty or otherwise', to all takers. Not far away from the camp were the ruins of the ancient city of On where, in the words of Guy Thornton, 'it was impossible to walk a step without treading on the bones of those who had been buried there five to six thousand years ago'.[21]

By 9 December the NZEF was practically complete in Zeitoun. That day, General Godley thanked the men for the efficiency of the disembarkation, and gave them credit for the good condition and low losses among the horses during the voyage from New Zealand. He encouraged them to continue their good behaviour and bearing, but then spoilt the effect somewhat by reminding them of the importance of smartness of dress and saluting.[22]

The 'Latrine Wireless' had been the name given to shipboard rumours, and the name stuck in Egypt, as Alfred Cameron recorded. 'Last week some wag erected a mock wireless aerial over the latrines lines, and it has created much fun & comment.' Rumours circulated endlessly: William Lynch was told 'by men who know their business that the war could *not possibly* last more than a year'.[23]

The first consignment of mail from New Zealand arrived in mid-December, 'about 6 tons, I'm told, for the New Zealanders, four wagon loads'.[24] Volunteer Aid Societies and Patriotic Funds in New Zealand and England sent gift packs of socks, tobacco, food and other luxuries. In January 1915, 3 1/2 tonnes of donated plum puddings arrived for the New Zealanders. There was a scandal when it was alleged that some donated goods were being sold for profit. 'There has been a lot of discontentment among the troops with regard to the gift goods. Only yesterday an Australian here said he had bought a tin of … tobacco at the canteen with a label on it "With the compliments of the people of N.Z.".' In another case a man 'went into Cairo and … bought [a sewing kit] and on opening it in Camp found a note saying it was made by his mother and given to the Authorities'.[25]

While the horses regained their strength, they could only be led around quietly. This was a bonus for Claude Pocock and others 'because we are all heavier than when we embarked. I myself have gained eleven pounds and many more are the same'.[26] Despite their weakness, many of the horses were still a handful for the troopers to control. 'Our mounts are in great fettle,' wrote Pocock, 'even better than when we left New Zealand and two is enough for one man to hold for when they are not rolling they are rearing and bucking like lunatics … The horses simply revelled in rolling in the sand and every five minutes would just fall down and roll over about a dozen times.' Edwin McKay recalled two occasions when 'the desert around the camp was dotted with frolicking animals that had broken loose. It was not a stampede either time: they reminded us of youngsters when school breaks up for the Christmas holidays; they were just happy and tomorrow was another day. They always returned at feeding time, so no real harm was done.'[27]

The care of the horses was everyone's responsibility in the mounted regiments, but some men had special duties. Each squadron had a farrier quartermaster sergeant, and each troop a farrier sergeant. Their first major job was to replace the shoes on hundreds of horses. To avoid the worst of the heat, they worked from 6 a.m. until noon, then rested until 3 p.m. In the OMR the farriers were compensated for this arduous work in the hot sun by receiving two pints of beer per day, paid for out of regimental funds.[28] The farriers were also the horse 'medics', dealing with cuts and bruises and other minor injuries and illnesses. The horses had left New Zealand with a winter coat, which they lost while sailing through the tropics. Within three months of reaching Egypt, they had grown a complete new winter coat. This caused them to overheat in the high daytime temperatures in Egypt, so the horses were clipped.

In January 1915 two veterinary sections arrived from New Zealand, and one of them was attached to the NZMR Brigade. The equine equivalent of the field ambulance, it had the capacity to treat 250 horses for minor ailments before returning them to the regiments. More serious wounds or illnesses were dealt with at larger veterinary hospitals. Sick parades were held every morning for the horses. Several epidemics went through the horse lines in the first few months, including influenza and ringworm. Five thousand horses were sick with influenza, and 50 died; 80 per cent were affected by ringworm. According to William Lynch, many horses were destroyed. 'My word they are killing a terrible lot of horses here. Today three were done in. Tomorrow they are going to do away with six or seven. To my certain knowledge twenty seven have been destroyed. Isn't it an awful shame? It is not as though they were injured some of them were a bit thin that was all.'[29]

The initial horse ration in Egypt was a mix of chaff, oats, bran and hay. Millet and Indian corn were sometimes added, and fresh green fodder (berseem) was often available. Once the high-quality food brought from New Zealand ran out, the horses had to get used to the inferior local stuff. 'When a change was made to "Tibbin", an Egyptian apology for our chaff the horses did not appreciate it, and consequently lost condition, particularly as the issues were very irregular and the tibbin itself very often contaminated with a considerable quantity of dirt.'[30] For a few weeks, the horses did poorly on the new diet. Claude Pocock wrote that 'one can see it the moment our mounts get a bit of solid work there is no stamina in them and the coats are all rough like the horses are when in bad health … when we go out in the morning they are all spirit but one good gallop and their heads are down and you can feel the quiver of their frames'.[31]

Once the horses got over their initial friskiness and lost their fussiness over their food, they settled down and became very contented – with one exception. Most never lost their mortal fear of camels, donkeys and mules. 'The Nelson squadron had a stampede at lunch time, the horses taking fright at some camels. One horse was killed, another broke its leg, and I hear one man was badly hurt.' As long as these 'monsters' were nowhere within sight or smell, the horses were happy: 'there they stood in long and polished rows, chewing the succulent berseem and munching the dry and uninviting tibbin, which apparently caused the horses much less concern than it did the anxious troopers'.[32]

The Arabian racehorses at Heliopolis were much admired by Claude Pocock and many others. 'These pure blooded horses the Arabs will not part with and if you begin to ask how much they turn away and won't listen. They are not big horses the majority standing about fifteen hands and a sculptor could not carve a better model from marble.' On 16 December Godley visited the 1st Australian Light Horse Brigade's camp at Maadi and had a look at its horses. 'They certainly have got a most beautiful lot of horses – better looking than ours, especially those from Queensland, but I do not think that they will be any more serviceable when it comes to the point. I am quite satisfied with our own.' Edwin McKay and the other mounteds quickly grew very fond of their horses. 'When the gruelling test came later in Sinai and Palestine we loved our horses with a feeling that went deeply into our beings. They were more than mounts to shift us from spot to spot – they were cobbers.'[33]

Very few of the New Zealanders had experienced anything like Cairo before. In 1914 the city was already ancient: people had lived in the area for at least 10,000 years. At just over 700,000, its population was only a little less than the entire population of New Zealand. Cairo had been ruled by many different dynasties over the centuries, and most of them had left architectural evidence of their reigns. Ancient Egyptian temples and enormous pyramids, Islamic mosques, palaces and tombs, and Coptic Christian churches dominated the skyline. There were vast cemeteries and equally large rubbish piles. Modern suburbs with wide European-style streets lined with imposing buildings were surrounded by thousands of rough tenements, shacks, markets and shops, linked by narrow, dark and dirty alleyways. 'It is a gay old city, is Cairo. It is the home of Eastern curios, priceless fabrics, beautiful pottery, good coffee, bad liquor, donkeys, dirt, vermin, ear-splitting noises, and rampant vice. You can get as much of each of these goods as you like.' It 'was a place of great interest and greater contrasts, where modern electric tramcars clanged furiously to clear the swaying camel from the track; where European sewerage systems penetrated curiously insanitary vile hovels, patched and restored against time's ravages, where the twentieth century courtesan in Paris modes jostled the veiled women of the Egyptian harem in concrete steel emporiums with the latest eccentricities of fashion'.[34]

Knowing that there was much in Cairo to tempt his men, Godley made sure there were plenty of wholesome leisure activities in the camp or nearby. 'We had amusement and recreation in plenty, between concerts at night, tennis, football, etc. on the desert by day. We even ran a gymkhana once, and played polo and wrestling on horseback – with donkeys as mounts…. Add to this boxing, and Church Parade on Sundays, and you will have a fair idea of how we put in time when we weren't training.'[35]

No doubt encouraged by Godley, many English civilians in Heliopolis and Zeitoun went out of their way to be hospitable to their visitors. Some opened their homes for use as reading and writing rooms. The 'Zeitoun Minstrels', a singing group of eight women and six men, gave free concerts for the soldiers. According to William Lynch, 'The English ladies of Zeitoun have opened a new tea shop at Helmia, they serve themselves and every thing is cooked by them. So you can imagine the little shop is well patronised.' D. McGregor wrote home: 'Nearly every second house is a restaurant & in between is a hotel & it is the same in Cairo. It is a real good place to go to the devil quickly but it isn't troubling the New Zealanders much…. At Heliopolis there is one of the best "Wonderland" outfits in the world, complete with water chute, scenic railway, helter skelter, etc. It only costs about 1/6 [one shilling and sixpence] to do the whole turnout & is a real cheap place to spend an evening.'[36]

Amateur archaeologists found much to interest them in the immediate neighbourhood. Little of what they dug up was authentic, but that did not seem to matter much.

In their time off many of the New Zealanders spent their hours with an entrenching tool, digging in the sand or excavating at the bottom of the masonry shafts which were dotted all over the desert. Scarabs, blue pottery beads, and other relics were frequently found. Astute Egyptians 'salted' these deposits, and for a few piastres they were willing to lead you to a grave where most excellent scarabs were to be found. If you paid the money and accompanied the guide, half-an-hour's not very strenuous digging would probably bring to light a dozen or more scarabs, which if taken to a dealer would cause amusement to one party and discomfiture to the other. These objects were made by the bushel in Austria and Germany before the war.[37]

These harmless local attractions could only hold the men's attention for so long, and Cairo was within easy reach. Regular 'gharries' (horses and carriages), electric and horse-drawn trams and trains meant that getting there was no problem.

There was plenty to do in the city. Sightseeing was usually the first occupation. Popular tourist spots included the Zoological Gardens, where Lizzie the 'bewitching' hippopotamus was a favourite, the Ezbekiah Gardens where British military bands entertained, the Citadel, the Egyptian Museum and the pyramids at Giza. The 'desire to climb to the top of the great pyramid of Cheops consumed them; no less than seven men [New Zealanders and Australians] fell in attempting it. Four of them were killed

Waikato mounted riflemen at the Giza pyramids.

outright; and another was maimed for life.'[38] Those who made it to the top carved their names into the stone alongside those of Napoleon's soldiers, who had been there in 1798.

The simple delights of tourism also wore off quickly. Once the men had 'scaled a pyramid, had their photo taken on a camel, set eyes on a biblical site or two, and tried their luck at digging up ancient treasure on the desert sands, they went to town'.[39] The British soldiers in the small pre-war garrison had spent little money in the shops and bazaars of Cairo, and the war was keeping the rich American and European tourists away. These lost financial opportunities were more than compensated for in December 1914 by the arrival of thousands of well-heeled Australians and New Zealanders. They had money burning holes in their pockets, and many of them were not too particular about what they spent it on.

They could gamble at the horse races, purchase dubious 'antiquities,' get drunk, and consort with prostitutes. When they ventured onto the streets of Cairo the men were quickly besieged by 'an army of boys and men trading walking-sticks and swagger canes by the thousand; antiques made out of Nile mud; ancient Dervish weapons with the dust of Birmingham still upon them; foreign postage stamps on sheets; scenic postcards and questionable pictures; dainty little fly-whisks and "pieces of the true Cross"'. Guy Thornton wrote that 'The streets swarm with pedlars, who accost each passer-by with earnest requests to buy. They are an unspeakable nuisance. … It is impossible to travel a couple of hundred yards near Shepheard's Hotel without being pestered by sellers of flower-stands, highly coloured Soudanese beads, walking-sticks, peanuts, muslins, silks, or photographs, some of which are good, but others vile beyond words.'[40]

To lure New Zealanders inside, canny hoteliers and bar owners put up signs inscribed 'The Balclutha Bar', 'The Waipukurau Reading Rooms' and the 'Wellington Hotel – very cheap and breezy'. Fred Waite complained that a man could not sit down anywhere without being 'attacked by a swarm [of boys wanting to clean their boots] which had to be literally kicked away'.[41] In the opinion of another New Zealander, 'There was only one thing to do – let them clean them. It was no good trying to dodge those boys; they were out to black your boots, and they meant to black them or perish in the attempt. You gained nothing by bolting into a pub or a restaurant; no sooner were you seated comfortably than they had you bailed up by the leg and their brushes going at forty horse-power.'[42]

The questionable hygiene of the Cairene merchants and their cruelty towards animals took some getting used to. The recollections of Captain Guy Thornton, the chaplain of the AMR, paint a fascinating picture. 'The guileless Egyptian has the unfortunate habit of cleaning the luscious-looking strawberries by the simple and effective process of placing them in his mouth, and licking them vigorously and thoroughly.' The cab driver 'is … absolutely pre-eminent in his lack of brains. Certainly his cruelty to his horses is past belief.' Thornton once took a cab which, after an hour's driving, ended up where it had started from. When he finally reached the correct destination and paid the fare for the intended journey only, the cab driver swore at length: 'until he had finished his remarks I did not realise how unutterably base, vile and filthy were my ancestors for at least a dozen generations. He evidently knew a great deal more about them than I did.'[43]

Those in authority made ill-advised attempts to keep the soldiers out of some of the better hotels. The British troops put up with this, but the wealthier and less class-conscious New Zealanders and Australians would not. 'Such rules had never been imposed on them in their own country…Crowds of privates and non-commissioned officers invaded the bigger hotels, and in a matter of a few weeks the authorities responsible for the mandate realized their mistake, and the proprietors of the hostels saw new and large avenues of profit opened up for them.' As a result, 'Astonished Staff Officers, with red tabs, gold braid, and eye-glasses found themselves rubbing shoulders with democratic but wealthy young Colonials in resorts which had never been so desecrated before.'[44]

Many New Zealanders were appalled by the immorality of Cairo, describing it as 'beyond description, dirty, evil smelling, immoral and loathsome' and 'wicked beyond the imagination of ordinary mortals'.[45] Most of the concerns related to prostitution. This was an accepted fact of life in Cairo, but the easy availability of sex for sale surprised many of the New Zealanders. 'Just behind the Esbekia Gardens was the prostitutes' quarter. It contained more than 3,000 licensed prostitutes; no one could put a figure on the number of unlicensed, though estimates said about 20,000.' Quite a few of the men quickly got over their embarrassment and partook of the services on offer, despite being urged not to by their officers, doctors and chaplains. They were particularly likely to visit brothels once they had had a few drinks. 'As anonymous members of a huge group of men, all dressed alike, all with nothing to do off duty but enjoy themselves, the soldiers could indulge themselves as they never would at home in their own towns and rural areas.'[46]

For chaplains like Guy Thornton, the sights were almost unbearable. 'Nearly every window has a balcony, and since many of the houses are three-storied, a large number, sometimes ... over twenty women, may be seen in one house leaning over the balconies, in every stage of undress, shouting out their foul invitations to passers-by ... any afternoon after 4 p.m. and evening thousands of soldiers promenade the street beneath, gazing at and passing remarks upon these shameless creatures.' Thornton could not bring himself to accept that men would choose to visit prostitutes, and he came up with many alternative reasons to account for their 'inexplicable' behaviour. He thought that alcohol 'benumbed their judgement, lessened their self-control, deadened their consciences, and quickened their passions'. He accused bar owners of drugging the drinks served to the men. 'I have time and again seen men walk into a liquor bar as sober as men could be, and after one or two drinks behave like sexual maniacs.' He also blamed the commanders for placing 30,000 'innocent' Australians and New Zealanders within easy reach of such a 'notoriously evil Oriental city'. Although naive, Thornton was certainly a brave man, at least according to his own recollections. He patrolled the brothel districts at night, shaming those soldiers that could be shamed, abusing the brothelkeepers and, occasionally, even beating pimps and touts.[47]

General Godley was more realistic. He recognised that he could not keep the men away from prostitutes. In a letter to New Zealand's Minister of Defence, he wrote: 'Really the only trouble I foresee is venereal; I am afraid we are almost bound to lose about ten per cent of the men through it. The women here are all full of it.'[48] Instead of trying to ban the trade, he instituted measures to control it and to limit its consequences. '[Godley] marched them through the Wazza, hoping that a daylight look at the women would reveal what was hidden behind the façade of night-time glamour. He told the officers to keep warning the men, and to set them an example. "Dangle parades" to identify infected men were held once a week. ... the General also arranged for the medical officers of each battalion to have a supply of syringes for urethral irrigation.'[49] Men infected with sexually transmitted diseases were placed in isolation wards in the Venereal Hospital behind barbed wire, and some were sent home in disgrace. Others were banished to hospitals on Malta to free up their beds in Egypt for men with 'honourable' wounds or sickness. But the problem persisted until the soldiers were moved away from Cairo later in the war.

The New Zealanders and Australians did not feel welcome in Egypt. 'The bitterness of the Egyptians is very much on the surface,' Claude Pocock noted, 'and the way they expectorate on the ground when they see us in uniform is a good insight into their feelings.' In return, the soldiers ignored the Egyptians or treated them with contempt. Benjamin Colbran wrote: 'Yesterday our major gave us a bit of advice & warning about the natives & their drinks, telling us to treat them with authority & let them know we are their masters. ... One can hardly help regarding the niggers as animals, when you see them lying about.'[50]

The New Zealanders also formed strong opinions about other nationalities that they encountered. Before Gallipoli it is hard to find a good word about the Australians in New Zealand letters and diaries. They were generally considered to be undisciplined troublemakers who badly needed to be knocked into shape. According to Walter Carruthers, 'The Australian troops have got a great reputation for roughness since they have been here'. Claude Pocock thought they were 'always making disturbances in the town which reflects upon the whole of the colonial forces'. Charles Bean commented: 'Some New Zealand officers were encouraging their men to have nothing to do with the Australians, but to show by their neat dress and sobriety that there was a wide difference between the two forces'.[51] New Zealanders' impressions of British soldiers are harder to come by. In a letter home William Lynch described the English as 'a very small lot, the average is not above 5ft 2. They think we are giants. There is always a lot around trying to get a ride on a N.Z. horse – their own are a lot of scrags.'[52] The New Zealanders were beginning to see themselves as different from other nationalities. A sense of national identity was starting to develop.

Ill-disciplined behaviour became more frequent as the men continued to train with no immediate prospect of fighting. It was considered good sport to offer bottles of beer to donkeys, ignoring the protests of their outraged owners, until the animals were too drunk to stand up. Young Egyptian newspaper sellers were coached by mischievous New Zealanders to call out, 'Very good news, Sergeant ____ dead'. His newspapers would sell like hot cakes, until the subject of the fake report found out about it: 'The poor unfortunate boy never knew why he was kicked out of the lines by some irate N.C.O.'[53] The New Zealanders had to be prohibited from making cab drivers drive at a gallop, because of the harm this did to the overworked and malnourished local horses. NZEF Headquarters also warned that a continuation of the theft of private cars in Cairo could result in the city being placed out of bounds.

Many men were caught and tried for such offences. Those sentenced to detention usually served their time in Abbassia Detention Barracks. 'The place is just like a prison,' said Alfred Cameron. 'The men have to sleep on the bare concrete floor and are altogether treated the same as an ordinary prisoner in N.Z. except pack drill is what they have to do instead of stone-breaking.'[54] The worst punishment that could be awarded was to be sent home to New Zealand in disgrace, and quite a few men suffered this ignominious fate.

The average working day in Egypt for the New Zealanders consisted of various combinations of parade-ground drill, field exercises, shooting, lectures, inspections, vaccinations and parades. In the mounted regiments, a typical day in camp began with 'Reveille' at 5 a.m., usually announced by the Auckland regiment's band playing 'John Peel'. After coffee and a muster parade at 5.30 a.m., 'stables' (cleaning out the horse lines and feeding and watering the animals) followed until 7 a.m. Breakfast and ablutions took until 8.30, when the units paraded. Drill consumed the next three hours, then it was stables again until lunch at noon. From 2 until 4 p.m., there was more parade-ground work. Stables followed until 5.30, with 'Retreat' sounding at 5 p.m. After evening stables, the soldiers were usually free from 6 until 10 p.m., unless they were on guard or horse picquet duty (which came around every third or fourth night). 'Last Post' was sounded at 10 p.m. It was an exhausting schedule. 'Some of the mounted men were even heard to envy the "foot-sloggers" or "beetle-crushers," since the latter had no horses to look after.'[55]

In addition to all of this, guards had to be found for the railway sidings, the stores depots and the hospitals. Ammunition escorts were always needed, and the regiments also had to provide mounted orderlies for brigade headquarters. Frank Hobson 'was on Police duty at Brigade headquarters, principally keeping natives and others from going near the Brigadier's gardens … and getting plenty of exercise in the military art of saluting and feeling inclined to put my fingers to my nose at some of them'. The men usually had Saturday afternoons off, 'also Sunday from the conclusion of Church Parade, besides an odd whole day or two, for which we had to get a special pass'.[56]

On 18 December Egypt was declared a British Protectorate, formally ending Turkish influence in the country. The next day the Khedive of Egypt, who 'has adhered to the King's enemies', was deposed and replaced by a more compliant figurehead. The Australasians were on the alert for trouble, but the Egyptians reacted with calm indifference, as William Pyle noted. 'We had ammunition served out in readiness for trouble but everything passed off quietly.'[57]

On 21 December Lieutenant General William Birdwood arrived from India to take up the command of the Australian and New Zealand contingents training around Cairo. His job was to train them so they could take the field against the German Army in France and Belgium as quickly as possible. Birdwood wanted the forces grouped

William Birdwood, the British commander of the Australian and New Zealand Army Corps (ANZAC).

into a corps of two standard infantry divisions and one mounted division. The NZMR Brigade and the 1st Australian Light Horse Brigade would form the nucleus of the mounted division, which would be completed when two more light horse brigades arrived from Australia. The War Office 'wasted no time in rejecting so revolutionary a proposal', so Birdwood had to think again.[58] He put the three Australian infantry brigades into the 1st Australian Division under Major General Bridges, and everyone else into a hybrid New Zealand Division under Godley's command. The latter division initially consisted of the New Zealand Infantry Brigade, the Field Artillery Brigade, the 1st Australian Light Horse Brigade and the NZMR Brigade. The whole force was named the Australian and New Zealand Army Corps, or ANZAC. Before long, its troops were universally known as 'the Anzacs'.

On 23 December the New Zealand Division marched through Cairo as a show of force but, as Percy Doherty records, they 'had some sport after leaving camp, the horses being fresh and not having been out of camp before, everything was new to them, and when we met some camels at a corner there was no end of shying and bucking. It was just the same when we met the donkeys, and as the tarred macadam road was slippery, a few had some awkward spills.' The reaction of the Cairenes was muted, according to Gordon Harper. 'The route was packed with fezzed men and veiled women who watched us closely without the semblance of a smile or a cheer, but every indication is that they are petrified with British rule.' William Peed described the ride back to camp. 'The way we came back through Cairo was through the thickly populated quarter. It is dangerous to go through there at night time as one might get knifed as soon as the niggers think it is worth while. We arrived home at half past one & were glad of a spell.'[59]

When the Second Reinforcements sailed from New Zealand in mid-December

Mounted riflemen riding through Cairo as part of the show of force, 23 December 1914.

1914 Frank Hobson was among them. 'Mounted men left [Trentham Camp] about 8 o'clock and rode into Wellington … Embarking horses all this afternoon, after feeding and watering them and getting them used to steam-engines, motors and women.' He was not impressed by the conditions on board. 'Horses are all standing between rails with no room to lie down, and men are lying between benches with no room to stand up. I'd sooner be a horse on a troopship.' Even on a morning when the swell was 'not so heavy … a lot of men can't stand the smell of breakfast…. Horses having a very bad time getting their sea legs. Moustache making decided progress.'[60] The Second Reinforcements reached Zeitoun on 30 January 1915, and each mounted regiment received about 105 reinforcements and 130 remounts.

Christmas Day passed quietly for the men of the NZEF. After morning church services, they had the rest of the day off.

Christmas Day on the edge of the desert, within sight of the Pyramids of Gizeh! The very last place in which I ever thought I should celebrate the festive season. And the outlook was far from 'Christmassy': A big wide stretch of yellow sand; a rough, trampled track styled a road; a straggling collection of low, flat-roofed, mud-built native houses that looked as if they had been chucked from aloft and stuck where they happened to perch; a few vines, date palms, and fig-trees, disputing the right to live in company with some sun-baked nectarines and loquats; a foreground made up of tents, both military and native, wooden shanties and picketed horses; a background of camp stores, mechanics' shops, and corded firewood, closed in by a line of dusty poplars; in the distance the desert, a vast study in monochrome, the horizon line broken in places by an Arab village and cemetery, a camel train, and the forbidding wall of some Egyptian grandee's harem; overhead a scorching sun shining in a cloudless sky; underfoot the burning sand.[61]

On 29 December Captain James Bell, of the Mounted Brigade Field Ambulance, died of a brain haemorrhage. He was buried with full military honours, including a firing party of 100 men from the WMR. During the return to camp from this funeral, the horse of Trooper George Burlinson reared and fell on him. He died the next day from his injuries. His funeral in the English Cemetery was described by William Peed. 'Everything was got up properly. The Gun Carriage for the body & a pall bearing party & also a firing party & the troopers horse done up well with white and black ribbon & his boots in stirrups turned with spurs to the front.'[62] These impressive military funerals were soon dispensed with when the number of deaths on Gallipoli made them impossible.

Another NZEF parade, of 6330 men and 3165 horses, took place on 30 December. This time it was for Clutha Mackenzie's father Thomas, the New Zealand High Commissioner from London. According to one report, 'The men were much pleased with the visits of their London representatives, and cheered them to the echo when they departed'. Percy Doherty was not so thrilled. 'It might be all very fine for Sir. Thos. MacKenzie to stand at the saluting point and watch us all march past him, but I'll bet he didn't know how we cursed him and his inspection. Its no joke groping about in the dark looking for your horse and gear, and turning out in marching order with just a dry piece of bread and some strong mix-up called coffee, for breakfast.'[63]

As 1914 drew to a close the men of the NZEF were still expecting to complete their training in Egypt soon and then go on to the Western Front. They had no interest in defending the Suez Canal forever. 'It beats me,' wrote Alfred Carruthers, 'why anyone would want to fight for a place like Egypt. It is nearly all sand & heat.' However, 1915 opened with no immediate prospect of fighting for the bored and restless men of the NZEF and AIF. Joseph Law's diary recorded that 'New Years day came in with much band playing, carol singing & drunkenness'.[64]

4

When will we fight?

*If it was generally known that we would not leave here
before three months and if there was a boat leaving for N.Z. tomorrow
every man jack of us would board her.*

WILLIAM LYNCH

*The worst had come to pass. The infantry had gone away and left them, the
mounted men, to sweat and swear in the desert till the war was over, and Heaven
only knew when that would be.*

CLUTHA MACKENZIE

GENERAL GODLEY WANTED THE NZEF to be ready to fight in Europe as quickly as possible, so he began a progressive training programme almost immediately. He worked his men hard, setting more demanding training objectives and higher standards than the Australian commander, Major General Bridges. The infantry battalions tramped off into the desert every morning on route marches, and spent hours shooting on the rifle ranges. The gunners practised setting up and firing their field guns. Dismounted training and shooting was also the lot for the mounted riflemen for the first two weeks while their horses were acclimatising to Egyptian conditions. They also led the horses on increasingly long walks to build up their fitness, and there was even a bit of route marching and bayonet fighting thrown in for good measure. For some of the men, it all came as a bit of a shock. 'In New Zealand the men of the force had been subjected to a training which they thought was severe enough, but the time there had been too short to allow of many long route marches or attack practices. The work had mostly been confined to physical drill and bayonet exercise, and small arms exercises. Now, in Egypt, they got the first taste of the really strenuous side of soldiering in war-time.'[1]

By 17 December the horses were strong enough for mounted training to begin. Claude Pocock thought it was 'real good to get into the saddle again ... a lot of

90

AMR men and horses resting at 'The Virgin's Breasts'.

Tommies came out to see us mount and were much surprised when none of us were bucked off and some of our horses had a good go … they told us that if their horses were like ours they would be more often on the ground than in the saddle, I can quite believe it after seeing them ride.'[2] The mounted regiments concentrated on moving quickly across the desert to dismount points, from where they would advance on foot under the cover of machine gun and artillery fire. The mounted field ambulance trained its medics in first aid and the treatment of shock, while its doctors lectured all ranks on topical diseases. The machine gunners practised deploying on horseback to a flank, dismounting from the gallop and bringing their Maxim guns into action as quickly as possible. The signallers trained in the use of semaphore flags and the heliograph. Mounted officers practised the fine arts of issuing orders, navigation, map reading, sketching and fire control. The NZEF officers and men had a lot to learn. In his brigade Russell saw much room for improvement, especially in his junior officers. 'Troop training – many young officers as yet by no means understand how to lead – and many are ignorant of details they should have at their fingertips.'[3]

Not everyone was impressed with the quality of the training. To Charles Bean, it was 'simply the old British Army training. Little advice came from the Western front. The Australian and New Zealand officers had to rely almost entirely upon themselves. They had not seen a bomb [hand grenade]; they had scarcely heard of a periscope.'[4]

Most of the training took place on the Cairo–Suez track and around features such as the Petrified Forest, the Red and Black Hills and the Virgin's Breasts. 'All day and every day was spent in the Desert – protection on the move – at rest – attack and defence – night operations, etc., etc. – till we could have found "Tower No. 3" and "the Virgin's Breasts" and other landmarks, blindfolded.' Percy Doherty considered the desert 'a great training ground, plenty of room and sand hills for cover, and there are also plenty of dry small canals and holes here and there, which put a good many riders to the test, and not a few on their "nuts"'.[5]

Cross-country riding skills were practised constantly, as John Wilder recorded. 'Tas and I had a few real good jumps, some of our Troop had a go – one chap jumped a wall, but the horse did not!'[6] The horses quickly became accustomed to standing near the artillery as it fired, or beneath the shells as they whizzed overhead. It was a constant source of amazement for the troops that, wherever in the desert they were, as soon as a halt was called, Egyptians immediately came running from all directions, selling 'oringies, very beeg, very sweet', hard-boiled eggs, cakes and other delicacies.

The mounted riflemen had to be able to swim their horses across rivers, and they practised this skill at the Nile Barrage. This was a very pleasant green spot after the baking desert, and the mounteds enjoyed these periods. 'It is quite beyond me to

Swimming horses across the Nile.

express in writing how we relished the little time spent in the gardens & on the lawns, after being so long on the glaring deserts & among the stinking native quarters.' '[At the Nile Barrage] we camped on G.R.A.S.S. – yes – real green grass under lovely high trees. It was fun chasing scores & scores of bats… we were like schoolboys.'[7]

Most men soon agreed with the decision to train in Egypt. The days were long, the weather was fine but not yet too hot, and there were limitless areas available for training. To top it off, there was the ever-present possibility of fighting against the Turks, who were known to be lurking not far way in Syria. But Egypt had its disadvantages as well, particularly as the temperature rose. 'Very hot today,' wrote Percy Doherty on 14 December. 'If this is supposed to be winter, I'm sure I don't want to see a summer here.'[8] Clutha Mackenzie described conditions in Zeitoun Camp as the heat increased.

The camp lay listless in the glaring heat of high noon. Long rows of tents gleamed dazzlingly in the sun. Saddlery, horse-rugs, nose-bags and gear were untidily scattered about. Except for the sleepy figure of the horse-picket, attempting vainly to keep his lanky person within the shade of the feed-trough, there was no one in sight. The horses needed little attention. With heads low and legs crooked, they dozed in every attitude of siesta. Within the open tents lay the human element, more or less replete after the seldom varying meal of sandy stew and bread. Most of the men slept, stretched full length upon rush matting on the shady sides of the tents. Some wore trousers, some shirts and some neither.[9]

Route marches raised dense clouds of fine grey dust that quickly coated men and horses. This, and the daytime temperatures, caused intense thirst. Orders stated that no one was allowed to drink any water before noon, and this discipline gradually acclimatised the men and their horses to going without water for long periods. Both gradually got used to hardship and short rations, as Percy Doherty noted. 'It is surprising how little one can live on and feel satisfied when used to it. After eating a couple of biscuits and a drink of tea one feels as if he has had quite a big tea now.'[10]

In early January Godley told the New Zealand government that the mounted rifles brigade was 'under orders to be ready to go out at a moment's notice to a place called Wadi Natrun, about 100 miles north-west of Cairo, in the desert, to watch for Bedouins and Senussi from that direction'.[11] Nothing happened. As the weather got hotter and the training dragged on into 1915 with no end in sight, the New Zealanders began to lose heart. Uninformed rumours continued to raise false hopes. A hopeful Gordon Harper wrote, 'If nothing comes of the Turkish advance we will be sent across to Marseilles in Feb. & gradually get up to the front when it gets warmer'.[12]

The attractions of Cairo had quickly palled, and more men began to spend their leisure time in camp with their mates. 'People can say what they like about the sights here, but I wouldn't give the lot for a good trip around Rotorua or a bit of bush scenery.'[13] As life in the NZEF began to sour, the men took out their frustrations on each other and on the Egyptians. 'Grousing was rife in the camp and the troopers were nervy,' wrote Clutha Mackenzie. Offended by the proprietors of the camp picture theatre, some men 'showed their displeasure by partially burning the building'. One evening, 'to break the monotony, some of the men surreptitiously extracted a couple of casks of un-watered beer from the brigade canteen. They rolled the barrels some distance across the sand, and proceeded to enjoy themselves.... A small Armenian general goods shop chose to over-charge, with the result that the vainly-expostulating merchant found his lean-to razed to the ground before his eyes.'[14]

One day Percy Doherty and a few friends had an unexpected brush with danger. 'While taking up a position in an old dry canal today, we were suddenly called into action with fixed bayonets against a snake that came wriggling along amongst us. It was about 2 ft. 6 ins. long, but we soon had it chopped up. This being our only "kill" since arriving in Egypt, I wonder if we will get a medal for our bravery.'[15]

As training moved away from parade grounds and into the desert, some dress rules were relaxed. 'Tonight an order came out from Headquarters that has sent us all rejoicing. It is, that no brass work on any of our gear is to be cleaned; it must be allowed to go dull, and its only a shame how easy it will be to carry that order out to the letter. Some of the boys spent the night in the canteen drinking each others health on the strength of it. ... On orders this morning that officers must wear bandoliers the same as troopers, also puttees in place of leggings, the idea being to cut down conspicuousness, so that they won't be able to be picked off by the enemy.'[16]

On 9 January squadron training ended and regimental training began. 'We had a strenuous day today,' William Peed recorded in his diary for 24 January 1915. '[The WMR] regiment had to attack the low hills that were supposed to be entrenched by 200 infantry. Dummy targets were put up. We had a very long run & were quite fagged when we got the order to charge with bayonets. One man got wounded in the leg by a stab from a bayonet. Our attack was covered by the artillery and machine guns.' Percy Doherty of the CMR described riding *a long way out into the desert with the usual advance and rear guards … Dummy men were stuck up in the sand dunes representing the enemy whom we were advancing on.… We were trotting along nice and quietly in troop column when the advance guard signalled back 'enemy in sight'. We were then halted and a message came galloping back with a despatch explaining position and all about the enemy. The next order was 'gallop' and off we went helter skelter for about half a mile.*

In the second last section of the troop, Doherty found it 'almost impossible to see, the stones and grit thrown up by the other horses in front almost blinding you'. The men closed their eyes, lay on their horses' necks 'and let them go till we heard the whistle with the signal "Halt" "Action dismount"'. After tumbling off, they handed their mounts over to the No. 3s 'and took cover under a ridge not far away. We advanced in short stages running from ridge to ridge taking as much cover as possible till we were within about 400 yards of the dummies when we opened fire. After firing about 10 shots per man we retreated a troop at a time till we got back to the horses.… After this … we were supposed to be suddenly attacked by cavalry, so when we came in sight of the enemy we tumbled off the horses, fixing bayonets as we doubled out to the front taking up a horse shoe formation in front of each troop. We fired another 10 rounds here rapid. This concluded the practice.'

Suddenly, in the midst of the interminable training, there was a chance of real fighting. Doherty thought 'we will very soon be in action, as the Turks have mobilized and are about to march on Egypt. We are all hoping that it is true.'[17] For once, the Latrine Wireless was correct.

While the Anzacs toiled in the desert around Cairo, Germany convinced Turkey to launch a force from Syria into Egypt to block, or at least threaten, the Suez Canal. This would interfere with the flow to Europe of troops and food from Australia, India and New Zealand, and it would also force the British to hold soldiers back from the Western Front to protect the canal. On 15 January 1915 25,000 Turks and Arabs advanced from Beersheba, reaching the Suez Canal in 10 days without loss. Awaiting them at the canal were 30,000 men, mostly Indian Army battalions, supported by artillery and warships. The New Zealand Infantry Brigade was deployed from Cairo to the canal defences on 26 January, and it took part in the battle. The mounteds were not required, much to Percy Doherty's disgust: 'the Mounted Men feel a bit dejected at being left behind, but horses would be of little use there, so we won't be sent there unless it is absolutely necessary'.[18]

The Turks attacked the canal defences in the early morning darkness on 3 February 1915. A few hundred succeeded in crossing to the western bank before they were killed or captured. The attacks were easily repulsed, and the expected uprising by the Egyptians did not eventuate. The Turks broke off the attacks and withdrew, leaving about 200 bodies and 700 prisoners at the canal. Thirty British and Indian soldiers (and one New Zealander) were killed. Even after the Turks had withdrawn, some of the eternal optimists in the mounted brigade thought that they would still be needed at the canal. According to Percy Doherty, 'Capt. Talbot of the 10th M.R. is supposed to have told someone that he thinks we are likely to go to the Canal this week, probably about Wednesday'. Like most other rumours, nothing came of this one. 'Usual training. We are all getting very sick of it.'[19]

During the excitement of the canal raid, 2000 saddles and bridles arrived for the NZMR Brigade. Half of them, Godley reported, were 'quite useless, as they are tiny little saddles of a rotten flimsy American pattern, which would only do for arab ponies. However, we have one thousand excellent ones.' These were 'a great success, and Russell had no sore backs during the long trek that he made last week, when he was out for four days'.[20] New bandoliers were also issued to the mounted riflemen to replace the inferior ones they had brought from New Zealand. Percy Doherty and his mates 'soaked the pouches on our bandoliers in water then filled with ammunition while wet to stretch them, as they are too small at present to hold ten rounds in clips. The bandolier carries 150 rounds of ammunition and it is surprising how heavy it is. It will be no pleasant task carrying a full bandolier all day.'[21]

On 27 January the New Zealand Division was renamed the New Zealand and Australian (NZ&A) Division to recognise the addition of the newly arrived 4th Australian Infantry Brigade.

As winter became spring, training was moved from the middle of the day to the early mornings and late afternoons. According to William Johns, 'The climate was lovely when we first came here, but now it is practically unbearable. The desert near the camp has been pulverised on the surface until drilling on it is practically impossible. Then the heat is getting cruel. We perspire even lying in our tents almost naked.'[22]

Sandstorms made life very trying. 'The strong hot wind raised an enormous grey pall of sand, through which the sun shone redly. Inside a tent was no better than outside. The very atmosphere consisted of hot sand.' They had been told 'that February was the month noted for sand-storms. Well, we ran across two – or, rather, they ran across us. We didn't like them a little bit. There was only one thing to do – get under cover straight away and stay there until the beggars blew themselves out. You would see them coming, for all the world like a big yellow smoke-cloud stretched right across the desert. Then it was a case of hop into your tent, fasten up the flap, and pray that someone else had driven the pegs home.'[23]

On 1 February, while the infantry brigade was away at the Suez Canal, the mounteds began brigade training. Clutha Mackenzie considered brigade and divisional training to be 'inventions of the devil'. Percy Doherty described it as 'a grand sight and we only wished that we were really on trek instead of just playing soldiers'.[24] The higher the level of training, the more important it was for the senior officers, and the less interesting it often became for the men. From the long-suffering trooper's perspective a typical divisional exercise went like this:

> *Move out of camp sometime between 4 a.m. and 8 a.m.; proceed leisurely for about two hours; halt when found to be mixed up with other troops; wait here half to three-quarters of an hour; move on for half an hour; halt one and a half hours (good sleep); move quarter of an hour; halt; told to put nosebags on horses; in five minutes ordered to move at once; move rapidly quarter of an hour; halt one hour; make dismounted attack on sand hill three miles away; move at the double across the sand for two miles; fall down and fire off half a dozen blank cartridges; fix bayonets and charge remainder of distance to hill; find hill occupied by staff who make audible comments about slowness; horses brought up by horse-holders who ask if it was hard work running in the sand; officers fall out to be lectured by the General; men mount and return to camp by the shortest route, the R.S.M. in charge.[25]*

Clutha Mackenzie wrote that each rank was 'roundly condemned to everlasting perdition by the rank immediately below it' until 'bad-tempered and dishevelled, the troops would set off on their homeward march, the final straw being added to the annoyances of the infantry by the passage to windward of the mounted rifles ... who would be home two hours before them'.[26]

Later in February, the Canterbury regiment conducted a sham bayonet charge against some British soldiers. Percy Doherty described what happened.

> *At last word was passed down the line to fix bayonets and be ready to charge. Col. Findlay was very keen and he could hardly constrain himself to wait for the bugle. With his 'Now,*

Canterbury, up and at 'em' every man jumped up like one and following the Colonel's lead, made for the trenches, which were held by the Tommies. The row we made was enough to frighten anything, some were yelling, others were giving a haka, and the Colonel in front was making more row than anyone. Well, we scared the very devil out of those Tommies. They hopped out of the trenches and ran for their lives…. The colonel said to us before we started 'Now boys, whatever you do don't stick a bayonet in my bottom'. Probably that is why he ran so hard to keep out of our way.[27]

In late February the 3rd Australian Infantry Brigade suddenly left Cairo for a secret overseas location. Something was going on, but no one yet knew what it was and the rumours continued. Percy Doherty recorded many of them in his diary. On 1 January: 'Another [rumour] that we are all going to be turned into Infantry, as Mounted Rifles are practically useless at the [Western] Front'. On 27 February: 'Rumour has it that we go to Jaffa in Palestine, but I think France will be our destination'. On 28 February: 'Some say we are going to Servia [Serbia], some say the Dardanelles [Gallipoli] and some think France'. On 14 March: 'Rumoured now that we are going to Salisbury Plains [in England] after all. Another rumour is that the Mounted men will not leave Egypt at all, so we don't know "where we are".'

On 26 March the Third Reinforcements, numbering 2210 men (including 439 Maori) and 933 horses arrived from New Zealand. Each mounted regiment received 115 new horses, some of which were not in good condition. 'The horses are a poor lot & not up to the previous standard of reinforcements.'[28] On 1 April 73 invalids, including 16 mounted riflemen, sailed from Suez for New Zealand. With them were 24 men who had been dishonourably discharged; three were mounteds.

Men were still pouring into the mobilisation camps back in New Zealand, and larger reinforcements were offered. New Zealand's Minister of Defence told Godley: 'We also propose to send you some more men. We have suggested a Mounted Brigade. I am not sure how far they [the British War Council] will desire mounted men but it is easier for us to send these than attempt an Infantry Brigade. I am afraid this latter is beyond our capacities.'[29]

The Anzacs were becoming increasingly angry at being marooned in Egypt while the war seemed to pass them by. Rumours suggesting that they were destined to stay in Egypt as a permanent army of occupation did not help matters. 'Hence the growing feeling of discontent, the constant grousing, and the daily lament of "Kitchener hasn't got any use for us; we're a 'Ragtime Army,' 'An Army standing by'"… In a word, we had attained to that top-notch pitch of condition in which we felt we must fight some one – or burst.[30]

The discontent and tension finally came to a head on Good Friday (2 April), a day off for the troops. That afternoon a serious riot broke out in the brothel district of Cairo, known as the Wazzir. The trigger for the riot could have been anything. Various stories circulated: a New Zealander was stabbed; a group of Australians was robbed; and an angry Australian or New Zealander who had contracted venereal disease had returned to the brothel and started a fight.[31] The rioting spread quickly, and many passers-by in the neighbourhood joined in. Buildings were set on fire, shops were looted and Egyptians were assaulted. Many men recorded their impressions of the riot. 'Hither and thither rushed the lightly-clad love-ladies screaming as only Eastern women can, and stopping only to hurl a bottle or other missile at some grinning Vandal who ducked quickly, then went on enjoying himself'. Claude Pocock 'saw one of our fellows came walking serenely down the street not knowing he was so near hostilities till a bedstead lighted on his head and he passed into oblivion'. Egyptian fire engines tried to put out the fires, but they did not have a hope. 'Another sound – the clang of a bell – broke on our ears as the fire-engines came racing up. Out came the hose; the police, who had hitherto remained in a state of "armed neutrality," endeavoured to clear a way for the native firemen. That settled them; no Colonial will stand the touch of a nigger's hand on his shoulder…. The hose was cut, and the engines were captured.' The Egyptian Militia, 'in their resplendent uniforms and mounted on their beautiful grey Arab horses', could do nothing, wrote Jim McMillan.[32]

British mounted military police were then sent in to quell the disturbances. That was a mistake, for the Anzacs hated the 'Red Caps', considering them to be

a little coterie of well-fed, rather pampered, and intensely self-consequential johnnies. … They seemed to imagine that they had a mob of English Tommies or niggers to deal with, but when they began trying to force their horses on top of the crowd they soon dropped down to the fact that they were up against something tougher. They were told pretty straight to go home and eat pie and not come meddling around where they weren't wanted. They didn't like being treated that way and showed it, so they had to be shoo'd off. At this they seemed to lose their top covering altogether, and, being armed with revolvers, opened fire on the crowd. It was now hell with the lid off. A number of the boys were hit, which sent the rest fair mad. You should have seen those Red Caps do a scoot! I don't think they got away unharmed; one I heard never got away at all.[33]

The riot was finally broken up after four hours by Anzac mounted troops. According to one witness, the growing thirst of the rioters was another factor in ending it. While a few men recorded their disgust at the day's proceedings, most seem to have been quite satisfied with the results. Duncan McDonald wrote: 'to my everlasting sorrow, I missed it'. There is no firm evidence of fatalities, but many Egyptians and a few British 'Red Caps' were badly beaten. 'There was certainly a biggish lot of damage done, and the natives who saw the scrap got the scare of their lives. But I fancy there weren't more than a house or two burned down – more's the pity!'[34]

Leave was stopped for all ranks, 'which in its turn resulted in the cinema catching fire and the canteen being raided'.[35] On 4 April Benjamin Colbran's diary recorded: 'Tonight the canteen started charging 1 1/2 P [piastres] for a pint of beer & the troops considered it too much so they took the matter into their own hands & pulled the tent down & took all the beer. After this we started on the dry canteen to pay off old wrongs. This place was a wooden building but it did not last long. The tents were soon full of biscuits fruit & other articles. After pulling down the restaurant tent things quietened down.' The next day he reported that the 'officers have got wind of a plan to stampede the horses tonight so there are hundreds of guards around the lines. This is a mean thing to do & I hope the guards will not fail to use their rifles if an attempt is made.' A Court of Inquiry could find no one to blame for the riot, but it nonetheless recommended that the New Zealand and Australian governments offer compensation for the damage done. This was agreed to, and New Zealand duly paid the sum of £1,759 to the Egyptian government.

The Wazzir riot and its aftermath showed that some of the men were becoming unmanageable, and many others appeared willing to follow them in any mischief that might occur. 'The troops were weary to sickness, both of Cairo and of the desert,' Charles Bean wrote. 'Years later they looked back on them as a paradise such as the contingencies of war were likely never to place in their way again.' David Scott put it all down to 'Too much to drink and not enough to do'. Claude Pocock believed that the riot was the inevitable result of the men being 'so utterly tired of being kept here, and being treated like children, we are made to do so much and so many things that are silly and useless … The sum total up to date is the men have had enough …it is my opinion that nothing but marching orders will quieten them.' Godley admitted as much in his report. 'It is unfortunate that this should have happened just before we left, but, really, one can only be thankful that nothing of the kind happened before.'[36]

For most of the Anzacs, their time in Egypt was almost over. In late February, General Godley was secretly warned to prepare the NZ&A Division for a move at short notice.[37] On the day before the Wazzir riot, Godley was told that his division would begin to embark at Alexandria the following week. Its destination was Gallipoli.

In August 1914 the Turkish Empire encompassed the modern states of Turkey, Israel, Lebanon, Jordan, Syria and Egypt, and parts of Libya, Iraq, Saudi Arabia and Yemen. Turkey controlled the Suez Canal and Russia's only warm-water route to the Mediterranean, as well as the newly discovered oilfields around the Arabian Gulf. In addition, the Turkish Sultan was the worldwide leader of the Moslem faith. These factors made Turkey a very desirable ally, despite its military weakness. Germany convinced Turkey to side with it in the coming war, and in August 1914 a Secret Treaty of Alliance was signed between the two empires. Turkey declared war on the Allies in November. Its first major act of war was to launch 150,000 men into the Caucasus against Russia.

On 2 January 1915, while the men of the NZEF were digesting their New Year's Day dinners and wondering if they would ever get to fight, Russia appealed to the British and the French to draw Turkish forces away from the Caucasus, where the Russian Army was under heavy pressure.

Russia's plea for help struck a responsive chord in England. Germany was already proving to be a tough nut to crack on the Western Front, where, by Christmas 1914, nearly 100,000 British soldiers had been killed, wounded or captured. Winston Churchill, the First Lord of the Admiralty, was keen to support any plan that offered an alternative to this deadlock, especially if it gave his underemployed warships something useful to do.

Within a week, military planners in London agreed to provide what Russia asked for and more. Turkey was believed to be a particularly weak member of the enemy coalition (the Central Powers), and it was thought that an attack on it might knock it out of the war. That might bring the neutral countries of Italy, Romania, Bulgaria and Greece into the war on the Allied side. Turkey's defeat might even lead to the collapse of Germany. The Secretary of State for War, Field Marshal Lord Kitchener, and Churchill suggested that the best way to achieve these grand objectives was to send the Royal Navy to the Turkish capital Constantinople, where its mere appearance was expected to convince the Turks to surrender.[38] After this the Allies could advance up the Danube River and across the plains of Hungary against Austria-Hungary,

Turkey.

and Russia would have guaranteed warm-water access to the rest of the world. The concept was approved by the British War Council.

To reach Constantinople the fleet first had to get through the Dardanelles, the 50-kilometre-long seaway linking the eastern Mediterranean Sea to the Sea of Marmara, the Bosphorus and the Black Sea. It was bounded on its west by the Gallipoli peninsula and to the east by the Asian part of Turkey. Turkish forts mounting heavy coastal artillery guns overlooked the narrow seaway from both shores, and the channel was mined. Many of the coastal guns were obsolete, and little ammunition for them was on hand. The garrison was small and lightly equipped, with only a few machine guns and little field artillery. These deficiencies were highlighted when British warships bombarded the outer forts in November 1914. German technical advisers were sent to the peninsula to help correct the problems, and by February 1915 the defences were in much better shape to withstand any renewed attack. Several hundred mobile field guns and the fixed fortress guns were supplemented by howitzers that could provide deadly plunging fire against unprotected ships in the restricted waters of the Dardanelles. They could not be hit themselves as they fired from behind hills. Anti-

WHEN WILL WE FIGHT?

submarine nets and several new lines of mines were secretly placed in the waterway (see map on p. 108).[39]

No land forces could be spared from the Western Front, so the first Allied plan of attack on the Dardanelles was a purely naval affair. Naval bombardments of the forts at the tip of the peninsula in February and early March 1915 had limited results. In mid-March, a large fleet of mostly old and expendable French and British battleships and minesweepers sailed up the seaway towards the Narrows, the most heavily defended part of the Dardanelles. The battleships were supposed to pound the forts and their guns into dust, after which the minesweepers would clear the mines. The fleet would then sail on to Constantinople and victory. Ten thousand troops, including the 3rd Australian Infantry Brigade which had mysteriously disappeared from Cairo at the end of February, were waiting on the nearby Greek island of Lemnos, ready to occupy the shattered forts. Another 30,000 Anzacs in Egypt were warned out for possible service as an occupation force.

Sixteen British and French battleships took part in the naval attack on 18 March. After early success against the forts, it ended in failure. The high-trajectory howitzer shells, though little more than a nuisance to the heavily armoured battleships, were deadly against the unprotected minesweepers, which withdrew after clearing only a few mines. Three British and French battleships were sunk and others were damaged by Turkish mines and by fire from the shore guns, and nearly 700 sailors were killed. The Narrows were never seriously threatened.

The attack showed that the fleet could not force a way through the Narrows without help. It was decided in London that a large military force would have to be landed to hunt down the elusive mobile howitzers and to ensure the destruction of the forts by attacking them from behind. The 10,000 men already on Lemnos were returned to Egypt to be reorganised, and other French and British troops, including the Anzac troops in Egypt, were confirmed for the attack.

The Mediterranean Expeditionary Force (MEF), as the Allied invasion force was known, was nearly 75,000 strong by the date of the landings. In addition to the 30,000 Australians and New Zealanders in the ANZAC, the MEF also included the British 29th Division, the Royal Naval Division and a French force of divisional size. Its command was given to General Sir Ian Hamilton.[40]

After the March attack, Turkish defensive efforts were redoubled on the peninsula. They knew that the enemy would be back, and that their next attempt would probably involve a landing. On 25 March, a German cavalryman, Major General Otto Liman

Otto Liman von Sanders, the German commander of the Turkish 5th Army at Gallipoli.

von Sanders, was appointed to command the new Turkish 5th Army, which was responsible for the defence of the Gallipoli peninsula and the Asian shore opposite. More troops were brought down to the area, more hospitals were prepared and more ammunition was brought forward. Labour battalions of Jews, Christians and Armenians worked at night on new defences and roads, while the combat regiments practised anti-invasion and counter-attack drills ceaselessly.

With only 84,000 men at his disposal, Liman von Sanders could not properly defend all the possible landing beaches. He thought the main Allied attack would come at Bulair, at the neck of the peninsula, so he placed two infantry divisions there. Another two divisions were sent to the Asian side of the Dardanelles, leaving two to defend the Gallipoli peninsula itself. One of them, the 19th Division, was commanded by the as yet unknown Lieutenant Colonel Mustafa Kemal. Liman von Sanders covered the most likely landing beaches with light forces, which were well dug in and protected with barbed wire and a few machine gun emplacements. Inland, he positioned regimental-sized groups to counter-attack the enemy troops once they had landed, and throw them back into the sea.

General Hamilton knew almost nothing about the enemy defences awaiting his invasion force. He had no detailed maps of the peninsula. The Turks were not regarded as a serious threat. Their unimpressive fighting performance at the Suez Canal in February, in Mesopotamia and in earlier wars, had convinced most Allied planners that the invasion of Gallipoli would be a pushover. London downplayed the decades of military assistance the Germans had provided to the Turks, and detailed reports about the defences of the Dardanelles and about the Turkish Army were ignored or forgotten.

As it turned out, the invasion would play to the strengths of the Turkish Army. By modern European standards, this conscript force was badly trained and inadequately led. It had lost most of its artillery in earlier wars. These characteristics made it ill-suited to modern mobile warfare, but the toughness and courage of the soldiers, especially the ethnic Turks from Anatolia, made them ideal for static trench warfare. Most of the men in the Turkish divisions waiting at Gallipoli were experienced regulars, and many had previous combat experience. They were well armed with modern German rifles and machine guns. The fact that infidels were invading the Turkish homeland guaranteed a stubborn defence. According to Tim Travers, the defenders of Gallipoli were 'often poorly fed and badly clothed but still willing to fight to the death'.[41]

General Hamilton planned to land his best troops, the Regular Army men of the British 29th Division, at Cape Helles on the southern tip of the peninsula, where the Royal Navy could best support them. This force was expected to capture the hilltop of Achi Baba on the first day. It would then advance up the peninsula to the Kilid Bahr plateau, overrunning the coastal forts along the way. A secondary landing was to be made by the ANZAC, 20 kilometres up the western coast of the peninsula at a sandy beach between Gaba Tepe and the high ground of the Sari Bair range. The job of the ANZAC was to seize the lower southern foothills of this range, then advance right across the Maidos Plain to the Narrows between Mal Tepe and Maidos, cutting the Turkish lines of communication and trapping the Turks defending Cape Helles.

Diversionary landings on the Asian side of the Dardanelles by the French, and further north at Bulair by the Royal Naval Division, were also planned to keep the large Turkish forces there pinned down away from the real landing beaches until the assault troops were safely ashore. According to the British official history, it was anticipated that the heights overlooking the Narrows would be overrun within three days of the landings.[42] Once the forts and mobile howitzers were dealt with, the Royal Navy would be able to clear the mines without interference. The plan was clever but complicated, and it demanded much of the forces executing it.

The MEF was poorly prepared for the battle ahead. Hamilton's headquarters staff was hastily cobbled together from whoever could be spared from the War Office. It was not well briefed and was woefully inadequate for the monumental task of planning and executing a complex operation like an opposed amphibious landing. The naval and army planning staffs worked in isolation from each other until a few days before the invasion, and the logistics and medical planning officers on Hamilton's own staff were sidelined and ignored. Many of the men in the MEF were inexperienced, and none of them were used to working together. Several commanders were pessimistic about the prospects of success, and they were not slow to tell Hamilton so.

Hamilton had little in the way of artillery, his supply of shrapnel shells was very limited and he had no high-explosive ammunition at all. The only fire support that he had in abundance were the heavy guns of the British and French fleets. His infantry divisions did not even have enough rifle ammunition for a serious fight. The ships and boats for the landings, which would presumably be made under enemy fire, were vulnerable and slow. Hospitals were prepared on Lemnos and in Egypt, and hospital ships were assembled, but they were not expected to deal with many casualties. Because trench warfare was the last thing Hamilton expected, the men of the MEF had no grenades, trench mortars, periscopes or other essential stores. There were few engineers and no materials to build wharves. Security was hopeless: letters addressed to members of the 'Constantinople Expeditionary Force' arrived in Egypt through the ordinary mail. The Egyptian press published details of the arrival of units with impunity, and some senior MEF officers even gave interviews about the invasion. Hamilton considered that the initial landing would be the only difficult part of the operation. Everything about the plan suggests that a swift Turkish collapse was expected as soon as the MEF set foot on enemy soil. As Chris Pugsley notes, 'No questions seemed to be asked about what the MEF would do if they did not'.[43]

When War Office planners were looking around for soldiers for the Gallipoli invasion the NZEF, New Zealand's national army, was conveniently handy and unemployed in Egypt. On 3 April the men of the ANZAC received orders to hold themselves in readiness to leave Egypt at short notice as part of the MEF. In the NZ&A Division, only the two infantry brigades (one Australian and one New Zealand) and the artillery brigade were required. The NZMR Brigade and the two Australian Light Horse brigades were to continue training in Egypt. Two squadrons of the Otago Mounted Rifles Regiment were included in the landing force, and another 50 Otagos were selected to provide a dismounted escort for General Hamilton.

There were several factors behind the decision to leave most of the mounted regiments behind. There was not enough water for the horses, and the intended landing sites did not favour mounted work. It was also explained that mounted troops would not 'normally' be required for an opposed landing and capturing of a beachhead.[44] MEF planners may also have decided that the mounted troops would not be needed to help defeat the Turks, who had performed so poorly on the banks of the Suez Canal a few months earlier. The canal still needed to be guarded, and a mobile force could perform this task with the least manpower, thereby freeing up infantry for the Gallipoli invasion.

Godley did not anticipate ever needing his mounted regiments in Turkey. 'This is an infantry and artillery war – exactly the opposite to South Africa, and mounted troops are at a discount. Their only chance will be if, after getting through the Dardanelles, we get on to the plains of Hungary.' He thought it 'unlikely that the New Zealand Mounted Rifles Brigade and the 1st Australian Light Horse Brigade will ever return to this Division, as it is understood that they are to form part of a newly formed Mounted Division'.[45]

Most of the mounted riflemen, including Clutha Mackenzie, were heartbroken to be left behind. 'The worst had come to pass. The infantry had gone away and left them, the mounted men, to sweat and swear in the desert till the war was over, and Heaven only knew when that would be.' The mounteds 'were grieved to the very depths of their souls to be left behind to stagnate on this sun-baked Sahara'. Some mounteds, including Claude Pocock, regretted joining a mounted unit. 'I must admit are sorry now that we are mounted here we are kicking our heels with nothing to do and can't get away and can't get into the infantry I am certain that if volunteers for the infantry were called … every man would step out … I would give a great deal to get marching orders.'[46]

Rumours quickly spread about what would be done with the NZMR Brigade. Percy Doherty wrote that 'all sorts of wild rumours are flying about that we are going to be left behind for Mounted Police etc., but it remains to be seen. Surely they won't treat us like that.' A week later he noted: 'The latest rumour now is that we are to leave for England about the 4th May and we are to be trained as cavalry – bow wow! We would kid ourselves galloping along waving a sword about. I'm afraid there would be a fair number of lop-eared horses after the first week.'[47] According to Claude Pocock, there was another rumour that 'the people of Cairo have petitioned the Military Authorities to have the N.Z. Troops left to Garrison duty here instead of the Australians', but the Cairenes would be sorry if that happened.[48] The mounteds seized upon any story that gave them hope of employment. Percy Doherty attended a lecture on Turkey where 'The lecturer raised our hopes a little higher by saying that mounted men would be wanted there after the battleships with the aid of Infantry had silenced all the forts, as the Turks would have to be kept on the run, so as not to allow them to entrench themselves too strongly against attack, and he thought it would be our lot to march right into Constantinople (loud cheering you can bet)'.[49]

Beginning on 9 April, the New Zealand infantry battalions, artillery batteries, engineers and transport units slipped away from Zeitoun. 'On the night of the

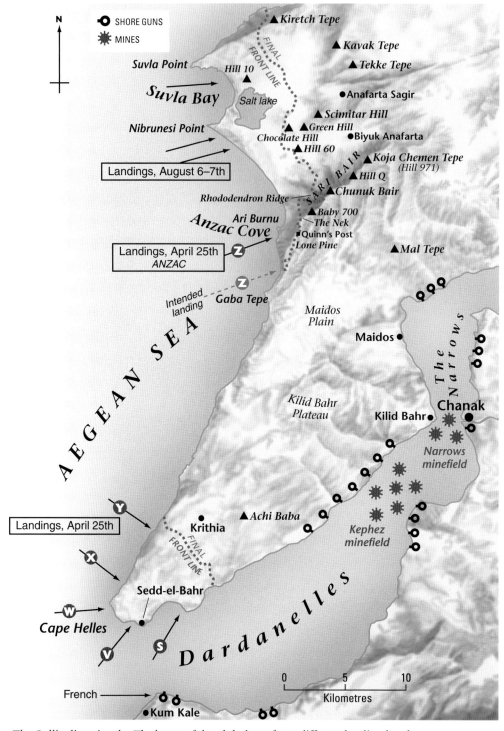

N
SHORE GUNS
MINES

Kiretch Tepe

Kavak Tepe

Tekke Tepe

Suvla Point
Hill 10
Anafarta Sagir
Suvla Bay
Salt lake
Scimitar Hill
Nibrunesi Point
Green Hill
Chocolate Hill
Biyuk Anafarta
Hill 60
Koja Chemen Tepe
(Hill 971)
Landings, August 6–7th
Hill Q
Chunuk Bair
Rhododendron Ridge
Ari Burnu
Baby 700
Anzac Cove
The Nek
Quinn's Post
Landings, April 25th
Lone Pine
ANZAC
Mal Tepe

Intended
landing
Gaba Tepe

Maidos
Plain

Maidos

The Narrows

AEGEAN SEA

Kilid Bahr
Plateau
Kilid Bahr
Chanak
Narrows
minefield

Achi Baba
Krithia
Kephez
minefield

Landings, April 25th

FINAL FRONT LINE

Sedd-el-Bahr

Dardanelles

Cape Helles

0   5   10
Kilometres

French

Kum Kale

The Gallipoli peninsula. The letters of the alphabet refer to different landing beaches.

departure [of the infantry] troopers searched for friends along the ranks that loomed through the darkness, grasped hands they never were to touch again, and went back to the same tiresome tasks of the horse lines.'[50] Three days later 11,142 men and 2218 horses of the NZ&A Division embarked on troopships at Alexandria, bound for Gallipoli. Two squadrons of the OMR went to Alexandria and embarked with the rest of the Gallipoli force. Their ship left the wharf at 7 a.m., but its sailing orders were cancelled and it returned to the wharf four hours later. The disappointed Otagos were told that they would sail in 10 days, but they were the last of the mounted rifles regiments to reach Gallipoli.[51]

Some of the mounteds tried to get away with the infantry. Clutha Mackenzie and a few mates wangled local leave from Zeitoun. Avoiding the military police, they caught a train to Alexandria, where they hoped to sneak aboard a troopship. The only troopship still tied up to the wharf was too well guarded, so they hired a Greek boat to try boarding a transport moored in the harbour. When the boatman put them aboard an American warship that was going nowhere, they admitted defeat and spent the rest of the day sampling the delights of Alexandria, before returning to Cairo on the night train.[52]

After the departure of the MEF for Gallipoli, and with the steadily rising daytime temperatures, the daily work routine eased a little for those left behind. 'The "Mounteds" are putting in a lot of foot drill now as the horses can't stand the heat. The heat & the flies are worrying the devil out of them.'[53] The early morning routine was the same, but less drill was conducted, and the afternoons usually consisted of a leisurely ride out to a cultivated area, where there was a short period of training followed by a nap under the palm trees. The columns returned to camp at about 4 p.m. Long-distance treks became more common. 'To counter the natural discontent and restlessness, [the mounted rifles and light horse brigade commanders] held inter-brigade manoeuvres and trekked for days at a time, often to places of interest like Memphis.' The fed-up mounted riflemen were not impressed. As William Lynch wrote, 'If it was generally known that we would not leave here before three months and if there was a boat leaving for N.Z. tomorrow every man jack of us would board her'.[54]

The landings at Gallipoli began before dawn on Sunday 25 April 1915. The 1st Australian Division landed first. It was supposed to seize the Third Ridge (later known as Gun Ridge) of the Sari Bair range, as far north as Chunuk Bair. Godley's NZ&A Division was then to land, advance across the peninsula and seize the hill of Mal

Tepe, overlooking the Narrows. The ANZAC infantry brigades were put ashore a little north of their intended landing beaches, in the middle of the steep terrain of the Sari Bair range instead of at its foot. This completely upset the plan, and both divisions were soon committed to fighting among the incredibly steep and rough hills on the seaward side of the range. Turkish counter-attacks were unrelenting and fierce. Losses were tremendous on both sides, and Birdwood's ANZAC barely managed to gain a precarious foothold on the edge of the Second Ridge. Nearly a quarter of the New Zealanders who landed at what would soon be known as Anzac Cove were killed or wounded that day.[55]

The British and French landings at Cape Helles were a little more successful, but none of the Allied objectives for the first day were reached. For the next two weeks, both sides fought almost continuously, but to no advantage. 'The hope of a short campaign, crowned by a splendid victory, had ended in disappointment. The invading army, everywhere held up by superior numbers, could do no more until heavily reinforced. … At Anzac the Australians and New Zealanders were hemmed in by superior numbers within a thousand yards of the beach. Every unit had suffered heavy losses; there were no reserves left; and the supply of ammunition was nearly exhausted. Nothing accomplished by the army had been of any help to the fleet, and the guns of the fleet were powerless to help the advance of the army.'[56] By 4 May the ANZAC alone had lost 10,000 men. The Turks had lost even more, and were desperately short of gun ammunition. Both sides paused briefly to regroup their forces.

When news of the landings filtered back to Cairo, the mounteds 'resembled dogs in leash in their anxiety to get away to the aid of the Force which had suffered so severely'. According to Walter Carruthers, 'The Mounted Rifles are still awaiting the call to arms & are beginning to think that it is not going to come'.[57] The publication of the first casualty lists and the sight of the large numbers of wounded men arriving back in Cairo for hospital treatment did not seem to worry the mounteds. Their comrades in arms were in action, and the Anzac horsemen envied them. The thought of going home without having been 'blooded' in combat did not bear thinking about. 'The men scanned the casualty lists … and cursed their luck, but a change was coming.'[58]

With the invasion stalled and MEF casualties mounting alarmingly, it became vital to get more men across to Gallipoli quickly. In Egypt there were three Anzac mounted brigades (the 1st and 2nd Australian Light Horse (ALH) Brigades and the NZMR Brigade) and two single regiments, the 4th Light Horse and the OMR. On 30 April General Birdwood suggested to Hamilton that these brigades should be asked for 1000 volunteers to temporarily reinforce the exhausted and understrength Anzac infantry.[59] In Egypt, General Maxwell asked Russell and Chauvel (the commander of the 1st ALH Brigade) what they thought about their brigades going to Gallipoli as infantry without their horses. They replied that they would go willingly, but only as complete brigades. They also insisted that, in the event of 'mounted troops being required on Gallipoli, their brigades were to have first preference and have their horses sent over to them'.[60] Maxwell supported their position, and forced it through in the face of considerable opposition from Hamilton and Birdwood.

The men of the NZMR Brigade received their orders to move to Gallipoli as infantry on Wednesday 5 May 1915. Approval was general, but not unanimous. Frank Hobson had never seen 'such a lot of smiling faces in camp as there are to-day'. William East wrote: 'We had to give up our horses altogether and train as infantry in the desert. That was a terrible thing after being on horseback so long.' Clutha Mackenzie thought 'it was not too good leaving the horses; they would have preferred going into action with the "prads" [horses] but they didn't mind doing anything to get out of this God-forsaken country and into the real thing'.[61] William Pyle would be 'sorry to see the last of my nag. He is looking very fit just now. Its hard luck after all these months of looking after them to abandon them, but it appears they would be of no use over there.' Hobson detected 'Something different in the air when the bugle goes now.... Some of our men are being left behind, somewhere around 10%... They had an ingenious or silly method of letting us know who were to be left behind; each man's saddle and horse kit was placed upright behind a horse cover and the officers passed along noting the owners and those who were to go their saddles were left upright, while those who were to be left their saddles were turned down.'[62]

A lot of work had to be done quickly to get the mounted riflemen ready for Gallipoli. 'Surplus stores were handed in, the troops were attired in battle order with packs ready, farewells said to the horses, most of which were never to see their riders again, while the officers put away their swords and distinctive dress to don the ordinary issue uniform.'[63] No proper infantry web equipment was available, and the best substitute that could be found in time was an ungainly brown canvas pack with two arm slings, to be worn on top of the bandoliers. Awkward and uncomfortable, the packs were quickly discarded on Gallipoli.[64] Clutha Mackenzie 'overhauled his [equipment] with much care and thoughtful consideration. Into his base kit went those things which would come in handy in Constantinople.... Into a barley sack went his saddlery, with a reserve of many straps, buckles and horse-brushes, all collected at odd moments. Rifle, revolver, field-glasses, everything underwent a thorough overhaul. Ammunition was clipped and forced into the leather pouches of bandoliers, which equipment appeared neither to be meant for nor accustomed to such practical use.'[65] Percy Doherty wrote: 'Tonight we filled our bandoliers with ammunition, 150 rounds. I wonder how many Turks that lot will answer for. Tomorrow I am going to put a very sharp point on my bayonet so that it won't require so much energy to push it in. It is hard to describe the general feeling every one has at the present. Everyone is so keen in seeing that his rifle is clean and that his gear is correct…. It is hard to believe that we are really going to fight. We have been fooled about so long, but we are going to get it in earnest I believe this time. The Turks are very strong in the Peninsula at present and will take a bit of driving back.'[66]

Brigade Headquarters, the three regiments, the field and signal troops and the field ambulance, totalling 1865 men, left Zeitoun in 'merry mood' on the evening of Saturday 8 May, 'delighted to have the opportunity of assisting their brothers of the Infantry'.[67] They took 277 horses (a few officers' mounts, the rest to pull wagons) in case there was room to use them on Gallipoli. According to Percy Doherty, 'Every one [was] in great spirits today; one would think that we were going on a pleasure trip somewhere'.[68]

Clutha Mackenzie described the last night in Zeitoun:

Forty-eight hours after the first warning, the last night came. A subdued murmur arose from the camp. Some busied themselves with final preparations; some glided silently away from the zone of flickering candle-light, towards the horse-lines to give a parting pat to their faithful horses, a sad farewell for many; some joined the cheery crowd who were making the most of their last moments at the canteen; and others, less careless and more sober-minded, sought a few moments of sleep. At eleven o'clock they fell in on their last parade in Egypt, though few regretted that…. A rough crowd they looked, these amateur infantrymen, overloaded with awkward, extemporized gear. They stood silent, for thoughts ran deep now that they were at last on the brink of the real thing, a moment towards which they had looked so long. The roll was called. Mac mentioned that he had left something, and slipped away to give the old mare a farewell stroke. Words of command echoed through the stillness, and soon the whole brigade was marching, as best it could, down the road towards the station…. The column turned to the left, and gradually the reverberating tread of heavily-laden men grew fainter in the distance. So went the mounted brigade.[69]

5

At last, Gallipoli!

We arrived in the middle of the night and couldn't see a thing. We really didn't know where we were. We hadn't been told anything. General Godley finally turned up and told us to do our best for King and Country. That was about all.

WILLIAM EAST

In less than twelve hours with the bullets crashing around the trench all night in the polluted air and one look over in No Mans Land in daylight, all the glamour in war for me was lost.

KEN STEVENS

WHEN THE MOUNTED RIFLEMEN and light horsemen left Cairo on 8 May 1915, the Allied situation on Gallipoli was still perilously insecure. The MEF was ashore, but it held little more than shallow beachheads. At Cape Helles the British and French were still nowhere near their first day's objective of Achi Baba. Twenty kilometres up the western coast at Anzac (as the position was already known), the Australians and New Zealanders were stuck on the edge of the Second Ridge below Battleship Hill, Baby 700 and Chunuk Bair, all of which remained firmly in Turkish hands. South of Baby 700, the Anzacs held Walker's Top, Pope's Hill and three small posts (Quinn's, Courtney's and Steel's) perched on the edge of the ridge above Monash Gully. The Turks 'needed only to drive back the invaders a distance of five yards to hurl them into the valley'.[1]

Anzac was a tiny beachhead, just over three kilometres long from Chatham's Post in the south to No. 2 Outpost in the north. The furthest point inland was Quinn's Post, only 1200 metres from the beach (see map on p. 114). For the thousands of men already there, the place seemed like a prison. 'Practically we are like a rat in a trap. The rat cannot get out and the owner of the trap does not like putting his hand in, and can only annoy the rat by pushing things through the bars.'[2] The New Zealanders

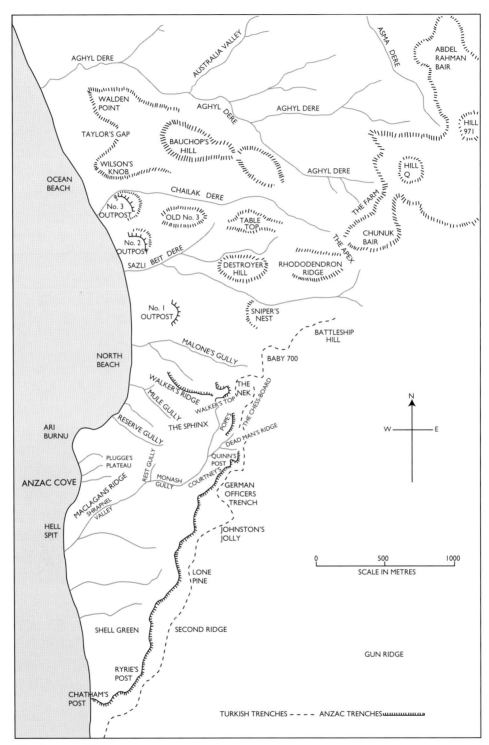

The Anzac position.

and Australians at Anzac had already suffered heavy casualties in a series of poorly planned attacks, and they were exhausted.

In late April General Hamilton decided to launch a major attack at Cape Helles to capture Achi Baba and the nearby village of Krithia. The Anzacs up the coast were told to keep the Turks opposite them busy in order to hold them back from Cape Helles. The first attacks at the cape resulted in nothing except more loss of life. Further attacks were ordered, and the two strongest brigades at Anzac, the New Zealand Infantry Brigade and the 2nd Australian Infantry Brigade, were sent south on 5 May to take part in them. The New Zealanders were replaced at Anzac by two weak brigades of the Royal Naval Division. At Cape Helles on 8 May both Anzac brigades were thrown into a series of hastily planned and badly co-ordinated attacks across open ground towards Krithia. The New Zealand brigade suffered over 800 casualties in a few hours. This took the total number of casualties in the New Zealand Infantry Brigade, which had been 3400-strong at the landings 14 days earlier, past 2000. By now the Anzacs as a whole had suffered 8500 casualties, over 2300 of whom were dead.

As the shocked survivors of the Anzac infantry brigades rested at Cape Helles the next day, 1865 men and 277 horses of the New Zealand Mounted Rifles Brigade arrived at Alexandria, along with a similar number of Australians in the 1st Australian Light Horse Brigade. Most of them boarded the *Grantully Castle*, while the horses and a

Canterbury mounted riflemen waiting to board the Grantully Castle *at Alexandria, 9 May 1915.*

few hundred men to look after them were embarked on the *Kingstonian*. That evening they set sail for what was still officially called 'an unknown destination'. Gallipoli was an unknown in one sense: the mounteds knew almost nothing about it. They left Egypt in a state of optimism based on near-complete ignorance of what lay ahead.

The mounted riflemen and light horsemen were tightly packed on the *Grantully Castle*, and there were no bunks or hammocks on the ship, but no one minded much. Many of the mounteds were quietly relieved at not having to worry about the horses for once. Over the next three days, as the ships crossed the Mediterranean Sea, most of them filled their time by sleeping, reading or playing cards. 'Those who had money wanted to get rid of it. It was of no more value.'[3] The more practical men sewed socks into the shoulders of their tunics to ease the load of the heavy packs, stocked up on necessities from the ship's canteen or repacked their kit. Percy Doherty noted that 'Officers and N.C.Os are cutting all their stars and stripes off and coming out like troopers ... We are pulling the wires out of the Service caps, so that the top does not show a stiff shiny surface, which is more easily picked up in the distance.'[4]

The troopships arrived off Cape Helles at 5.30 on the morning of Wednesday 12 May. 'This morning is very foggy and drizzling with rain, so that we can see very little,' wrote Frank Hobson. 'Breakfasted off porridge and tea and butter, within sound of the guns, the dull booming of which could plainly be heard.'[5] Another mounted rifleman wrote: 'At last, Gallipoli! The Trooper regarded it suspiciously. It looked miserable and he felt likewise. After the long, bright months in Egypt, the damp penetrated to his bones, and he hadn't had breakfast. Anyhow, he supposed it wouldn't be so bad, and went off downstairs for a wash.'[6] At noon the troopships weighed anchor and sailed up the coast to where the ANZAC was fighting. An attempt to land the men there in daylight was frustrated by Turkish artillery fire, so the ships backed off and waited for nightfall before trying again.

The mounteds arrived at Gallipoli 17 days after the first landings. They had guessed from the casualty lists that the invasion had not gone entirely to plan, but they were still surprised to see that the front line was 'simply on the cliff-tops above the beach',[7] so close that Turkish shrapnel pellets and bullets were landing among them as they approached the shore. 'A continuous roll and rumble could be heard, and now and again, as the breeze came from the land, the sharp crackling of rifle fire used in earnest, a sound new to the ears of so many of those eager boys.'[8] Arthur Batchelor wrote: 'Bullets splashing all round us. Rotten feeling at first soon get used to them. Only two chaps hit.'[9]

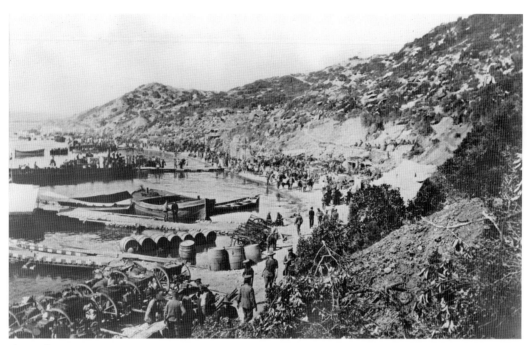

Anzac Cove.

The horses and most of the men aboard the *Kingstonian* were sent back to Egypt, leaving 1500 mounted riflemen and a similar number of Australian light horsemen to be landed. First they were transferred from the *Grantully Castle* to destroyers and torpedo boats. Charles Nicol and the rest of the AMR 'with those ridiculous brown packs up, and all manner of things from shovels to pannikins appended, tumbled down the gangway on to her deck'. Some of the heavily laden men had to clamber down swinging rope ladders. 'Imagine his feelings on finding himself on a rope ladder, dangling twenty feet above a dancing torpedo boat.'[10] When they were within 1500 metres of the land the men were transferred into barges towed by small boats and taken in to the beach. Some of the mounteds were disoriented by the strange sights and sounds. 'Many lights from the bivouacs on the seaward slope gleamed like a miniature Wellington across the water. War seemed difficult to reconcile with so serene and perfect a night. ... The whole thing was weird, yet beautiful – the still glory of the night, the eerie, echoing rattle from above, and the flickering light of the bivouacs.'

The mounteds landed on a temporary jetty at Anzac Cove at 6 p.m. and 'gathered in ragged lines along the beach to await orders. What was expected of them that night, none knew.'[11] William East was not impressed. 'We arrived in the middle of the night

117

and couldn't see a thing. We really didn't know where we were. We hadn't been told anything. General Godley finally turned up and told us to do our best for King and Country. That was about all.'[12]

The beach was a fascinating sight for the new arrivals. 'The narrow beach ... was a seething mass of humanity and mules. ...They appeared out of the darkness and passed into it again with an air of steady practical purpose. Ant-like, they passed in continual streams from barges to stacks of boxes, whose size rapidly increased.'[13] James Harvey 'could hear the rifles cracking on the ridges above the landing. Most of us thought we would be into it straight away.'[14] While they waited to be told what to do, men collected shrapnel bullets and shell casings as souvenirs.

The official story was that the new arrivals were welcomed with open arms. 'Every face on the beach was wreathed in smiles,' wrote Fred Waite. 'Whatever the trudging infantry men had thought in Egypt as the mounted men swept by, to-day there was nothing but the good-humoured banter of "Where's your horses?" ... Never were troops more welcome.'[15] General Birdwood reportedly said to Lieutenant Colonel Mackesy of the AMR: 'Thank God, you have come'.[16] Their reception was not entirely like that. Some men on the beach did welcome the mounteds, then 'immediately launched into long-winded accounts of previous fighting. With an air of conscious superiority, they gave them hints and advice, and told vividly of trials, troubles and dangers. All this the new-comers accepted unchallenged and with deep respect.'[17] Others ignored them or even swore at them, perhaps because many of the new arrivals greeted them warmly and boisterously, not understanding 'how offensive the bounding, super-abundant animal spirits of fresh troops can be to men who are tired beyond all telling'.[18]

When orders were finally received, the mounteds shouldered their uncomfortable packs and tramped around Ari Burnu Point and up into Reserve Gully below the Sphinx. Gordon Harper wrote: 'We made our way in single file up a very pretty gully, in a dry, winding creek bed, and through dense green scrub, much the same as our native growth. The whole time, on the ridges on either side of us, the terrific fusillade kept up without ceasing. It was almost impossible to hear one speak, the continuous crackle was so loud.'[19] Ken Stevens spent his first uncomfortable night ashore on steep scrub-covered slopes 'amongst some graves, and the air was not very fresh', while Clutha Mackenzie and his mate Smokey 'forced themselves under a holly bush, enveloped themselves in their oil-sheets, and braced their feet against stems of shrubs to prevent their sliding down the fifty degree slope'.[20] Few of them could sleep for the

Walker's Ridge (left), the Sphinx (centre) and Walker's Top (right skyline) from Plugge's Plateau. Table Top is the flat-topped hill in the left background. The NZMR Brigade spent its first night ashore perched on the steep slopes in the foreground.

noise of rifle and machine gun fire from the ridges above them. Many thought a major fight was in progress, but it was actually a quiet night by Anzac standards.

The 13th of May dawned fine, and after a hasty breakfast some of the mounteds had a quick look around. It did not look quite so strange in daylight. 'Lovely day & splendid scenery,' wrote William Dawbin. 'Small green cultivated patches (said to be mined) scattered among the scrub. Constant rifle & shell fire all night & day. Newly made graves everywhere.' Gordon Harper thought it 'a strangely peaceful setting for the horrors of war, these green hills and fields, red and yellow with poppies and wild flowers, and the blue Aegean coming right to their feet'. For another new arrival, 'The scene was not half-bad – a sapphire sea meeting a widely sweeping beach, a green, tree-dotted flat, and scrub-covered hills, all sparkling with dew and bathed in the clear, tempered sunshine of an early Aegean summer morning'.[21]

Godley's New Zealand and Australian Division was responsible for the northern part of the Anzac line (No. 3 and No. 4 sections), with the 1st Australian Division to its south. No. 3 Section, at the head of Monash Gully, included Quinn's Post, Courtney's Post and Pope's Hill. No. 4 Section included Walker's Top, Walker's Ridge and Nos 1 and 2 Outposts. In the absence of the New Zealand and the 2nd Australian infantry brigades, two weak naval brigades were holding these parts of the line. Godley sent the mounted riflemen to No. 4 Section and the Australian light horsemen to No. 3.

After breakfast the Wellingtons led the brigade up Walker's Ridge, the only direct route from the beach, via a steep and narrow path and onto Walker's Top, where they relieved the men of the Naval Brigade, Royal Naval Division. As they neared the forward trenches they came under heavy Turkish fire. 'The sun was hot, and the way was steep, not to mention a weighty burden of equipment. The cool sea drew farther away as they soared gradually skywards, panting and perspiring. They reached their trenches at last, pushed themselves along ditches too narrow to take simultaneously them and their gear, casting loving epithets at telephone wires, which caught their rifles, and waited interminable times for the man ahead to move on. Towards midday … they collapsed in their appointed positions.'[22]

Four troops of Wellingtons occupied the firing line, with four in support and four in reserve. 'The A.M.R. followed in like manner towards the left-wing trenches, and the C.M.R. relieved the other troops on the lower slopes of Walker's Ridge to the sea.'[23] According to James Harvey, the men of the Naval Brigade 'were not too keen on the trench fighting and did not do too much shooting. The enemy were very careless in exposing themselves and enabled us to get a good shot or two.' The mounteds found their part of the front line to be in a filthy state. 'The trenches were anything but clean, and flies swarmed everywhere.'[24]

The view from the high ground reminded some New Zealanders of home, as Fred Waite noted. 'The men of the Wellington regiments recognized a strong resemblance to the view from the Paekakariki Hill, looking out towards Kapiti and the long white stretch of the Otaki beach.' Sightseeing was a dangerous pastime in the front line, as machine gun fire from the enemy trenches 30 to 50 metres away ripped across the mounteds' trenches and Turkish artillery shelled the rearward slopes. Snipers were another deadly threat, as Alfred Cameron noted. 'The Turkish snipers are very good shots, hard to locate and very cheeky.'[25]

The CMR was also put in charge of Outposts No. 1 and 2 on lower ground to the north. These isolated outposts were not occupied until after nightfall, because to attempt to do so in daylight invited death. The outposts were well placed to guard the northern approach to the Anzac beach, which was otherwise open to Turkish attack.

The mounteds quickly turned the weak outposts into well-protected strongpoints, which were never threatened with capture throughout the campaign. Leslie Smith, a CMR signaller, quickly learned that standing up and waving semaphore flags at the outposts with Turkish snipers about was not a good idea.[26]

Ken Stevens was shocked the first time he saw dead bodies. 'Looking back at our first day in the trenches – The stench of the unburied friend and foe in No-Mans-Land – Digging trenches at night amongst them – shocking.' Bill Callaghan turned to Stevens and said, 'If their mothers could see them this war would end today'.[27]

For most of the mounteds, their first night in the front line was another sleepless one, as Turkish flares and rifle and machine gun fire kept them awake. One CMR man, Trooper William Hay, was killed and another two were wounded in a patrol of volunteers sent out to bury 40 dead Australians who had been lying in a beached boat near No. 2 Outpost since the landings. Hay, the first battle casualty in the NZMR Brigade, was killed by a sentry, another Canterbury man, who failed to recognise him in the dark. According to Percy Doherty, Hay did not respond to the challenge of the nervous sentry, who shot him through the head and bayoneted him.[28]

That same night Major George Hutton and a raiding party of 100 Canterbury men were landed near Suvla Bay before dawn to see if a Turkish artillery observation

William Hay, accidentally killed by a New Zealand sentry on 14 May.

post there had been reoccupied since an earlier raid. The commander of the destroyer that landed them explained that they 'worked the land like beating for birds,' but nothing was found except three sheep, one of which was captured alive, one shot and a third bayoneted. When the men returned to Anzac with their 'prisoners', General Birdwood ordered them to hand the live sheep over to the Indians, who would not eat meat they had not killed themselves.[29]

The first priorities on Walker's Top were to deepen the existing trenches and to extend the front line towards the Turks so that the 'dead ground' there could be observed and covered by fire. Two saps

Anzac and British soldiers on the edge of Walker's Top (later renamed Russell's Top) overlooking North Beach.

(shallow trenches) were dug straight out into No Man's Land, far enough so that all the ground in front could be seen from the trench. The next step was to link the saps up in a new front line. Sapping was grim and dangerous work, as Francis Twisleton recorded. 'The ground around is covered with dead which have to be pushed to one side with sticks, you can't show yourselves. The smell is the worst feature of that job.' Percy Doherty wrote: 'The sap that we were working on was a very dangerous one. It was not safe to hold your finger up, and if anyone bobbed his head up, it meant certain death as the place was alive with snipers, and the dirty dogs have already got a number of our fellows. With a periscope, one can see all around with safety, and it was the saddest sight I have ever seen. On both sides of the trenches … were dead bodies of Turks and N.Z. infantrymen, and there they lay just as they had fallen in action. … Some still had hold of their rifles and one man had his bayonet stuck right through a Turk, but he was still hanging on to his rifle.'[30]

Marksmen were stationed in the trenches to keep the enemy snipers' heads down while the work went on. The trenches were cleaned up and deepened. Some sections were roofed in with timber, and dugouts were excavated to provide some protection from shrapnel. Charles Powles recalled a sergeant who took cover under a thin blanket

Three unidentified Anzacs killed on Gallipoli.

during an early shrapnel bombardment was not amused when others safe in dugouts laughed at him. It sounded 'cold-blooded to see humour in what is probably costing men their lives, but without humour war would be unbearable, and all concerned would soon be raving lunatics'.[31]

The mounted riflemen quickly learnt the essentials of fighting and surviving on Gallipoli. The fact that they had received little training in the finer points of trench warfare did not matter. All that was required of them was a strong back for digging and carrying supplies, a stronger constitution and a good shooting eye. 'Within a few days the troopers realised that to be able to dig is one of the first qualifications of a soldier.'[32] There was no timber or iron available for supports so the men simply dug into the stony clay and hoped that it would not fall down on top of them under shellfire. Some men got carried away and made their trenches so deep that they could neither shoot from them nor climb out to charge.

Walker's Top was separated from the very strong Turkish front line positions of Baby 700 and The Chessboard by The Nek, a narrow saddle the size of three tennis courts hemmed in on either side by steep gullies. Walker's Top was a small area, gently sloping downhill from The Nek towards cliffs overlooking North Beach. The distance from the front line to the edge of the cliffs was only about 30 metres. Walker's Top

The track up Walker's Ridge, linking North Beach to Walker's Top. The terraces below the track were home for the mounted riflemen when not in the front line.

was everywhere exposed to fire and observation from higher Turkish trenches, yet it was the key to the security of Anzac. Its loss would be a disaster because there was nothing between it and the sea. If the Turks captured Walker's Top they would overlook the Anzac rear areas along the beach and also be able to fire into the backs of the defenders lining the edge of the Second Ridge above Monash Gully. 'If [the Turks] could hold that position, the Australian and New Zealand Army Corps would be forced to withdraw, if it could, from the Peninsula, and would probably be crushed in making the attempt.'[33] There was little room for artillery on the plateau, and only one Indian Mountain Battery supported the brigade at first. The Indian gunners 'worshipped their little guns, and lay round them at night with their long curved

swords at their hips.' Even the mountain guns could do little because of a shortage of ammunition. Naval gunfire was of no help because the opposing trenches were too close together and were not visible from the sea. 'Summed up it was far from being a comfortable position.'[34]

Trench life on Gallipoli was a more compressed and unpleasant experience than on the Western Front. The battlefield was so small and the terrain was so difficult that support trenches, if they existed at all, were usually very close behind the fighting line. In many places there were only one or two trench lines between the Turks and the beach. There was very little artillery available to either side, and the Allied gun positions were sometimes within a few metres of the front line. All of the hospitals,

No. 2 Outpost (left) looking south towards Plugge's Plateau.

supply depots, wharves and rest areas were within artillery, and sometimes rifle, range of the Turks. No Man's Land was much narrower, too; ranging from a few hundred metres wide at best to a few metres at worst.

Men in the front lines spent their lives below ground level. During the day sentries could not look over the parapet and live, so they used loopholes and periscopes. Even in the rear areas men above ground were always vulnerable to snipers, machine guns and shrapnel. The men on Gallipoli faced the ever-present possibility that a strong Turkish attack could break through the front line and be among the rear areas in just a few minutes. The Anzacs knew that at any time they could be driven into the sea. The continual tension and stress caused by this knowledge was unique to Gallipoli, though the closeness of the opposing trench lines did offer some advantages, as Thomas Catchpole noted. 'The safest place of the lot is in the firing line, as the trenches are practically shrapnel proof, and also too close to the enemy for them to shell.'[35]

Because a surprise Turkish attack from such short range had to be stopped immediately, the firing trenches were always full of men. There would be no time for support troops to get up the steep tracks from the beach and valleys. Reserve troops worked nearby during the day and slept at night as far forward as possible, fully

No. 1 Outpost below the cliffs of Battleship Hill.

dressed and armed. The trenches and tracks were often so crowded with sleeping men that messengers could not pass through without stepping on them.

The usual routine in daylight was for one squadron to man the fighting line. Another squadron would be nearby in the supports, and the rest of the regiment would be 'resting' or working. At night, when Turkish attacks were more likely, the front-line manning would increase by 50 per cent or more, with all other troops kept closer at hand. The whole front-line garrison 'stood-to' on the firing steps for an hour before dawn and at dusk, when enemy attacks were thought to be most likely.

The squadrons out of the firing line did not have an easy time. These men worked harder than those in the firing line. They toiled endlessly to improve the tracks up Walker's Ridge and elsewhere, and they carried water, rations and ammunition to the front line. As soon as the track was good enough, two 18-pounder guns of the New Zealand Field Artillery were dragged up onto Walker's Top. The gun positions were almost on top of the firing line. It was all very strange.

The trenches forming the front line of the Anzac position supported each other. In isolation, any trench could be attacked and taken with relative ease. What saved them from this were interlocking arcs of fire, particularly of machine guns and artillery. The machine guns on one position, Walker's Top for example, were sited to fire across the front of adjacent trench systems such as Quinn's Post and Pope's Hill, and vice versa.

Bombs (which we call grenades today) became a vital weapon in the close trench warfare on Gallipoli. The Anzacs had none initially, so they were forced to improvise by making them out of empty jam tins stuffed with nails and bullets around a core of gun cotton and a fuse. The Turks had plenty of real 'cricket-ball' bombs, and they were very generous in their use. Bombs landing in Anzac trenches were often picked up and thrown back. If this was not possible, greatcoats were thrown over them to suppress the blast. The Turkish bombs had long fuses, and this gave the defenders a few seconds to pick them up and throw them back. The rule of thumb was: if the fuse was still burning, pick it up and throw it back; if not, cover it and stand well back. Some men even caught bombs in mid-air and threw them back. The Turks quickly grew wise to this, and shortened the fuses. Some Anzacs made a game of this, but it was deadly serious. When a bomb detonated near men in the close confines of a crowded trench, the resulting wounds from blast and shrapnel were serious.

In daylight Turkish snipers shot any man careless enough to show his head above the parapet. Most of the mounteds on Walker's Top learnt this lesson quickly. Those who did not were killed within a few days. On the Anzac side, marksmen in the regiments immediately began hunting careless Turks. This had not been the habit of the previous occupants of the trenches, and the Turks quickly realised that their new opponents were altogether more aggressive. It was soon noticed that the enemy trenches opposite Walker's Top were being deepened and widened, and many new sandbagged loopholes were being built for their snipers. The trenches were so close together that the noise of the Turkish picks and shovels was clearly audible.

The mounteds quickly adjusted to the new life 'and in three days they might have been at it for ever. ... The first week on Walker's Ridge passed fairly uneventfully, and by the end of it its holders looked war-worn veterans.'[36] They lost their innocence just as quickly, as Ken Stevens noted. 'In less than twelve hours with the bullets crashing around the trench all night in the polluted air and one look over in No Mans Land in daylight, all the glamour in war for me was lost.' The death of friends quickly became a commonplace occurrence. Clutha Mackenzie wrote 'always there came the momentary sadness, and, maybe, the remark, "Poor old Bill. They hooked him this morning. He was a good old sport." That was his requiem and, save for a few stray thoughts in the silent watches of the night, old Bill went unremembered.' Percy Doherty wrote on 19 May: 'Yesterday, Captain Bluck and Sergt. Major Marr of the 4th Waikatos went out to try and get at a sniper, but they were both shot dead'. Some unlucky men were killed by their own side. William Dawbin recorded the death of 'Bromley, A Squadron, [who was] killed today by premature burst of mountain gun shell'.[37]

At first the New Zealand Mounted Brigade Field Ambulance worked on Lemnos Island, treating casualties evacuated there from the peninsula. It sailed to Gallipoli on 31 May but was not allowed to land. The medics spent the rest of the day on a destroyer, sailing endlessly in circles to avoid submarine attack, before being sent back to Lemnos. In early June, they accompanied 1266 wounded men on a hospital ship to Malta. After two trips to Alexandria with more wounded men, they finally landed on Gallipoli on 24 July. When they did get ashore their greatest difficulty was finding somewhere safe to set up their hospital tents. By then, there was little unoccupied land left that provided cover from enemy fire. The ambulance was forced to establish itself up close to artillery batteries, and the medics inevitably suffered from enemy fire aimed at the guns.

For five days there was little enemy action on Walker's Top, and this gave the mounteds time to sort themselves out. Already the monotony of trench life was getting to some of the troopers and they longed for something serious to do. Some of them even envied their friends in the shattered infantry brigade. Their wish to be 'blooded' was granted on 19 May when the heaviest Turkish attack of the entire campaign broke over them.

6

The Defence of Anzac

*The Turks came on in their usual close formation, and were simply
mown down.... In some cases, however, they did actually get into our front fire
trenches, but were immediately bayoneted to a man. In other places they
reached our parapets – only to be pulled by the legs into the trench by
one man and bayoneted by another.*

'ANZAC'

*Some of the poor chaps have been lying out there dead for a month now
and the stench is awful... Some of the sights of our poor chaps
I will never forget in a lifetime.*

JACK MARTYN

AFTER DEFEATING THE BRITISH attacks at Cape Helles in early May, General Liman von Sanders was ordered to launch a massive attack to finish off the invaders once and for all. He decided to drive the Anzac forces into the sea first before turning his full force on to the British at Cape Helles. The Turkish 2nd Division was brought down from Constantinople and the 3rd Division came across from the Asian shore for the attack, which was scheduled for 3 a.m. on 19 May. Instead of concentrating his 40,000 men on one or two vulnerable points, Liman von Sanders decided to launch them in a surprise attack all along the Anzac front line. His aim was 'before day-break, [to] drive the Anzac troops from their trenches, and follow them down to the sea'.[1] Facing the Turks were 12,450 Anzac riflemen backed by 43 artillery pieces and many carefully sited machine guns.

A few days before the date of the attack Royal Naval Air Service scouting aircraft spotted strong Turkish forces moving towards Anzac. This reconnaissance had been ordered after the Turkish trenches had been suspiciously quiet after two weeks of constant activity (they were conserving ammunition for the attack). This early warning gave time to take steps at Anzac to ensure the failure of the coming attack. Extra artillery pieces and machine guns were brought forward onto Walker's Top and elsewhere, and reserve troops slept in the forward trenches with bayonets fixed. The machine guns were secretly and carefully sited to fire along the front of the Anzac trenches, and loose barbed wire was hidden in the brush in front of some of the trenches to trip up attackers. What was left of the 2nd Australian Infantry Brigade, back from Cape Helles, was placed in reserve in Shrapnel Valley, and 16 spare machine guns down on the beach were ready to be sent forward at a moment's notice.[2] Morning stand-to on Wednesday 19 May was brought forward from 3.30 to 3 a.m.

Awaiting the attack on Walker's Top were the Auckland and Wellington mounted rifles regiments. Canterbury detachments were out at No. 1 and No. 2 Outposts. On Walker's Top two incomplete saps ran straight out towards the Turkish trenches at The Nek. These narrow and shallow ditches were manned by the 3rd Auckland and 4th Waikato squadrons of the AMR on the night of the attack. The third AMR squadron was behind them, and to their left some flanking trenches were manned by Wellington mounted riflemen with a machine gun. Behind the saps the main trenches were packed with troops. 'There was probably a bayonet to every yard [of trench].'[3] Facing them was the Turkish 19th Division commanded by Mustafa Kemal. Included in the ranks of this division were a number of young trainee officers sent down from Constantinople to gain experience.[4]

At 5 p.m. on 18 May the Anzac trenches received the heaviest shelling yet experienced on Gallipoli. Everyone stood to arms but nothing happened. Nonetheless, Ken Stevens thought it 'was obvious they were going to attack because we could hear a loud hum over in their front lines'. The defenders awaited the onslaught in tense silence, wondering how they would react to their first fight. Frank Hobson wrote: 'It is an uncanny feeling to be looking out of a trench in the dark, waiting for an enemy's approach and thinking over the possibilities of the situation'.[5]

The Turks attacked first in the north, creeping down the ridges towards the outposts soon after sunset on 18 May. 'The anxious [CMR] garrisons detected sounds of men scrambling down the gullies. Around the posts alert ears heard the undertones of voices. It was some time before the listeners could determine the mutterings as definitely Turkish. Into the mysteries of the scrub volley after volley was poured. The attackers, feeling they were "in the air," squealed and disappeared in the direction of the Suvla Flats.'[6]

From midnight until 3 a.m. the Anzacs on the main position came under heavy

A New Zealander firing a Maxim machine gun at Gallipoli. Weapons such as this, firing 600 rounds per minute, killed hundreds of Turks on 19 May.

fire from Turkish rifles and machine guns, and hundreds of cricket-ball bombs were hurled into their trenches. Just before 3 a.m. 'the sleeping men were awakened, and in their greatcoats, with bayonets fixed, lined the front and support trenches, while the reserves formed up and waited in the valleys'.[7]

The Turkish attack was not announced by the roar of covering artillery or machine gun fire. Between 3 and 3.30 a.m. the Turks crept forward in silence. Then, bugle calls and appeals to Allah were heard as thousands of Turkish infantrymen surged forward with fixed bayonets: 'a great shouting was heard, cries of 'ALLAH' and the fire ceased & the enemy charged our left opposite The Nek throwing bombs & firing their rifles as they came'. The call to Allah was 'a really fearsome battle-cry, until one gets used to it'.[8]

The attackers were hard to see, but the glint of the early morning light on their bayonets and the muzzle flashes from their rifles gave them away. The Anzacs held their fire as the masses of yelling Turks came closer and closer. According to Frank Hobson, one AMR machine gunner 'was sitting behind his machine gun … calmly reading *The Auckland Weekly News* and waiting for the Turks to come up'. There was no order for rapid fire 'until the first line of attacking Turks was 20 yards away'.[9] Then, as Charles

Bean wrote, the Turks 'fired their rifles and threw bombs as they rushed, while the Aucklanders … fired at the flashes, but without being able to stop the advance. As the Turks passed down both sides of the sap, the men in it faced each way and continued to fire. Three rushes of the enemy along its western side were one after another swept away by their rifles and by a machine-gun of the Wellington Regiment.' Advancing 'in great strength, line after line', the Turks formed 'an ideal target for machine gunners, who … took full advantage of it, the Turks being mowed down in hundreds, making room for hundreds more, to be wiped out in their turn.'[10]

The Auckland mounteds manning the shallow forward saps were very exposed, as the Turks 'poured through the gap into the centre between the two forward saps. In both saps the Mounteds stood, kneeled, lay out in the open or wedged themselves with a boot into the earth wall, firing at each wave as they passed.'[11] According to Ken Stevens, 'The blaze from the rifles and machine guns lit up our front and it was open slather; we firing at the Turks and they firing at us as they charged'. In the words of the official AMR history, 'The end of the left sap became a very warm corner. Here Lieutenant Weir and some of his troop put up a desperate struggle, in which bayonets were used, and drove off three rushes.' Fred Waite wrote: 'Again and again they advanced, but, caught by the loosely-strewn barb wire, they dropped like flies and were beaten to the earth by the machine guns. The din was indescribable.' Rifle and machine gun barrels grew too hot to touch, and rifle bolts began to jam. 'The men in trouble [with jammed rifles] were possessed of the healthy belief that if their particular rifles were out of action everything was lost.'[12] In several places the charging Turks took cover immediately in front of the Anzac trenches. Some observers were convinced that this was all that stopped them from breaking through.

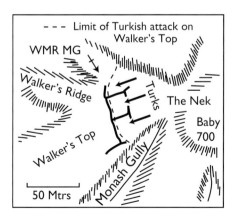

The defence of Walker's Top on 19 May.

The Waikato squadron of the AMR was on the southern side of Walker's Top. Lieutenant John Roberts had received the command of this squadron only that morning, after Captain Alfred Bluck, the previous squadron commander, was killed by a sniper. Roberts had only a few hours of daylight to work out where to place his men to best effect. He placed the Whakatane Troop in the incomplete forward sap, with two other troops behind

133

Cornelius James, killed on 19 May.

them in the old front line, and a troop in reserve. The Whakatane troop leader, Lieutenant Cornelius James, was ordered to hold the sap for 20 minutes at all costs 'and he and his men well knew what the cost would be'. The men could not fight from the shallow, narrow ditch, so, when the attack came, they leapt out into the open and fired lying on their stomachs. 'Soon they were at point-blank range, and dozens of Turks were shot down at a distance of 10 feet.' The Turks should have overwhelmed the little band, but they did not. 'Within a few minutes two-thirds of the troop had become casualties.'[13]

As soon as the squadron was reinforced the men charged the Turks who had taken cover just in front of them, 'to meet Abdul with the bayonet'. In the face of this onslaught, 'the Turks ran back, the New Zealanders following them. … The handful of Aucklanders who followed the running Turks through the scrub were met by a growing fire from Baby 700. Having cleared the space in front of the trenches, they therefore returned to their own line.'[14]

There was no finesse in this fight. It was a matter of kill or be killed, 'a battle of bullet and steel'. As Charles Bean wrote, 'All along the trenches infantrymen whose station was not in the firing line were begging for a place on the fire-step, offering in jest sums of money for a "place" which they knew no money could buy'.[15] The mounteds fought in grim silence, although a Maori haka was heard at one stage. Most of the killing was done by the Anzac machine guns, which had been sited to create a lethal barrier of bullets between the opposing front lines that could not be penetrated. The machine gunners poured belt after belt of bullets into the lines of Turks as they attacked the Aucklanders.[16]

'The Turks came on in their usual close formation, and were simply mown down. They just melted away in places like a snowball in hell. Mostly they failed to reach our trenches, being cut down and beaten back by the terrific fire. In some cases, however, they did actually get into our front fire trenches, but were immediately bayoneted to a man. In other places they reached our parapets – only to be pulled by the legs into the trench by one man and bayoneted by another.'[17] According to Clutha Mackenzie, 'They brought their packs & rations with them when they came, indicating that they meant to stay.'[18]

Lieutenant Colonel 'Old Joe' Mackesy, the commander of the AMR, was an active participant in the fight. 'He first appeared, with rifle and bayonet, in the advanced sap on the right. After firing for a time he made his way to the left sap, and finding no room on the parapet, climbed to the parados [the mound of earth behind the trenches], which was the highest and most exposed point in the vicinity, and from there emptied several magazines.' During the fighting Mackesy countermanded a suspicious order to cease fire because there were Australians in front of the trenches with the words, 'Australians be damned! Ask where the order came from.'[19]

The main attack was over by 5 a.m. As the sun rose smaller Turkish attacks were launched, but they were easily stopped. Turkish survivors spotted while trying to get back to their own lines were shot without mercy. Men sat on the parapet of the trench or stood behind it, shooting with little thought for their own safety, until increasingly heavy and accurate Turkish fire from Baby 700 and The Chessboard forced them back under cover. The defenders smoked cigarettes and chatted excitedly as they awaited the renewal of the Turkish attacks after dawn.

Mid-morning the CMR detachment at No. 1 Outpost spotted Turks massing for another attack in the head of Malone's Gully. 'The rifles of the 10th Nelson Squadron, assisted by the machine gun, brought a devastating fire to bear … For a few minutes a stream of lead played up and down their ranks, causing awful havoc. The mass heaved and swayed convulsively, then broke and stampeded to the rear, assisted in their flight by the ever-watchful guns of the torpedo-boat destroyers, while the watchful machine guns … poured belt after belt into the enemy reserves.'[20]

The Turkish attack was a disaster, largely because the Anzacs knew it was coming. To make matters worse, the assaulting troops were not familiar with the layout of the trenches they attacked. On Walker's Top they were confused by the unexpected saps pointing straight at them. They attacked different parts of the line at different times. There was no attempt to co-ordinate the assaults along the line, or to concentrate on one or two weak points. 'The Turks did not seem well-trained. There was no attempt at covering fire, and so our men could sit right out on the traverses of the trench, or even the parapet, and shoot for all their worth.'[21] There was no doubting the courage of the Turkish infantry as they charged forward unhesitatingly into the storm of artillery, machine gun and rifle fire. According to one Turkish survivor, 'military discipline, patriotism and military fervour had all played their part ... but he emphasized the influence of a military band concealed in a forward position which had played martial music throughout the action'.[22]

At 1.25 p.m. General Godley ordered 100 men of the WMR to attack two lines of enemy trenches at The Nek: 'Light as possible, fifty rounds of ammunition only ... First and second trenches ... some machine guns and a few Turks ...Clear them out and come back.'[23] No one could believe that Godley was serious. No Man's Land at The Nek was so narrow and open that an attacking force would have to bunch together to cross it, inviting destruction on a grand scale, as the Turks had just demonstrated coming the other way. The very strong enemy positions at The Chessboard, Baby 700 and German Officer's Trench all overlooked The Nek, and, because fighting had ceased everywhere by now, the Turks would be able to give any attack across it their undivided attention. 'It was considered by all occupants of our trenches that the order was an impossible one. The intervening ground was devoid of cover, and it could be raked by the enemy at will from numerous well-posted machine guns, the flying bullets of which would form a network, through which it would be impossible to penetrate for even a short distance.' In other words, 'They were to attempt to do, with a hundred men in broad daylight, what thousands of Turks had failed to accomplish in the dark! And to what object?'[24]

Lieutenant colonels Meldrum and Mackesy both protested to Brigadier General Russell. He agreed that the attack was pointless and would result in almost certain death for the 100 men concerned, and told Godley that he would not order the attack. Godley insisted on the attempt being made, and Russell refused again. While the debate raged, Meldrum readied his men, taking 'an equal part of this forlorn hope from each of the three squadrons, to obviate the risk of one being wiped out. To have any chance at all of success, it was painfully obvious that it must have as a leader, one of the highest order whom the men would implicitly trust and follow. This dubious honour was conferred on the gallant Captain W.J. Hardham, V.C.'[25]

[The assault troops] filed silently and with set faces to their assembly positions. They were in for something serious. They had all seen the waves of advancing Turks in the early morning dissolve away to nought. ... [They] slipped over the parapet, and lay, awaiting the word, among the many dead, Turkish and Australasian, of last night, and of three weeks earlier. Minutes passed slowly, five, ten, twenty, thirty – what on earth did this mean? The sun blazed fiercely on the flattened figures, the smell was awful, and the firing

slackened not a bit. The Trooper had examined his breech a dozen times, adjusted and readjusted his ammunition to facilitate its easy handling, and had made certain several times of the firmness of his bayonet. … He longed to be off, even into that hail of bullets which whizzed low over his head.[26]

Another trooper recalled: 'As if they knew what was in the wind, the Turks opened up as the fateful hour approached, sweeping our lines with bullets. They were rattling on the parapet like hail as we crouched in the trench waiting the time to go over.'[27]

In the face of such determined opposition from his subordinate commanders as well as from the Turks, Godley grudgingly allowed Russell to cancel the attack. Russell did so just before it was due to be launched. 'Then came orders along the line. What – what in the deuce – Crawl back – Lord! Surely they didn't mean it. Yes, it was so, but the Trooper couldn't quite gather in the situation. Having made up his mind to do it, and stood the forty-five minutes' strain of waiting, it seemed a bit tough not to be repaid with a whack at the Turks. They wormed themselves back over the parapet, gathered hazily that the attack had been deemed inadvisable, and sauntered tiredly back to their old place in the communication sap.'[28]

Arthur Batchelor wrote: 'Thank Goodness as 90 men could have done nothing & few would have returned as murderous fire was opened on them'. Ken Stevens thought the attack was called off because there was no rum left to give to the men to fortify them before the attack. 'There is little doubt that had the attack been carried out, few, if any, men would have returned to our trenches.'[29] This fact was demonstrated three months later when 374 out of 450 light horsemen were killed or wounded when they attacked across this same ground.

Many Gallipoli veterans believed that Godley punished Lieutenant Colonel Mackesy for refusing to support the counter-attack by sending him back to Egypt to look after the horses. Ken Stevens certainly thought so. 'What did Colonel Mackesy know about sick horses? Our officers were tight-lipped on the question. We in the ranks came to the conclusion that he must have refused to send us into a brainless slaughter.'[30] No evidence to support this belief has been found, and it seems there was another reason for Mackesy's departure from Gallipoli. On 12 June Godley's headquarters sent a memo to Russell. 'Now that it seems likely that your Brigade will remain dismounted for some time, and that the horses and a considerable number of details will be left in Egypt, the G.O.C. thinks that a Regimental Commanding Officer, of the rank of Lieut. Colonel, should be placed in charge of them … will you please

The CWGC Walker's Ridge Cemetery. Twenty of the 29 mounted riflemen buried here were killed on 19 or 20 May.

detail one of your Commanding Officers for this duty.' Russell picked Mackesy: 'I have just returned one of my Colonels to Cairo to look after the horses – not a bad old fellow, and plucky enough, but too old (over 60) to tackle this kind of job'.[31]

Twenty-seven men were killed and 32 were wounded in the NZMR Brigade as it fought off the Turks on 19 May. The Aucklanders suffered the most, losing 23 killed and about the same number wounded. The ANZAC as a whole lost 160 men killed and 468 wounded. Many of the casualties occurred when the Anzacs climbed out of their trenches to fire into the backs of the retreating Turks after daybreak.[32]

The trenches were so tightly packed with riflemen that the wounded and dead could not be removed from the trenches until well after dawn. It was lucky that there were only a few wounded mounteds, because the brigade's field ambulance had not yet landed. The regimental doctors and stretcher-bearers did what they could to get the badly wounded men down to the beach.[33]

The attack involved about 40,000 Turks. It was their biggest effort of the campaign, and their heaviest defeat: 10,000 became casualties, at least 3000 of whom were killed or mortally wounded. Dead and dying Turks lay in heaps in front of the Anzac trenches. Gordon Harper's comment summed up the Anzacs' reaction: 'I can only say about it that we revenged our lost friends whose little wooden crosses we are

Blindfolded Turkish prisoners under guard at the NZMR Brigade headquarters at the top of Walker's Ridge, probably after the 19 May attack.

now living amongst'.[34] The 19 May battle became known officially as 'The Defence of Anzac' and Walker's Top was renamed Russell's Top in recognition of his brigade's efforts. Anzac riflemen and machine gunners fired almost a million bullets during this attack, and the artillery batteries fired nearly 3000 rounds.[35]

When a Turkish prisoner revealed that a heavy follow-up assault was planned, the New Zealand Infantry Brigade's return from Helles was hastened, and all ranks were warned to expect more of the same.[36] On Russell's Top tired but elated men closed the gaps in the new front line, and the saps were quickly converted into proper firing trenches. On the night of 20 May searchlights from warships played over the enemy trenches. No further attacks developed, allowing the mounteds to take a breather. A few days before he was killed, Frank Hobson wrote that he took his bandolier off 'for the first time for some days. So far we only take off our boots when we manage to get a swim.'[37]

The survivors of the New Zealand Infantry Brigade got back to Anzac the day after the attack. Leslie Smith went down to the beach to meet the returning Canterbury infantry. 'Many of our pals are dead, wounded or missing. Not half of them got through and the rest of them look very worn out.' According to Smith, it took several days for the infantry to lose the 'hunted look'. Cecil Malthus, one of the returning infantrymen, 'felt it rather as a grievance that these newcomers [the mounteds] should have had such an opportunity while we, for all our heavy losses, had had so few chances of damaging the enemy'.[38] The same day two more Australian light horse brigades and the first squadron of the Otago Mounted Rifles (OMR) Regiment arrived from Egypt.

Even without the element of surprise, had General Liman von Sanders concentrated his superior numbers on a small part of the enemy front line, perhaps at The Nek, he could have broken through and overwhelmed the entire Anzac position.[39] As it was, their bloody defeat convinced the Turks that it was not going to be easy to push the invaders back into the sea. The attacks at Anzac and at Cape Helles in the first three weeks of May 1915 marked the end of the first phase of the campaign. The MEF was ashore and safe. To eject it would take more troops and artillery than were immediately available to the Turks.

As Charles Bean noticed, the attitude of the Anzacs towards the Turks changed after the attack and the subsequent armistice: 'from being bitter and suspicious they became admirers and almost friends of the Turks – "Jacko" or "Abdul", as they called them – and so they remained until the end of the war'. He regarded the altered attitude as extraordinary. 'They were very savage the first day … but since the slaughter of May 19th, and since they have seen the wounded lying about in front of the trenches they have changed entirely. They are quite friendly with the Turks; anxious to get in the wounded if they can – give them cigarettes.'[40] This new respect for their fellow sufferers did not, however, stop the Anzacs from killing them at every opportunity.

On the afternoon of 20 May white flags were seen in the Turkish trenches opposite The Nek, Quinn's Post and Courtney's Post. Turkish interpreters called out that they wanted a truce to bury their dead and recover their wounded. At The Nek 30 Turks under a Red Crescent flag emerged from their trenches to discuss an armistice with the Aucklanders. Ken Stevens and others 'thought the whole Turkish army was going to surrender, but were very disappointed when we learned they only wanted an armistice to bury the dead in No Mans Land'.[41] While these informal negotiations were proceeding, Anzac observers noticed that other Turks were massing in their forward trenches. Others were spotted collecting rifles and ammunition from their dead in No Man's Land. It was decided that the truce was a ruse to cover preparations for another attack, and the Turks were told to get back into their trenches. According to Clutha Mackenzie, 'We ordered them to halt which they did but they moved forward again & someone perceived them to be dragging rifles with their feet. So we gave them a few

THE DEFENCE OF ANZAC

rounds and they cleared back a bit & then came on again, & we could detect the sound of entrenching tools at work, so we gave them a few more rounds. ... On being asked their business, they said they desired half-an-hour to carry away a wounded doctor. We gave them two minutes to disappear & then turned on our rifles. We killed half-a-dozen. Later we discovered that under the wounded doctor pretence they brought up a machine gun on a stretcher. ...It is practically certain that we shall be attacked tonight.'[42] After two minutes' grace, firing resumed all along the front line. Forty Turks who were too slow were shot down by a New Zealand machine gunner. Ken Stevens witnessed one Turk who 'did not hurry to get down and one of our men shot him and he rolled over into his trench. None of us who saw what happened approved. That was not war.'[43]

The Turkish attacks along the Anzac line on 19 May had greatly increased the number of corpses on the ground between the opposing trenches. As the days passed, hundreds of wounded Turks lying untended out in the open died, adding to the number of bodies. The danger of disease spreading from the decomposing corpses was obvious, but they could not be buried or burned during the fighting. Moving the front line back a little was not an option at Anzac. The smell became so bad that Sergeant John Black took to wearing a sock over his nose. Ken Stevens described how bodies within reach of the Anzac front lines were dragged in and buried. 'With a hook on the end of a stick we collected as many Turks as we could reach from our trenches. One we hauled in had lain less than a yard from our parapet and he hardly hit the bottom of the trench before he threw his hands up and pleaded for mercy. There was not a scratch on him and he was the cause of the only laugh we had on that day of sad and sordid events. He became a prisoner instead of having a rope put around his neck and dragged along the bottom of our trench to the huge trench grave we dug for Turks.'[44]

Formal negotiations for an armistice to bury the bodies began on 20 May. The armistice finally took place four days later, once detailed procedures had been agreed.

Monday 24 May was a 'most ghastly day'. Wet and misty at first, the weather cleared up by mid-morning. Rifle fire and shelling continued until a few seconds before the appointed start time of 7.30 a.m. When it stopped, an eerie silence fell across the battlefield. White flags were hoisted on both sides, and men nervously appeared above their trenches. Fifty from each side laid out a demarcation line down the middle of no man's land from the beach up the Second Ridge as far as The Nek. Sentries were posted by the white flags to show both sides where the line lay. A 'most

'A most ghastly day'. Anzacs burying dead Turks during the armistice on 24 May.

awful sight' greeted New Zealand doctor Lieutenant Colonel Percival Fenwick when he reached a plateau. 'The Turkish dead lay so thick that it was almost impossible to pass without treading on the bodies. The awful destructive power of high explosives was very evident. Huge holes surrounded by circles of corpses, blown to pieces. One body was cut clean in half; the upper half I could not see, it was some distance away. … Everywhere one looked lay dead, swollen, black, hideous, and over all a nauseating stench that nearly made one vomit.' At The Nek in front of the mounteds there 'was a narrow path, absolutely blocked with dead, also a swathe of men who had fallen face down as if on parade – victims to our machine guns'.[45]

Most of the dead were Turks. 'Only a few New Zealanders were found unburied, these having apparently sold their lives dearly, for dead Turks lay around them.' 'In front of the Walker's Ridge line lay an Australian bugler, a mere boy, with his bugle slung across his shoulders. Nearby lay the body of a New Zealand infantryman, his hands still grasping an out-stretched rifle, the bayonet of which was in the body of a Turk.'[46]

By 10 a.m. the demarcation line was in place, and burial parties and medical teams began burying the dead. Groups of up to 200 men from each side cleared sectors about 1000 metres long. Both sides appeared to have chosen their biggest and most impressive soldiers for the work. The Anzacs 'had been ordered to be shaved and smart in appearance to impress the Turks'.[47] They could carry only water bottles, shovels and stretchers. The opposing trenches remained fully manned throughout the armistice, and senior officers on both sides took advantage of the opportunity to have a close look at the enemy's defences.

The agreed plan was for enemy dead to be carried across to the centre line for identification and burial by their compatriots. However, the decomposed bodies were often too far gone to be moved without falling apart, so they were buried where they lay, or in handy abandoned trenches and saps. Somtimes all that could be done was to heap dirt over the bodies, or, at best, to scrape a shallow grave next to them and tip them in. This meant that many dead Anzacs on the Turkish side of the demarcation line were never identified. Identity discs were collected from accessible bodies, and regimental padres conducted hasty burial services throughout the day.

When a German officer accused New Zealanders burying bodies of digging trenches, Dr Fenwick's response was understandable. 'I lost my temper ... and told him that the corpses were so decomposed they could not be lifted and our men were merely digging pits to put the awful things into. He was a swine, this particular German.'[48]

Jack Braithwaite took the opportunity to examine the clothes and weapons of the dead Turks – 'Most of them are quite old ... and are dressed in any sort of old clothes' – and Clutha Mackenzie noticed that 'Their rifles are well worn & their clothes very tattered & torn & strongly reinforced with Aus. and N.Z. stuff taken from our dead.' On the NZMR Brigade front 136 British rifles and the bolts from 54 Turkish rifles were collected. A few men 'attempted conversation with the Turkish parties, but ignorance of each other's language proved a difficulty. Still they smiled and gesticulated and exchanged cigarettes.'[49] Some Turks and Anzacs fraternised, 'and sometimes exchanged samples of their rations. But the majority of our men were too overcome at the sight of the dead, sometimes literally lying in heaps, to have much concern with the living.' One Turk told a New Zealander that 'our fighting had astonished them all & that they had expected practically no resistance from us, believing us to be an uneducated, untrained, unarmed colonial rabble'.[50]

It was a terrible, unforgettable experience. Many men wore handkerchiefs over their noses in a vain attempt to keep the stink out, while others shoved scented cotton wool up their nostrils. William East wrote: 'The smell of the dead was dreadful, especially when you put bayonets into them. You had to bayonet the bodies to let the gas out. Otherwise they were too swollen to be shifted. Our dead were dumped

The medical officer of the CMR, Captain Robert Guthrie, on the edge of Russell's Top during the armistice. At any other time, such exposure would have cost him his life. The Sphinx is behind him.

on blankets and dragged back to be buried on our side of the line.' 'Some of the poor chaps have been lying out there dead for a month now,' wrote Jack Martyn, 'and the stench is awful... Some of the sights of our poor chaps I will never forget in a lifetime.' Another wrote: 'I never saw so many bodies crowded into the same space before; there were literally thousands of them. And the condition they were in! I dare not describe the sights I saw. We scraped out shallow holes, edged the things gingerly in and covered them up as quickly as possible. It paid to smoke hard all the time.'[51]

The luckiest men at Anzac that day were those who were not required for the burying parties. It was a hot day, and the chance of a swim in the sea without running the risk of being killed by shrapnel was too good to miss. By noon 'the Anzac beaches were crowded with the battalions from the trenches'. After a dip, Bob Orr commented to Ken Stevens that 'All we need is some nice girls to hand round some things good to eat'. Stevens recalled that the 'peace and quietness everywhere was a treat'.[52]

At 4.25 p.m., with over 3000 Turks and several hundred Anzacs buried, the armistice ended. The enemies parted on good terms and returned to their trenches. After a few minutes silence 'both sides delivered tremendous volleys at nothing in particular, and settled down quietly for the night'.[53]

The day after the armistice, as the mounteds were being relieved by Australians on Russell's Top, the old Royal Navy battleship *Triumph* was torpedoed. The ship sank quickly but with little loss of life. 'The troopers ate their lunch in stony silence. It seemed they had lost an old friend.' The understandable Turkish reaction angered Ken Stevens. 'A sickly feeling came over me when I heard the Turks screaming with delight, and we saw them waving their hats as the *Triumph* turned over.'[54] The *Triumph* was sunk by a German submarine. Earlier in the month, General Hamilton heard that an enemy submarine was loose somewhere in the Mediterranean, so he withdrew most of the naval ships and transports to the submarine-proof harbour of Lemnos Island. Only a few warships, including the *Triumph*, were still anchored off Gallipoli when the submarine arrived and went to work. Two days after the sinking of the *Triumph*, the *Majestic* was sunk by the same submarine off Cape Helles. This drove the remaining ships to safety at Lemnos and Egypt, leaving only two destroyers to guard the northern and southern flanks of Anzac.

The loss of the heavy guns of the warships did not have the disastrous effect predicted. Large calibre naval gunfire, though spectacular and terrifying, was not particularly effective at Gallipoli because of the flat trajectory of the shells, their poor fragmentation, their short supply and the closeness of the opposing trenches. Nevertheless, the Anzacs felt abandoned by the Navy, while the Turks opposite them were greatly encouraged. Both sides soon learnt that the smaller destroyers were quite as effective as their larger consorts had been.

As May drew to a close the daily toll of death and injury continued to rise remorselessly. On the 26th Percy Doherty wrote: 'Hunter of the C.Y.C. was shot to-night when going out on outpost (dead). I haven't mentioned that two days ago, Sgt. Boden and Sergt. Johnston of the 10th were both shot dead. The former was entering the trenches from the front at night time, which is certain death, as we shoot at sight, so he was shot by one of his own men. Johnston was shot by a sniper. Happer (C.Y.C.) was also shot the other day.'[55]

7

No. 3 Outpost

If the Turks assailing the post had attacked with determination
the garrison must have been overwhelmed.

CHARLES BEAN

We feel we have lost a lot of our best men all for nothing.

CLUTHA MACKENZIE

———————————————

BY THE END OF May, commanders on both sides had realised that frontal assaults against trenches defended by determined men backed by machine guns and artillery could not succeed without many more troops and high explosive artillery ammunition. Lieutenant Colonel Meldrum, a chess player, likened the situation to being 'not unlike perpetual check'.[1] On the Allied side there was no likelihood of reinforcements or more ammunition arriving soon, so General Birdwood began to look for some other way to break the deadlock at Anzac.

He and other officers wondered if there might be an unguarded route from the northern outposts onto the Sari Bair hills above and behind the formidable enemy trench systems on Battleship Hill, Baby 700 and The Nek on the Second Ridge. If a strong Allied force could capture the hilltops, it might then be able to take those trenches from behind. This ought to force the Turks to withdraw from the whole of the Second Ridge. Once this ridge was secure, the Anzacs should be able to resume their barely started advance eastward towards the Narrows. Theoretically the idea held glittering prospects for success, but to be certain it would work, someone needed to go and look.

While these thoughts were germinating in the minds of the generals, scouts from the South Island garrisons of No. 1 and 2 Outposts were already busily exploring this area. They were led by Major Percy Overton, the second-in-command of the CMR. In civilian life Overton was a 38-year-old high country sheep farmer who had earned

Percy Overton, killed on 6 August.

a reputation as a scout in the South African War. The country around Anzac reminded him of New Zealand. 'The country here is very hilly and is broken with deep gullies, the sides of which are very steep and covered with dwarf oak and stub holly but will suit us down to the ground as it is what we are accustomed to.'[2]

On 15 May Overton undertook the first of many daring scouting expeditions into the tangled foothills below the Sari Bair hilltops. He quickly found that this flank was not well guarded by the Turks. The rough ground was a difficult obstacle, but he found passable routes along three valleys, the Sazli Beit, Chailak and Aghyl deres. These gave access onto two ridges, Rhododendron Ridge (named by Overton for its rhododendron-like scrub cover) and Damakjelik Bair. These, in turn, led upwards to the three key Sari Bair summits of Chunuk Bair, Hill Q and Hill 971 (also known as Koja Chemen Tepe). Overton once climbed Rhododendron Ridge almost as far as Chunuk Bair, and he confirmed that an Allied force on this hilltop would be above and behind the Turkish trenches on Battleship Hill, Baby 700 and The Nek.

Three more New Zealand patrols went out on 27 May. Two of them did not get far, but the third, under Overton's personal command, thoroughly explored the lower reaches of the Aghyl Dere over 36 hours. He took tremendous risks along the way, barely avoiding strong Turkish patrols or camps more than once. 'We had a most exciting and interesting time dodging Turkish outposts. I was able from what I saw of the country to make a map and gain much information as to the movements of the Turks, and would not have missed the experience for worlds.'[3] This time he found what he considered to be a feasible route up onto Hill Q north of Chunuk Bair. He also reported that the enemy outposts in the foothills were manned only at night.

Overton's reports, when added to information obtained from Greek refugees from nearby villages, showed that there were passable and relatively unguarded routes up onto the crest of the Sari Bair ridge overlooking the northern corner of the Anzac perimeter. This was just what General Birdwood, who had been thinking more and more about an outflanking attack, wanted to hear. He chose to overlook the negative aspects of Overton's reports: the strong Turkish posts on either side of the Chailak Dere which would need to be captured, and the steady reinforcement of Turkish positions on the hills and in the valleys. By the end of May Birdwood, with General Hamilton's approval, was well along the way to developing his scheme into a detailed plan.

By now Birdwood had 25,000 troops at Anzac, more than he needed to defend the current front line. He thought he could capture Chunuk Bair with the surplus troops already under his command, reinforced with the Gurkhas of the 29th Indian Brigade, which was available in Egypt. The mounteds were front runners for the attack. They were already in position on the left flank, 'they knew the ground and were already itching to end the deadly monotony of trench life at Anzac'.[4] Hamilton and Birdwood planned to launch the attack in early July.

To their disappointment, most of the South Island mounteds had played little part in defeating the massive 19 May attack, but a chance to prove themselves was not long in coming. A new Turkish trench, on a low spur of Rhododendron Ridge below Table Top, was discovered on 27 May. Overton's scouting activity, careful though it was, probably drew Turkish attention to the area and prompted them to dig the new position. It was about 300 metres inland from No. 2 Outpost and invisible from it. It was very close to higher Turkish positions on Table Top, Destroyer Hill and the lower end of Rhododendron Ridge.

Enemy snipers in the new position quickly made a nuisance of themselves, so Godley, perhaps at Russell's suggestion, decided to capture it. It appears that Godley failed to gain his corps commander's approval, which he would not have received, given Birdwood's interest in the area for future operations. Russell convinced Godley to let the NZMR Brigade make the attack. The AMR and WMR were already available, having just been relieved on Russell's Top by the Australian light horse. When the last squadrons of the OMR arrived on 28 May, Russell put them into No. 1 and 2 Outposts, replacing the CMR. Russell thus had all three of his regiments available for the attack.

At 10 p.m. on Friday 28 May the 1st (Canterbury Yeomanry Cavalry) squadron of the CMR seized the new enemy position. Its garrison of about 20 Turks 'ran like blazes & left most of their gear…. We were all keen as mustard & rather enjoyed the operations.'[5] At a cost of one man killed and five wounded, the operation was apparently a complete success.

The Manawatu squadron of the WMR immediately relieved the CYC squadron in the captured trenches, now named No. 3 Outpost. It seems they took no machine guns into the post. With pick and shovel they began to prepare the position for the inevitable Turkish counter-attack. They were not seriously molested until dawn on 29 May, by which time they had excavated a semi-circle of trenches facing the high ground to the east.

As soon as the sun rose it became apparent that No. 3 Outpost was going to be a very difficult prize to hold. Turkish snipers and machine gunners on the high ground overlooking the outpost began firing down into the trenches, and artillery lashed the position with shrapnel. Nothing could be done to halt this fire, so the defenders had to stop digging and take cover during the daylight hours. The Wellingtons took no casualties that day, but the need to stay below ground allowed Turkish counter-attack forces to creep very close to the post without being seen.

On the evening of 29 May Colonel Mustafa Kemal seized the opportunity presented to him and attacked No. 3 Outpost in strength. It had just been taken over by 98 men of the Wellington East Coast squadron under the command of Major Selwyn Chambers. The new men had barely got themselves settled 'when sounds of movement were heard. Presently, showers of hand-grenades descended on the post. Calling on "Allah," the enemy, numbering many hundreds, surrounded the post.' At 10 p.m. Chambers reported that the post was surrounded and under attack by a large body of Turks. 'The Wellingtons had no hand-grenades … so had to depend upon their rifles. Rushing up to the parapet and yelling their eerie cries, but never daring to press the attack home, throwing hand-grenades and then retreating, the Turks let the precious hours of darkness slip by.'[6] At the same time as they launched these weak attacks against No. 3 Outpost, the Turks isolated it from reinforcements by digging blocking trenches between it and No. 2 Outpost.

At midnight the 2nd (Queen Alexandra's Wellington West Coast) squadron, under the command of Major Jim Elmslie, was sent to help the besieged garrison. They had to approach along the southern side of the ridge. The crest was blocked by a new enemy trench, and the northern side was dominated by Turkish fire from the hill on the far side of the Chailak Dere. On the way Elmslie dropped off one troop of men between Nos 2 and 3 Outposts. This troop was fiercely attacked and driven back to No. 2 Outpost, closely followed by the Turks, who tried 'to gain our trenches under cover of the Wellington troop, but we managed to get a cross fire in behind [the] Wellingtons and beat them back, the foremost Turk falling about 3 yards from the trenches'.[7] The rest of Elmslie's squadron was held up by stronger Turkish forces in the new trenches encircling No. 3 Outpost. The fighting outside the outpost raged for hours, often at very close range. 'Sergeant Con. McDonald … grasped the muzzle of a rifle which was pointed at him, in time to divert the bullet from his body, but it struck his right hand and traversed upwards to the elbow, shattering the bones en route.' Because the Wellingtons were fighting in the open, casualties mounted quickly. Soon after daylight, Captain Bill Hardham VC was seriously wounded. Lieutenant Duncan McDonald, who was shot in the stomach while assisting Hardham, died of his wound a week later.[8]

Francis Twisleton spotted the Wellingtons 'penned in a little valley and unable to move; they had a lot of wounded and one or two killed'.[9] Major Elmslie distinguished himself by his courage and leadership. 'The men think there is no one like him. During the fighting, he was walking amongst us as though he was going to get the cows in'. Jimmy Moore 'was severely wounded in a leg and lay helpless. With bullets tearing up the ground everywhere, Major Elmslie ran to his help and bandaged up the fearful gash, under fire at close range. Elmslie had his cap shot off, another bullet drilled his pocket book and three others the folds of his tunic. Quite unperturbed, he finished bandaging Moore, then, putting him on his shoulders, carried him back to safety.'[10]

From dawn onwards the defenders of the post came under renewed artillery, machine gun and sniper fire from the surrounding hills. Artillery and long-range machine gun fire from the Anzac perimeter tried to keep the Turks at bay, but much of the ground around the beleaguered post was hidden from view. At 7 a.m. the Manawatu squadron was sent back to break through and relieve the garrison, but it got no closer than Elmslie's squadron had. Both relief squadrons were pinned down by Turkish fire for the rest of the day, and No. 3 Outpost remained cut off and surrounded. As Francis Twisleton wrote, 'They were still going at it hammer and tongs at No. 3'. According to John Wilder the mounteds endured 'a regular hell … we hardly had a moment's peace, we were absolutely surrounded by Turks who were just beneath us under the cliff

Norman Cameron, killed on 30 May.

Victor Christophers, killed on 30 May.

with a covering fire on the other side of a gully. The Turks were almost close enough to touch, but the covering fire kept us down and they just threw in bombs as they liked.'[11] The telephone line back to No. 2 Outpost was cut repeatedly. Turkish artillery fire blew in part of the trench line which, according to James Harvey, was only '3 feet deep and a foot to 18 inches wide.... [Lieutenant Norman] Cameron was killed by a rifle bullet through the head; he was standing speaking to me at the time. The whole of the 24 hours was put in on our knees.'[12] Wilder wrote: 'It was pretty hot work as we could not look over the top at all where we were, a few tried before we arrived, but nearly all were shot. The Turks were under a ledge just beneath us, not more than five yards away. They threw in bomb after bomb and till we got used to them they did a lot of damage. The only thing to do was pick them up and throw them back at the enemy.... I saw one chap throw back four in no time.'[13]

As the official WMR history recorded, 'The wounded had to take care of themselves, and many of them continued to fight when suffering from grievous injuries.' James Harvey wrote that 'It was an awful job getting the wounded to a small space where we could lay them; we had to drag some of the poor beggars down the trench on their stomachs or backs'.[14] Sergeant 'Tassy' Smith, the brigade's champion heavyweight boxer, and a fine horseman, was killed by a bomb while picking up a second one. According to Harvey, he 'was blown up in the groin and stomach, and his legs were badly cut about; he died a very hard death and was in great pain'.[15] William Pyle wrote: 'Poor old Vic Christophers was shot dead ... last night. ... Vic's death is hard on any one who knew him. He was one of the best chaps I ever knew & us fellows who were pals of his are very cut up. There are so many good fellows gone, though.'[16]

The trenches of No. 3 Outpost were on the very edge of the steep hillsides, and the men defending them could not see or shoot down the slopes without exposing themselves. To do so invited quick death from Turkish snipers and machine gunners on the hills around them but, with no grenades to throw, the defenders could do little else but rely on their rifles. In these circumstances, machine guns could not have been used even if they had been taken into the post. 'The Turks were closing in and

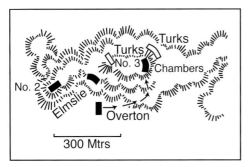

The fight for No. 3 Outpost, 28–30 May.

ammunition was running short when, providentially, Captain Spragg unearthed some thousands of rounds of our own ammunition, which seemed like a gift of the gods.'[17]

As the day went on, 'the magnitude of the folly of ordering a small force to hold this isolated and badly-sited salient became more apparent'. The defenders expected a final, annihilating bayonet assault at any moment, but it never came. 'If the Turks assailing the post had attacked with determination the garrison must have been overwhelmed.'[18] Some mounteds thought the vigour of their defence convinced the Turkish commander that he faced a much stronger garrison than he in fact did.

The besieged post was covered in a haze of dust all day, thrown up by the bullets and bombs. 'About 5 p.m. on Sunday evening,' wrote John Wilder, 'the Turks sapped under one corner of our trench and blew it up, and the fire being too hot to build it up again we had to retire to the first two corners and build barricades. When this happened and the Turks got in at the other end we thought it was all up, but they did not seem too keen on coming at us.'[19] By sunset on 30 May, 14 of the 98 men in the post were dead. Fifteen others were wounded. They could not be evacuated, and several died in front of their helpless friends.

Further attempts to relieve the post were postponed until after dark. Even after night fell the two frustrated Wellington squadrons could not get past the enemy blocks on the ridge, so two Canterbury squadrons tried another way. One of these squadrons, commanded by Percy Overton, found an approach route that was not blocked by the enemy, and it relieved the Wellington East Coast squadron at 10.30 p.m. on 30 May. Laughlin Bain was one of the men in the relief force. 'We had to go over a piece of ground covered by a machine gun and several rifles. … After a hundred yards of that we had to go sneaking and crawling up gullies and round hills with Turks all around us and we got to the trench where the Wellington MR were.'[20]

The Turks attacked immediately and the reinforced defenders had to fight them off for several more hours before the Wellington squadron, covered by the Canterburys, could evacuate its wounded. General Godley wanted the relief force to stay in the post, but Russell had already authorised its abandonment once the besieged defenders had been rescued. Godley countermanded Russell's order, but was overruled by

Birdwood. By the time the withdrawal was officially approved at midnight, it was already under way. The commander on the spot had decided that the post could no longer be held. The wounded were carried out on overcoats. When the survivors of the Wellington East Coast squadron withdrew, they had been fighting continuously for 28 hours.

As soon as the Turks detected the withdrawal, they surged forward after the mounteds. According to Laughlin Bain, 'if you can imagine 500 beagles and a few huntsmen's horns you will have some idea of the noise they made. When we thought they had come far enough we climbed a bit of a hill to a trench and pasted them. We gave them "Allah, Allah".' A hand-picked rearguard covered the withdrawal, 'calmly and methodically picking off any too adventurous enemy'.[21]

The Turks were stopped by a vigorous defence from most of the NZMR Brigade lining the newly dug sap that linked the main Anzac position to the outposts. Faced with a reinforced and determined foe, the Turks did not press their attacks but

The CWGC No. 2 Outpost Cemetery. Eight of the 24 mounted riflemen buried here were killed in the fight for No. 3 Outpost in May. The new No. 3 Outpost is in the background.

153

withdrew in triumph to their recaptured post, where nine dead New Zealanders had been left. 'As daylight advanced it was seen that they had stripped some of the dead New Zealanders and flung them from their trenches; the naked body of one hung head downwards on the cliff below the parapet. This incident greatly embittered the troops.'[22] As Clutha Mackenzie wrote, 'They shall suffer for that!' Next morning the bodies were blown up by a destroyer, 'with a few well-directed shots ... and gradually the deed was forgotten'.[23]

Leaving a squadron of Aucklanders to keep an eye on things, the exhausted troopers 'trailed homewards, carelessly trampling the dewy wild poppy heads on their way. A bathe and a drink, and then a long, long sleep.'[24] Two days later a new No. 3 Outpost was established on a knoll immediately north of No. 2 Outpost. The post recaptured by the Turks was renamed Old No. 3 Outpost.

The prolonged fight for No. 3 Outpost was a terrible experience for many of the mounteds. 'To the highly-strung men, many of whom had not slept for three days, the yelling of the Turks, the ghostlike sea lapping on the beach in the background, and the enemy leaping from bush to bush in the moonlight, the whole business resembled a frightful nightmare.'[25] It was a worse experience than the 19 May attack, when the men could shoot down the charging Turks from the relative safety of their trenches. This time they were at a disadvantage. The NZMR Brigade lost 23 killed and 57 wounded, mostly in the WMR (18 killed and 52 wounded).[26] The Australian war correspondent and historian Charles Bean considered this casualty list 'not heavy for so sharp a fight'.[27] Maybe so, but it was heavy enough for such a futile operation. By the end of it, the entire mounted rifles brigade had been dragged into what had started out as a seemingly simple

The temporary grave of Alfred Dickenson (WMR), killed on 30 May. This grave was later lost.

'A hopeless position'. Old No. 3 Outpost from Table Top. With Table Top remaining in Turkish hands, the outpost could not be held.

squadron operation. The attack on Old No. 3 Outpost should not have taken place, as Russell admitted afterwards. 'I did not like the position at all and thought that it was too exposed, and finally got leave from G.O.C. [Godley] to withdraw into another position – a consent very reluctantly given.'[28] Many men who took part agreed with Russell's judgement. Clutha Mackenzie believed that the whole thing had been undertaken 'rather too lightly'. He thought 'it was all caused by a foolish error of judgement in putting a weak outpost, entirely unsupported, a long distance from our main position. We feel we have lost a lot of our best men all for nothing. ... The outpost we all knew was in an exceedingly dangerous position surrounded as it was on three sides by the enemy with nothing to prevent them cutting it off on the fourth side & with no supports whatever.' Fred Waite agreed. 'It was a hopeless position for us – away out on a salient – and should never have been attempted.'[29]

Had Godley or Russell looked at the ground closely from No. 2 Outpost before ordering the attack, they should have seen that No. 3 Outpost could not have been retained while the Turks held the adjacent higher ground of Table Top and Destroyer Hill. Approving the attack was Godley's second serious tactical error to affect the mounteds after the 20 May counter-attack order. In both cases, he ordered attacks that had little or no chance of succeeding. Godley was already unpopular in the NZ&A Division, but these two incidents led many mounted riflemen to question his tactical ability.

This failed operation also warned the Turks that this flank was vulnerable to attack. They quickly improved their defences at Old No. 3 Outpost, on Table Top and on Chunuk Bair. Mustafa Kemal was not satisfied; he wanted a strong garrison to close the northern route completely, but was overruled by his senior commanders. On the Allied side, Percy Overton was so discouraged that he predicted any subsequent attack up this route 'is doomed to fail, as the element of surprise will be lacking'. His commanders were less concerned, but they did prohibit further activity (except patrolling) on the northern flank of Anzac. The aim was to convince the enemy that their recent improvements to its defences made it completely secure against attack.[30]

As May became June and summer drew near, life at Anzac settled down to a prolonged quiet period while both sides prepared for major operations. By the end of May all the mounted regiments had experienced combat, and their losses had been considerable, but their reputation as reliable fighters was growing.

8

Life and death on Gallipoli

Death came along pretty regularly. You'd hear someone had been killed,
someone wounded, and you couldn't take it too much to heart.
You just said, 'Poor devil' and got on with your day.

WILLIAM EAST

We live in holes dug into the ground and live like fighting cocks. Many of
the Christchurch men I knew have all gone, but they all died hard.

ALEXANDER ROBBINS

———————————————

THE CLIMATE ON GALLIPOLI in April and May 1915 was ideal – fine but not too hot – but it grew more unpleasant as summer approached. July was the hottest month of the year, with daytime temperatures in the shade averaging 31 to 33°C. The narrow trenches became furnace-like in the still hot air. The climate 'was now becoming a remorseless enemy. The heat of the noon-day sun was intense; there was little or no shade; and the scanty water supply in the trenches was rarely sufficient for men with a parching thirst.'[1] As Percy Doherty noted, occasional summer thunderstorms 'made everything uncomfortable. The trenches which are cut in clay were nothing but slush, and the clay sticks to everything, making a horrible mess.'[2]

Despite the worsening climate, life on Gallipoli soon settled into a 'not unpleasant routine', according to Clutha Mackenzie. 'The fresh, bright, beautiful dawns were slightly chilly, the early mornings were far from unpleasant, though the noonday hours were warm, and afflicted with flies and smells; but, beneath the shade of outstretched blankets and oil-sheets, the troopers whiled away the time, sleeping mostly, some writing and some playing cards. ...'

For breakfast the men dipped a few biscuits into jam and chewed them until they could be swallowed. They tidied the bivvy, shook out their blankets and then it was time for the daily 'wash'. A few teaspoons of water sufficed for cleaning teeth and washing

Troopers Bridge and Strachan (both WMR) in a trench on Walker's Ridge.

the face, and for the occasional shave. Lastly, the men stripped and cleaned their rifles, rewrapping the bolts in protective cloths. 'The afternoon hours dragged drowsily past, until, with the lowering sun, they woke to prepare the evening meal, the largest of the day. ... the cool, clear evenings were spent ... in sniping and artillery practice, and by [the Turks] in expending wastefully large amounts of small arms ammunition against the opposite parapets.'[3]

Inevitably, food was the topic of many complaints on Gallipoli. There was no lack of it, but its quality and suitability left a lot to be desired. A few men thought the rations were fine. Lieutenant Colonel Arthur Bauchop, a South African War veteran, was quite satisfied. 'The rations issued in this campaign have been of the most luxurious sort. ... I question if British troops have ever been so well fed. Delicacies unknown before in the history of an army in the field have been lavishly distributed. About a month ago there were two issues of ham & eggs!'[4] Trooper Vic Christophers also thought the food was quite good. A week before he was killed he wrote, 'We are very well fed here, better than we've been since leaving New Zealand'.[5]

Bauchop and Christophers were in the minority. Most men were scathingly critical of the food. Jack Martyn's section 'went up before the Major and made a complaint about our rations. They are not sufficient to keep a man in form and the potatoes and onions are not enough for a sparrow. On occasions all I could shit was a raisin.' Ken Stevens and his mates 'loathed the food, salt bully and bacon, hard biscuits, watery jam and cheese' and 'were starving because of the lack of vegetables and fruit'. The biscuits were so hard that many men nibbled their edges and then threw them into No Man's Land. According to George Ranstead, 'We hate the things and try to make all sorts of patent dishes out of them. We have boiled biscuits, fried biscuits, toasted biscuits, biscuit puddings.'[6] As the daytime temperatures increased, the cheese melted and the salty bully beef was discarded because of the thirst it caused. Biscuits and jam with the ever-welcome tin of tea became the standard summer fare on Gallipoli. The jam was always either plum and apple, or apricot, and the men hated it.

In a more temperate climate, or in a war of movement, where the rations could have been supplemented by the local purchase of fresh fruit and vegetables, the rations would have been all right. Stuck in trenches on Gallipoli with summer drawing on and with little water, the men 'had little appetite for the over-salted "bully", which, in the heat of midday or afternoon, slipped in its own fat across the platter or mess-tin, swamping stray flies as it went; or for the thin apricot jam on tasteless biscuit; or for the cheese, greasy from exposure to the sun and filling the dugout with an odour sickeningly reminiscent of that exhaling from the corpses in No-Man's Land'.[7]

Men longed for simple delicacies from home. Francis Twisleton yearned for 'a slice of buttered toast.... I've got an intense longing for apple pie and rice pudding'. Ken Stevens wrote: 'Cakes from home were a welcome change of diet, but no one thought of sending such eatables as potatoes, onions, tinned fruit or fish.... At meal time ... we would talk of all going down to the Waverley Hotel in Queen Street and have a good meal of fish, roast beef, pork or lamb with green peas, potatoes, kumeras, and then plum pudding and fruit.' George Ranstead missed 'the bread, oranges and eggs-a-cook that we got in Egypt'.[8]

Clutha Mackenzie was able to spice up his diet. 'The possibilities of the larder were considerably spun out by barter with the Indians, who had plenty and to spare of good food, by the use of one's wits and by purchase at exorbitant prices of certain articles from sailors.' Curry powder was particularly sought-after from the Indians. 'Our fellows,' George Ramstead explained, 'collect the enemies rifles and sell them to the sailors at a standard price – a few packets of cigarettes, a loaf of bread and a tin of condensed milk.' Ken Stevens bought a dozen eggs from sailors, paying well over the odds for the privilege. As he was carrying his precious cargo back to his bivouac, a passing mule kicked his haversack and broke all the eggs except one. Undeterred, his section picked out as much dirt and eggshell out as possible to make scrambled eggs. When they added the last unbroken egg to the mixture, it was rotten.[9] 'People going to Mudros [on Lemnos Island] or Imbros were loaded with commissions and made the

Greek traders rich by buying tinned figs, pineapples, and milk at fabulous prices, and paradoxically, fowls eggs that were fresh and only one shilling a dozen.'[10]

There were occasional official efforts to improve the variety of the rations. Fresh bread and eggs were sometimes distributed, and extra jam, rice and dried fruit appeared now and then. So did Maconochie's, 'a line of meat goods packed with a few slices of potatoes, carrots and beans'.[11] Rum and lime juice was sometimes issued, but never in large quantities.

Any change in the ration issue was cause for comment in letters and diaries. 'We are now getting issued with 4 packets of cigarettes 2 of matches & about an eggcupful of rum & lime juice per week. Today we got bread.' Tinned milk was brought across to Gallipoli, but it was withheld until the men cleared up the piles of cheese. There were never enough of these goodies to go around, and the men in the front line thought those down on the beach got most of what did arrive. Ken Stevens 'met a man after the war who said he had had plenty of bread and fresh meat. Later I found out he was a member of the A.S.C. [Army Service Corps].' According to William Watson, a ship called the *Osmanieh* that plied the route between Gallipoli and Lemnos Island 'had her holds full of the most priceless foods and stores, such as Huntley & Palmers biscuits, hams, bacon, oatmeal and flour, jams and tinned butter and whiskey etc. ... the ship I was told went regularly at night time to Gallipoli, where the fighting men were nearly starving, but never discharged any of her priceless cargo'.[12]

Francis Twisleton thought 'there ought to be a first-rate canteen ship where men could get what they need in order to vary the diet. If they could get milk and rice there would be fewer men getting sick. It is a pity that the powers that be stopped the daily issues of rum. A large proportion of the men have been used to a certain amount of alcohol every day, and to have it stopped makes them unstable, though they might not think so themselves.' For another trooper, the rum issue, 'when not stopped by the higher command or absorbed by the A.S.C. and quartermasters, was occasionally a relieving and pleasant interlude'. In May, Vic Christophers wrote: 'We get supplied with tobacco and matches and get rum served out twice a week. We don't think much of the prohibitionists who want to stop our rum and beer. It's the one luxury we have. I have never met a prohibitionist in the army.'[13]

There were no kitchens or trained cooks in the mounted regiments. Rations were issued to sections of four men, who could cook and eat them when and how they liked. 'Each section has their own billy,' Robert Tuke wrote, 'and we take turn about cooking. We sometimes powder the biscuits up in empty Turkish shell cases and make imaginary porridge.' According to Percy Doherty, 'We are all getting to be expert cooks, as every man has to cook his own now, and we make some great concoctions out of soaked biscuits and jam and sugar. We are issued every day with 4 tins of bully beef, one tin of jam, an allowance of biscuits, tea and sugar and 8 potatoes, also a small piece of bacon for each section of four men. The only trouble is the scarcity of water.'[14]

Water was always in very short supply on Gallipoli. 'Water was very scarce, and a shave, much less a wash, [was] altogether out of the question. In a moment of wild extravagance Mac had burst a couple of tablespoonfuls on cleaning his teeth.'[15] The daily ration seldom exceeded 2 1/4 litres per man, for all purposes. Most was consumed in the form of hot tea, with a few teaspoonfuls being used for washing and shaving. There were hardly any wells and springs inside the Anzac position. In late May water diviners in the OMR discovered a reliable and abundant water supply in a dry riverbed near the regimental bivouac at No. 2 Outpost.[16] Men from the main Anzac position would often risk Turkish snipers and machine gunners to get to the outposts for a taste of this crystal-clear cool water. Most of the fresh water was brought on barges from Malta and Alexandria, pumped ashore into storage tanks in the gullies and transported to the trenches on the backs of mules or men. When the seas were rough salt water contaminated the fresh water in the barges which 'made it very unpleasant for drinking'.[17]

The health of the Anzacs was good until the end of May. After that the heat, flies, poor diet, disease, lack of fresh water, cramped living conditions, heavy work and lack of real rest combined to destroy the health of most of the men stuck there. 'During June and July the strength of the troops visibly declined. The great frames which had impressed beholders in Egypt now stood out gauntly; faces became lined, cheeks sunken.' Ken Stevens could spot new reinforcements 'by their sleek complexions, new clothes and fat on the ribs'.[18]

By mid-June 'not only the spirits but the physical health of the troops began to be affected by the squalid misery of their surroundings. The daily number of sick was increasing by leaps and bounds; and there was scarcely a man on the peninsula who was not a victim to the prevailing epidemic of dysenteric diarrhoea.' Francis Twisleton wrote: 'Men are not too fit now. It would be alright if you could sleep during the day, but the flies are here in countless millions …You can't sleep in the daylight for them, which makes the night work feel more severe.'[19]

As the official history of the New Zealand medical services recorded, 'In the first

William Lynch, killed on 9 August.

week of June, the evacuations by sickness from the Anzac corps amounted to 456; but during the last week of the month, 818 sick were evacuated from the beach – a sickness wastage equivalent to 35 per 1000 per week, or one brigade a month'.[20] Noel Trolove wrote: 'Most of the men were weak and suffering from dysentery and septic sores on hands and joints'. Lieutenant Colonel Fenwick, a doctor, was 'in terror for our men. I can't protect them from disease.'[21] By late July, between 100 and 200 men per day were sent to hospital, usually with dysentery or enteric fever. Cecil Malthus was 'infuriated because we understood that a quantity of sick diet, mainly condensed milk … was all grabbed by those we called the "backstairs boys" at the foot of the hill'.[22]

The 24 May armistice was not repeated, and unburied bodies posed a serious health risk as the weather warmed. Flies bred in their millions on the rotting corpses. Dense humming clouds of the bloated insects would rise from the bodies when disturbed by explosions, only to settle quickly back to their feasting or buzz across to the latrines or the trenches where the men were trying to eat. There was 'such a loathsome plague of huge flies (known to the troops as "corpse-flies") that it was difficult to eat a mouthful of food without swallowing the pests.' According to James Harvey, the flies 'argue for every bite one eats'. 'Shrapnel and sniping were often severe, but they did not drive men to distraction as did the flies'.[23] By the beginning of June, the millions of flies began to affect the health and the morale of the troops. Minor wounds inevitably became infected by flies, and there were no medicines to treat them. William Lynch had his own remedy. 'Do you remember giving me the small bottle of sheep dip before I left? Well it has proved a regular God-send, for every little scratch one gets, it festers and won't heal, but a dab of the dip makes a difference.'[24]

As the trench lines expanded, they cut into the graves of men buried in the May armistice, and decomposing bodies often became part of trench walls. 'In one place the lower leg and boot of a dead Turk stuck out from the corner of a trench, and at another a bony hand protruded. Grim humorists shook it as they passed,' wrote Clutha

Mackenzie. 'There are other things in our trenches that we don't care overmuch to have as company. Maggots – maggots crawling in battalions about a chap's feet and dropping from the sides of a trench down his neck. Maggots from the dead!... We have dead Turks right on our very parapets. Only this morning a bullet pitched into one lying close handy, and the putrid matter (of the consistency of porridge) was "spattered" right over us. They say you can get used to anything. Well, maybe so. But its hard to get used to that.'[25] 'Round No. 2 Sap ... was a sight one wishes to forget. Fourteen dead Turks were lying in a space of probably six square yards. The sap was crawling with maggots, and the stench was abominable. Yet this sap had to be held day and night.'[26] Noel Trolove wrote: 'The floor of the trench was springy to walk on in places where dead had been buried none too deeply underfoot, and in some places sundry pieces of equipment and human anatomy protruded from the trench walls'. Even after the May armistice and following the improvements to sanitation, the stink of rotting bodies and human waste was ever-present. The smell of chloride of lime also became characteristic of Anzac. 'Chloride of lime ... was scattered thickly on all decaying matter, and the scent of Anzac drifted ten miles out to sea.'[27]

Because the men were unable to change their clothes, lice and fleas bred in the seams of shirts and trousers. There was no steam disinfection available on Gallipoli and before long, practically every man was infested with these disease-carrying pests. It became common to see men at rest with their clothes off, killing the insects thriving in the seams of their uniforms.

Survival, not sanitation, had been the top priority in the first few months after the landings. Once the position was more or less secure, strenuous efforts were made to improve hygiene. The piles of refuse and horse manure behind the front line were buried, and the trenches were cleaned up and kept that way. Proper latrines were dug and their use was enforced. Corpses within reach were dragged into the nearest trenches with grappling hooks and buried or burnt. Fly screens were placed over sleeping accommodation, and wells and water tanks were guarded to prevent accidental contamination.

Determined not to let their mates down, many Anzacs would allow themselves to be evacuated only if they were too sick to prevent it. Ill and wounded men who were evacuated from Gallipoli were sent to hospitals in England, Malta or Egypt. They never knew where they would end up, and their units back on Gallipoli completely lost track of them. There was a great deal of medical muddle throughout the campaign. Men were held waiting for hospital ships that never arrived or were embarked only to be offloaded again within hours. Casualties were sent to hospitals and convalescent camps that were no longer there. The sick or wounded could be gone for months on end. Knowing this, commanders tried to keep their sick men with them on Gallipoli for as long as they could, and this encouraged the spread of infectious diseases.

In addition to the obvious illnesses and infestations, there was a gradual and more insidious deterioration in the health of the Anzacs. In late July an Australian medical report stated that the men's health was poor and getting worse, and that the decline could not be halted by further improvements in sanitation. It was characterised by gastro-intestinal upsets, lung inflammations, rapid pulses, loss of weight and enlargement of the heart. The doctors concluded that the men were working too hard for too long without proper rest, on inadequate rations and in hot and filthy conditions.[28]

Two New Zealand military hospitals were set up in Egypt in June and July. Until then New Zealanders had been treated in the former Egyptian Army Hospital in Cairo. The first hospital was set up in Port Said, with beds for 600 patients. The second hospital took over the Egyptian Army site in Cairo and expanded its capacity to over 1000 beds. A convalescent hospital was also set up in 1915, first in Alexandria and later at Heliopolis in Cairo.[29]

It was becoming too hot to sleep during the day, even if the crawling lice and swarming flies had permitted it. On most nights men were either in the front line or in working parties to the rear. The work was heavy, monotonous and dangerous. There was no chance to really get away from the front line: they were always within range of enemy artillery fire. 'The units in "rest" lived under the

Men of the Mounted Brigade Field Ambulance.

same conditions as those in the line; they enjoyed no "spells" among civilians, women and children, as in the rest areas in France; there were no daily papers, no cafés or cabarets.'[30]

Swimming was the one officially approved recreation on Anzac, and it served a useful therapeutic purpose. The sea was so close to the front line that everyone got to swim in it at least occasionally, and to wash their clothes. According to Jack Braithwaite, 'The sea is shallow and the bottom is clean white sand and one can walk 100 yards out before getting out of depth'.[31] Although Anzac Cove was largely out of sight of Turkish observers, swimmers often attracted enemy artillery fire. Despite a few deaths and many injuries, Birdwood refused to ban the practice. As Francis Twisleton noted, 'The men will risk anything for a swim, the days are hot, there is little water, and unless you get into the sea you can't wash'. Cecil Malthus wrote that swimming in the sea 'gave a delicious relaxation, as well as relief from heat and thirst. … We chanced the occasional shell, but if a couple of snipers got to work on us it was time to withdraw. There were a few casualties, but the Command wisely decided that the benefits justified them.'[32]

A few units enjoyed brief respites on Imbros or Lemnos islands, but none of the mounted regiments did until much later in the year. It was not thought possible to send many men away from Anzac for a rest in case the enemy attacked while they were gone.

Despite the arrival of reinforcements, by the end of July, the WMR could muster only 362 men for duty, 200 less than its established strength; the CMR could muster only 72 men. Overall, the mounted rifles brigade had lost 93 men killed, 321 wounded and 443 sick since 13 May.[33] As bad as this sounds, it could have been much worse. Typhoid and smallpox inoculations proved their worth at Gallipoli, with very few casualties from either disease.

Most men seemed to accept the appalling living conditions without complaint; it was the boredom and lack of action that upset them and lowered their morale. 'Even hard work and hourly risk of death could not relieve the monotony of existence on those barren, sun-baked hillsides; and as week followed week with no change in the situation, and no sign of the promised advance from the south, it needed all the philosophy of which the troops were capable to keep their spirits from drooping. Cooped together in stifling trenches or shadeless gullies, tormented by flies, tortured by thirst, stricken by disease, and ignorant of the reasons which condemned them to inactivity, it was difficult to keep light-hearted as the early hopes of victory gave way to disillusionment.'[34] Francis Twisleton thought that 'we do too much digging in and waiting for events to happen. There is a lot of good cavalry country around here, and if we only had our horses we could flank their position and put the fear of death into them.' Clutha Mackenzie wrote: 'Our great desire is for action, get into it & get the thing through'. The men were trapped and they knew it. Leo Acland told John Barker that 'we are in the same position as if a man was on top of Mt Cook with his night shirt on and had to wait till someone came to take him down'. Leslie Smith wrote: 'We are all sick of the whole thing & would not care if peace was declared tomorrow'.[35]

In the midst of the horror at Anzac, some still found things of beauty to appreciate. 'The prettiest sight of all is the Hospital Ship at night,' wrote Francis Twisleton. 'It has a belt of green lamps around it so close together that the light merges, with a big white light amidships. The water is always so calm that everything is clearly reflected and makes a picture one is never tired of looking at.' For Clutha Mackenzie, 'Night time at the Cove was always beautiful. The starry brightness above the blackness of the sea, the steep rising face of the hill, with the twinkling lights and flickering fires of the bivouacs, the throng of toilers among the great piles of stores, the mules and water-carts crunching along the gravel, the wounded awaiting embarkation ... what might be called the throbbing heart of Anzac.'[36] The animal life of Anzac was also written about. 'Lots of big tortoises there. Out scouting one night I thought I was being followed. Waited for who was tracking me, shot at it and bullets flew off. It was a tortoise.' Fred Waite: 'Out on the Suvla Flats, red foxes played in the sun with their cubs. On the prickly scrub, the little praying mantis held up her supplicating green hands and prayed as if we were all far past redemption.'[37]

The disciplinary record of the mounteds on Gallipoli was good. On 31 May Trooper Marshall was charged with the serious crime of sleeping while on sentry duty. He was found guilty, and sentenced to 14 days' Field Punishment No. 2 (hard labour and detention). According to Chris Pugsley, 'the leniency of the sentence recognised the enormous strains placed on men in these conditions. It is the only known court martial in Russell's New Zealand Mounted Rifle Brigade on Gallipoli.'[38]

Now and then mail came from home and its arrival was cause for celebration. 'Letter day is undoubtedly our Day of Days here,' William Pyle wrote. 'The mails are weeks overdue,' Percival Fenwick recorded on 14 May, 'and we all want news from home. It is a great pick-me-up to get a letter.' On 9 June Benjamin Colbran 'got a letter from Uncle Sam dated March 28th and I don't think I was ever so pleased at getting a letter before. A little news from home goes a long way here now.' Clutha Mackenzie

Sergeant Major Charles Brown (left) and Trooper Bailey (right). Brown was killed on 27 August.

described the 'buzz of excitement while a mail-bag was being sorted, and then a strange quiet would hang over the terraces while every one in his dug-outs eagerly explored his pages'.[39] Letters from home discussed a wide variety of topics: wool and meat prices, family births, deaths and marriages, business dealings, news of other family members joining up, and so on. Most men wrote letters home whenever they could, but a lack of paper and an inefficient postal service didn't help matters. All outgoing mail had to be passed by regimental censors. John Wilder went 'around to Canterbury Camp and got their censor to pass my letters as [deleted] is too d--- lazy and was going to leave ours until next mail; he said openly that he was just going to do the Officers'. He's a cad of the deepest dye.'[40] These letters would often give news of relatives or family friends met overseas, and brief accounts of action (if they escaped the attention of the censors), usually with an assurance that the writer was fine and not to worry. Some items of homeward-bound mail caused problems, and orders were issued in September forbidding the posting home of shells, grenades, cartridges, fuses and detonators.[41]

Newspapers were not often seen, and the men were almost totally ignorant of what was going on in 'the outer world & of the progress of the war in other theatres'.[42]

Rumours were the lifeblood of the MEF: 'I don't know how many rumours are circulated here per minute but I should think that they reached three figures easily'. In May, for instance, Walter Carruthers wrote: 'We have just got the information that we are fighting against a large body of Germans.' Later that month 'a most delightful beach yarn' said that the division was to be relieved 'and to return to Egypt en route

for France. Awful pity it is not true. We should all like a rest and a sight of France. …
I suppose we must stick it out until the end of the war.' Later came 'Strong rumours
that we will be going back to our horses soon. All keen to do so … this rabbit life
[is] no good to anyone.'[43] In early June it was claimed that the Russians, who were
allegedly bombarding Constantinople, had given the Turks a few days to abandon the
Dardanelles, and that General Hamilton had gone to Constantinople. 'We all hope
it is true as most of us want to get out of this already.' On the anniversary of the
Battle of Waterloo (18 June), the story went about that '25,000 Highland Regulars
[were] reported landed between here Anzac Cove and Cape Helles'. All hope of an
early departure seemed to be dashed when the mounteds received proper infantry
equipment in July. 'This looks like the end of horses for us. Very disappointing to
all.'[44]

The men talked about all sorts of subjects, but, according to Fred Waite, there
were three favourite: oysters (which were best?), medals (what medals would be
awarded?) and the horizon (if a man could see the upper decks of a ship whose hull
was below the horizon, did that mean that he could see over the horizon?). 'Late in
the afternoon, when the little groups assembled behind the firing line to prepare the
evening meal, men would talk of their favourite foods, and speculate as to where the
first big meal would be eaten when the great work was complete.'[45]

Sunday church services were a regular feature of life at Anzac, but not everyone was
happy with their content. The men of the Otago regiment were mostly Presbyterians,
but the padre was an Anglican, and their commanding officer lost patience 'with his
constant effort to shove his "doctrine" down the throats of the Presbyterians'.[46]

Uniforms quickly went by the board on Gallipoli. All badges of rank were removed
to save the wearers from being picked off by Turkish snipers. 'Tunics were the first to
go, and bit by bit the soldier shed his garments until he stood only in his boots, his
shortened trousers, a shirt and a cap. Riding breeches, cut well above the knee, made a
most roomy pair of shorts.'[47] As the weather got hotter the 'majority of the men were
almost naked, a pair of shorts and boots and a hat completing their wearing apparel.
The exposed parts of their bodies became almost black, and this became known as the
"Anzac uniform".'[48]

The Turks opposite the Anzacs enjoyed several advantages over their enemies.
They rotated their battalions out of the front line to safe rest areas and replaced them
with fresh troops. They had access to unlimited supplies of clean fresh water and
good food. Not knowing this, the Anzacs sometimes pitied the Turks. 'The Turkish

prisoners and dead are not too well clad, some of them wear pieces of goat's skin sewn to cloth for boots. Their footgear is exceptionally bad, so if we can get them on the run we'll have them footsore and beat them in two to three days.'[49]

At night the Anzacs could sometimes hear the Turks opposite them talking and sometimes singing, 'to the accompaniment of a mouth-organ, and enlivened the trench life with various well-known tunes, including the "Marseillaise" and "Tipperary". A gramophone in the Turkish trenches could also be plainly heard.'[50]

Francis Twisleton thought little of Turkish tactics but respected the individual Turkish soldier. 'The Turk is a good fighting man on the whole,

'Johnny Turk'. Turkish soldiers and a religious adviser (second from right) in a trench at Gallipoli.

but jumpy at night. They will charge right up to the trenches, when they do no possible good to themselves. If they charge in a body they come under the machine guns and get wiped out. Machine guns are a deadly affair: they can be set at evening on to any position where men are likely to be working in the dark and put a blast on at any time.'[51] Most Anzacs hated the Turkish snipers. 'They are the best shots of the Turkish army and they are hidden in the bush and the trees … [One sniper] was painted green from head to foot. Green face, gun, boots and clothes. We put 6 shots in him all at once and he fell from the tree. Another day we got a female sniper, but she was shot before we knew she was a woman. There have been a lot of women snipers about. They are good shots.'[52]

Charles Bean noticed 'a clear and interesting difference between the N. Zealander and the Australian. The New Zealander regards the Turk much more kindly than our men. "Kind hearted beggars, the N. Zealanders", said one of our chaps the other day; "a Turk snipes them and then they catch the beggar and take him by the hand and lead him down to the beach".' Bean also wrote: 'undoubtedly the N.Z. fights more with his gloves on than the Australian: the Australian when he fights, fights all in … The N.Z. man is a good trustworthy soldier; but he has not the devil of the Australians in him.'[53] A New Zealander observed that 'the Australians [when fighting] always made more noise than the New Zealanders. Often Australian units, when desperately engaged with the enemy, shouted like a crowd of football barrackers. This was not usually the case with the New Zealanders. When at grips with the enemy they were comparatively quiet, and they fought with a grim determination, never underestimating their foe.'[54] General Hamilton thought they were 'fine men all of them, but very different (despite the superficial resemblance imparted by their slouch hats) when … seen shoulder to shoulder on parade. The Australians have the pull in height and width of chest; the New Zealanders are thicker all through, chests, waists, thighs.'[55]

The mounteds took great care of their weapons. Francis Twisleton wrote of 'the affectionate care each man has for his rifle; every rifle in the Regiment is kept in a spotless condition without any inspection or orders'. 'Machine guns were very reliable,' Ernest McRae recalled. The Maxim gun was 'heavy but dependable. … Had to be kept right … looked after it like a baby, oiling, cleaning, dismantling and putting back together. Determined guns wouldn't let them down.'[56]

Grenades, or bombs as they were known, were in very short supply at Anzac, and the MEF was too low in the War Office pecking order to receive them in any numbers. To meet the shortfall, a 'bomb factory' on the beach at Anzac manufactured 'jam tin' bombs. These home-made weapons were fashioned from anything that came to hand, including artillery fuse containers and empty tobacco tins. To make best use of this scarce and unreliable weapon, bomb throwers were trained in their use. The cricket players of the Otago regiment were found to be the best at this job. Trial and error determined that the most effective method was for the thrower to lie on his back. As soon as enough bombs were available, orders were issued that every Turkish bomb landing in the Anzac position was to be immediately answered with two thrown in the opposite direction. The men 'took part in the new game of "two for one" with great zest, and as the trenches at the Nek were only some twenty yards apart good practice was made'.[57]

New weapons were occasionally introduced. The Garland Bomb Thrower was 'a good mortar with an excellent little bomb'.[58] When four Japanese trench mortars arrived in late May these proved very effective, lobbing a 14-kilogram bomb a good distance. Their use led the Turks to roof over some of their front-line trenches with

Manufacturing home-made bombs from empty tins on the beach at Anzac.

heavy timber, as the Anzacs would discover in August. However, when the 2000 bombs, called black cats by the Turks, ran out, no more were delivered.

On 18 July flannel gas helmets and respirators were issued, following reports that the Turks might employ poison gas. According to Benjamin Colbran, 'we do not know how to use them'. Many men thought them unnecessary – 'the prevailing winds would soon disperse any gas, & the mountainous ground would only cause a problem for gas in the low-lying gullies etc' – and 'the general feeling was that gas helmets were just so much extra to carry'.[59] The precautions proved needless. Although poison gas was employed on other fronts in 1915, it was not used on Gallipoli.

In the early months the Turks had relied on 'manpower and rifles rather than on machine guns and artillery. In particular artillery ammunition had to be carefully husbanded because of limited quantities on hand.'[60] Fortunately for the MEF, the Turks remained short of howitzer and mortar ammunition until the last few weeks of the campaign. It was only the lack of Turkish artillery shells that allowed life to continue on the beach at Anzac. What artillery the Turks did have was mostly used to bombard the front-line trenches. Leslie Smith recorded that one Turkish gun which regularly shelled the Anzacs at dinner time was called 'Tucker time Liz'.[61]

When mortar bombs were fired at the Anzacs, they could see the projectiles curving through the air towards them, with the fuse burning and the bomb tipping end over end. Ken Stevens wrote: 'in the darkness they seemed a long time coming over, and I used to think every one was going to drop on me'.[62]

When he returned to Egypt from Gallipoli on 15 June, Lieutenant Colonel Mackesy became the commanding officer of the NZMR Brigade Details back in the desert. The details received reinforcements and remounts from New Zealand and convalescent men from the hospitals in and around Cairo, sent them on to Gallipoli when they were fit enough, and looked after the horses.

Mounteds recovering from wounds or sickness in Egypt visited the horses if they could, and their reports were always of interest to the others when they got back to Gallipoli, as Percy Doherty's diary entries show. In June he noted: 'Lieut. Barker back from Hospital (Egypt) yesterday. He says horses are not looking bad as reported. They are looking well but have changed colour.' In November Doherty himself was in Egypt: 'The Main Body horses are all kept in stables, or rather, sun shelter sheds, and on the whole are looking very well and are as fit as fiddles … The horses are pretty fit and buck the natives off, but they don't seem to get hurt; they scramble on again as if nothing had happened.'[63]

The horse lines were well maintained. Shelters were built from rushes to protect the horses from the worst effects of the desert sun. The horses became completely acclimatised to the Egyptian climate and the fodder, and this served them well in the years to come. Most of the Egyptian grooms were unused to properly fed and energetic horses, and occasionally resorted to physical abuse to control them. As a result a few horses were nervous and man-shy.

Exercising the horses could be an entertaining affair. 'Rode out in charge of the natives while exercising this morning,' Percy Doherty noted in his diary, 'and it was good sport watching the poor devils getting pitched off. Horses seemed to be loose and galloping everywhere, but they all eventually get back to their own stables'; 'Usual exercise in morning and afternoon and usual number of niggers getting bucked off and run over etc'; 'Reinforcements allotted their horses this morning … some of the horses pretty fresh and one or two men dismounted without orders'.[64] Clifton Bellis had another story to tell:

> Some of the [Egyptian] boys could ride well; others had only ridden donkeys before, and when they tried the same tactics with a horse, sitting well back and digging their heels into the flank, the boy and his mount soon parted. ... When we turned for home trouble really did start; at least forty horses bolted, with each boy holding on for dear life and yelling to Allah. There were several bomb-trenches and water-troughs to be negotiated near the camp, and one or more boys ended up in every one. One boy collided with the end of the mess hut; he never moved again. Another of our boys, a good rider, decided when his mount got a bit out of hand to make a wide detour at full gallop, and come in at the back of the stables – not realising that Transport had dumped a huge stack of fodder, in sacks, in his path. The horse shot around the end of the stack, the boy went over the top, calling on Allah, and got an awful fall. He got up very slowly and remarked, 'Horrass a bastit! [Horse a bastard!]'.[65]

In July 1915 a second riot took place in the brothel district of Cairo. Afterwards, General Maxwell had the following order read out to all troops in Egypt: 'A certain number of men are reported to have behaved like savages and have thus brought discredit on you all. ... Are you going to allow it? ... Have you no thought for the brave dead of your country? Is their reputation nothing and will you allow it to be blackened by a few blackguardly brothel frequenters?'[66] Other problems included assaults, breaking into houses, insulting women, begging in the streets and one case of murder. Tram car companies complained that men refused to pay fares, rode on the roofs and abused the conductors. Typical crimes and punishments in the NZMR Brigade Details included: throwing food in the mess hall (fine of two days' pay); drunk in town (10 days' confinement to barracks); absent without leave (seven days confinement to barracks and fine of one day's pay); late for stables (fine of one day's pay); galloping horses in the desert (fine of one day's pay); and insolence to an NCO (six days' confinement to barracks and a fine of three days' pay).

Meanwhile, for the thousands of Anzacs and others back on Gallipoli, the summer months passed slowly. While they watched and waited for something to happen, the men grew weak and dispirited as disease, poor food, ceaseless work and constant stress sapped their strength and their morale. With no prospect of victory, they began to despair of ever getting away from Gallipoli alive.

9

Interlude

If I can read the signs at all, methinks we won't see our horses for a space yet a while.

JAMES HARVEY

As the long, hot, dusty July days came to a close, the pulse of Anzac seemed to quicken.

CLUTHA MACKENZIE

AFTER THE FIERCE FIGHTING and heavy losses of the May battles, the next two months at Anzac were relatively quiet. General Hamilton was waiting for major reinforcements and planning the operations in which they would be used. He had adopted Birdwood's plan for a breakout to the north of Anzac and prohibited any large-scale fighting by the Anzacs which might focus Turkish attention there.

This did not, however, mean that standards were allowed to slip. The generals demanded constant vigilance and ongoing small-scale offensive action. According to Hamilton, 'A purely passive defence is not possible for us; it implies losing ground by degrees – and we have not a yard to lose. If we are to remain we must keep on attacking here and there to maintain ourselves!'[1] Various memos and directives constantly reinforced this message. 'It is of the first importance that the offensive spirit of our troops should be kept alive. Nightly patrols should go out and worry the enemy's sharpshooters, and locate his trenches and guns.... When an enemy sharpshooter has been detected, every effort should be made to kill him with the first shot.'[2] Officers and NCOs were ordered to make sure that firing trenches were well equipped with periscopes and bombs; that company officers lived in the trenches day and night; that snipers operated in pairs; that support troops practised daily getting into firing lines quickly; and that every man in the fire trench had his bayonet fixed. Men apparently also needed to be reminded that single unarmed Turks coming into the trenches were to be taken prisoner, and not shot. One directive closed by stating that the enemy 'must be made to feel that better men and finer soldiers than themselves are against them, and are going to drive them from position after position until they give up the struggle'.[3]

Both sides made the most of the quiet months to strengthen their defences. According to the official British history, 'the most important work carried out by the Anzac corps in June and July was the continuous mining and tunnelling by which the front trenches were protected from Turkish mines and the strength of the whole line very greatly increased'.[4] Underneath the trenches Turkish and Anzac miners drove long shafts into the earth, at the far end of which they placed explosive charges to blow up the enemy positions above them.

Turkish snipers remained a threat, moving forward and around the flanks of the Anzac trench lines in search of unsuspecting new targets. The 'fall of bullets from new & unexpected angles was the cause of many casualties on the beach and lower slopes of Walkers Ridge'. As Claude Pocock noted, 'to put your head up here is to gamble with life'.[5]

Anzacs in the front line came up with inventive ploys to keep the Turks opposite them awake and nervous. 'Sometimes at night,' wrote Robert Tuke, 'we used to make the Turks waste thousands of rounds of ammunition, this is how we did it. We would all send up a loud cheer and fire about seven or eight rounds a man, and Mr. Turk used to think we were charging their trenches, and would right along their line keep firing at nothing for sometimes an hour or more. We did have a smile at them.'[6]

The Turks sometimes tried to convince the Anzacs to give up. 'About this time an enemy aircraft dropped propaganda circulars into our trenches, the papers, which greatly amused our troops, stated that the Turks had no grievance against the Colonials, and England was using them only for their own ends, also that communication by sea would be cut off by German submarines, and that we would be compelled by hunger and thirst to surrender or be driven into the sea. They had plenty of provisions and would treat us well.'[7] Gordon Harper remembered another message: 'You are cut off, your ships have deserted you, your supply ships can't reach you, you will be eaten by flies. Come over and be well fed instead of being shot.'[8]

On 1 June the New Zealand Infantry Brigade took over No. 3 Section from the Australian light horse and occupied Quinn's Post and Courtney's Post. Lieutenant Colonel Malone, the commander of the Wellington Infantry Battalion, made his name as the 'landlord' of the posts. Under his energetic leadership, both were transformed from a collection of shallow trenches perched on the lip of Monash Gully into well-organised fortresses. The infantry wrested control of No Man's Land from the Turks, but several Anzac raids from Quinn's Post in early June resulted in heavy loss of life and a lowering of morale in the brigade.

The men of the mounted rifles brigade and the OMR spent the early summer on Russell's Top, Walker's Ridge and at the northern outposts. 'Normal life on the Peninsula embraced night post duty, night patrols, day observation, sniping, digging, wiring, ration and water carrying. ... Night post duty consisted of watching tactical points on the trench system, to stop a rush, give the alarm and observe and listen for enemy movement.'[9] The regular rotation of forces from the front line to 'rest' areas continued into the summer months. 'Periods of duty were 24 hours as garrison to Nos. 1 and 2 Outposts, 24 hours in the main line trenches and 24 hours in support, and so back to the Outposts again. The supporting troops did the work in the communications trenches, on the track up the hill and on the beach, those in the trenches deepened and extended their own positions.'[10]

Getting to the outposts was still a dangerous trip, as Benjamin Colbran recorded. 'We left camp at dusk ... loaded with our packs and equipment plus 200 rounds of ammunition which weighs over 100 lbs besides this I carried 25 lbs water ... With this load we had to run along a sandy beach with bullets whizzing amongst us. We arrived safely at the outpost and lay down and went to sleep.'[11]

Units out of the firing line were worked almost until they dropped. 'There was no rest from shell fire, and no rest from toil. When a regiment was sent to a beach gully for "rest" it meant that it was treated to a more liberal allowance of shrapnel, and more work than usual.' According to Clutha Mackenzie, 'The days were spent on road-work or on big communication saps, and at night, more often than not, there were sapping fatigues in the front firing line, squadron supports,

Frederick Overton, killed on 1 June.

Ernest Snow, killed on 6 June.

heavy pieces of artillery to haul to their emplacement, and the like'. As the official CMR history explained, 'Rest Camp on Anzac was "one of those things no man can understand." A unit goes into rest camp. Then the messages begin to come for work parties. Every officer and man is soon employed with pick and shovel. More messages still come for more men, and the Adjutant gets "strafed" for not being able to supply them. And so it goes on till everybody is glad to get back to the front line.'[12]

Battle casualties mounted slowly through June and July, as sniper, machine gun and artillery fire cut down the unwary and the unlucky on both sides. One night William Pyle had a very unpleasant experience. 'We were just changing guard when a shot came over the trench & killed the man standing beside me. The force of the shot deafened me & when I looked around, here was this poor chap lying against my legs, shot thro' the head & dying. He died before we got him out. His name was Snow.' On 1 June Frederick Overton was killed in front of Robert Tuke, who was 'just having a yarn with him when the gun went off. I rushed up to my dug-out, and poor old Bill sang out for everyone to take cover, but he was too late himself and the brass cap of the shell went right through his body. I think he was undoubtedly the most popular sergeant in the Wellington Regiment.'[13] Men out of the line were not safe. It was 'not unusual for a resting battalion to have as many casualties in 24 hours as a battalion in the front line'. William Pyle: 'Down at Anzac on fatigue. Turks shelled heavily & killed 8 and wounded 41. They come over without any warning. 50 men is a big number to lose without a hit back.'[14] With over 25,000 men crammed into an area of less than 2 1/2 square kilometres, there was little room to hide, and many men had close shaves with death, as Percy Doherty noted. 'J. M. Hampton got shot through both legs this morning while washing his clothes on the beach … The bullet passed right through one thigh and stuck in the other, but it does not seem to be serious.' He had a near miss himself: 'I was washing our dixies on the beach this afternoon and a sniper's bullet passed clean through the dixie that I had in my hand, but it didn't touch me'.[15]

Despite orders to avoid the area, a few essential patrols continued to take place to the north of Anzac. On 9 June Francis Twisleton and 12 men of the OMR undertook a scouting patrol in the foothills beyond the outposts. The scouts were returning along the sand hills along the beach when they were spotted by the enemy and 50 Turks raced to cut them off: 'leaving the cover of the sand mounds they took to the hard wet sand at the water's edge and set off at a run. In breathless excitement the troopers on the hill watched the race.'[16] The Turks were driven back just in time by fire from a motor torpedo boat offshore and from a mountain gun, and Twisleton and his scouts got back safely.

On 27 June Russell's Top came under unusually heavy artillery fire, with over 400 Turkish shells exploding on the plateau. The trenches were badly damaged and observers in No. 1 Outpost reported that the enemy trenches opposite Russell's Top were full of Turks with fixed bayonets. Surprisingly, no Turkish assault eventuated for another few days. Then, at 1.30 on the morning of 30 June, after 90 minutes of artillery and rifle fire, a new enemy regiment from Constantinople was launched across The Nek against the 3rd Australian Light Horse Brigade on Russell's Top. Some NZMR machine gunners and work parties were with them. 'In the moonlight, about an hour after midnight, the Turk, calling on his God, surged forward to the attack on No. 4 Section. In the half light the machine gunners found the range, and mercilessly cut up the attacking waves. But they were not to be denied. On and on they pressed, right up to the parapets.' The light horsemen sent away the New Zealand work parties. 'As one Australian laughingly put it, "this is our show, you New Zealanders just leave it to us".'[17]

It was another disaster for the Turks. Light horse and mounted rifles machine gunners cut them down in swathes. A few reached the trenches, where they were killed. Afterwards 200 dead Turks were counted in front of Russell's Top. Hamilton described the attack. A 'very serious assault – very serious for the enemy – was suddenly launched against the Anzac left, the brunt of it falling on Russell's New Zealand Mounted Rifles and Chauvel's Australian Light Horse; a bad choice too! Our victory complete; bloodless for us. Their defeat complete; very bloody. Nine fresh enemy battalions smashed to bits; fighting went on until dawn; five hundred Turks laid out and counted.'[18] Leslie Smith wrote that some Turkish prisoners 'were in rags & had boots practically in pieces. Several had stabs in calf of leg & explained that they had been driven to attack by their officers.' He also reported that 'after a second attack the Turks attended to our wounded men & then sent word to our lines for us to go & get them. Our experience so far is that [the] Turks play the game properly.'[19]

'What a sight No Man's Land presented that morning of June 30!' wrote Fred Waite. 'The majority of the … Turkish troops lay dead or wounded out there in the open; and of the dead men on the parapets, each had a rough haversack filled with dates and olives, the ever-present Turkish tobacco, and filled water-bottles.' The New Zealand mounteds buried more than 200 of these 'noisome dead' on the night of 2–3 July.[20] This was the last Turkish attempt to break the Anzac line. From then until August, they busied themselves covering the slopes of Baby 700, Battleship Hill and The Chessboard with lines of new trenches, and with tunnelling and mining operations.

At the end of June the Fourth Reinforcements landed, the first mounted rifles to arrive since the brigade had landed on 12 May. Russell received 420 men, bringing his strength up to 1212. In early July 477 Maori of the New Zealand Native Contingent also arrived from Malta. They were attached to Russell's brigade and sent out to garrison No. 1 Outpost, which was quickly renamed 'the Maori Pa'. Their first job was to broaden the Main Sap, a trench that linked the outposts to the main position, to a width of 1.5 metres to allow two-way traffic for the forthcoming offensive.

(Left to right) Lieutenant Beamish, Lieutenant Colonel Bauchop and Major Chambers at No. 2 Outpost. Bauchop and Chambers were both killed in the August offensive.

Work continued without pause on saps, tunnels, communication trenches and dugouts. Some trenches were covered over with timber to protect them from shrapnel and bombs, but there was very little wood available for this purpose. What little timber that did come ashore had to be guarded 'like the Bank of England' to stop Anzac pilfering. Wire netting was erected in front of some trenches to protect them from Turkish bombs. It was not possible to place conventional barbed wire barriers in No Man's Land. The trenches were so close together that men could not crawl out and hammer in pickets without being heard and shot. Instead, portable X-shaped frames were manufactured on the beach, wrapped in barbed wire, carried up into the trenches and heaved over the parapets at night. Long sticks were then used to push them out into no man's land. In some places, searchlights were mounted.[21]

Russell's Top was subject to continuous harassing fire from Turkish artillery around Anafarta and on the slopes of Chunuk Bair. New enemy gun positions and trenches were spotted on the Sari Bair range, Chocolate Hills and Salt Lake Ridge. Men could sometimes see British shells exploding on the Achi Baba hill to the south: each time they hoped they heralded the great attack from the Cape Helles front that would finally push the Turks off the peninsula.

On 12 July the Turks were fooled into believing that an attack was to be launched against them from Russell's Top. Dummy men were hoisted above the parapets, flares were fired and whistles were blown. A platoon from the Maori contingent, brought in for trench-fighting experience, joined in with a haka.[22] The overall effect must have been convincing, because the Turks opposite Russell's Top fired heavily across No Man's Land for 20 minutes, and were 'jumpy' for the rest of the night.

According to the Wellington regimental diary, on 29 July the Turks opposite Russell's Top set fire to the bodies of their dead after pouring a 'strange liquid' on the bodies. The glow from the macabre fires lit up no man's land from 2 to 3.30 a.m. A day later, news of the Allied capture of Baghdad was greeted with a compulsory cheer along the Anzac perimeter. The noise upset the Turks, who immediately opened up with heavy machine gun and rifle fire, and brought men forward into their communications trenches in anticipation of an attack.[23]

Life and death in the trenches continued. 'July was a quiet month in the front line with plenty of time to write the very short letters or keep a diary and it was a very common sight to see the firestep in the trench lined with naked men hunting "greybacks" [lice] in their shirts and pants,' wrote Ken Stevens. 'Went into No. 5 sap. Very quiet night except at intervals when machine gun fire raked our trenches. Got my bayonet blown off,' Claude Pocock recorded on the 7th. 'We are all the time looking for blood, the more the better,' William Lynch wrote home. I have been more excited over shooting Turks than wild pigs. So far I have got 37.' 'Great excitement about 12 last night,' William Pyle noted on the 16th. 'Stood to arms about midnight. It was just a lot of silly rot. A few Turks had opened fire & one of our heads [senior commanders] had lost his, & roused us all out. Some of our chaps were very unnecessarily excited.'[24] Sentries grew to love the destroyers cruising offshore. 'They would creep close in [at night] and throw their searchlights over the ground in front of the trenches. One cannot describe the relief of a sentry looking anxiously out to his front, on a pitch dark night, his imagination making every scrubby bush a moving enemy, suddenly finding everything flooded by an intense white light.'[25]

By the end of July the Anzacs were not in good shape, as Clutha Mackenzie recorded. 'The Regiment was getting tired of continually sapping without any excitement to break the monotony, other than the more or less frequent arrival of shells in their vicinity, and the attentions of snipers on the beach. Moreover, the flies increased in their countless millions, the ground was getting very dirty, the stench in parts was almost unendurable, and practically everyone was more or less affected by stomach trouble. The troops grew daily thinner. ... With dark olive skins, cadaverous faces and often a good growth of beard, they were a hard-looking lot.'[26]

Birdwood's relatively simple and small-scale July surprise night attack evolved into Hamilton's complex and massive northerly breakout employing almost all the MEF, as well as large reinforcements. Birdwood and Hamilton had intended to use the New Zealand mounted rifles and infantry brigades, plus the 29th Indian Brigade, for their July attack. This plan went out the window when Hamilton was offered more reinforcements than he immediately knew what to do with. There was neither space nor water for all of them within the Anzac position, so Hamilton decided to secretly land the 13th Division, the 29th Brigade of the 10th Division and the 29th Indian Brigade at Anzac, and the 10th and 11th divisions further north at Suvla Bay. The offensive would begin on 6 August, when the moon would not rise until 2 a.m.

In its final form the plan consisted of one main and several supporting elements. The main effort was to be a breakout to the north of Anzac and the capture of the hilltops of the Sari Bair range, including Chunuk Bair, by Birdwood's force. This, it was thought, would make the Turkish positions further down the ridge untenable. In order to deceive the Turks as to the direction of the real attack and to commit their reserves elsewhere, the Sari Bair attacks were to be preceded by Australian feints at Lone Pine and elsewhere on the right, and by British attacks at Cape Helles. As soon as Chunuk Bair was captured, the assault forces there were to attack south along the ridge towards the rear of Battleship Hill and Baby 700. Simultaneously, there would be a frontal attack across The Nek against Baby 700, launched from Russell's Top.

The final supporting element was the landing of the two new British divisions at Suvla Bay. They were part of IX Corps, which was placed under the command of General Sir Frederick Stopford. An old man recalled from retirement for this important command, Stopford lacked aggression and drive, and needed strong direction. Unfortunately, Hamilton was not the man to give it to him. Stopford's 10th and 11th divisions were supposed to be ashore at Suvla Bay by noon on 7 August. Hamilton wanted them to capture the Suvla plain as a base of operations, and also to assist Birdwood's forces on the Sari Bair hills by capturing Turkish gun positions. This required them to advance inland quickly to seize the Chocolate and W Hills and the more distant foothills around the edge of the plain. Unfortunately, the second part of Hamilton's intention was not conveyed clearly enough to General Stopford.

According to Charles Bean, a suggestion was made to land a regiment of light horsemen, on their horses, to the north of Suvla Bay: they would ride inland to attack the Turkish rear areas. This 'wild-cat' scheme was not adopted, probably because of the difficulty of landing the horses.[27]

Birdwood put Godley in charge of the northern breakout. In addition to the NZ&A Division already under his command, he was allocated the 3rd Australian Light Horse Brigade, two brigades of the 13th Division and the Gurkhas and Sikhs of the 29th Indian Infantry Brigade. In total, Godley had 20,000 men available. Birdwood retained the remaining brigade of the 13th Division and the 29th Brigade of the 10th Division as his reserve. Most of these men had to be secretly landed and hidden within the Anzac perimeter in the first few nights of August.

Apart from the 3rd Australian Light Horse Brigade, which was to remain inside the Anzac perimeter, everyone else under Godley's command was earmarked for the night advance onto the Sari Bair heights. It was a challenging command.

The capture of the Sari Bair crest was to be achieved in two stages. The first phase was the clearance of the weak Turkish defences from the foothills on the seaward side of the range. These defensive positions dominated the valleys of the Sazli Beit, Chailak and Aghyl deres, up which the attacking forces had to move in order to approach the hilltops. The job was given to the NZMR Brigade and one brigade of the 13th

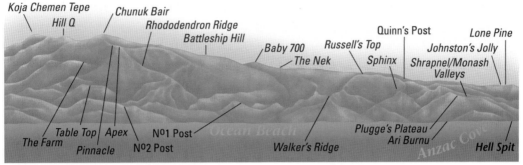

The Sari Bair range viewed from the west.

Division, known as the Right and Left Covering Forces respectively. The mounteds were ordered to capture the entrances to the Sazli Beit Dere and the Chailak Dere. This required them to seize the Turkish positions on Old No. 3 Outpost, Destroyer Hill, Table Top, Bauchop's Hill and Walden's Point. Birdwood thought that two regiments of the NZMR Brigade would be enough for this task, but Godley convinced him that the entire brigade of four regiments and the Maori contingent were needed.

The 13th Division brigade forming the Left Covering Force was to secure the Damakjelik Bair, to the north of the Aghyl Dere, to protect the northern flank of the advance up onto Hill 971.

The foothills had to be cleared by 11 p.m. to give the main assault columns enough time to reach the crests before dawn, so surprise and speed were essential. Once they had captured their objectives, the covering forces were to garrison them to provide cover and a fallback position for the 10,000-strong assault force heading for the top of the Sari Bair range.

The assault on the Sari Bair summits was the second part of the Sari Bair plan. The New Zealand Infantry Brigade, under the command of Brigadier General Francis Johnston, was ordered to ascend Rhododendron Ridge and seize Chunuk Bair by dawn on 7 August. Its routes onto the ridge were along the Sazli Beit Dere and the Chailak Dere. The infantry were to leave their assembly areas at 11 p.m., and were expected to be on Rhododendron Ridge, within reach of Chunuk Bair, by 2.30 a.m. The summit was to be attacked immediately, whether or not the whole force was assembled.

The objectives of the other main assault force were Hill 971 (Koja Chemen Tepe) and Hill Q, both to be reached via the Aghyl Dere. This task was given to Brigadier General H. V. Cox, who commanded the 4th Australian Infantry Brigade and his own

Supplies pile up on the beach at Anzac Cove.

29th Indian Brigade. The Aghyl Dere, unlike the more straightforward valleys to its south, was composed of many winding and narrow branches, issuing from as many as 30 steep, brush-choked ravines and gullies. It had barely been scouted at all; even Overton had explored only part of its lower reaches. It is aptly described by Robert James as 'mad country'.[28] Cox's task was the most demanding of all. In just three and a half hours 'the column for 971 was to penetrate three miles [nearly 5 kilometres] of unreconnoitred hill-country [at night], by a route about twice as long as that to be covered by the Chunuk Bair column and infinitely more difficult to follow. The strongest factor for its success was that Major Overton himself was allotted to it as guide. Birdwood hoped that this summit would be reached at the same hour as Chunuk Bair, at any rate that it would be attacked about dawn.'[29]

As soon as all of the Sari Bair summits were captured the assault troops were to dig in and link up with each other. Reinforcements would then be pushed forward to fight off enemy counter-attacks, and to conduct the final phase of the operation.

Part of the force on Chunuk Bair (a brigade of about 2500 men) was to move south along the ridge, taking the strong Turkish positions on Battleship Hill and Baby 700, in co-ordination with an attack across The Nek from Russell's Top by the 3rd Australian Light Horse Brigade.

These light horsemen faced a daunting task. 'Baby 700 was the strongest position at Anzac. Across its summit the enemy's trenches lay one above the other, affording tier after tier of fire. The only direct approach to it lay along the narrow Nek, not thirty yards wide, which led to Russell's Top.' Altogether, the enemy defences consisted of 'nine lines of trenches in front and several to the flank, comprising in all at least forty separate trenches and saps'.[30] The Nek attack was to be launched at 4.30 a.m., one hour after Chunuk Bair was meant to be in New Zealand hands. Other Australians were to make supporting attacks against Turkish Quinn's and The Chessboard.

In summary 'the offensive would begin in the southern zone [Cape Helles] at 3.50 p.m. Lone Pine would next be attacked at 5.50. Farther north still the main blow would be launched at 10. At the extreme north the Suvla force would then begin landing. If all went well, daybreak would find Sari Bair and Tekke Tepe in Hamilton's hands, with Suvla behind as a base and the old Turkish position in front of Anzac outflanked and crumbling before a further advance. A final thrust would block the enemy's communications on land, and guns and searchlights would prevent his sea-transport across the straits.'[31] That was the plan. The timings were very tight, and a long sequence of phases had to be accomplished if the whole concept were to succeed.

The plan was compromised from the start because of a lack of detailed knowledge of the ground. Even the scouts of the mounted rifles regiments could not cover the area with sufficient thoroughness 'owing to the activity and alertness of the enemy'.[32] Mounted rifles scouts who knew the territory were sent across to Lemnos Island to train the new battalions assembling there in the finer points of night marching. The commanders of the assault columns were only permitted to study the ground from the decks of destroyers cruising off the shore, too far away to be useful.

It was impossible for news of the approaching reinforcements to be kept secret, and the Turks knew that Hamilton had to do something soon. General Liman von Sanders considered Cape Helles and Anzac secure, and he ruled out the rough ground to the immediate north of Anzac as a viable enemy attack route. He thought the enemy would land at Gaba Tepe, south of Anzac, on the Asiatic coast or at Bulair. This led him to disperse his 16 divisions to cover all these areas, as well as Anzac and Cape Helles.

Light forces were also moved to Suvla Bay. Colonel Mustafa Kemal believed that the Sari Bair range was the most likely target for the expected attack, but his concerns were ignored. Despite these less-than-ideal dispositions the Turks were well placed to fight off the coming offensive. Altogether, Liman von Sanders had about 110,000 troops in the Gallipoli area: 40,000 at Cape Helles, 30,000 at or near Anzac, 20,000 up at Bulair and another 20,000 on the far side of the Dardanelles.[33]

Secrecy was strictly enforced during the build-up to the new offensive. The men were told nothing, but the evidence before their eyes indicated that something was brewing. For Clutha Mackenzie, 'As the long, hot, dusty July days came to a close, the pulse of Anzac seemed to quicken'. James Harvey wrote on 26 July: 'If I can read the signs at all, methinks we won't see our horses for a space yet a while'.[34] 'Reserves of water and rations were being stored up. New bivouac areas were being dug in every hillside and terrace, with nobody to occupy them, and officers commanding regiments were being taken out on destroyers to view the country beyond our left flank.' Another observer recorded: 'One notices a general preparation on all sides, the supply depot below us is increasing in size. … All communications trenches are being widened; a road along the shore to No. 2 outpost is being made. Last night a complete howitzer brigade came ashore, 18 guns. Men are practising hill climbing, Anzac beach and foreshore are piled up house high with all sorts of stores and ammunition. All this work is done at night time.'[35]

Anzac already held over 20,000 troops, and this number would double before the offensive began on 6 August. Thousands of reinforcements and many artillery batteries came ashore over three nights, all hidden away by dawn. Many of these new arrivals had no idea of where they were or what they were expected to do. Few of them had conducted a night advance even in training, let alone in the mad country of Gallipoli and against a live enemy. Claude Pocock observed: 'Troops landing every night. It is now fully anticipated that a general advance is to be made within a week. Rum is to be issued till further notice many comments as to the cause of this act.' The men filled their spare time 'by practising cliff climbing. … Digging had ceased. Strange troops occupied all the odd gullies within the lines. Batteries of guns appeared in every corner.' Francis Twisleton cynically noted that 'The men are being better fed than usual'.[36] One day in late July Lieutenant Colonel Meldrum mentioned to General Godley that the men were hoping for some action soon. 'He remarked with a smile "Well I can promise you that they will have their battle soon." This went round the lines as did numerous rumours from other sources of big events to come, and bucked the men up wonderfully.' As the likelihood of battle increased 'the Anzac sick parades diminished; men already evacuated tried to "desert" back from ship, hospital or base'. Most were 'far from fit and at least 30 per cent, who had been suffering for weeks from the prevalent dysentery, were more ready for hospital than an offensive operation'.[37]

They certainly had their work cut out for them, as the following passage from the British official history makes clear. 'No account of the operations … can hope to convey any adequate idea of the extreme difficulties of the undertaking if the reader does not first try to visualize the bewildering nature of the country through which the troops were to move. The spurs and gullies were so contorted, so rugged and steep, and so thickly covered with dense prickly scrub', that they were difficult even for 'an unencumbered tourist provided with a good map and setting out in the full light of day'. In August 1915 'the only available maps were very inadequate, and these arduous routes had to be traversed at night by heavily laden men, who were harassed by an invisible enemy and led by guides who themselves had little real knowledge of the ground'.[38]

Just before the attack began, General Birdwood encouraged the men to push on whatever happened around them.

Two or three days hard fighting may, we hope, clear the Turks from these hills around us, and I know that everyone will do his best to make success a certainty. … [The NZ and Australian Division] will have a hard and difficult time of it, and I know that nothing will stop them … Remember, men, the order of the day must be "shove on and keep shoving on" until we are in complete possession of the heights above us … Though they [the Turks] are terrified of the Australian and New Zealand soldiers in the open, yet there is no doubt that they will always fight well when behind trenches. … Let us hope they will again do as our men said they did when they landed on the 25th April – run faster than they had ever seen men run before.[39]

10

The Covering Force battle

We are to attack tonight. We move off some time after dark and are to take
a big ridge ahead of us. Hope we get thro' alright.

WILLIAM PYLE

… during the whole of the Gallipoli campaign few troops showed a flair to match
that of the New Zealand Mounteds on the night of August 6.

LES CARLYON

AT NOON ON THURSDAY 5 August Brigadier General Russell handed over No. 4 Section to the 3rd Australian Light Horse Brigade and brought his three regiments down from Russell's Top and Walker's Ridge in preparation for their role in the long-anticipated offensive. Ken Stevens was 'glad to leave Walkers Ridge and the filthy conditions. The little cemetery at the back of the trenches was full.'[1]

On paper Russell had at his disposal about 1900 fighting men, including the Maori contingent and the OMR,[2] but many of these soldiers were 'sick with almost universal and continuous dysentery and other troubles. Their spirits had risen to the attack, but many looked like scarecrows'.[3] Few of them would have admitted to being sick, though. 'As usual when there was "something doing" sick parades fell off; men simply would not go near the M.O. [Medical Officer] for fear of being kept back.' Harry Browne was typical. 'Speaking for myself, I was thin, but in good hard fighting trim.'[4]

The Auckland, Wellington and Canterbury regiments joined the Otagos, the Maoris and the engineer troop at the outposts. Maori platoons were attached to each of the regiments, and the second Maori company was held in reserve. Twenty-five sick or lightly wounded men took over the defences of the outposts, allowing everyone else to rest until dusk on 6 August. They made the most of it, relishing the change from the noise and the stink of the fighting trenches. They wrote letters, brought their diaries up to date and cleaned their weapons for the umpteenth time. Arthur Curry wrote: 'Everyone is busy today sharpening bayonets, sewing white labels in their tunics, inspecting respirators and field dressings and having a last good feed before the great slaughter'. Officers studied the enemy positions through periscopes.[5]

'Officers as well as men carried rifle and fixed bayonet. They had no steel helmets … They wore shirt and trousers only; tunics were an encumbrance.'[6] Each man carried one day's rations and water and at least 200 rounds of rifle ammunition (none of which was supposed to be fired before dawn the next day). Picks and shovels, sandbags and jam-tin bombs were also taken. Ken Stevens 'carried 300 rounds of ammunition in a bandolier and an extra belt, a haversack with two days rations, one filled with jam tin bombs, a brass rifle grenade, field glasses, water bottle and rifle. As ordered, our tunics were rolled and our paybooks were sewn in our shirts. The official history says we travelled light.'[7]

The first shots of the August offensive were fired at Cape Helles. The men waiting up the coast at Anzac were too far away to hear this, but at 4.30 p.m. they did hear the sound of an artillery bombardment much closer to hand. It was followed an hour later by the sound of heavy rifle and machine fire, signalling the 1st Australian Infantry Brigade's attack on Lone Pine.[8] Its purpose was to draw as many Turkish reserves as possible towards the southern part of the Anzac front line, away from the Sari Bair hilltops. Unfortunately, it achieved this aim a little too well. The Turks were so alarmed at the attack that the local commander was reinforced from two directions. All his reserves, including men who should have been guarding Chunuk Bair, came to help, but so did two regiments from another Turkish division south of Gaba Tepe. These latter units arrived at Lone Pine at midnight to find that they were not needed there. Unfortunately for the Anzacs, that meant that they were much closer to Chunuk Bair than they would otherwise have been.

At dusk the Maori platoons held a religious service at No. 1 Outpost. According to Harry Browne, 'they gathered around their native chaplain in fighting array, and a brief service was held in their own tongue. … After a few words the hymn "Jesu Lover of My Soul" was sung in Maori to a tune of their own. The parts blended beautifully. The Contingent had 25 tenors in its chorus. The chaplain in a splendid voice sang the solo, the rest supplying the obligato. … The hymn ceased. There was a silence that could be felt and then Maori and Pakeha heads were bowed while the native prayer and benediction were pronounced.'[9]

As they waited for the word to move out, many of the mounteds must have

William Pyle, killed on 6 August.

thought of home and their chances of seeing it again. They knew some of them would not survive the next few days. 'Action at last,' wrote William Pyle. 'We are to attack tonight. We move off some time after dark and are to take a big ridge ahead of us. Hope we get thro' alright.' Pyle was killed within hours of writing these words.[10] In Clutha Mackenzie's words, 'The Regiment, water-bottles filled and in final trim, stood leaning on their rifles. Occasionally some one gave a hitch to his gear, others talked in subdued tones, or gazed solemnly out to sea.' Percy Doherty noted that 'no rifles must be loaded and the magazines empty. All work must be done with the bayonet. We didn't relish the idea of going out with empty rifles … but orders had to be obeyed, so there was nothing for it.' As Fred Waite recorded, 'Officers spoke to their men. The principal injunction was to press on up the hill. If any man lost touch, he was to join the nearest party and go resolutely on.'[11] The mounteds had just two and a half hours to secure their objectives.

As soon as darkness fell at 8.30 p.m., 381 men of the Auckland Mounted Rifles Regiment stood up, checked one other's kit for the last time and silently moved out. Their route was up the Sazli Beit Dere south of No. 2 Outpost. Their task was to capture Old No. 3 Outpost, which had been turned into an 'immensely strong' position by the Turks after they took it back from the mounteds at the end of May.[12] It was protected on its western and southwestern sides by rows of barbed wire, and 28 mines had been laid in gaps in the entanglements. Two lines of trenches and several strongpoints protected its southern face, and hundreds of Turkish reserve troops were encamped on the far side of the position.

Despite these formidable defences, the outpost was captured easily, largely because of a clever ruse. For weeks past, a destroyer just off the beach had turned its searchlight onto Old No. 3 Outpost and shelled it from 9 until 9.10 p.m., and again from 9.20 to 9.30 p.m., every night. The guns then switched their fire onto Table Top. The aim was to get the Turks into the habit of evacuating their front-line trenches until the illuminated bombardment ended. The Aucklanders' assault on the night of 6 August was timed to take place at 9.30 p.m. when the enemy trenches should be empty.

As the Aucklanders waited for the destroyer to open fire, 'the silence in that dark

The Sazli Beit Dere. Destroyer Hill (right) was captured by the Manawatu squadron of the WMR on the evening of 6 August.

ravine was uncanny, and time was measured by heart beats'.[13] At nine on the dot the guns on HMS *Colne* opened fire. The noise of the exploding shells masked the approach of the Aucklanders as they crept up the hill in the shadow of the searchlight. The men reached their assault positions, below the less-protected southern side of the post, without loss. According to Ken Stevens, 'The shells seemed to have a very nasty crack and crash, above our heads, into the trenches and I could not help feeling that one would fall short on us'.[14] A small advance party of bayonet fighters crept further up the hill and overpowered a sentry post, bayoneting its four occupants. The main assault group then came up the hillside and lay down 20 metres short of the enemy sandbags. By now the destroyer's guns had begun firing on the rear of the enemy position, but its searchlight stayed fixed on the post.

As soon as the destroyer switched her gun and searchlight onto Table Top at 9.30 p.m., the Aucklanders leapt to their feet, fanned out and charged into the outpost. 'Eight Turks, in a detached post, were bayoneted almost before they were aware of the presence of danger, and the troopers, without the slightest hesitation, dropped down through openings in the overhead cover into the absolute blackness of the trench. ... the trench was far from being empty, and some desperate hand-to-hand fighting took place in the dark.'[15] As Fred Waite explained, 'The trenches were roofed

Auckland mounteds resting in Old No. 3 Outpost after recapturing it on the evening of 6 August. Note the timber roof to the trench.

… with heavy baulks of 8 x 3 [inch] sawn timber covered with sand bags. The guns on the destroyer had made no material impression on this cover, as shells striking it had glanced off and buried themselves uphill. In the front trenches was discovered a dugout with a complete equipment for electrically firing the 28 small square iron mines placed in front of the posts.'[16] The Turk who sat in the dugout ready to explode the mines was killed before he could lift a finger. Some Turks 'were concealed feet foremost in holes in the trench walls, from which they fired until the steel did its work'. In the dark confines of the trenches it was a grim, brutal hand-to-hand fight. The Turks stood no chance, although not every Auckland bayonet found a live target. 'One Aucklander, in dashing down the trench, bayoneted in fine style a roll of blankets and two or three sacks.'[17]

As the Aucklanders consolidated their gains, some of them faced a bayonet charge by a small group of Maori attached to the Wellington regiment. When an Auckland officer shouted at them in their own language 'the Maoris grinned, and went to search for Turks somewhere else'. According to Peter Buck, 'The Auckland Mounted Rifles took Old No. 3 but dug-in without cleaning it out. Captain Dansey, with 70 Maoris, asked Major Chapman … to give him another 50 men and he would clean up the position. This was refused, and Dansey did it with his 70 men, losing only seven killed and several wounded … We got our blood up that night … We went right up and into it with the steel. Hand-to-hand fighting was the thing. It was like the days of our forefathers.' The Maoris 'went grimly for those Turks, bayoneted them in their lines, they burst into a tremendous haka when they had cleared the trenches – "Ka mate, ka mate, ka ora, ka ora!" – then silence as they pressed on to the next point'.[18] This

Old No. 3 Outpost from Table Top, photographed in 1918. Left and right are the Sazli Beit and Chailak deres. Just visible are the terraces of the Turkish campsite overrun by the North Auckland squadron of the AMR on the evening of 6 August.

war cry echoed across the dark hills often that night, and its effect on the frightened Turks can be imagined.

While the Waikato squadron and the Maoris cleared the trenches the North Auckland squadron ran past them and straight into about 400 Turks moving back towards the outpost from their campsite on the Chailak Dere side of the hill. Although they heavily outnumbered the New Zealanders, the Turks turned and ran for their lives. New Zealand bayonets and bombs killed any Turks that were too slow. Sergeant Major James Milne reportedly killed or wounded five fleeing Turks with one bomb.[19] The Aucklanders took very few prisoners that night.

So far all had gone to plan. Old No. 3 Outpost had been captured quickly and at

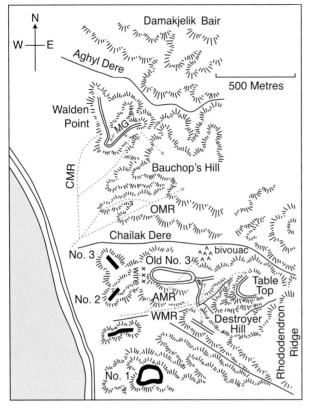

The Right Covering Force battle on 6 August.

little cost in New Zealand lives. 'About 100 of the enemy were killed, while the Aucklanders lost only Lieutenant H. F. E. Mackesy and 6 men killed and 15 wounded. Within a quarter of an hour they had worked through all the trenches, and by 10 p.m. not a Turk, except a few prisoners, remained alive within the position. The Auckland Regiment spent the rest of the night transforming Old No. 3 into a New Zealand post, facing upwards towards Chunuk Bair.'[20]

Three hundred and forty-six Wellington mounted riflemen followed the Aucklanders into battle at 8.45 p.m. As the men filed out of the Main Sap they were met by the regimental padre, who 'with a "God bless you, my boy" ... shook each by the hand as they passed out into battle'.[21] While the Aucklanders were closing in on Old No. 3 Outpost, the Wellingtons moved past them along the Sazli Beit Dere.

Major Charles Dick and his Manawatu squadron led the WMR along the dere. Their task was to capture Destroyer Hill and a communications trench linking it to Old No. 3 Outpost. With them was Harry Browne. 'Sharply at 9 p.m. in single file we started up and into the darkness of the narrow water course. Further up our walk broke into a double, and then the enemy opened fire. A machine gun was sweeping the water course and passing a certain spot the bullets were striking fire on the stones. Here the first casualty lay moaning. After that several were hit.'[22] The mounteds were forbidden to fire, so they simply charged straight at the trench, losing four men killed and seven wounded along the way. Those Turks caught in the trench were killed. Two Manawatu troops then climbed the northern slopes of Destroyer Hill, bayoneting 20 Turks and capturing eight more as the summit was cleared and picqueted.

'Mad country'. Table Top from the Sazli Beit Dere. The WMR made its way up this dere in complete darkness.

Tragedy and farce went hand in hand that night. 'For a time we manned a little ridge in the gully, expecting a counter attack,' wrote Harry Browne. 'Near me lay Joe Chamberlain, in agony and calling for morphia pills, but we didn't have any. In the darkness … he had run into a cluster of four [Turks], bayoneted two, but the others shot him in the stomach. He did not die until the next morning. … Major Dick was wounded in the hand and went back to have it dressed. Returning later with Quarter[master] Lodge they heard some Turks jabbering in the darkness.

Giving orders to imaginary men, they called out to the Turks to surrender, which they did, an officer and five men. We laughed when we heard how the wounded Major and the Quartermaster had surrounded the enemy.'[23]

The last objective of the WMR that night was Table Top. This flat hilltop was shelled for 20 minutes by the destroyer and by artillery firing from the old Anzac position. Clutha Mackenzie watched the bombardment. 'The overhanging crag, her summit rent by an inferno of shell fire, her inaccessible escarpment lit by the lurid glow of scrub fires, and the fantastic smoke clouds eerily revealed by the searchlight, made altogether a wild night battle scene of weird glory.'[24] At 10 p.m. the bombardment ended and the ship's searchlight was switched off. This was the signal for Table Top to be rushed and captured. A steep and crumbling clay cliff face in the centre was flanked to the northwest by a narrow ridge joining it to Old No. 3 Outpost, and to the southwest by a less steep but densely vegetated slope. Whichever way an assault force went, it was bound to be a slow job.

Table Top from Old No. 3 Outpost. The dotted line indicates the intended line of ascent. The unbroken line indicates the actual route taken by the WMR on 6 August. Chunuk Bair is on the skyline directly above Table Top.

Two WMR squadrons reached the foot of Table Top after bypassing an unguarded barbed wire barrier across the dere. It was a moonless night, but Table Top stood out clearly, its steep clay sides faintly illuminated in the starlight. The first attempt to scale its gentler southwestern face was frustrated by the thick scrub there. Lieutenant Colonel Meldrum then led his squadrons up a side branch of the dere towards the western face of Table Top. He intended to climb 50 metres up the bare clay face to the northern ridge, and gain the summit from there. As they moved along the gully, a stray Turkish flare set fire to a bush on the ridge above them. The men were sitting ducks. 'Word was sent back along the line to lie down. For fully five minutes the scrub blazed, lighting up both the ridge and Table Top. We expected any moment to be seen but the low bushes along the side of the ridge must have thrown a shadow across the Dere which kept us out of sight.'[25]

Once the fire went out the troopers zigzagged their way up the steep clay slopes,

'It seemed like war made easy'. WMR men resting in trenches on Table Top after its capture on 6 August.

cutting steps with entrenching tools and bayonets. All the way up they prayed that they would not be seen or heard. Major Jim Elmslie led the way. 'He went in front and cut the steps up with his own hands. Only his training on one of the wildest bush farms in New Zealand made this feat possible – in the dark – in silence.' As Meldrum wrote: 'The hillside here was of dry clean earth, free from stones and no sound was made by the falling earth as the steps were cut. On getting over the top of the ridge a halt was made till some 20 men had assembled. With bayonets fixed these went on up the hill to the trench at the rear of Table Top.'[26] The scrub-covered summit was almost unoccupied. Most of its defenders had gone down the Chailak Dere to see what was happening at Old No. 3 Outpost and elsewhere. A few unwary Turks were found in a trench along the southwestern edge of the plateau and killed, and the hilltop was secured just before midnight.[27]

The Wellingtons spent the rest of the night digging in on Table Top. They cleared the scrub to gain good fields of fire and scraped ledges on the seaward side to shield them from the Turkish shrapnel fire already being directed at them from the heights of the Sari Bair range. According to Clutha Mackenzie, 'so steep was the cliff that he only managed to make a ledge sufficiently wide to sit on, while his legs dangled over the abyss, and the sun blazed on him [the next day] in undiluted fury. … In a hollow at [his] feet half a dozen dead Turks turned black in the sun.'[28]

A well-used track was found on the northern side of the hill running down the ridge towards Old No. 3 Outpost. Over the next few hours many of the Turks who had gone down this path to see what was going on returned, blissfully unaware that Table Top was in enemy hands. By dawn, 150 of them had been rounded up. 'The prisoners … beamed with happiness, offered cigarettes, biscuits, money and mementoes to their guards, and embarrassed them by crowding around in an effort to shake their hands.' The prisoners 'were a sturdy crowd, though there were some old ones among them. … Most of the enemy were big men but this one wasn't and the poor little beggar was scared out of his life.'[29]

General Hamilton lauded the capture of Table Top. 'The angle of Table Top's ascent is recognised in our regulations as "impracticable for infantry". But neither Turks nor angles of ascent were destined to stop Russell or his New Zealanders that night…. No General on peace manoeuvres would ask troops to attempt so break-neck an enterprise. The flanks of Table Top are so steep that the height gives the impression of a mushroom shape of the summit bulging out over its stem.'[30] It was a very tidy piece of work, but luck and surprise also played a major part in its success.

The work of the Aucklands and Wellingtons was over for now. Their casualties had been slight. The AMR lost seven or eight dead and 15 wounded. The WMR suffered between four and six killed and nine wounded, almost all in that first rush at the communications trench in the Sazli Beit Dere. The Maori platoons lost as many as 13 killed. The Wellingtons captured at least 158 prisoners. According to Lieutenant Colonel Meldrum, 'it seemed like war made easy'.[31]

The two South Island regiments had a much harder fight that night. 'Otago was to advance northward until opposite the nearest spurs of Bauchop's (the next ridge north of No. 2), and then turn inland to attack it. Canterbury was to continue along the shore until opposite Walden Point, a half-detached triangular hill forming the north-western extremity of Bauchop's, and then, similarly turning, seize the point, advance inland, and rejoin Otago further east.'[32] As soon as the destroyer searchlight illuminating Old No. 3 Outpost was turned off at 9.30 p.m., the Canterbury and Otago regiments advanced from No. 2 Outpost onto the flat and open ground to the north.

The Chailak Dere from Old No. 3 Outpost. Just visible (centre) is the barbed wire barricade cleared by the OMR. Bauchop's Hill is in the background.

By that time the sounds of battle around Old No. 3 Outpost must have alerted every Turk within earshot.

Some of the Otagos turned inland into the Chailak Dere, the valley immediately north of the outposts. There they 'found themselves held up by a barbed-wire erection of unexampled height, depth and solidity, which completely closed the river bed … The entanglement was flanked by a strongly-held enemy trench running right across the entrance to the Chailak Dere. Here that splendid body of men, the Otago Mounted Rifles, lost some of their bravest and best.'[33] Murray Richards wrote: 'We moved into the creek but the Turks must have had wind of our intended attack; just as we got into the creek they opened fire … we did not fire a shot as we went out without any cartridge in our rifles. We were told to take the place with the bayonet and by jove we did in great style … two Turks came around a bush and I got them both.'[34] Francis Twisleton took charge of clearing the wire. Engineers cut the barbed wire into sections and attached grappling hooks to the sections, which Maori teams hauled away from the cover of the dry creek bed. When the engineer officer was wounded, Twisleton went out himself to attach the grappling hooks to the wire six times. Although under rifle and machine gun fire from a trench 70 metres away, he was not hit.[35]

Meanwhile the rest of the OMR captured trenches and eliminated an enemy machine gun post on nearby Wilson's Knob. Most of the Turks fled ahead of them, but 40 were killed by Otago bayonets. The regiment then advanced up the southern slopes of Bauchop's Hill. It had already lost many men to enemy fire.

The last regiment to cross the start line was the CMR. They knew that they faced a difficult task. 'Of course every man realised that we were booked for one hell of a fight,' wrote Noel Trolove, who gave a detailed account of the night's events. 'The little problem allotted to our Squadron looked tough enough to suit anybody, I assure you'. Before they left their assembly area 'my section buried a few extra eatables we had, such luxuries as a half bottle of Lea & Perrin's, a tin of condensed milk and some personal belongings, beside a scrub bush, with the understanding that if any of us came through they should dig them up and post the letters etc addressed to relatives. Incidentally I was the only one left to perform this duty for the other three, which I did a fortnight later. The other three were all killed.'[36]

The Canterburys moved through the sand hills beside the beach and up a dry stream bed. They were led by a few scouts. Four of these met an enemy patrol of four men, with whom they fought a silent bayonet duel. It ended with all four Turks dead and two Canterbury scouts wounded, one in the chest, the other in the jaw.[37]

The CMR's first objective was Walden's Point, a low knoll at the northwestern end of Bauchop's Hill that barred the way into the Aghyl Dere. The Canterburys had about 500 metres of open ground to cover. They crossed the first 300 metres without loss while the Turks on Walden's Point were blinded by the searchlight of another destroyer. They then stopped and waited for the searchlight to be switched off, at which time they were to rush Walden's Point. Noel Trolove wrote: 'While waiting here word was passed for the No. 3 of each Section, who carried the Section wire cutters, to report in front. As my No. 3, Trooper R. Lusk, passed me he grabbed my hand and whispered "Goodbye old man, I won't see [you] again". I said, "Rot, Bob". "No! Something tells me I'm for it", he said and was gone in the dark. Sure enough, he was right, for next morning he was found dead before the muzzle of one of the machine guns on Walden's with his wire cutters still in his hand. ... Trooper F. Jarman also handed me a letter at this time, saying he thought that I would come through, but he wouldn't. He was right too, for he was mortally wounded five minutes later.'[38]

Apparently the searchlight accidentally illuminated the waiting Canterburys, alerting the Turks to their danger. 'Hell broke loose everywhere, and the enemy trenches defined themselves with flashes of fire. Two machine guns on Walden's were spouting streaks of flame and Sergeant Cotton and Trooper Jarman, left and right, went down in the first burst. We blundered and stumbled on in the semi dark which was now lit up with flashes and flares and star shells.' Gordon Harper wrote: 'A deafening crackle of rifle and machine guns met us out in the open, but the line never wavered'.[39] Lieutenant Colonel Findlay, the commander of the Canterbury regiment, was shot through the thigh.[40]

The regiment split: the 10th squadron charged straight at Walden's Point while the 1st squadron raced to the right into Taylor's Gap and then back onto Walden's Point from behind. With no covering fire to keep the enemy's heads down, the men ran straight at the machine guns as fast as they could. As Daniel Laurenson wrote, 'It was then a case of go for it'.[41] When the 10th squadron men reached the base of the hill they gained some cover.

Noel Trolove takes up the story again.

> Luckily the guns on the top could not depress far enough to harm us as we came close under the hill … we made our way up the slope and gathered under the parapet of the trench which ran along the lip, and lay there for what seemed quite a long time, to get breath back, while the Turk garrison who could not see us poked their rifles over the parapet and fired at random. Some of our fellows caught the rifles as they came over and had a tug-of-war. We lay there probably only a minute or two, with the whole countryside away back to Anzac in an uproar. Then a whistle blew and we were over the parapet with a rush and in among the garrison. Those Turks died hard, and we lost a lot of splendid fellows around those two guns … Most of the garrison were bayoneted as no prisoners were to be taken that night. Troopers chased Turks over the flat top of the hill, some of the Turks squealing, and one in particular as he dodged and twisted and turned with several men after him. It wasn't a pleasant sound.[42]

Gordon Harper and his fellow troopers found it impossible to hear any commands, and at this point many were hit. 'The machine gun was just above us and its fire deafened us, while huge bombs from trench mortars shook the ground under us. The whole place seemed to burst into fire from a hundred points, and then came the rush. Straight up the hillside they went into the scrub on top, and in the yellow grass many a figure sank and rolled back, while the rest went on like a wave, leaping the scrub parapets as they gained the crest, and there the silent swish of the bayonet did its work. The fire slackened, the machine gun stopped short, and we found ourselves on

Francis Davison, killed on 6 August.

the other side of the trench, and what were left of the defenders were rushing headlong into further blackness.'[43]

Canterbury men raced along the captured trench towards the Aghyl Dere, killing any Turks they met along the way. Lieutenant 'Mickey' Davison was killed leading a group of men against another machine gun. 'For a moment we lay and listened,' wrote Gordon Harper, 'and then the Lieutenant's voice rang out, "At them with the bayonet!" The answer was a burst of flame from the scrub opposite and a spitting of dust in our eyes as we went down the clay face towards them. On we went and again their fire was cut off short, and the bayonets slashed among the bushes and the black retreating figures, till all was quiet.' Fred Waite wrote: 'The keen bayonets did their silent work, and the gun ceased its death-dealing tapping'.[44] After four smaller trenches were similarly dealt with, Walden's Point was in the hands of the Anzacs.

The Canterburys then crossed the saddle linking Walden's Point to Bauchop's Hill and headed up its northern slopes. 'The ground was so broken, the twists in the gullies so confusing, that all cohesion was lost. But the troopers knew that their duty was to press on up the hill, so up the hill they went.' The mounteds cleared row after row of enemy trenches, with surprised Turks fleeing before them 'leaving all their gear behind. Silver swords, silk quilts etc.'[45] On the way up the hill the leading Canterburys met Lieutenant Colonel Arthur Bauchop with an advance party of his Otago regiment. About 30 of them joined forces to clear the top of the hill. 'On the down-slope in rear of it were found the [abandoned] bivouacs of two battalions. A Nordenfeldt gun was captured, together with the regimental stores.'[46] Few prisoners were taken and at least some surrendering Turks were killed. Noel Trolove captured two Turks, but claimed Bauchop told him that no prisoners were to be taken. Trolove said his prisoners were then killed by another Otago man.[47] Wounded men were left where they fell, and some of them were killed by Turks who had infiltrated back onto the spur behind the New Zealanders.

Bauchop sent Trolove and another man down the hill towards the Chailak Dere to see if they could find any Turks there. Trolove found the dere 'packed with Turks.

There were a hundred or more and I could hear a lot of low jabbering.' He withdrew to make his report after throwing a jam-tin bomb at the enemy.

Bauchop set the men to work digging defensive trenches around the crown of the hill. They were not left in peace for long. The first counter-attack came from the north. 'Bauchop's orders were: "Let them come boys, till they show above the scrub – I'll give the word – then five round[s] rapid [fire]. Yell like hell and into them with the bayonet".' The men lay quietly and waited, hearing the noise made by the Turks as they crept nearer. When Trolove could see about six Turks in front of him, Bauchop gave the order to open fire. After firing more or less blindly, Trolove and his comrades leapt from their trenches and attacked with fixed bayonets. 'I don't think we shot many, but I don't think the rest finished rolling and tumbling through the scrub until they reached the bottom of the dere.'

Bauchop's Hill was declared secure at 1.10 a.m. The small party spent the rest of the night on alert. Bauchop told them to 'cheer like dervishes' to create the impression that they were present in great strength. The Turks attacked a few more times, but with no success. Bauchop passed the early morning hours chatting to his men as they scratched trenches in the hard ground: he talked to Noel Trolove about tennis. As dawn approached, Bauchop ordered his men to remove their conspicuous white patches. Just after that, 'he stood up and shouted: "Come, boys, give one more cheer". He got as far as "Hip, Hip" when there was a flash from a patch of scrub … The Colonel staggered and fell. Several of us picked him up and carried him to a little depression near the summit. When asked by the Otago officer if he was hard hit, he answered, "Yes, I'm done, but don't worry about me, carry on". He was shot through the body.' Bauchop died on a hospital ship on 10 August, and was buried at sea.[48] According to Trolove, 17 of the 30 men who defended the top of the hill that night were killed or wounded.

As dawn broke the men on Bauchop's Hill came under long-range machine gun and shrapnel fire and casualties increased. Daylight also revealed to Trolove the scale of the operation around him. 'When it was day someone said, "Good God, look!" and pointed to the rear. Looking that way we were astounded to find the whole sea from Suvla Bay to Anzac covered with a great fleet of transports and warships, both large and small. The beach was alive with boats and men.' Back on Old No. 3 Outpost Ken Stevens 'was in high glee and felt sure we would win Gallipoli in a canter'.[49] The reality was somewhat different, as will be seen in the following chapters.

The South Islanders captured their objectives in complete darkness in a series

'There was much close fighting, even wrestling'. Turkish corpses (some in bare feet) on Bauchop's Hill.

of small-scale and deadly hand-to-hand fights. Fred Waite recorded 'Many a duel between surprised Turk and desperate New Zealander was fought that night in the tangled scrub' and Charles Bean described 'much close fighting, even wrestling. ... Major Hutton, who commanded the [Canterbury] regiment after Findlay was hit, himself fought a bayonet duel in which, after lunging at his opponent four times, he fell, and was only saved by a companion who bayoneted the Turk.'[50] As the official CMR history would note, 'From the moment of the first charge till men found themselves on Bauchop's Hill, nobody can say exactly what happened. All they knew was that they struggled and fought with Turk, with scrub and with hill, they fell down gullies, were fired at always, and eventually found themselves at their objective.'[51]

The casualties in the South Island regiments that night were much heavier than in the WMR and AMR, although the exact numbers are difficult to pin down. Commonwealth War Graves Commission records state that 24 Canterburys and 29 Otagos were killed on 6 and 7 August, most of whom would have lost their lives during the night. About 180 others were wounded. The NZMR Brigade, including the OMR and Maori detachments, began the night of 6 August with about 1900 men. By dawn about 80 of them were dead and another 230 were wounded.[52]

Otago mounteds digging trenches on Bauchop's Hill on 7 August.

The work of the mounted riflemen was over, at least for a short while. Their efforts that night attracted widespread praise. 'By this magnificent feat of arms, the brilliance of which was never surpassed, if indeed equalled, during the campaign, almost the entire Turkish defence north of Anzac was for the moment swept aside and the way cleared for the infantry to advance up the valleys to Chunuk Bair.' Hamilton agreed: 'No words can do justice to the achievement of Brigadier-General Russell and his men. These are exploits which must be seen to be realised.' The official British history found it 'difficult to praise too highly the conduct of the New Zealand troops engaged in these encounters'.[53] In part this effusive praise reflects the fact that practically nothing else in General Hamilton's great offensive went according to plan. Nonetheless, the success of the mounted regiments that night is remarkable. With empty rifle magazines and fixed bayonets they charged into concentrated rifle and machine gun fire. They had no covering artillery or machine gun fire of their own, and they did not fire a shot until after they had secured their objectives. In this way they seized six enemy positions.

Only a few of the men had ever traversed the country before, and they had to make converging attacks in the dark while adhering to very tight timings. To be fair to the other units who enjoyed less success, the mounteds had the shortest distances to cover that night, over ground that was familiar to at least some of them. They enjoyed the great advantage of surprise and, at Table Top, a measure of good luck. Perhaps, too, some of the Turks in the lower outposts felt isolated and abandoned, and felt little urge to remain and fight.

The Left Covering Force enjoyed similar success. Two battalions of the 40th Infantry Brigade moved past the Canterburys on Walden's Point and seized the Damakjelik Bair on the far side of the Aghyl Dere by 1.30 a.m.

This meant that the vital entrances to the Sazli Beit, Chailak and Aghyl deres were all in Allied hands. All was ready for the two assault columns to enter the deres and climb the ridges and spurs to capture the hilltops of the Sari Bair range. There were two problems. The covering force battle had taken longer than it was supposed to. At 1 a.m. Brigadier General Russell reported to Godley that the line Old No. 3 Outpost–Table Top–Bauchop's Hill was secure. Brigadier General Travers, the commander of the Left Covering Force, made a similar declaration 30 minutes later. The plan required the foothills to be in Anzac hands two hours earlier than that, by 11 p.m. The second problem was that the mounteds had missed quite a few Turks in their advance, especially in the Chailak Dere and in Taylor's Gap. This became apparent when the assault columns ran into them as they advanced.

Still, three hours of darkness remained. There was still time for the Right Assault Column to capture Chunuk Bair before sunrise, but only if it moved quickly and its commanders acted decisively.

11

Chunuk Bair

The whole Regt. stopped in a slight hollow for hours while the Turks shelled and sniped us. Men were killed and wounded all around me. Legs, arms and other portions being blown off.

JOSEPH LAW

When the enemy charged us everyone stood up and it was just plain open slather, shooting as fast as possible at them running towards us.

KEN STEVENS

THE SHORT SUMMER PERIOD of darkness meant that the two assaulting infantry columns needed to move very quickly if they were to capture the Sari Bair hilltops by dawn on 7 August. Any delays would be fatal to the plan, but many of the troops in the columns were sick or inexperienced, the covering forces had not been able to clear the Turks out of the deres completely and none of the commanders had scouted the routes up which they were expected to lead their men in the dark.

The four battalions of the New Zealand Infantry Brigade that made up the Right Assaulting Column had six hours from 10.30 p.m. to capture Chunuk Bair. The Otago, Wellington and Auckland battalions were to ascend the Chailak Dere, while the Canterbury battalion was to follow the more restricted Sazli Beit Dere. They were all to meet on Rhododendron Ridge, from where the Wellington and Auckland battalions would assault and capture the Chunuk Bair summit.

After being held up by a 'traffic jam' in the Main Sap for two hours, the Canterbury Infantry Battalion made its way along the Sazli Beit Dere towards Table Top. When the leading infantrymen reached the apparently impassable cliffs at the base of the hill, there were no mounteds there to tell them that this was the way to go, so they turned back. As they stumbled back down the dere, some mounteds pointed a few platoons in the right direction. The rest of the battalion went all the way back to its assembly area in Happy Valley below Walker's Ridge before turning around again.[1]

Meanwhile, in the Chailak Dere the men of the Otago battalion were held up early on by barbed wire and scattered enemy fire. 'They were easy enough to overcome … but each little affair cost a few men and, even worse, ate into the precious time.'[2] The advance up the narrow and difficult dere was a very stop-start affair, and the leading Otago infantrymen had only just reached the summit of Table Top by 3 a.m. Some of them started to jump into the trenches dug there by the mounteds, but Meldrum told them there was no room for them and sent them on towards Rhododendron Ridge. Lieutenant Colonel Malone's Wellington infantrymen were not far behind the Otago battalion. The Auckland and Canterbury battalions were still down in the Chailak and Sazli Beit deres respectively. Dawn was about an hour away.

As the sky brightened in front of them, the leading Otago and Wellington rifle companies reached a small knoll on Rhododendron Ridge later known as The Apex. In front of them was a narrow saddle about 200 metres long which rose to a second point called The Pinnacle. From The Pinnacle the ridge dipped again before rising in a continuous and exposed incline up to Chunuk Bair, 300 metres further away. The New Zealanders were very close to their objective, but they were almost out of time.

There was only a handful of Turks up on Chunuk Bair at that time, along with German officer Colonel Hans Kannengiesser, who saw the first New Zealanders creeping up the ridge below him near The Apex and ordered the Turkish soldiers to fire a few volleys at them.[3] That was enough to halt the New Zealanders' cautious advance up Rhododendron Ridge. Instead of pushing on for the top immediately, as he had been ordered to do, Brigadier General Johnston hesitated. His tired men sat down, ate their breakfast and waited.

As the first New Zealand infantrymen reached The Apex, Australian light horsemen in the mounteds' old trenches back on Russell's Top were getting ready to attack the Turkish trenches across The Nek and on Baby 700. This was supposed to be co-ordinated with a New Zealand attack on the same trenches from Chunuk Bair. But the New Zealanders were not even on Chunuk Bair, let alone ready to attack from it. An earlier Australian attack against German Officers' Trench, which was supposed to silence machine guns there, failed. The Turks opposite Russell's Top were alerted, so surprise was impossible. Birdwood nonetheless ordered the attack across The Nek to take place, apparently to help the New Zealanders below Chunuk Bair.

The Turks opposite Russell's Top had a few minutes to get ready after the preliminary

Telephoto view of The Nek from Old No. 3 Outpost. The trees on the skyline indicate where the Australian light horsemen were massacred on 7 August.

bombardment ended. They 'manned their trenches two-deep in anticipation of the assault which they knew must be imminent. One line seated on the parapet and the other standing behind it, they nestled their rifles to their shoulders, took aim, and waited. Their machine-guns here and there rattled off a dozen shots as they made ready for action.'[4] At 4.30 a.m. the first of 450 Australians from the 8th and 10th light horse regiments climbed out of their trenches and charged across The Nek towards the Turkish trenches. The New Zealanders over on Table Top and Rhododendron Ridge heard the Turkish fire rise to a roar four times as successive lines of Australians were shot down. Ken Stevens watched the massacre from Old No. 3 Outpost. 'We did not see one of them reach the enemy trenches which were only twelve yards in front of them. The Turkish machine guns raked No-Mans-Land for nearly an hour after any Australians were left standing.' By the time the attack was called off 236 light horsemen were dead or dying and another 138 were wounded.[5] The Turkish trenches were never in any danger from this pointless attack. According to Waite, 'in military history there is no more splendid record of sacrifice than was enacted that fatal morning' but Lieutenant Colonel Meldrum's comment of 'No greater record of crass stupidity!' is closer to the mark.[6] Supporting attacks from Quinn's Post and Pope's Hill also failed. The attacks at The Nek, Pope's Hill, Quinn's Post and German Officers' Trench cost the Australians 650 casualties out of 1250 who attacked. And it was all in vain, for Chunuk Bair and the other Sari Bair summits remained in Turkish hands.

Below Chunuk Bair the New Zealand infantrymen were still waiting for orders. To the north they could see the Suvla Bay invasion force coming ashore and they were greatly encouraged by the sight. Brigadier General Johnston was not so happy. He had watched the Australian attack at The Nek fail. In the other direction, he could see that the Left Assaulting Column was nowhere near its objectives of Hill Q and Hill 971. The cover of darkness was gone, and his brigade was under increasing fire from Chunuk Bair. With only half of his brigade close at hand, he felt isolated and vulnerable. Taking all these factors into consideration, Johnston decided against a daylight attack on Chunuk Bair. When a message to this effect reached Godley, he ordered Johnston to attack at once. Johnston did as he was told and gave the job to the Auckland Infantry Battalion and a stray Gurkha battalion that had turned up on Rhododendron Ridge from the other assaulting column.

When the attack finally began at 11 a.m. hundreds of Turks were waiting for it up on Chunuk Bair. The Auckland infantry platoons advanced over The Apex towards The Pinnacle in close formation, in broad daylight and with little covering fire. They

Selwyn Chambers, killed on 7 August.

immediately came under heavy enemy rifle, machine gun and shrapnel fire, and 300 of them were killed or wounded in 20 minutes. The survivors gained a little cover in a shallow trench on The Pinnacle. The Gurkhas were unable to support them.

Two companies from the Canterbury battalion had been brought forward to support the Aucklanders. While they waited in the open, Turkish fire killed or wounded more than 100 of them. Both these battalions were effectively destroyed as fighting units, and they took no further part in the Chunuk Bair battle. Godley wanted another attempt to be made, but Lieutenant Colonel Malone refused to send his Wellington battalion forward. Johnston had no choice but to tell Godley that he did not support further daylight attacks. Godley reluctantly agreed to postpone any more attacks for the time being.

Back down the ridge the mounteds were digging in on the positions they had captured the night before. Not long after dawn a stray bullet found Major Selwyn Chambers, the commander of the Wellington East Coast squadron of the WMR, as he rested on Table Top. Hit in the throat, he bled to death in minutes.[7]

Further north, Brigadier General Cox's Left Assaulting Column, consisting of the 4th Australian Infantry Brigade and the 29th Indian Brigade, was in serious trouble. The Australians were trying to get to Hill 971, about five kilometres from their start line, across very rough ground that no one had scouted in detail. This brigade was probably the sickest formation at Anzac, and John Monash, its commander, was not at his best. Writing after the event, Ken Stevens was 'certain that no battalion of men, no matter how fit they were, could reach Koja Chemen (971) in darkness in the five hours allotted to them. Owing to the narrow gullies they would have to travel in single file for most of the journey … In darkness it was madness to try even if there were no enemy bullets to contend with. As an ordinary route march in broad daylight it may have been possible, with men in good physical condition.'[8]

The Australians were being guided by Percy Overton, who was apparently convinced by a local villager to take a shortcut to the Aghyl Dere. This took them along a narrow valley (later known as Taylor's Gap) between Walden's Point and Bauchop's

Hill, instead of around the seaward side of Walden's Point as planned. Overton had not scouted this difficult route, and there was still some enemy activity along both sides of the valley. As the valley rose towards its summit the track narrowed, and the men were forced to thread their way in single file around boulders and through dense and prickly scrub. At one point pioneers had to come forward to hack a path through the dense scrub. It took them three hours to traverse the 600 metres of Taylor's Gap. By the time the advance guard of the Australian assault force reached the Aghyl Dere in the early morning, the moon was rising and they were under increasing enemy fire from the low hills in front of them. Overton pointed the leading Australian battalions in the direction of the Abdel Rahman Bair, their route to Hill 971.

Overton then went back to bring forward the 29th Indian Brigade, which had become separated from the Australians. Overton led the Indians through Taylor's Gap and directed them towards their objective, Hill Q. He probably sent them the wrong way, but he was shot dead before he could discover and correct his mistake.[9] For the rest of the day, most of the Australian and Indian battalions wandered lost and exhausted in the Aghyl Dere and on the lower foothills, under increasing enemy fire. Neither brigade ended the day anywhere near its objectives. The Australians were still two kilometres away from Hill 971, while the Indians were just reaching the foot of the main range below Hill Q.[10]

The landings to the north in Suvla Bay started well. They completely surprised the Turks, and by noon on 7 August 16,000 men of the 10th and 11th divisions were safely ashore. Then it all went wrong. A few thousand Turks, ably commanded by the German Major Wilhelm Willmer, were able to hold the inexperienced British soldiers off with a few lines of snipers and some light artillery fire. They quickly ran out of water. General Stopford failed to push forward with any speed, believing that he had already achieved all that was expected of him. The British captured a few minor hills late in the day, but they failed to advance far enough to give the men up on the Sari Bair hills any assistance at all. They might as well have stayed aboard their ships for all the good they did. Clutha Mackenzie, watching from his perch on Table Top, wrote 'the troops on shore were scarcely moving. During the whole day only a few small bodies advanced a small distance, with little opposition it seemed, at any time. Why did they not make a general advance?'[11]

As soon as General Liman von Sanders heard about the Suvla Bay landings he realised that Sari Bair and Suvla Bay were where Hamilton's main effort was being made. He ordered every uncommitted unit within reach to march towards Anzac, and five divisions were soon on their way. The forces already at Anzac and Suvla Bay were told to hold the line for 36 to 48 hours until these reinforcements arrived. This defined the length of time Hamilton had left to secure his victory.

General Godley decided to attack Chunuk Bair again in the pre-dawn darkness of Sunday 8 August. This gave the Turks an extra 18 hours to protect the hilltops with an impenetrable barrier of machine guns and barbed wire, but they did not do so because most of their reserves had not yet arrived, and because the Turkish commanders had still not figured out exactly what was going on. Their units were scattered and mixed up all over the battlefield, and it took time to sort them out and work out what was happening in front of them.

Godley did not really know what was going on either. Instead of concentrating all of his forces against Chunuk Bair, where success was within reach, he decided to renew the attack against all three major summits of the Sari Bair range. The exhausted 4th Australian Brigade was to try again to capture Hill 971, and the 29th Indian and 39th Infantry brigades were to seize Hill Q. What was left of Johnston's New Zealand Infantry Brigade, reinforced by the Maori Contingent, two regiments of the NZMR Brigade and two British battalions, was to seize Chunuk Bair. The assault was to be preceded by a 45-minute artillery and naval gun bombardment.

At 3.30 p.m. on 7 August, Godley told Russell to be prepared to bring forward two regiments and the Maoris. Russell chose the Auckland and Wellington regiments, leaving the weaker Otago and Canterbury regiments to guard the foothills. The Auckland mounteds were the first to go forward, at 1.30 a.m. Two hundred and eighty-eight of them joined the Wellington and Otago battalions, half of the Maori Contingent and the 7th Gloucesters and the 8th Welch Fusiliers at The Apex at 3 a.m. on 8 August.

The pre-dawn bombardment of the Sari Bair crest was heavy and accurate, and it scattered the Turkish defenders. About 4.45 a.m. the Wellington Infantry Battalion and half of the Gloucesters, about 800 men in all, walked onto Chunuk Bair without firing a shot and almost without loss. Colonel Kannengiesser had been wounded by shellfire earlier and most of his soldiers abandoned the hilltop just before Malone's men arrived. The New Zealanders, the Gloucesters and a few Welshmen occupied a shallow line of Turkish trenches on the crest of the ridge, about 200 metres to the south of the Chunuk Bair summit. Ahead of them in the distance they could see the Narrows of the Dardanelles. The Auckland mounteds remained at The Apex with the Maoris and the Otago infantry for the time being.[12]

Chunuk Bair (centre skyline), with The Apex and The Pinnacle in the foreground. The open slope below Chunuk Bair was swept by Turkish fire during daylight hours.

As soon as they had light enough to see, Turkish machine gunners and snipers firing from Hill Q and Battleship Hill closed the route from The Apex to Chunuk Bair. The rest of the Gloucesters and the Welshmen were caught in the open on their way up Rhododendron Ridge and shot to pieces.[13] The Turks then threw everything they had at the men on the crest. Fortunately for the New Zealanders, 'everything' was not yet very much. Only small numbers of Turkish reinforcements were immediately available, and these were fed into the fight piecemeal as they arrived.[14]

There was no room in the shallow trench on Chunuk Bair for everybody, so Malone set half of his battalion to work digging another trench about 20 metres behind it. He sent 80 men over to the far side of the ridge to provide early warning of Turkish counter-attacks, but they did not last long once the sun rose. The Turks soon reclaimed most of the crest-line trench too. Undaunted, Malone and his men fought on from the support trench. The Wellington infantrymen 'disguised their lack of ammunition, bombs and adequate support by the sheer aggression of their defence'.[15] Turkish bombs that rained down on the men in the shallow trenches were picked up and thrown back, or smothered. When the bomb throwing eased off, a Turkish bayonet charge usually followed. Malone dealt with these by getting his men out of the trench and counter-charging. The Turks would not face these ferocious attacks, and Malone's men fired a volley into their retreating backs before returning to the trenches, always fewer in number, to await the next onslaught. Before they could get back into the trenches, they had to clear them of the newly dead and wounded. In this way they defeated at least six Turkish bayonet charges before noon.[16] All the while, they were being shot at from both flanks and shelled. The Turks tried to get around their flanks to attack them from behind, but they were always seen in time and shot down by Malone's vigilant men and by New Zealand machine gunners down on The Apex.

For most of the day the New Zealanders up on Chunuk Bair remained cut off from substantial reinforcements, and their wounded could not be evacuated. Wounded men fought on until they were killed, or dragged themselves into shelter behind the firing trench. 'The wounded lay exposed to the sun at the rear of the trench, and many there died. One man went raving mad, and ran along an exposed place with a tunic over his head, but he fell into the trench before he was hit.' Most of the wounded men died untended because the medics and stretcher bearers were all casualties themselves. Ken Stevens would 'never forget the wounded calling for help on Chunuk Bair when there was none available'.[17] The sun blazed down on them all day, and their water ran out after only a few hours. Communications back down the ridge were maintained by the signallers laying and relaying telephone lines under fire. Corporal Cyril Bassett won the only Victoria Cross awarded to New Zealanders on Gallipoli for this work.

Godley's other attacks towards Hill 971 and Hill Q got nowhere. The Australian, Indian and British troops were still exhausted from the night before, the ground was incredibly difficult to get through, and light Turkish forces were able to block them without difficulty. This allowed the Turks to concentrate their efforts against the enemy on Chunuk Bair.

By noon the pressure on the dwindling defenders of Chunuk Bair was so heavy that Malone called for reinforcements. Two squadrons of the Auckland Mounted Rifles Regiment, under Major Samuel Schofield's command, and a party of Maoris had been trying to get up the exposed ridge to help them since 9 a.m. The Aucklanders 'dashed by "eights" across the narrow saddle to The Pinnacle; but near that point the whole regiment was pinned down by the enemy's fire into the shelter of a slight rise for some hours. Here, lying on the scrubby saddle, it was observed by the enemy's artillery. Whenever a man stirred, two guns, firing at extreme range from the direction of

Frank Chapman, killed on 8 August.

Anafarta, were turned upon the saddle. By their shells Major Chapman and several others were killed.'[18] It took the Aucklanders seven hours to reach Chunuk Bair, advancing in small groups and in short rushes. 'At 1 o'clock … Major Schofield led the regiment in another advance towards the firing line. This was effected by crawling forward along the saddle, making gradually to its southern side so as to reach the edge overlooking the Sazli Dere, and thence dropping down into the head of the dere, in the shelter of which large numbers of wounded from the summit were now lying. There the regiment deployed and prepared to charge by half-squadrons up the remaining 200 yards of exposed slope to Malone's position.'[19] Two hundred and forty-eight Auckland mounteds made it to the top.

Trooper Joseph Law was one of them. 'Roused up at 1 o'clock & moved up the gully again, stayed part way up a hill until daylight. Some more climbing & then a run over the side of a hill with bullets raining around us like hail from machine guns…. The whole Regt. stopped in a slight hollow for hours while the Turks shelled & sniped us. Men were killed and wounded all around me. Legs, arms & other portions being blown off…. After waiting 7 hrs without moving, we went from the jaws of death into the "Valley of Dead" (6 or 700 wounded & dead here) on into the Mouth of Hell, charged up the side of "Chunik Bair" to relieve the Gloucesters & others.'[20]

As the Auckland mounteds moved up Rhododendron Ridge, they came across increasing numbers of wounded men, lying in cover if they could reach it, or in the open under fire. Trooper John McKinnon may have passed the body of his brother Ken, an Auckland infantryman who had been killed earlier in the day. If he did, he cannot have mourned for long, for he was killed on the same day.[21] Under the intense enemy fire the Maori contingent, like the Gurkhas before them, had veered off down the hill towards The Farm, where it stayed.

When the mounteds eventually made it to the top of the hill at 4 p.m. they found the Wellington infantry 'at the point of exhaustion. The firing line, only three-and-a-half feet in depth, was now so full of dead and dying that the men had to leave it and endeavour to scratch another trench immediately behind it.' The Aucklanders took over the trenches on the right flank of the position, and Major Schofield joined Lieutenant Colonel Malone in the headquarters trench. At 5 p.m. Schofield was seriously wounded and Malone was killed by artillery fire.[22] Captain Ferdinand Wood took over command of the Auckland regiment until his arm was shattered by a Turkish bullet.

Soon after the Aucklanders arrived 'there began a very violent bombardment of the slope by Turkish batteries ... followed by a succession of attacks – hand-grenades coming over fifty at a time, the enemy getting out of their trenches and advancing with officers at their head, the New Zealanders shooting them as they rose. This effort of the enemy, like its predecessors, was beaten back.'[23]

Ken Stevens wrote a detailed account of the AMR experience on Chunuk Bair that day:

The sky was cloudless, the sun was scorching and the air was dead calm and filled with acrid fumes from exploding shells, bombs and rifle fire. ... The air seemed to be electrified with the crackle of bullets and the Turks were bombing our men some of whom I [was] surprised to see picked up live bombs with fuses burning and threw them back at the enemy ... As well as returning Turkish bombs we threw all the stones we could reach and any we could dig out of the side of the trench with a bayonet. ... Our line was L shaped and about 200 yards long, the short sections being on my left extending about 50 yards and rising up to the crest of Chunuk Bair. ... Straight in front of us from three to twenty-five yards was dead ground unless we stood up and made targets of ourselves for the enemy that was practically on three sides of us. The plan of Turkish attack was to assemble in the dead ground in front, then a group would attack us with bombs then charge, while another group would scramble up to our left on top of Chunuk Bair. ... When the enemy charged us everyone stood up and it was just plain open slather, shooting as fast as possible at them running towards us. ... When we halted a charge by the enemy, what were left of them dropped down into the short scrub just in front of our trench and we got down out of sight as much as possible. Then we both started sniping at each other. ... The number of casualties caused by bombs was only a small fraction of that from the deadly rifle fire which was from a range of three yards to less than one hundred. ... As we had no sandbags I piled a couple of dead men on my left to block the view of me for the enemy on the hill. ... As the day wore on the scrub was all cut away by bullets and bombs. ... My throat was parched, my lips and tongue were sticky and the sun seemed so slow going down that I wished it would drop out of the sky and let them bring water up to us. Perspiration was streaming down my face and my sweat rag was saturated and it was getting difficult to see on account of the salty perspiration in my eyes. … A bullet broke my bayonet off, but as there were plenty of Turkish rifles and ammunition I used one of theirs and it was a blessing as it did not kick like ours and my shoulder was very sore.[24]

Godley had a foothold on the crest of the Sari Bair hills and he intended to make the most of it. The hopeless attempts to capture Hill 971 were abandoned. The New Zealanders on Chunuk Bair were to be reinforced by the Otago Infantry Battalion and the Wellington mounteds on the night of 8 August. Together they were to seize the rest of the Chunuk Bair summit and then expand their position southwards towards Battleship Hill. The British and Indian brigades stuck in the deres around The Farm were to climb up and seize Hill Q and the saddle joining it to Chunuk Bair. Lastly, a strong British force was to move up Rhododendron Ridge to the Chunuk Bair position during the night, and attack north at dawn to link up with the British and Indian forces on Hill Q. The attack was to be preceded by a bombardment of the crest line and the far side of it from 4.30 until 5.15 a.m. on 9 August.

Meanwhile, two Turkish divisions had arrived from Bulair on the night of 7–8 August after a very rapid forced march of 40 kilometres. General Liman von Sanders wanted them committed to the battle immediately, and he sacked their commander when he asked for time to rest his tired men. That evening these new divisions and the Turks already at Suvla Bay and on the Sari Bair hills were placed under the command of Colonel Mustafa Kemal. Three other Turkish divisions were approaching the battlefield from the south and east. Hamilton's period of grace was almost at an end.

While Godley's staff wrote out the orders for the new attacks, the day passed slowly on Chunuk Bair. 'All sense of time was lost – it seemed that they had been fighting for an eternity.' At last the sun set and the immediate crisis passed. 'The trenches were still held at dusk, when the situation became – as always in Gallipoli – much easier. The moment darkness fell, men carrying bombs, water, and ammunition from the Chailak Dere, who during the day had not been able to go farther than The Pinnacle, reached the advanced position without hindrance.'[25] Harry Browne wrote: 'The hills were strewn with dead and wounded … in the darkness one was in constant dread of stumbling over a wounded man. No words can describe the heroism of the severely wounded. They cheered us on as we passed them and if you apologised for kicking against one they would reply "It's alright mate, I know you did not mean to".'[26]

At 10.30 p.m. on 8 August the Otago Infantry Battalion and 173 men in two squadrons of the Wellington Mounted Rifles Regiment joined the remnants of the Wellington infantry, the Auckland mounteds and the British battalions on Chunuk Bair. One of the WMR reinforcements was Clutha Mackenzie. He found 'a line of shallow holes, some a foot deep, some eighteen inches, aided a little by a few almost useless sandbags. The cliff brink was six or eight yards away, and under it lay the enemy.' A support line, five metres behind the front line, consisted of 'half a dozen holes whose fine garrisons lay dead within them, except a few who raved in delirium for water that was not to be had. They and their arms lay prostrate across each other, many half-buried by flying earth from shells and bombs.'[27] Harry Browne had 'seen many pictures of dead in the trenches, but never one like that trench and the communication trench leading from ours into it'.[28]

Only 70 of the 760 Wellington infantrymen who had captured Chunuk Bair that morning were still unwounded. The exhausted survivors who withdrew back down the ridge were in a pitiable state. 'They had had no water since the morning; they could talk only in whispers; their eyes were sunken; their knees trembled; some broke down and cried like children.'[29] The remnants of the AMR stayed put.

For the rest of the night the New Zealanders dug furiously in the hard rocky ground and dodged Turkish bombs. According to Browne, 'our little trench was very shallow and this proved to be our salvation, for when the grenades dropped into our trench … Sandy and I would hop out the back and fire there till the bombs had exploded … We were fighting in our shirt sleeves so there were no overcoats or anything to throw on the bombs.'[30] Joseph Law wrote: 'Our men fell like fruit from a tree in a gale. The Turks rushed us with bombs, only to be mowed down by our men. One came up with the white flag & a party of bomb throwers. They all fell…. The Turks came on during the night only to be wiped out. We held the front while reinforcements dug a trench & then came back into it. … [Trooper Alfred] Kent had dozens of wounds, but was quite cheerful. I bound him up in 6 places, he thanked me but died about two hours after.'[31]

Clutha Mackenzie described the scene:

Lit fantastically by flickering flames, which were licking slowly through the scrub, was a small, ghastly, battle-rent piece of ground, not one hundred yards in width. … The Turks lined the far edge, their ghostly faces appearing and vanishing in the eerie light, as they poured a point-blank fusillade at the shattered series of shallow holes where the remnants of the New Zealanders were fighting gallantly. Sweeping round to the left was the flashing semicircle of the enemy line, bombs exploded with a lurid glare ... Above the rending of the bombs, the rattle and burr of the rifles and machine-guns and the crash of shells, sometimes sounded faintly men's voices – the weird 'Allah, Allah, Allah' of the enemy in a chanted cadence, and the fierce half-humorous taunts of the attackers. Everywhere lay dead and dying men – mostly the former, Turkish and British [including Anzacs]. Equipment and rifles were strewn in the greatest confusion over the torn earth, and all the time the creeping flames cast weird lights upon the passing drama.[32]

Chunuk Bair was still in New Zealand hands, but strong Turkish reinforcements had already arrived, and more were on the way. It was only a matter of time before their full weight was turned onto the troublesome defenders of the hill top. Fortunately for the New Zealanders, the first major counter-attack by the Turks took place elsewhere, giving them another 24 hours' respite. Those hours would later be described as New Zealand's finest.

12

New Zealand's finest hour

*Physical fear is a strange thing. While all are more or less affected by it
in a tight corner, most manage to contain it, but in some cases
it causes them to lose all control over themselves.*

HARRY BROWNE

*Bombed, shelled, sniped, raked with machine-gun fire, suffering extremely
from thirst, they utterly refused to be dislodged, but they could only get some relief
from time to time by getting out and charging with the bayonet, or catching the
Turkish bombs and hurling them back. And all day the sun blazed down on
their agony. This was perhaps New Zealand's finest hour.*

CECIL MALTHUS

LIEUTENANT COLONEL WILLIAM MELDRUM took command of the Chunuk Bair position
at 11 p.m. on 8 August, after the commander of the Otago Infantry Battalion was
wounded. In addition to 173 of his own mounteds, he had under his control 400
Otago infantrymen, 85 survivors of the AMR and a few British soldiers.

At midnight the Turks almost succeeded in another attempt to get behind the
position. 'There was a shout of "Allah! Allah!" and a rush of Turks both from left rear
and from [the] front. The New Zealanders kept their heads, faced round and fired, and
the assault melted.' For the next few hours the enemy attacks eased off. 'The enemy,
although not heavily attacking, had been constantly breaking into bursts of fire, either
upon alarm or as a demonstration; once there had been a scuffle at the regimental
headquarters itself, a party of the enemy having apparently crept round thither from
Chunuk Bair in the dark.'[1]

At 4 a.m. the Turks launched a major attack. Meldrum recorded what happened.
'They started with shrapnel and bombs and sniped at us from both flanks and front.
The bombs did us the most harm. The Turks swung them in long woollen socks and

they came hurtling through the air for 30 or 40 yards, rolling into our trenches and exploding there. Many men were wounded. Some jumped behind the trench and lay or knelt behind the parapet; and then with rifle fire and bombs, we fought them all along the trench line'.[2] As Charles Bean wrote, bombs 'fell continuously among the New Zealanders. On the flanks the enemy had to expose himself to throw them, individual Turks constantly running forward only to be shot down. … In front of the bomb-throwers had come two or three lines of skirmishers, who ran forward in open order and flung themselves down, the bombers then mostly throwing from behind them.'[3] This Turkish attack cost the Wellington mounted riflemen and the Otago infantry half of their remaining strength. Two brothers from Taranaki, Michael and Richard Murphy, were among those killed that day. It is probably this attack Meldrum was referring to when he wrote: 'Remember them at Chunuk Bair when after a fierce Turkish attack had been driven back at a cost to ourselves of half our numbers. The order "Smoko" was passed around and all cares dropped from them in a moment, just as at Smoko in a shearing shed.'[4]

At 5.15 a.m., while Meldrum's force was still fighting off this attack, the Gurkhas and a few hundred British soldiers made it up onto the ridge joining Chunuk Bair to Hill Q after the artillery and naval bombardment cleared the crest of most of the Turks. The Gurkhas drove off the few remaining enemy soldiers in a brief and bloody hand-to-hand fight. Then five high explosive shells, probably fired from British guns, burst among them, killing many. The Gurkhas and some of the British soldiers apparently panicked and ran back down the hill, leaving a dozen men on the saddle. These few were quickly driven off by a Turkish attack, and the saddle was lost.

There was no sign of the other British force that was supposed to come up to Meldrum's position from The Apex and then attack northwards to link up with the Gurkhas. They had been sent the wrong way and got nowhere. As dawn broke, these battalions were wandering lost and exhausted in the ravines of the Aghyl Dere, below The Farm, where they were of no use to anybody. A few of them did make an attempt to reach the crest line, but they were stopped by enemy fire well below The Pinnacle.

That was the end of Godley's last attack. The only part that Meldrum probably noticed was the preliminary bombardment, several rounds of which landed on his own position. Harry Browne witnessed the result:

A man was blown thirty feet into the air by a naval shell, his limbs outspread, his whole body silhouetted against the sky. Yet another shell and the charred trunk of another man's body fell near us. Simultaneously the enemy attacked fiercely his hand grenades taking deadly effect. ... One moment they were working their rifles like men possessed, and shouting defiance, and the next they lay crumpled up in the trench. Two only survived from that trench. ... Some New Zealanders left their positions and ran back down the hill. In the midst of it all I was shouting 'Come back the 6th.' And 'Come on you black cow' to the Turks. ... A– suddenly cried 'Come on Boys, retire'. I turned on him 'you cow, I'll put a bullet in you' I said through the din, Sandy shouted 'You ... coward, I'll bayonet you'. He knew it was meant and subsided. ... Another British shell landed right amongst the boys. In the flash of the explosion we saw them hurled backwards from it. Poor old Hughie Pringle was killed, his throat ripped by a piece of it and presently there came groping past us Clutha McKenzie [sic] blinded, young Mel Bull his jaw smashed and another unrecognizable. As they passed us their faces were covered in blood and seemed to hang in tatters. Physical fear is a strange thing. While all are more or less affected by it in a tight corner, most manage to contain it, but in some cases it causes them to lose all control over themselves.[5]

Clutha Mackenzie described his own wounding: 'there was an awful lurid flash close in front of him, on the level ground almost in his face, and it seemed he had been hit across the head with a bar of wood, and he could not see'. He heard one of his friends say, 'Old Mac's a goner'. Mackenzie survived the war, but he was blinded for life.[6]

According to Bean, 'The situation for a moment looked critical. But Colonel Meldrum of the Wellingtons with his adjutant Captain Kelsall, and Major Elmslie, rallied the men. The brave Elmslie led forward a troop of his squadron to reoccupy the empty sector of trench. Before he could reach it he was hit by a bullet through shoulder and neck. He fell, picked himself up, gained the trench, and there, smiling at some of his men, "I'm afraid I can't help you much further, boys, but you're doing well – keep on ..." he said, and died. Kelsall, leading back the men who had retired, also gained the trench, but was soon afterwards killed by a bomb. Both on right and left, however, the position was completely

James Elmslie, killed on 9 August.

reoccupied.'[7] Meldrum recommended Elmslie for a posthumous Victoria Cross, but it was not awarded. Elmslie's death was a great loss to the men of the Wellington regiment. As Cecil Allison wrote, 'Jim proved himself a splendid soldier and a first class officer. He was the idol of the regiment. Old Mr Elmslie ought to be the proudest man in the country to think he had such a son.'[8]

By dawn on 9 August only 22 of the Auckland mounteds were still able to hold a rifle, and Meldrum sent them back down the hill.[9] At dawn, just before he lost his sight, Clutha Mackenzie described 'a ghastly scene ... the decision must come soon, for this desperate more or less continual hand-to-hand encounter could not last much longer'. Harry Browne and the other tired men were 'now and then casting longing glances back down the gullies wondering if help would come'.[10]

Throughout the day the Wellington mounteds and the Otago infantry held off repeated Turkish attacks. Cecil Malthus wrote that they 'suffered throughout the day an ordeal even more intense and dreadful than Malone's men had endured. Bombed, shelled, sniped, raked with machine-gun fire, suffering extremely from thirst, they utterly refused to be dislodged, but they could only get some relief from time to time by getting out and charging with the bayonet, or catching the Turkish bombs and hurling them back. And all day the sun blazed down on their agony. This was perhaps New Zealand's finest hour.'[11]

It was a ruthless fight with no mercy given or expected. Harry Browne 'could not help laughing at the grim purpose displayed in the face of a big infantryman and the poise of his rifle and bayonet, as he rushed past [after] someone cried out that a Turk was trying to sneak away from behind our lines and sure enough there was his crouching form making for the left shoulder of the hill, but shortly a despairing "Allah" announced that the big man's bayonet had got home'.[12]

As Bean observed, 'The pressure on the New Zealanders clinging to their foothold was ... intense. Their main trench was now about five feet in depth, but casualties were so heavy that, to leave greater room in it, Captains Hastings and James and many of their men got out and lay firing over the parados.'[13] Harry Browne and the others knew 'that if hard hit they would probably die where they fell and lucky the man who was killed outright. ... We were standing on our own mates but they wouldn't mind and we were too exhausted to lift them out. ... If only Abdul had known how few were left in that gap, but there, he didn't and possibly he was as exhausted as ourselves. ... In the little neighbouring trench over which no Turk had come alive, the only sign of life among the many there, was the stump of an arm which now and

OMR stretcher bearers.

then waved feebly for help and a voice which called "New Zealand" to four listeners, who could give or get no aid to him. On the parapet above lay a hand. That hand had been throwing back Turkish bombs.'[14]

Meldrum called for reinforcements and more ammunition. Forty or fifty British soldiers reached him at noon, but they brought no extra ammunition with them.[15] All the men could do was rummage through the bandoliers and ammunition pouches on dead and wounded men. Despite his losses and dwindling ammunition stocks, Meldrum was able to hold the crest for the rest of the day because the Turks had lost some of the will to attack after their costly early morning effort. That was about to change.

Colonel Mustafa Kemal was now in command of all the Turks fighting on the Sari Bair range and on the plain around Suvla Bay, including the two divisions that had arrived from Bulair. Kemal decided to attack the British beachhead at Suvla Bay first. In the early morning hours of 9 August 16,000 Turks captured Tekke Tepe and part of Damakjelik Bair, but the attack did not draw any enemy forces down from Chunuk Bair as Kemal had hoped.[16] Kemal then rode south to Chunuk Bair, which he reached

Advanced Dressing Station in the Chailak Dere.

on the afternoon of 9 August. He decided that an all-out attack was necessary to take back Chunuk Bair, and it was scheduled for the following morning. Kemal spent the rest of the afternoon and the night gathering as many troops as he could get his hands on. The failure of his last attack meant that Godley had finally lost the initiative: what happened next would be dictated by his enemy.

During the day Hamilton offered Birdwood another division, but he and Godley declined. There was no room and no water for them, and the deres were already choked with wounded and dead men. Godley issued orders for the positions to be consolidated, and plans were drawn up to relieve the exhausted New Zealanders on The Pinnacle and up on Chunuk Bair. Meldrum told him that two fresh battalions would be enough to hold the line on Chunuk Bair.

The relief began after dusk. By 8 p.m. on 9 August the New Zealanders on Chunuk Bair had been replaced by the first of 900 British soldiers of the 6th North Lancashire and 5th Wiltshire regiments. Taking their wounded comrades and Major Elmslie's body with them, the New Zealanders made their weary way down Rhododendron Ridge to the head of the Chailak Dere. Meldrum left a few scouts and machine gunners behind to help the British soldiers settle in; few survived. Only 73 Wellington mounted riflemen walked off the hill. There was room for only one of the British battalions in the existing trenches. Instead of digging new trenches that night as Meldrum had urged, the tired men of the second battalion stacked their rifles and went to sleep in the head of the Sazli Beit Dere.

These two battalions were overwhelmed and destroyed early the next morning by Kemal's attack, which involved three Turkish regiments totalling perhaps 6000 men.[17] After recapturing the crest of the hills the Turks came down the western slopes. On Rhododendron Ridge naval gunfire, artillery and massed machine gun fire, including from the mounted rifles positions on Bauchop's Hill and Table Top, stopped them at The Pinnacle. Noel Trolove watched the onslaught. 'Later in the morning the Turks in thousands started to come down the bare shoulder of Rhododendron Spur towards our support trenches at the Apex. They seemed to come in double lines, shoulder to shoulder, right across the spur. Every ship in the bay opened fire; every machine gun within range opened up. The spur was one mass of bursting shells, and the lines seemed to melt away before they reached the Apex. … Some machine guns back on Bauchop's were firing incessantly, the position of one could be made out by the little patch of steam rising above the scrub, from the boiling water jacket.'[18] Stopped on Rhododendron Ridge, the Turks veered to the right, fell upon the British battalions around The Farm and wiped them out. According to their own casualty records, only about 250 Turks were killed or wounded in this counter-attack.[19] The new front line settled here, and the Turks turned The Pinnacle, Chunuk Bair, Hill Q and Hill 971 into impregnable fortresses.

The end of the great adventure. Dead bodies under British flags aboard a trawler alongside a hospital ship off Anzac Cove. The trawler sailed into deep water every morning to bury bodies at sea.

Many New Zealanders were upset to see their hard-won gains lost so quickly

'Trophy weapons', including a Maxim machine gun and a trench mortar, captured from the Turks in August. Note the graves in the background.

after their replacement by the British units. Daniel Laurenson wrote: 'to our utter disgust it was only about two hours before the Turks had taken the positions from them. It was simply disgusting and the poor tired out colonials were called on to make a new defensive position. My word our fellows felt it very much.'[20] This criticism is understandable but unfair. Had the New Zealanders still been on Chunuk Bair on the morning of 10 August, they would have put up a better fight, but they still would have been wiped out.

On 6 August the NZMR Brigade, including the Maori Contingent and the OMR, was 1900 strong. The arrival of 500 reinforcements during the battle brought their strength up to 2400. In six days they lost 151 men killed, 485 wounded and 53 missing.[21] The New Zealand Infantry Brigade suffered 1714 casualties and the Australians nearly 3500. Almost all the dead had to be left where they fell. Eighteen thousand of the 50,000 men committed to the fight by Hamilton were killed or wounded in five days. Most Western accounts state that the Turks lost up to 20,000 men in the same period, but several historians with access to Turkish records have concluded that Turkish casualties were no more than 3500 to 4500.[22]

Those who were killed outright were lucky in one sense. 'Throughout the four days' fighting, the sufferings of the wounded at Anzac, and in a lesser degree at Suvla, had been almost indescribable.'[23] The harrowing experiences of the April landing should have resulted in better medical planning for the August offensives, but this did not happen. Thirty new hospital ships had been ordered, but the War Office could not meet the demand and only a few arrived. Medical planning was particularly weak for the breakout to the north of Anzac. The difficulty of getting stretcher cases down the steep ridges and through the twisting deres to the dressing stations under shrapnel, machine gun and sniper fire meant that many wounded men died before they could be seen by the doctors. 'The sides of the gullies were lined with gravely wounded men, lying out in the blazing sun, choked by the dust of passing troops and mules, tortured by flies, and driven mad by thirst.'[24] Many wounded men got lost in the gullies and died there, unknown and alone. 'Up in these gullies of torment men died by the hundred – died of thirst, of awful bomb wounds and of exposure. … The Sazli Beit Dere and the Chailak Dere were crowded with walking cases; those who could not walk, waited in vain for stretcher-bearers, then born of desperation, crawled, crept, and rolled down the slopes into the gullies.'[25]

Even at the casualty clearing stations, the wounded were not safe. Rows of men lay out in the open, where enemy shells would occasionally explode among them, wounding or killing the already wounded.

There were not enough small boats to move casualties from the beaches to the hospital ships waiting offshore, and many of them died of neglect on the beaches. The few hospital ships were quickly full, and they sailed for Alexandria, Malta or Lemnos with insufficient medical staff. 'Many arrived at Alexandria and Malta with maggots crawling in the wounds that had never been touched since the field dressing carried by all soldiers had been hurriedly wrapped round them. It was not the result of neglect – unless the shortage of medical staffs was due to neglect.'[26]

Conditions on Lemnos were appalling, with many gravely wounded and sick men lying on bare ground. They were lucky if they had a blanket. The hospitals there, in Egypt and in Malta were all full by 13 August, and some casualties were sent all the way to Gibraltar or England. The hospital ships buried many men at sea, including Lieutenant Colonel Arthur Bauchop of the OMR. Benjamin Colbran watched him go over the side on 10 August. 'Twice a day we stop & bury 5 or 6. About 40 died in our 2¹/₂ day run to Alexandria. I saw our fine old colonel Bauchop go overboard.'[27]

The Sari Bair offensive was a failure. The MEF was no closer to the Narrows than it had been on 6 August. Godley's own analysis after the battle identified some of the problems:

To begin with, our objective was too ambitious. It was asking too much of the physically unfit troops to make the long night march and attack on Hill 971; it would have been better to have confined our effort to Chunuk Bair and Hill Q. Further, had I to make the attempt on Sari Bair again, I would … have given those troops which formed the covering force the main ridge as their objective. Had General Russell, who knew the ground better than anybody else, been given in addition to his own New Zealand Mounted Rifles, the Australian Light Horse, whose attack on the Nek met with such disaster, I have no doubt that he would have gained the ridge on the first night without difficulty. The New Zealand, 4th Australian, and Indian Brigades could then have relieved him, and established themselves on Chunuk Bair and Hill Q. The 13th Division, held in reserve, instead of being broken up, would have been available … for further reliefs or reinforcements.[28]

There was much more to it than that. At a time when bold leadership, aggression and a certain amount of risk-taking was required, key Allied commanders, including Godley, made bad decisions or no decisions at all. In open warfare, the soldiers' raw courage and determination were not enough. Their commanders needed to know where they were going and how to get there quickly. They also needed a sound grasp of tactics and an understanding of how to use ground to best advantage. Not many of the senior British and Anzac commanders on Gallipoli in August 1915 displayed these attributes.

If the offensive had been better planned and executed, the Turks could perhaps have been forced from their positions along the Second Ridge between Chunuk Bair and Lone Pine. However, this would probably not have led to their complete collapse on Gallipoli. Their strong reserves would have prepared another defensive line and waited for the attackers to come up against them there. On the Allied side there were not enough reserves available to exploit any success on the Sari Bair ridge. Ken Stevens recognised as much when he wrote of the view from Chunuk Bair. 'What did we see? Nothing but enemy trenches. I think it was lucky for us that the Turks did not let us get a mile or so further inland, because we could have never maintained an army in that rough country. It was bad enough as it was.'[29]

The capture and subsequent loss of Chunuk Bair remains one of the most controversial aspects of the Gallipoli campaign. Thousands of words have been written about how Malone sited his trenches, as if that made any real difference to the final outcome of the battle. The fact is that New Zealanders held those trenches against all comers for over 36 hours. Chunuk Bair was finally lost to a Turkish force so overwhelmingly strong that no defender had a chance of fighting it off, however well sited his trenches were.

The fight to hold Chunuk Bair on 8 and 9 August is one of the great achievements of New Zealand's mounted riflemen, yet their effort and their losses are largely unknown. Lieutenant Colonel Malone's leadership, and the destruction of his battalion, have taken the lion's share of the limelight. Their efforts are worthy of acclaim, but so are those of Lieutenant Colonel Meldrum, the Auckland and Wellington mounted riflemen and the Otago infantrymen. These men fought on Chunuk Bair for over 30 hours, repelling nearly continuous Turkish attacks.

Despite the undoubted heroism of the New Zealanders, they received very little recognition in the form of awards. Cyril Bassett's Victoria Cross was the only one awarded to a member of the NZEF. According to Major James O'Carroll, Brigadier General Russell would not recommend awards in his brigade. 'I spoke to the Brigadier about it, but as he says, everybody did well and lots were never seen.' Ken Stevens believed that 'General Godley was evidently so disgusted with the failure to capture Sari Bair ridge that twelve men who were recommended for the D.C.M. only received

The Chunuk Bair Memorial and statue of Mustafa Kemal.

Mentioned in Dispatches'. As far as Edwin McKay was concerned, 'it is hard to believe that only one New Zealander was outstandingly brave at a time when bravery was the normal routine'.[30]

Morale within the Anzac regiments and battalions was at an all-time low after the failure of the offensive on which so many hopes had rested. William East wrote: 'The ones left after that August fight were pretty dejected. They'd been in the fight for some time and it takes a long time to get over what they'd been through. Especially with the tucker we'd been getting. There was never enough food to build you up again. Just enough to survive on, that's all.' Contrast this with Hamilton's remarks: 'After all's said and done the troops at Helles and Anzac are still perfectly game'.[31]

Most of the forces who had taken part in the offensive on both sides were withdrawn and rested. The New Zealand Infantry Brigade never fought another serious battle on Gallipoli, but New Zealand's mounteds were not so lucky.

13

Anyone's mutton

*I felt as though I could scrape the smell of dead men out of my mouth
and throat and stomach in chunks.*

FRANCIS TWISLETON

*The magnificent brigade of New Zealand Mounted Rifles … had been worked
until it was almost entirely consumed.*

CHARLES BEAN

DESPITE THE FAILURE OF the Sari Bair offensive General Hamilton was not ready to give up. He brought two more British divisions ashore and ordered the British commander at Suvla Bay to use them to capture Kiretch Tepe and the inland ridges of Tekke and Kavak Tepe (see map on p. 108). Hamilton wanted to make the Suvla beachhead safer and, more optimistically, also usable as a platform for another attack towards the elusive Dardanelles. One hundred Anzacs were attached to the Suvla forces to help them deal with Turkish snipers. Jack Martyn was one of them, and he was unimpressed with what he found. 'These Territorials are more like a mob of sheep than fighting men and cannot act for themselves. The Turks have numbers of them terrified.'[1] Once again the Suvla Bay corps failed to deliver when it attacked on 12 and 15 August. Its commander, General Stopford, and other senior officers were sacked.

On 17 August Hamilton finally admitted failure. He asked the War Council to send him another 45,000 men to replace the losses in his existing force, and 50,000 more in new divisions. While this unwelcome request was being digested in London, Hamilton ordered another attack with more limited objectives. The veteran 29th Division was brought up from Cape Helles to capture Scimitar Hill and the 11th Division was ordered to capture W Hills and the plains to their south. The 2nd Mounted Division, brought across from Egypt without its horses, was held in reserve. In order to protect the right flank of this attack, to improve the boundary between the Suvla Bay and

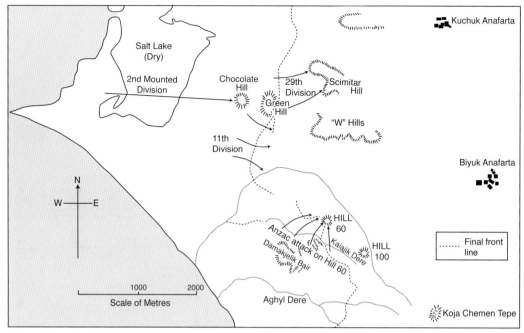

The Hill 60 plan of attack.

Anzac positions and to capture two wells, the Anzacs were ordered to capture Hill 60. In terms of the number of men committed, this offensive would be the largest fought on Gallipoli. It was scheduled to begin on Saturday 21 August.

Hill 60 is an unimpressive little knoll at the seaward end of a long and gently rising ridge. 'Except for a single stunted oak and a few mere bushes it was ... bare of trees but clothed in dense, prickly scrub with a few patches of grass or stubble.'[2] As usual, MEF planners knew little about the Turkish defences on the hill. 'No aeroplane photographs of the Hill 60 defences were available, and the sides and crest of that low flat-topped mound were so densely covered with scrub that the general lie of its trenches could not be properly seen from any part of the British line. But an idea persisted that the Turkish defences on the hill consisted of a girdle of trenches on its summit, and that the capture of this work would ensure the possession of the whole hill and a commanding view to the north. This belief was incorrect.'[3] After they occupied it at the end of the Sari Bair offensive, the Turks had turned Hill 60 into a strong redoubt with several interconnected rings of trenches. The redoubt was connected to depth positions and to Hill 100, further up the ridge, by communications trenches.

To get to Hill 60 from their front line on the Damakjelik Bair, the Anzacs had

Trenches at Hill 60.

to cross two low ridges and the Kaiajik Dere. The dere was overlooked by Turkish trenches along the ridge linking Hill 60 to Hill 100, and machine guns on Hill 100 were sited to fire straight down it. The communications trenches would need to be blocked to prevent enemy reinforcements from getting forward to Hill 60, and the Turks on Hill 100 and in the trenches between it and Hill 60 would need to be kept out of action if the assault on Hill 60 was to have any chance of succeeding.

Most of the Allied forces available for the attack on Hill 60 were either tired and sick veterans, or newly arrived troops with little training and less experience of battle. What remained of the New Zealand Mounted Rifles Brigade after the Sari Bair offensive was defending the foothills below Chunuk Bair. Closer to Hill 60 the front line was held by the 29th Indian and 4th Australian brigades under Brigadier General Cox, who was put in charge of the Hill 60 attack.

The headquarters and the two South Island regiments of the NZMR Brigade, each with a platoon of Maoris attached, were transferred to Cox's command on 20 August. The CMR and OMR had not seen action since the covering force battle on the night of

6 August. Although they did not fight on Chunuk Bair, they could still only field 400 sick and tired men between them. As Chris Pugsley notes, fitness 'was now measured in terms of a man's ability to stand and carry a rifle rather than fitness to fight'. Alan Holmes wrote 'today we are ordered for the front – it may be that I shall never return to the ones I love – please God may I do my duty to the last.'[4]

Cox decided to launch his attack on the afternoon of 21 August. Two Gurkha battalions and the Connaught Rangers were to capture the two wells to the north and west of Hill 60. Brigadier General Russell was made responsible for the capture of Hill 60. His 400 mounteds were to attack across the Kaiajik Dere to capture the hill, while 500 men from the 4th Australian Infantry Brigade were to attack the ridge joining it to Hill 100.

Cox intended to use the Anzac artillery to bombard Hill 60, Hill 100 and the ridge between them for 45 minutes. As the assault troops neared the hill, the guns would shift their fire on to targets behind the Turkish front lines. Unfortunately this fire plan was changed on the day of the attack, when it was decided to use the Anzac guns to help the British attack further north. After firing in support of the British attack, the guns would switch back to bombard the Hill 60 area for just 30 minutes. To give sufficient time for this reduced bombardment to have an effect, the start of the Hill 60 attack was delayed half an hour to 3.30 p.m.

Saturday 21 August was another hot and sunny day. In the mounted rifles brigade, 'Squadron and troop leaders spent the day observing the objective and the best lines of advance. They went back to their men, explained the position and made clear to everyone that the attack was to be by bayonet only, then bombs.'[5] As the assault troops moved into the trenches opposite Hill 60, they watched the artillery bombardment begin in the north. The British attack there started on time, but once again it failed. Little ground was captured and there were 5000 casualties.

The bombardment of Hill 60, when it began, did little damage to the enemy trenches. It did warn the Turks that an attack was coming. According to Francis Twisleton, the artillery 'gave it all to the Tommies we got none; not a shell and the trenches looked damnably sinister and silent'. The NZMR Brigade War Diary simply notes that there was 'very poor artillery preparation'.[6] As the minutes ticked by towards 3.30 the assault troops lay and waited and thought their private thoughts. Gordon Harper wrote: 'It is always rather a trying space waiting for the signal to jump out; and I could not help noticing Sergt. George Ferguson going round his men cracking jokes as we waited for the shells overhead to slacken, and allow us to advance. His body was the first we had to jump over as we left the parapet. His South African ribbons were still on his breast.'[7]

Promptly at 3.30 they went over the top. For the first time on Gallipoli, the mounted riflemen charged defended trenches in broad daylight without any covering fire 'across some very exposed ridges, in the face of exceptionally heavy machine gun and rifle fire, and in the later stages, high explosives and shrapnel', and they paid the inevitable price.[8] The CMR, led by Major George Hutton, was on the right of the mounteds' line. The OMR, commanded by Lieutenant Colonel Robert Grigor, was on the left. The two regiments had 700 metres and two minor ridges to cross before they reached the closest Turkish trenches on Hill 60. 'Down the slope went the Canterburys and Otagos,' Fred Waite wrote. 'Troop after troop dived into the hail of death and pushed on to the first ridge to collect their scattered fragments. Each troop made its fifty yard rushes and fell down exhausted. These men had lived for months on hard rations and were weakened by dysentery and fatigue. But on they swept again. It was a triumph of resolute minds over wasted bodies. Reaching the shelter of the gully, they reformed and commenced the steep ascent. Dozens of the troopers fell never to rise again.' In the words of the official history, 'It was simply a case of get there, and during the last part of this rush most of the casualties occurred'.[9]

As he neared Hill 60 Francis Twisleton saw that the enemy trenches ahead of him 'were evidently full of Turks with plenty of machine guns. Men of course began to fall on the parapet of the trench as soon as it was mounted. ... The roar of the rifle fire and machine gun fire was terrific; I could not make my voice heard. All orders had to be by signs. ... There was

Francis Twisleton holding his damaged pistol at Hill 60 on 21 August.

A dead Turk on the lip of a trench at Hill 60.

no hesitation on the men's part; as soon as I gave the signal forward, they dashed from cover and straight on though bullets simply rained down on us, and the men were going down fast, most damnably fast. ... At the foot of the last ridge before we tackled the stubble paddock, we struck a sunk creek, which gave wounded men shelter and allowed us to reorganise. In ten minutes out of our strength of 160 men we had lost about 90.'[10] Twisleton was wounded when his pistol was hit by a Turkish bullet. He dug several small pieces of metal out of his left hand and leg with a pocket knife, and carried on to Hill 60.

The survivors reached the forward enemy trenches on the edge of Hill 60 and leapt straight into them. They bayoneted any Turks they caught, threw bombs at those who fled and chased them down several communications trenches. 'The Turks in the trench were killed, and a machine gun was captured and immediately turned upon the Turks by the two Harper brothers of the Machine Gun Section.' An immediate Turkish counter-attack was beaten off, and 'the troopers stuck like limpets to their hardly-won position'.[11] They waved red flags to indicate the limits of their success.

The other assault troops were unable to keep up with the New Zealanders. On the left the Gurkhas lost momentum after most of their British officers were shot, although they did capture one well. The Connaught Rangers charged enthusiastically onto the lower slopes of Hill 60, where they were stopped by heavy Turkish fire from the summit of the hill. They fell back to the westernmost line of trenches. The Australians on the right had a much harder time of it. As soon as they showed themselves, Turkish machine gunners and riflemen from Hill 60 right along the ridge to Hill 100 opened fire on them. None of these enemy positions had been disrupted by artillery fire, and there was no covering fire from Anzac machine guns to keep the heads of the Turks down during the assault. As a result few of the Australians made it across the Kaiajik Dere alive. Some of their wounded men, lying helpless and under fire in the dere, were burnt to death when an artillery explosion started a fierce blaze. The Australians dug in for the night where they were.

At dusk the New Zealanders reported: 'Have captured about 120 yards enemy trench and one enemy machine-gun, which we are using against Turks, but cannot push on. Men exhausted'.[12] The mounteds were holding a tiny foothold on the lower slopes of Hill 60, but they were cut off from friendly forces to either side and from reinforcements. From 7 p.m. they were under increasing pressure from Turkish bomb attacks. The men spent the night digging communications trenches to link their positions to the old front line back on Damakjelik Bair. Many of them were only wearing shorts and shirts, so they had a cold and sleepless night. According to Twisleton, they were told to expect no relief for 36 hours.[13] The open ground behind them was strewn with bodies. It was starting to look like Chunuk Bair all over again.

About 11 p.m. several hundred Turks approached the New Zealanders perched on the edge of Hill 60, apparently wanting to surrender. As they came nearer, it was obvious that they were fully armed with rifles and grenades. Eleven of them got into the Canterbury trenches and were promptly taken prisoner. Some Otago mounteds climbed out of their trenches and tried to convince other Turks to give up their weapons and come quietly. 'The few New Zealanders were hopelessly outnumbered, but still they tried to indicate by signs and pantomimic gestures that the Turks must first lay down their arms.[14] Some of the Turks leant down and shook hands with New Zealanders in their trenches, and one particularly large Turk tried to pull Lieutenant Colonel Grigor out of his trench. Grigor broke free and ordered his men to fire on the Turks. A few of them were killed, and the rest ran back into the cover of the scrub. Grigor apparently walked all the way to the Turkish trench line to convince the Turks there to surrender. A Turkish officer tried to pull him in to the trench, but Grigor was having none of this, and walked back to his own lines unscathed.[15]

Twisleton did not think that these Turks had any intention of surrendering. 'Now a Turk knows how to surrender... no arms, and hands up. ... It suddenly dawned on me they expected us to surrender. I was suspicious that they meant to bomb the trenches, then charge, when we should have been in a queer position. I kept my eyes glued on the Turks and as soon as I saw some of them drop on one knee and heard their rifle bolts rattle, I gave the order to fire. ... It was the best five rounds rapid I have ever heard, only a few seconds and not a Turk was left standing.'[16] Major Herbert Hurst, who had taken command of the Canterburys when Major Hutton was shot, had a slightly different theory. He heard a bugle call, after which 'two or three enemy ground scouts appeared creeping through the scrub. I passed the order along not to shoot, but that the Turks should be allowed to come up to the parapet and pulled in. This was successfully done, and a few minutes later the main body of the enemy appeared, apparently deceived by the fact that no fire was opened on their scouts, who had evidently clambered into our trenches. I think they took this to mean that either our trenches were vacated or that we wished to surrender, and so came close up.'[17]

Soon after this strange incident New Zealand machine gun fire set fire to the clothing of a dead Turk. The flames spread to the brush, and the blaze threatened to force the New Zealanders out of their trenches. Trooper Andrew Barr jumped out of the trench to put the flames out with a shovel. 'Every Turkish rifle in the vicinity opened on him standing there in the light of the fire. Barr calmly worked on, extinguished the flames, and then jumped back into the trench.'[18]

By the end of the day, 'Very heavy casualties had been suffered; and all that had been gained, apart from the capture of the wells, was a precarious foothold on the slopes of Hill 60'.[19] When Russell came up and inspected the position that night he realised that fresh troops were needed if the rest of Hill 60 was to be captured before daylight. Godley reluctantly released the newly arrived and inexperienced 18th Battalion of the 5th Australian Infantry Brigade for the job. No clear attack objectives or orders were given, and no time was allowed for reconnaissance. Their 'desperate' assault was late in starting, and ended up taking place in broad daylight on 22 August. Although the battalion did not even know it was to attack until the last minute, it did so 'bravely, with little notion of what it was to do.' At first the Australians extended the New Zealanders' gain, but 'it was gradually driven back on them after losing half

Wellington mounted riflemen in the Chailak Dere on their way to Hill 60 for the second attack.

its men killed or wounded'.[20] The Australians did capture part of a trench. When they were aggressively counter-attacked at 9 a.m., the raw troops were forced to give ground and retreat. A few survivors of this Australian battalion moved to their right along the captured trench, linking up with the New Zealanders. Nothing more could be done and further attacks were called off.

The mounted riflemen and a few Connaught Rangers and Australians held about 200 metres of trench on the southern and western edges of Hill 60, well below the summit. Some of the trenches were held only partially, and sandbag walls were built across them to keep the Turks on the far side at bay. The Canterbury and Otago regiments were relieved by the Wellington and Auckland mounted rifles regiments on the night of Monday 23 August. The South Island regiments, which went into the fight for Hill 60 with 400 men, marched out with only 191 unwounded men between them. In all, out of the 4000 men who had attacked around Hill 60 on 21 and 22 August, 1300 were killed or wounded.[21] Of the several hundred mounted rifles

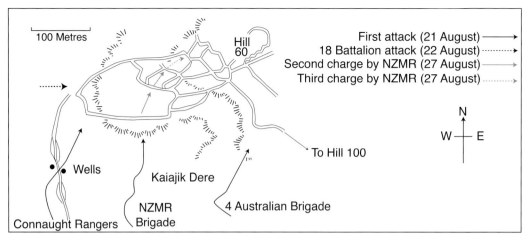

Hill 60, 21–29 August.

reinforcements who arrived on Gallipoli just before the relief, most went straight into the trenches.

General Birdwood was not satisfied. Despite the fact that the Turks were furiously improving its defences, he still wanted the top of Hill 60 captured. He ordered a fresh assault for Friday 27 August. In order to gather the 1000 fit men he needed, he called on no fewer than nine battalions and regiments to contribute. 'It was the last forlorn hope, probably the most forlorn of all.'[22] The 'entire' NZMR Brigade was included in the new attack because some of its men knew the trench layout on Hill 60. A hundred and fifty men in the Canterbury and Auckland regiments formed the first line of the centre assault force, with the same number of men from the Otago and Wellington regiments in the second line. These 300 men represented the entire fighting strength of the NZMR Brigade, and almost all of them were sick or lightly wounded.[23] Major James Whyte, the second in command of the WMR, led the assault force.

The mounteds were to be flanked on their left by 250 Connaught Rangers, and on the right by 350 Australians. Brigadier General Russell wanted to attack at night, but he was overruled. Instead he was promised a heavy, hour-long artillery bombardment to precede his attack, which was to be launched at 5 p.m. 'The gunners promised 500 H.E. shells over the space of 500 yards square.'[24]

General Godley gave the mounteds a pep talk before the attack, as Claude Pocock recorded. 'General Godley addressed us all. Complimented us upon what we had done & asked us to finish the job tomorrow, which will be done.' John Wilder was not as impressed. 'He was full of praise and soft soap, but it did not go down too well.'

Henry 'Bruiser' Taylor, killed on 27 August.

By now the New Zealand mounted riflemen were almost at the end of their endurance, as William East noted. 'The men lined up for the attack were all fairly disgruntled and dejected. They'd just about had it. We were only told that we were attacking the Turk trenches ahead and we would be given the signal to charge. Not what the attack was for, or anything else.'[25]

As he waited to go over the top, James Rudd was approached by Jack Bindon, 'a young chap [who] was as white as a sheet. Jack said "I'm going to be killed this afternoon". I said "A lot of us will be killed". ... With final checking of guns and ammunition completed, I can still remember the feeling as we looked at our watches and saw the time creeping nearer to five o'clock. The whistle went and out hopped the first line of men and they fell like ninepins, then the second row went out and my friend Jack Bindon's premonition was fulfilled.'[26] William East also took part in this charge. 'So we lay there waiting with our bayonets fixed. When the word came, our major, Major Bruiser Taylor, was right in front of me as he jumped to his feet. He had a sword he wasn't supposed to have – because of swords drawing Turk fire – and he blew his whistle and pulled his sword out and shouted "Charge!" That's all he said. The next thing he was flat on his face, shot through the head. I didn't know whether to go back or forward and I decided to go forward and all the rest were coming with me across an open piece of ground. We were just anyone's mutton.'[27]

Although the artillery bombardment seemed fairly effective, the attackers soon realised that the trenches opposite them were still packed with live and very alert Turks. Once again the enemy machine guns on Hill 100 were not knocked out by the artillery, and they had a clear line of fire into the Australians. Nothing was done to suppress the enemy artillery. Francis Twisleton wrote: 'As soon as our men mounted the parapet of the trench, the Turkish guns, which had been silent, opened out with a lot of beautifully placed shrapnel that was deadly in its effects'.[28]

Fred Waite described what happened. 'At 5 p.m. our men jumped out to advance and were immediately under a terribly hot fire from machine guns and rifles. But they never wavered, and with men falling everywhere they continued in one long straight line, magnificent in their courage, on into the first trench where they disappeared for 10 or 15 minutes, amongst a nest of live Turks. Finishing these off, without more hesitation, they rose again and advanced under the same withering fire, fewer in numbers, but dauntless in determination, only to meet a new foe in the enemy's shrapnel. The casualties were fearful. But still they pressed on to the second trench, then the third. Men were falling more quickly now. ... The little pink flanking flags were gradually moving forward as the artillery exploded their shells just in front of them.' As the official CMR history would explain, 'It seemed no distance to go, probably sixty yards, but every yard of ground was swept by enemy shrapnel and high explosives. Casualties were fearful, but the line reached the first trench and disappeared into it. It seemed minutes, but was probably some seconds only, before they reappeared. A short rush and they were over the second trench and into the third on the top of the hill. But mortal man could go no further. In each trench there remained many Turks in spite of the heavy bombardment from the Anzac guns. These were now killed and their bodies, together with those who had been slain by the bombardment, literally filled the trenches.'[29]

As the Canterbury and Auckland men dealt with the Turks in the first trench, the Wellington and Otago mounteds leapt over them and ran on for the next line of trenches about 40 metres away. When they reached it, they found it 'to be almost choked with Turks who had been killed in the bombardment'.[30] As the mounteds fought their way towards the top of the hill, they ran into increasingly heavy fire from an unsuspected maze of enemy positions. These were manned by fresh Turkish reinforcements who were coming forward along the uninterrupted communications trenches. Many enemy trenches remained to be cleared, so the reserve line of inexperienced Australian infantrymen was sent forward to finish the job. They made little headway and soon afterwards strong Turkish reinforcements began attacking the newly captured trenches. The brunt of this counter-attack fell upon the New Zealand mounted riflemen. According to General Hamilton, the fighting 'was almost entirely hand-to-hand and of a very severe nature'.[31] To the New Zealanders' left, British troops retreated, leaving the mounteds dangerously exposed. James Watson and other New Zealanders 'were very bitter against the English troops. Had they come at once we would not have lost so many men.' The Australians to the right again made little progress and lost many men, mostly to machine gun fire from Hill 100. The Canterbury regiment began this attack with 119 officers and men. A day later there were just 18 of them left.[32]

When night fell machine guns were hurried forward to the captured trenches, which were deepened and cleared of corpses – according to the CMR historian the enemy dead lay two or three deep – and more sandbag barriers were hastily erected to keep the Turks at a safe distance. All night, bombs flew between the opposing trenches. At last the New Zealanders were well supplied with this essential weapon, of which 'it is reported that five thousand three hundred were used on this hill during this night'.[33] Russell sent 100 men of the 9th Australian Light Horse Regiment into the assault at 9 p.m. in an attempt to capture some trenches to the left of those held by the mounteds. They achieved little and lost many men.

Early the next morning 56-year-old Chaplain William Grant of the WMR was killed when he went along a trench to help a wounded man lying among the scattered bodies. Just before he died, he was heard to remark to another clergyman with him, 'We are now most assuredly in the Valley of the Shadow of Death'. He was 'bayoneted instantly before [the Turks] recognised his Red Cross armband, but his comrade was spared. The Turks hoisted a white flag at once, and sent the padre's companion back with their apologies for their mistake in the heat of battle, then returned his body.'[34] Francis Twisleton wrote that Grant 'had no business there at all [but] it was a fine way for a soldier priest to die'. Grant's death was keenly felt. 'He was one of the finest men I have met,' one trooper wrote. 'Though well on in years, he was always in the thick of it, and where the fighting was hottest, there you would find him. At all hours of the day and night he would carry water and biscuits up into the trenches, and would always cheer the men up with: 'Fight on, boys, you can beat them. God is with you.' Every man would have laid down his life for the Padre.'[35]

Chaplain William Grant, killed on 28 August.

Father Patrick Dore, the Roman Catholic padre of the brigade, was also shot at Hill 60. He would have perished where he fell, but the Aucklanders insisted on evacuating him. He died in New Zealand while undergoing surgery.

The pressure eased off a little after dawn on 28 August. 'By daylight the enemy had expended his strength, and his attacks throughout the day were not so violent.' Instead the New Zealanders were heavily shelled by Turkish artillery all day. 'Their

Trooper Walter Cobb with a captured Turkish machine gun at Hill 60.

gunners knew the range to a yard, for these were his own captured trenches he was shelling. There seemed to be no escaping these terrible guns; man after man, group after group, was destroyed, but the survivors held stubbornly on.' Francis Twisleton wrote: 'The concussion caused by high explosive shells ... knocked out quite a number as well as robbing some of speech and hearing'.[36]

The mounteds spent the day clearing the trenches of the piles of dead Turks and strengthening their defences. Twisleton took command of a party of Australians and taught them how to throw bombs. 'I put them in parties of three, one to throw, one to light them, and one to act as a sentry.' In the same letter Twisleton wrote: 'In many places the parapet and parados of my trench was built up of dead men, Turks of course; the stench was appalling and got into my stomach. I had been unable to eat since the first trench was taken and I felt as though I could scrape the smell of dead men out of my mouth and throat and stomach in chunks.'[37]

AMR survivors of Hill 60.

At 2 p.m. officers from the 10th Australian Light Horse Regiment arrived to have a look at the position in preparation for another attack that night. Two hundred light horsemen from this regiment captured a new section of trenches, which they defended against vigorous enemy counter-attacks for the rest of the night. A hundred and sixty of them died or were wounded in the process.[38] Russell told his father: 'I'm working like a steam engine getting men killed ... I've eaten up three brigades here in the course of the day's fighting for an abominable little hill'.[39]

On 29 August the operation was finally called off. After handing over the position to a British brigade, most of the New Zealanders left Hill 60 on 3 September and moved to Cheshire Ridge, 'a fairly quiet place. The Turks had no inclination to attack, nor has the [CMR] Regiment the strength, though they annoyed each other with an intermittent rifle fire, but that was all. Although literally crawling with vermin, Cheshire Ridge was a haven of rest after Hill 60.'[40]

'So ended eight continuous days and nights of the hardest and most exhausting fighting the Mounted Brigade was engaged in during the whole war.' Much of Hill 60 was in Allied hands, but the Turks still held the vital ground on top of the hill. Birdwood thought it had been captured in its entirety, describing it as a 'big tactical scoop'.[41]

The New Zealanders captured 'Three machine guns and 46 prisoners ... three trench mortars, 300 Turkish rifles, 60,000 rounds of small arm ammunition, and 500 bombs'. According to James Watson, 'We gained about 400 acres in four days fighting. 1000 men killed and wounded. Land is very dear [expensive] here.'[42]

At least 236 New Zealand mounted riflemen lost their lives in the fighting for the 'abominable little hill' between 21 and 30 August 1915. As Bean wrote, 'The magnificent brigade of New Zealand Mounted Rifles … had been worked until it was almost entirely consumed'.[43] Even after absorbing 200 reinforcements, the regimental strengths on 29 August are pathetic. Officially, the AMR had 140 men, the WMR 128, the CMR 37 and the OMR 60 men on that day,[44] but the true situation was even worse.

Edward Brittan, killed on 28 August.

Henry Brittan, killed on 28 August.

When Godley visited the South Island regiments 'they told me they only had about eight or ten men who were really fit for duty in the trenches; this out of an establishment of 544.' Some squadrons almost disappeared entirely. Of the 33 men in the 2nd squadron of the WMR committed to the attack, only four emerged unscathed.[45]

Two Christchurch brothers, Edward (aged 24) and Henry Brittan (aged 27) were killed on 28 August. The Watson family of Dunedin also lost two sons at Hill 60: David Watson was killed on 27 August, five days after his brother Robert. Trooper Frank Clark, the great-uncle of New Zealand's Prime Minister Helen Clark, was killed at Hill 60 on 28 August.[46]

According to the NZMR Brigade's war diary, 1149 men became casualties between 5 August and 1 September 1915. Almost 40 per cent of them were killed or died of wounds. Percy Doherty wrote: 'We are a sorry broken-up looking crowd now, and it is hard to think of our mates who have gone'. Men looked for their missing friends for days, as Claude Pocock recorded. 'We who are left are looking for those who are missing, but except for those who have been sent down wounded cannot find any trace. … Still no more come in & no news, our Reg[iment] is cut to pieces … our

The CWGC Hill 60 Cemetery and Memorial. This stands on the ground fought over on 27–29 August.

faces wear a gloomy expression at the loss of our chums who have given their lives to get this hill. But I am proud to be one of them. … Those who watched the charge say it surpassed all. … Still no more men found. It is now nearly sure that they are away wounded or laying out on the hill side. We are but a handful left & all done up.'[47]

Men wounded at Hill 60 did not suffer as badly as those on Chunuk Bair. '[The stretcher bearers] followed every attack, and though it was nearly always impossible to remove the wounded, yet they bandaged them and marked the place where they lay. By night they searched the ground over which the troops had advanced in case any wounded had been missed. The call for "stretcher bearers" never found them wanting.'[48]

During 1915 public subscription in New Zealand paid for the outfitting of two hospital ships. His Majesty's New Zealand Ship *Maheno* left New Zealand on 11 July 1915 and arrived off Anzac on 26 August, just before the second Hill 60 battle. 'Many

Bones of dead Anzacs and Turks at Hill 60, photographed in 1918.

of the wounded ... were fortunate enough to be taken aboard our own hospital ship ...With what joy did the soldiers welcome the clean sheets, the hot baths, the thousand and one comforts and the sight of real New Zealand girls. After the hand-to-hand struggle at Hill 60, to lie at rest on the "Maheno" and watch the nurses was like creeping quietly into heaven.' The two operating theatres aboard the ship worked non-stop from the evening of 27 August until the morning of 29 August. The ship then sailed for Mudros with 445 patients.[49]

Insult was added to injury after Hill 60 when very few gallantry awards were made to the mounteds. 'General Russell has refused to recommend any individuals for rewards as he says every man is worth a V.C. and it is sufficient honour to belong to the brigade.' The regiments had lost most of their junior officers, but 'although repeated recommendations of N.C.O.'s were made for commissioned rank [General Godley] would not allow any promotions to commissioned rank as there were reinforcement officers on the way to the firing line from New Zealand'.[50]

The Hill 60 attacks were poorly planned and inadequately resourced. Although the objective was quite limited, it was beyond the capacity of the weakened troops. The Turks were able to reinforce Hill 60 at will throughout the battle and no diversions distracted them. Artillery was unable to damage the Turkish trenches. Historian R. R.

James has summed it up: 'For connoisseurs of military futility, valour, incompetence and determination, the attacks on Hill 60 are in a class of their own'.[51]

According to the official British war history, 'The bitter fighting on Hill 60, still regarded by the Australians and New Zealanders as perhaps their sternest trial on Gallipoli, had added the last straw. None of the units engaged had ever been so depleted as at the moment when the action began, and the men had only been able to carry on by sheer force of will … but the prolonged strain at Anzac – the fighting, the heat, the constant debilitating sickness – had made too prodigal a call upon their store of nervous energy, and at the end of August the Anzac Corps was temporarily incapable of further offensive effort.'[52]

14

So long Johnnie …

General Godley … hoped we would soon all recuperate
in strength so as to be fit to take our place on the Peninsula again. I will refrain
from writing what the boys think of him.

PERCY DOHERTY

Thank God we're leaving that bloody death-trap for ever!

UNKNOWN

IN EARLY SEPTEMBER 1915 the weekly evacuation rate of sick Anzacs from Gallipoli was
25 times higher than that of a similar-sized force on the Western Front.[1] 'The troops,
weakened by continual hardships and malnutrition, were an easy prey to dysentery
and similar ailments. The dressing stations were also kept busy by men troubled with
septic sores. Scratched by the prickly scrub, or with a meat or jam tin, the wounds
were healed with great difficulty, which was not surprising, as the men were not
strong enough to throw off or resist even the most trifling ailment.'[2] Worried doctors
told General Hamilton that the Anzacs who had been on the peninsula for more
than a few months were worn out, malnourished and sick, and that their incidence
of abnormal heart rates, shortness of breath, skin sores and diarrhoea was too high.
These men could no longer be considered fit for duty: they should be withdrawn
from Gallipoli immediately for a prolonged period of rest and recuperation. General
Hamilton agreed that he needed to rest his exhausted Anzacs properly if they were to
be of any use to him for further attacks, which he was already planning for the spring
of 1916. Once the arrival of the 2nd Australian Infantry Division had made the risk
acceptable, Hamilton sent the New Zealand infantry and mounted rifles brigades, and
three Australian infantry brigades, to Lemnos Island for a long rest.

On Monday 13 September 900 weak and exhausted New Zealanders left Gallipoli
on the *Osmanieh*. A few hundred gunners, engineers, medics, signallers and machine

All that was left of the CMR on Lemnos, 13 September 1915. Lieutenant Colonel Stewart is in the foreground.

gunners, who could not be spared, stayed behind. The balance of the thousands of New Zealanders who had landed on Gallipoli since April were dead, missing or already evacuated among the tens of thousands of MEF sick and wounded.[3]

In September the NZMR Brigade was probably the weakest of the veteran brigades at Anzac. As Russell noted in a letter home, 'the brigade is reduced to vanishing point'.[4] After 50 machine gunners were left behind, only 249 mounted riflemen made the voyage to Lemnos. Most were reinforcements: each regiment now contained fewer than two dozen Main Body men. The Canterbury regiment was in the worst state of all. Out of 677 officers and men who had landed on Gallipoli since May, just 28 went to Lemnos. The rest were dead (125), missing (46), already in hospital (466) or remained behind on Gallipoli (12).[5] William Watson described the appearance of the Anzacs as they left. 'I never saw such exhausted looking men. … The thing that impresses me is the brightness of their eyes. Some are very very thin with jaundice and dysentery. Some are boys with baby faces and huge great unhealthy stomachs, with dreadful fat looking faces. They all have that dreadful whiteness.'[6]

When it reached Lemnos the New Zealand Mounted Rifles Brigade came ashore on a single barge. The men slowly made their way to Sarpi Camp, five kilometres away. Typically, the camp was not ready, and there were not enough tents. It began to rain and the men spent their first night standing up in a few large tents with water flowing

Sarpi Camp on Lemnos.

around their feet. Initially there was little fresh food available and the men had to eat bully beef and biscuits for several weeks. Some men in the hospitals had to lie on the stony ground as there were insufficient beds or stretchers.

Despite all these inexcusable failures, the men relished the peace and quiet on Lemnos. Twenty-five mounteds went straight to hospital, where one man died from heart failure. A hundred and eight others already in hospitals on Lemnos rejoined the brigade while it was there. Sixty-seven men were found to be medically unfit for further active service. General Russell sent them back to Egypt to look after the horses, freeing up fit men from there to come across to Gallipoli.[7]

'The A.M.R. Band had arrived, and at one of the first parades of the handful of survivors it played, "Where are the Boys of the Old Brigade".'[8] On 16 September a French admiral inspected the brigade. 'The four regiments were drawn up in two lines in the camp, while he rode through. The total Brigade state was 151, including brigade headquarters. The Admiral asked General Russell if this was all that remained of his regiment. He did not realise at first that he was inspecting the remnants of four regiments. When he did so he turned round, looked at the men in wonder, gravely saluted and rode off.'[9]

Light training began for the Anzac brigades on 18 September. It consisted of 15 minutes of physical training before breakfast and two hours of drill and marching before noon. The afternoons were free.

On 5 October 1090 mounted riflemen in the 6th Reinforcements arrived at Sarpi Camp.[10] They were eager to get across to Gallipoli, but the veterans smiled sadly at them and shook their heads, saying nothing. Were it not for the graves of their friends there, none of them had any wish to see the peninsula again. 'To honour the veterans it was the custom to parade them in a file by themselves in front of the reinforcements … Words can hardly describe the feelings which the sight of the short lines in front of each squadron produced. In front of one squadron would be four men; before another, seven, and so on.' Another observer found it tragic 'to see the thin line of tattered, emaciated veterans and to contrast them with the lines of fit, stalwart, properly uniformed fresh troops'.[11]

The reinforcements trained separately for the first week, as the veterans were still not strong enough to join them in serious training. Training began in earnest on 12 October. 'The N.Z. Mtd. Rifles …formed practically a new brigade, and was trained for six hours daily.' The training syllabus included rifle firing, trench digging, marching, trench fighting, bomb throwing and small tactical exercises. Some of the veterans were still so weak that their packs were stuffed with paper instead of clothing.[12]

Russell still wanted to commission experienced veterans from the ranks to replace the officers who had been killed or wounded in the Chunuk Bair and Hill 60 battles, but Godley insisted on using inexperienced reinforcement officers to fill the many gaps in the regiments. This angered the veterans, many of whom by now hated Godley.

Some thought they had done enough, and that they should be sent home to New Zealand for good. Godley dashed these hopes in his typically pompous way, as Percy Doherty recorded. 'General Godley … made a speech, soft soaping us as usual, and said that the fine work the Mounted Brigade had done on the Peninsula was equal to any of the finest deeds of the Empire, especially the work we did on Hill 60, where important positions were gained against heavy odds etc. etc. and he hoped we would soon all recuperate in strength so as to be fit to take our place on the Peninsula again. I will refrain from writing what the boys think of him.'[13]

There was little good food available on Lemnos unless the men bought it themselves. Local villagers sold eggs, beer and wine, brown bread, fruit, figs, tomatoes and herbs. The men could also buy tinned fish, tinned fruit and tinned sausages in navy canteens. Gift parcels from New Zealand and England arrived, containing pickles, strawberry jam (a welcome change from the detested apricot jam of the Gallipoli ration), condensed milk, sweets, shortbread, magazines and other rarities. 'A gift particularly touching was a large consignment of sweets packed in tins by … school children.' The hot baths at Thermos were another undreamt-of luxury, as were the Canadian nurses. 'With their wonderful ways, their delightful accents, and their cute little naval capes, the memory of those nurses working away in that hell-hole of Mudros should never be forgotten.'[14]

After nearly two months of peace and quiet on Lemnos, the New Zealanders and Australians prepared to return to Gallipoli in early November. By then the NZMR Brigade (including the OMR) was 1559 strong, still 1000 men below its full strength.[15]

While the Anzacs rested and slowly regained their strength on Lemnos, the future of the Gallipoli campaign was being debated in London. General Hamilton's request for 95,000 reinforcements was refused. When he heard this news, he replied that he would have to give up either Suvla Bay or Anzac within a fortnight. On hearing soon afterwards that he would receive about 20,000 reinforcements, he amended this alarming prediction and told London that this would be enough to hold his present positions through the coming winter, but not enough to force the campaign to a victorious conclusion before then. By now, Hamilton's masters in London were losing confidence in his judgement, and anything he said was treated with suspicion. By now, some of his own headquarters staff and subordinate commanders were plotting to have him removed from command of the MEF.

The Turks on Gallipoli settled down for a quiet winter and began making plans for 'a violent and extensive attack to take place between Ari Burnu and Suvla. New reinforcements were assembled and experienced divisions removed from the line to train in practice trenches dug well away from the front. Berlin sent out special technical units to assist with these preparations. … Von Sanders hoped preparations would be finalised by late January.'[16]

New trenches appeared all over the high ground, concrete bunkers were built and dense barbed wire entanglements were put up everywhere. Some trenches in critical areas such as Chunuk Bair and The Nek were widened and filled in with barbed wire, creating impassable barriers. The Turkish commanders were looking forward to the winter. 'When the rains begin, unpleasant as they will be in our trenches and saps, they will be far worse for the British. For they will be stuck in the marshes and

Storm damage to Watson Pier, October 1915.

swamps on the low ground, and the rain and the floods pouring down the ravines that descend from our lines will swamp them.'[17]

In London, pressure began to mount for the abandonment of the Gallipoli campaign. Aside from the MEF's continuing lack of success and heavy casualties, there was growing concern about two new factors: the approaching winter and the effect of the likely fall of Serbia.

The MEF on Gallipoli was completely dependent on the sea; rough waters along the exposed west coast of the peninsula would prevent the landing of reinforcements and supplies, and the evacuation of casualties. Whenever the wind blew from offshore, the beaches were vulnerable. As if to emphasise this point, the first winter storm struck Gallipoli on 8 October, followed by others on 27 and 31 October. Each time, heavy seas damaged piers and smashed boats all along the beach. These were clear warnings of what was to come. Birdwood urged his men to quickly finish their winter preparations. Plans were prepared for large quantities of water, food and ammunition to be stockpiled on the peninsula. Extra hospitals were planned to look after casualties who would not be able to be evacuated.

On 6 September Bulgaria joined the Central Powers. As part of the sweetener,

Germany and Austria-Hungary agreed to help Bulgaria invade Serbia. When this became known to the Allies, a desperate plan was drawn up to help Serbia, in part because its loss would put the entire length of the Berlin–Constantinople railway under enemy control. This would allow more German and Austrian troops, artillery and ammunition to be sent to Turkey. The Allies knew that the MEF would be blasted off Gallipoli if heavy guns and large-calibre high explosive shells became available to the Turks in significant numbers. Accordingly, less than a month after he had asked for nearly 100,000 reinforcements, two of Hamilton's existing divisions on Gallipoli were taken from him and sent to the Greek port of Salonika. They achieved nothing there, and by 5 November the invading Central Powers had captured enough of Serbia to gain control of the last part of the Berlin–Constantinople railway.

Now there were only two realistic options for Gallipoli: either reinforce the MEF with enough men and ammunition for Hamilton to force a quick victory before winter storms and enemy artillery made life impossible, or give up and evacuate Gallipoli. On 11 October the Dardanelles Committee (the executive sub-committee of the War Council) asked Hamilton what he thought about evacuating Gallipoli. He replied that it was 'unthinkable' and that it would result in the loss of up to 45 per cent of his men and most of his artillery and stores. Unfortunately for Hamilton, his credibility had just been called into question again, this time by the Australian journalist Keith Murdoch, who had visited Anzac on his way to England. Murdoch told anyone in London who would listen that the Gallipoli campaign had been bungled from the start, and that the peninsula should be abandoned immediately. Plenty of influential people did listen to Murdoch, and to many others who loudly criticised the conduct of the campaign. It all came to a head in the middle of October, when Hamilton was relieved from command and 'recalled' to England. He never held another important command.

General Sir Charles Monro was appointed to the command of the MEF in Hamilton's place. When he reached Gallipoli on 28 October, Monro was dismayed by what he saw and heard. Taking account of the continued weakness of the men, the lack of artillery ammunition, the likelihood of an imminent increase in Turkish artillery power, the poor prospects of success against the strengthened Turkish defences and the closeness of winter, he recommended to London that the peninsula be evacuated at once. He warned Kitchener to be prepared to lose 40,000 men in the process.

This was not what Kitchener wanted to hear, so he went to see for himself. When he arrived on 12 November, just after the Australian and New Zealand brigades had returned from Lemnos, he was as appalled as Monro had been. 'The local conditions to which the Gallipoli army had long since grown accustomed – the open beach, the crazy piers, the landing of stores by hand from bumping lighters, the strings of kicking mules, the heavy dust, the cramped spaces, the jostling crowds on the narrow beach within range of the enemy's guns – filled him with blank amazement. Arriving later at Anzac Cove, where conditions were still more difficult, his wonder only grew.'[18]

The returning men of the NZMR Brigade disembarked at North Beach at dusk on Wednesday 10 November to find the beachhead transformed. 'The only likeness of the Anzac as the old hands knew it was the noise of rifle fire and bursting bombs.' The front lines on both sides were far stronger than they had been when the mounteds left in September. Everyone was working hard to erect winter quarters, to improve their protection against enemy artillery and to build up reserve stocks of supplies. Light railways ran along the beach and there were new roads and tents everywhere. 'Long terraces were dug on the hillsides and roofed over with iron, and inside these shelters short tunnels were bored into the hills, to be used when the bivouac area was shelled.'[19] The NZMR Brigade was sent to Waterfall Gully – 'where the waterfall was, no-one seemed to know' – on Bauchop's Hill, where the men dug winter quarters for two weeks. Because of the numbers of new reinforcements in its ranks, the brigade was treated as a new unit while the many inexperienced officers and men were introduced to trench life under supervision. According to Jim McMillan, 'The biggest job on hand was a vast tunnelling project at No.2 Outpost, to accommodate the Divisional Headquarters'.[20]

Fighting was now a low priority. 'Both sides were content to sit still and watch each other and neither appeared willing to launch an attack'; 'The men have lost their old keenness for sniping and observing. They lie about the trenches taking little of their old interest in the business of fighting'; 'With an increased readiness to live and let live above ground, the opposing forces dug deeply underground, defensively for dugouts and communications tunnels, offensively for mining activity'.[21] This 'live and let live' attitude meant that battle casualties in November and December were a fraction of those in earlier months: 105 New Zealanders died and 125 were wounded in those last six weeks.[22]

In late November the NZMR Brigade took over a section of the front line extending from Warwick Castle, inland from Bauchop's Hill, across the Aghyl and Kaiajik deres to Hill 60. At nearly two kilometres, the line was too long to be manned along its entire length, so the regiments established a series of outposts. The trenches between the posts were patrolled and listening posts and patrols were sent out in front of the firing line at night. In each regiment of about 300 men, a third was manning outposts with a similar number in support and the remainder resting. 'The sector was quiet, and very little sniping had been indulged in prior to our arrival. This fact was very evident, as on the first morning a Jacko went for a stroll over his front parapet, much to the amazement of our fellows, who promptly shot him down. After this, the Turks were not so casual.'[23]

At the same time as the Anzacs returned to Gallipoli, the first trainloads of Austrian heavy howitzers and German high explosive ammunition reached Turkey along the reopened Berlin–Constantinople railway. The guns and ammunition were immediately sent on to Gallipoli.

Kitchener finished his inspection of Anzac, Cape Helles and Suvla Bay on 14 November. He concluded that, without reinforcements, Gallipoli could be held through the winter against the Turks alone, but not if large numbers of German or Austrian troops, guns and ammunition arrived. To survive such a threat, the MEF would need substantial reinforcements and supplies but these were not available. Even if they were, Kitchener no longer saw any prospect of final victory at Gallipoli. He reluctantly decided that the evacuation of Suvla Bay and Anzac was the only sensible solution. This recommendation was telegraphed to London on 22 November. At the same time, Kitchener told Birdwood to start secretly planning an evacuation.

As if to underline the sense of this recommendation, winter storms struck Gallipoli with a vengeance five days later. Heavy rain, hail and extremely cold winds during the day were followed by snow that night. Overnight temperatures dropped to −5°C and 'Next morning the troops awoke to find everything white with snow'. For many Australians and Indians, this was their first experience of snow. 'The troops will long remember the small hours of November 28 as they were rudely awakened by the tarpaulin roofs of their never-too-elaborate dug-outs collapsing on top of them with the weight of snow.'[24] Soaking wet men on both sides huddled in the open around blazing fires, ignoring each other for a few hours. This informal armistice was brief; later that day some New Zealand machine gunners spotted large numbers of Turks in the open in a particular area. It seemed that the snowfall had caught them unawares, providing a white backdrop against which they were easily seen. Many of them paid for this error with their lives.

The mounted riflemen were caught out in this storm as they took over British trenches in Australia Valley:

Snow at Anzac Cove, 28 November 1915.

A fierce storm (bitterly cold wind and rain) was raging when the time arrived at 3 a.m. for the Regiment to move out to effect the relief, and we plodded along in the slush and mud carrying everything movable we could conveniently handle to reach our objective, which was accomplished about an hour before dawn, but we had to wait for daylight to take over the necessary posts. During the period of waiting, snow began to fall and continued throughout the relief, and also the next day and night. The Relief was completed about 9 o'clock, and the 'Tommies' moved out to the beach in the snow. Here they remained all day as transport was unavailable and many of the poor little chaps made their way back to our line for shelter during the night. Sad to relate quite a number perished from exposure in the open gully running up from the sea, and were found by our fellows the next morning. The trenches and bivvies taken over were in a deplorable condition … The place was a sea of mud.[25]

A bitterly cold northerly wind lashed the peninsula for two days, freezing the wet ground. Icicles hung from the trenches, and damp bedding froze. Jack Martyn wrote: 'As this day wore on it became terribly cold, and every man went into the trenches after dark. It was an awful night. It started snowing at midnight and a razor like wind cut the sentries faces.' As the CMR historian recorded, 'Every effort was made to keep the men in the trenches warm. Hot tea and coffee were sent up to them at night and rum when they came off duty in the morning.' Fred Waite reported that 'The most popular place after the blizzard broke out was the ordnance stores, as everyone was in want of extra clothing – and, thank goodness, it was available. It was amusing to see sentries on duty after their experience of the first night. It would have needed a very energetic bullet to penetrate the amount of clothing worn! This is a fair sample: – Hat, balaclava cap, (two if procurable) waterproof cape, greatcoat, tunic, cardigan jacket, shirt, two singlets, two pair of underpants, trousers, puttees, two pair of sox, straw or paper around the feet, and a pair of trench boots!'[26]

The men at Anzac suffered less from the cold than the men at Suvla Bay, where several hundred died from exposure or drowned in flooded trenches and dugouts. (Many Turks also perished or were injured.) There were 4211 frostbite cases among the 15,800 Allied troops evacuated from Gallipoli after the storm.[27] The doctors now had to deal with rheumatism, frostbite and colds, but the incidence of jaundice, dysentery and diarrhoea declined as the flies died off in the cold.

Edward Chaytor. He took command of the NZMR Brigade in December 1915.

On 29 November Australian infantrymen at Lone Pine were on the receiving end of the new Turkish heavy artillery. Trenches were blown in and dugouts collapsed. The men were battered and dazed, and 264 of them were killed or wounded. It was another grim warning for the MEF. Some Turkish prisoners cheerfully told their Anzac captors 'that a large number of heavy guns were being placed in position to blow us into the Mediterranean, which was understood to be very cold in winter'.[28]

General Monro witnessed both the storm and the bombardment. On 1 December he urged the War Committee in London to make up its mind quickly. Monro then left Gallipoli, after handing over command of the forces there to

Birdwood. Godley took over the command of the ANZAC, and Russell replaced him in command of the NZ&A Division. Lieutenant Colonel Meldrum stepped up as acting commander of the NZMR Brigade until its new commander, Colonel Edward Chaytor, arrived.

Chaytor was a professional officer who had served during most of the Gallipoli campaign as a senior staff officer on Godley's HQ. He had served with distinction in the South African War. Seriously wounded on Gallipoli, he had only just returned to duty. In October Godley had written that Chaytor was 'a most valuable officer and commander, and as the senior New Zealand officer, there is no question but that he should have the first Brigadier's appointment that falls vacant'. Not long afterwards Godley sent Chaytor to Egypt to assume command of the newly formed New Zealand Rifle Brigade. Then, when the command of the NZMR Brigade became available in December, Godley recalled Chaytor from Egypt and gave him this appointment instead.[29]

When the final decision to abandon the peninsula was made in London on 7 December, 5713 men and 12 artillery pieces had already left Anzac. Orders were immediately issued for the evacuation of Suvla Bay and Anzac as soon as possible; Cape Helles would be retained in the meantime. There were insufficient boats available to evacuate all three positions at once, and storm damage to piers at Cape Helles would take some weeks to repair. The northern evacuations had to be complete before the expected arrival of really bad winter weather in late December.

Evacuating a beachhead under the guns of an enemy on high ground is a very difficult military undertaking. 'Stated in its simplest terms, the problem involved in the evacuation of Gallipoli was the secret withdrawal and embarkation of an army of 134,000 men, 14,000 animals and nearly 400 guns. The enemy's trenches were in some places less than ten yards distant from the British positions; and the open beaches from which the troops must embark were within effective range of the Turkish artillery. The coast was believed to be watched by German submarines; it was the season of winter gales; and even a moderate sea would suffice to bring the embarkation to a standstill.'[30]

It was essential to fool the Turks into thinking that the MEF was staying put. False orders were issued for winter rest camps to be constructed on Lemnos Island, and this was publicly announced to the troops (and any listening spies) on 12 December. Attempts were also made to convince the Turks that reinforcements were landing. 'Parties of men were sent in the dark to the beach and marched back in daylight in full view of the Turks. Fires were lighted in those gullies used by reinforcements and kept burning daily until the end.'[31] 'Silent stunts' were begun to accustom the Turks to long periods of silence. The first of these was the longest, running for three days from 24 to 27 November. 'A mysterious order for forty-eight hours' silence was hailed with delight by the men. No work was to be attempted, not a shot was to be fired.'[32] Shorter silent stunts then became commonplace.

The real plan was treated with the utmost secrecy. If the Turks realised what was going on once the evacuation had begun, when the number of defenders was reduced, they would have a perfect opportunity to attack and overwhelm them. In order to preserve the great secret until the last possible moment, it was necessary to simultaneously thin out men right along the front lines at both Anzac and Suvla. 'The normal method, to fall back by stages to successive positions, was out of the question there, because the Turks in the centre, if once warned of what was happening, had only to thrust 300 yards in order to overlook the embarkation piers at North Beach. The only possible method was to deceive the enemy by holding all the front-line posts, however lightly, till the latest possible moment, and then to withdraw their garrisons in one final concerted movement.'[33] This made the plan much riskier and more complex.

The evacuation was to be accomplished in three steps. First, all non-essential men and supplies were sent away in early December. Then, on 13 and 14 December, one regiment or battalion in each brigade would be evacuated to Lemnos 'rest camps'. At Anzac that would leave a rearguard of about 20,000 men, who would be withdrawn on the nights of 19 and 20 December. This force had to be strong enough to stay on Gallipoli throughout the winter in case storms isolated them before they could be evacuated, but small enough to be able to be evacuated completely in just two nights. Brigadier General Russell was appointed to command the Anzac rearguard.

The men were kept in the dark about the evacuation, but of course they knew something was up. Percy Doherty, perhaps the NZEF's greatest rumour collector, wrote: 'All sorts of rumours are on the wing about no more reinforcements being sent to Gallipoli, the Colonial troops being withdrawn to do garrison duty for the winter, and finally one rumour says that the main body men are going to be sent back to N.Z. for a spell'.[34] The suspicious Anzacs watched as mildly sick men were evacuated at night instead of remaining in hospitals in the peninsula. During the day men were marched around purposefully, creating the impression that reinforcements were being landed. 'To the disgruntled troops taking part [who did not know it was a deception] ... it was just another foul-up.'[35] Surplus stores were given away, removed or destroyed, and the flow of new supplies ashore slowed to a trickle. 'Condensed milk that would have been invaluable earlier in the campaign was destroyed by punching holes in the tins with bayonets. Jar after jar of rum was smashed. Blankets by the thousand and piles of clothing were saturated with petrol ready to be burnt. Everything of value to the Turk was made valueless.'[36] Amazed men received butter, fruit and vegetables, cigarettes and canteen stores, sometimes for the first time in the campaign. Edwin McKay 'was handed half a dozen tins of condensed milk for my own use if I wanted them, and [I] could give none away as all my mates were similarly overloaded'. Fred Waite wrote: 'Parties visiting the beach found ordnance and supply officers astonishingly open handed. Tinned fish, condensed milk, different varieties of jam and other rarities could be had for the carrying away. Officers' coats, leather leggings, puttees, and many pairs of boots were appropriated. Men going back to the front line looked like itinerant hawkers.'[37]

On 12 December the evacuation plan was presented to the divisional commanders at Anzac. Russell's NZ&A Division in the north of the position would be evacuated from temporary piers on North Beach, while the two Australian divisions further south would leave from Anzac Cove. Timings were calculated to the minute, taking account of marching speeds and distances to travel from the trenches to the embarkation piers. Casualties incurred during the evacuation who could not be easily moved were to be left behind in dressing stations, and medical staff volunteered to stay behind to accompany them into captivity.

Although formal orders were not given to all ranks until 16 December, within 24 hours of their senior commanders being told everyone at Anzac knew about the evacuation. The reactions of the men varied. John Masterman was pleased. 'The Evacuation came as a surprise to all of us but we took it with glee as were anticipating a very bad winter.' An anonymous mounted rifleman wrote: 'Thank God we're leaving that bloody death-trap for ever!'[38]

More of the men were disappointed and angry. 'We hear that we are evacuating Anzac altogether & if so it hurts like the deuce & I can tell you I do not like it in the least,' wrote Walter Carruthers. 'My goodness, Mother, how it did go to our hearts,' wrote John Martyn, '– after all we had gone through – how we had slaved and fought – fought and slaved again – sizzled in the heat, tortured by flies and thirst and later

An almost deserted Anzac Cove on 17 December 1915.

nearly frozen to death. It was hard to be told we must give it up. But it was not our wasted energy and sweat that really grieved us. In our hearts it was to know that we were leaving our dead comrades behind. ... We thought too, of you people in New Zealand and what you might think of us. Believe me, it is far harder to screw one's courage up for running away than it is to screw it up for an attack!'[39]

As Charles Bean explained, 'The men hated to leave their dead mates at the mercy of the Turks. For days after the breaking of the news there were never absent from the cemeteries men by themselves, or in two and threes, erecting new crosses or tenderly "tidying-up" the grave of a friend. This was by far the deepest regret of the troops. "I hope," said one of them to Birdwood on the final day, pointing to a little cemetery, "I hope they won't hear us marching down the deres".'[40]

The AMR was the first of the mounted rifles regiments to go, leaving on 14 December for Lemnos. The final stage of the evacuation began four days later. Just before dusk on 18 December half of the remaining 20,000 Anzacs left their firing positions and lined up in the communication trenches. As darkness closed in they moved off down the Aghyl Dere and then south towards the embarkation piers along the carefully marked and controlled routes. They waited for a few minutes at the piers on North Beach until boats came inshore to pick them up. As they filed aboard, they dumped their new grenades into the sea. Most of the mounteds went to Lemnos with everyone else, but 182 Otago men sailed directly to Egypt.

By dawn on Sunday 19 December there were just 10,000 'die-hards', including 540 New Zealand mounted riflemen, left at Anzac. They were divided into A, B and C parties. The C Party, which would be the very last to leave, was to be made up of 'active gallant men'. Commanding officers were besieged with requests from men to be part of this group, even though it was very likely that they would not be able to escape.[41] Many veterans of the April and May landings felt it was their right to stay until last ('first in, last out') but most of them were too sick to be accepted. In the end, it was left to local commanders to determine who would be in the various parties.

The Turks still seemed to have no idea of what was happening in front of their eyes. The Anzac front-line trenches were now very thinly manned, and men scurried from firing step to firing step firing a few shots to simulate fully occupied trenches. Machine guns fired a few bursts before being moved to another position to fire another few dozen rounds. Men waved trench periscopes above the parapets, threw random shovelfuls of dirt into the air to indicate digging, and marched uphill with packs on their backs as if they were arriving reinforcements. Lanterns were left burning in empty bivouacs. Many of the medics who had volunteered to stay behind were evacuated as there were no new casualties for them to look after.

A feint attack in the afternoon at Cape Helles distracted the Turks for a few more hours, until dusk fell for the last time over the Anzac position. 'On that last day … Anzac seemed strangely desolate and empty, except at a few points visible to the Turks, where movement was specially maintained.'[42] Several times during that last day, the Turks fired shells into the deserted defences, causing the men of the rearguard to wonder if this was the start of an attack. It never was.

'The sun went down that evening on a wondrously peaceful scene. The peaks of Samothrace and Imbros were bathed in the glow of a glorious golden sunset. The sea was unruffled by the faintest breeze. Faint wisps of clouds floated lazily across the sky, fitfully obscuring the moon. As soon as it was dark men became very busy.'[43] At dusk the last guns were dragged down to the beach and embarked. The A Party of 4000 men (280 mounteds) left their trenches at 5.30 p.m., followed four hours later by the B Party of another 4000 men (160 mounteds). Half of the remaining doctors and medics were sent away with these parties, along with most of the machine guns. While these parties were embarking the 2000-strong C Party was cut off from the beaches by large barbed wire barriers in the deres and communication trenches. If the Turks attacked now, the C Party men were expected to fight and, if necessary, die where they were. If they could hold off the attacking Turks until 2 a.m. they were to conduct a fighting withdrawal down the ridges to the beach. Jack Rudd wrote 'Those of us chosen to leave behind were given a few hand grenades to put on our belts and told to stop the Turks from following us'. The A and B parties were afloat by 11.25 p.m. without incident, although Arthur Cox fell off Watson Pier into the sea after drinking a whole bottle of rum.[44]

Now only 2000 C Party men were left to defend the entire Anzac perimeter. Each of the mounted rifles regiments left 34 men, one machine gun and a few trench mortars. 'With a rifle and bayonet and a stock of hand grenades the men of the rearguards took up their positions in the front line. Machine guns were carefully looked to. Ammunition was plentiful. If the Turk did come over he would pay a big price. As one of the normal smells of Anzac was that of tobacco smoke, men smoked packet after packet, and pipe upon pipe.'[45]

Had the Turks attacked nothing could have saved these last few men. But they did not. They seemed to be too involved in digging and placing more barbed wire in front of their own positions. The 'die-hards' were too busy to reflect much on what might happen if the Turks rushed them. They ran around lighting candles in dugouts, firing rifles, trench mortars and machine guns, and generally making themselves look like a powerful army. Marksmen ran up and down the deserted trenches, firing from sniper positions. Twenty-four-year-old Sergeant Thomas Fawcett of the WMR was determined to get an enemy sniper before leaving. Colonel Davis 'told him to leave well alone at this stage, but he replied "I'll have one more go". The Turk fired first and shot Fawcett through the head ... he was probably the last man killed on Anzac.'[46] Some men left notes and signs for the Turks: 'Remember you didn't push us off, we simply went' and 'So long Johnnie, see you soon at the Suez Canal'. General Godley left a letter for the Turkish commander 'asking him to take special steps to preserve the graves of our men. I hope this will be effectual, and feel sure that it will, as they have behaved most honourably so far.'[47]

The last hours ticked slowly past without incident. The full moon lit up the nearly deserted trenches. Surely, thought some men, the Turks must notice something was amiss soon. At midnight some of the Wellingtons had a hurried meal of plum cake and brandy.[48] At 1.40 a.m. the first of the 100 C Party mounted riflemen buried their last trench mortar and filed quietly out of the trenches. They were followed at 10-minute intervals by the two remaining groups.

Barbed wire barriers were pulled across the communications trenches behind them, booby traps were armed and automatically firing rifles were set up. By 2.05 a.m. the trenches were completely empty. Behind the trenches the men unfixed their bayonets, unloaded their rifles and picked up their machine guns before walking down the Aghyl Dere to the coast. They covered the three kilometres to the embarkation piers on North Beach in eerie silence. The New Zealand infantry brigade and the Australians made their way to their own embarkation piers, and the last man was afloat by 4 a.m. One mounted rifleman was wounded slightly by a stray bullet through the lobe of his ear.[49] At 4.10 a.m. Anzac was officially abandoned. An hour later, so was Suvla Bay. Only the dead remained.

In some places the deserted trenches were within just a few metres of heavily manned enemy trenches, yet still the Turks suspected nothing; or, if they did, they did not test their suspicions. A few mines were detonated, followed by furious bursts of Turkish fire which spread right along the front line. Even after this the Turks were unsure of what was occurring. Finally, as dawn approached, a few suspicious Turks crept forward to occupy the craters left by the exploding mines on The Nek. They found in front of them empty enemy trenches. Word quickly spread, and a general attack was ordered for 6.40 a.m. This took place after a heavy shrapnel bombardment, and soon the Turks were swarming all over Anzac and Suvla Bay. They were disturbed in their victory celebrations by a last few naval shells fired at them from departing warships.

'Once on the warships the men were hurried below to a meal of hot cocoa, steaming pea soup, and every delicacy the ships' stores could offer.'[50] Most of the men were quiet and thoughtful as they steamed away from Gallipoli. 'At 4.30 a.m. we were heading for Lemnos, and we were a very silent crowd even then. All were busy with their thoughts and they were not all pleasant ones either, as it was hard to leave old Anzac where we had lost so many good friends and comrades.' For Jim McMillan, 'The only comfort to be derived was in the knowledge that the Turks had been so thoroughly hoodwinked and that there were no more names to be added to the long list of dead and wounded'. Jack Martyn found something to laugh at. 'The Turks were completely fooled and we laughed till we almost cried, to hear them blazing away at our empty trenches.'[51]

The last squadrons of the New Zealand Mounted Rifles Brigade reached Lemnos at 9 a.m. Two days later the mounteds sailed on His Majesty's Transport *Hororata* for

Alexandria, which they reached on 25 December. A day later they were back in their old lines at Zeitoun Camp in Cairo.

By 20 December 83,000 men, 4600 horses and mules, and 186 artillery pieces had been evacuated from Anzac and Suvla Bay, almost without a single casualty. On 8 and 9 January 1916, 35,000 men, 3600 animals, 128 guns and about 1500 tonnes of stores were withdrawn from Cape Helles, again almost without loss.

The evacuations succeeded against all expectations through excellent planning, good luck (the weather), and perhaps a little Turkish co-operation. 'Without good weather the best-laid plans would have been of no avail, and it was the season of winter gales. Yet from the moment the evacuation was ordered the sea remained as smooth as a village pond. Sixteen hours after the last boat left the shore a fierce gale sprang up, which, 24 hours earlier, must surely have led to disaster.' It is possible that some senior Turkish commanders knew that evacuations were likely in December.[52] If they did, they did nothing about it, and it seems most likely that the evacuations caught them by surprise.

Almost one million men fought over Gallipoli in 1915, and nearly half of them were killed or wounded there. Out of approximately half a million Turks, 68,000 died and 161,000 were sick or wounded.[53] Of the 489,000 British, Indian, French, Australian

All that was left of the 500 Main Body AMR men who landed on Gallipoli in May 1915, at Zeitoun in December.

and New Zealand soldiers sent to Gallipoli over the nine months of the campaign, more than half became casualties, including 46,000 who did not survive. Nearly one in four of those who died were Anzacs (2721 New Zealanders and 7594 Australians). Another 23,252 Anzacs were wounded.[54] Apart from the Turkish statistics, these totals do not include casualties resulting from non-fatal illness, which afflicted practically everyone who was there before the end of August.

The original New Zealand Mounted Rifles Brigade and the Otago Mounted Rifles Regiment were effectively destroyed on Gallipoli. Almost half of the 4000 mounted riflemen who served there between May and December lost their lives (727) or were wounded (1239). As almost all of these casualties occurred between May and the end of August, when 2920 mounted riflemen served on Gallipoli, the true casualty rate is two-thirds. The Auckland, Wellington and Canterbury regiments suffered equally, while the Otagos lost slightly fewer men.[55] The Commonwealth War Graves Commission (CWGC) database lists a total of 727 mounted riflemen who died between May 1915 and May 1916.[56] Those men who died after the evacuation in December 1915 almost certainly received their wounds or fell sick while on Gallipoli, hence their inclusion in the casualty totals.

Some histories state that around 476 mounted riflemen died on Gallipoli. This number appears to exclude the deaths in the Otago regiment (which was not formally part of the NZMR Brigade), and some of those who died after the evacuation. One hundred and sixty-two mounted riflemen are buried in named CWGC graves in Turkey, while 107 others lie in named graves on the islands of Lemnos and Malta, in Egypt, Gibraltar, England and in New Zealand. The remaining 458 mounted riflemen have no known graves and are commemorated on Gallipoli memorials. They were buried at sea, their graves on Gallipoli were lost or their bodies were never positively identified.

Troopers Jeffrey Harney, Ronald Gowland (both AMR) and Archie Morice (CMR) were the only mounted riflemen among the 25 New Zealanders taken prisoner by the Turks during the Gallipoli campaign. All of the New Zealanders were wounded when they were captured, and six of them died in Turkish captivity. Harney and Morice were repatriated at the end of the war, but 19-year-old Ronald Gowland died of disease soon after arriving in Istanbul.[57]

The destruction of the Wellington Mounted Rifles Regiment between May and December 1915 is illustrated in the following chart.

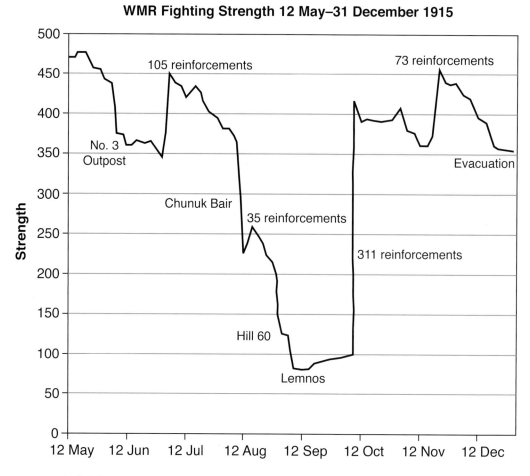

WMR Fighting Strength 12 May–31 December 1915

Decreases in fighting strength are due to men being killed, wounded or sick. Significant increases are due to the arrival of reinforcements, with lesser increases reflecting the return of men from hospital. Source: WMR War Diary, WA Series 42/1, Archives New Zealand.[58]

The WMR regiment landed on Gallipoli in May with 476 officers and men; during the campaign it absorbed 524 reinforcements; 360 Wellingtons were evacuated from Gallipoli in December. That means the regiment suffered 640 casualties in just over seven months (most of them in the first four months). The WMR is illustrated because its records are the most complete. The other three mounted regiments were much the same.

Dreadful as this toll is, it is important to recognise that four out of every five mounted riflemen who served on Gallipoli lived through the experience. Half of those survivors bore the scars of Gallipoli wounds for the rest of their lives. Many of them almost certainly had their lives shortened as a result of the wounds or sickness they suffered in 1915. The emotional and psychological damage caused by such terrible experiences is less easy to assess, but it is clear from the recollections of many veterans that Gallipoli was an experience that they would sooner forget, if they could.

The trenches of Gallipoli were certainly not what New Zealand's mounted riflemen had in mind when they joined up in August 1914. They went there willingly because there was a job to be done, and because they were needed. New Zealand's mounted riflemen did not consider themselves heroes, and they would be embarrassed to hear themselves described as such now. After the war Lieutenant Colonel Meldrum described them as 'wonderful fighters – but they were not great talkers and they didn't want any heroics about their work – what they did was part of [the] day's work to be got through and done well – but that was enough'.[59] Perhaps that should be their epitaph.

For the men of the New Zealand Mounted Rifles Brigade, the war had only just begun. Those Gallipoli veterans who were still fit enough to fight faced three more years of war against the Turks. The epilogue that follows this chapter summarises those years, but the full story must await another book.

Epilogue

On Boxing Day 1915, 1391 men of the New Zealand Mounted Rifles Brigade arrived back in Cairo, where they were reunited with their horses. Many others were still in hospital or convalescing in Egypt or England, and hundreds were already home in New Zealand, unfit for further service. Brigadier General Edward Chaytor, now in command of the NZMR Brigade, immediately began the task of rebuilding it. By New Year's Day 1916 the brigade was well over its authorised strength, on account of the many hundreds of reinforcements who had been held back in Egypt during the closing stages of the Gallipoli campaign.

In April 1916 most of the NZEF, in the form of the newly raised New Zealand Division, finally sailed for the Western Front. The Otago Mounted Rifles Regiment, reduced to a squadron, went with them. The NZMR Brigade remained behind in Egypt to help defend the Suez Canal against the Turks. Two thousand mounted riflemen, mostly reinforcements but including many Gallipoli veterans, were compulsorily drafted into the division that went to France. These transfers, combined with the losses from Gallipoli, meant that the brigade left in Egypt contained only a small proportion of original 1914 Main Body mounted riflemen. The riders had tasted defeat at the hands of the Turks on Gallipoli: they felt they had a score to settle.

The NZMR Brigade was one of four mounted brigades making up the new Australian and New Zealand Mounted Division (commonly known as the Anzac Mounted Division) in the Egyptian Expeditionary Force (EEF).[1] The commander of the EEF, General Sir Archibald Murray, was responsible for the defence of Egypt against the Turks, who were expected to follow up their success at Gallipoli with another invasion from Syria. Murray decided that the best place from which to defend Egypt was from the Syrian border, and this is what he set out to do in mid-1916. The mounted troops had made the most of the intervening months to learn the art of desert survival.

The Anzac Mounted Division led the way across the Sinai Peninsula in 1916, almost single-handedly defeating the Turks in three battles along the way.[2] The Battle of Romani on 4 August 1916 was the mounteds' first fight as a mounted brigade. The battle was won but a complete victory was denied through stubborn Turkish resistance

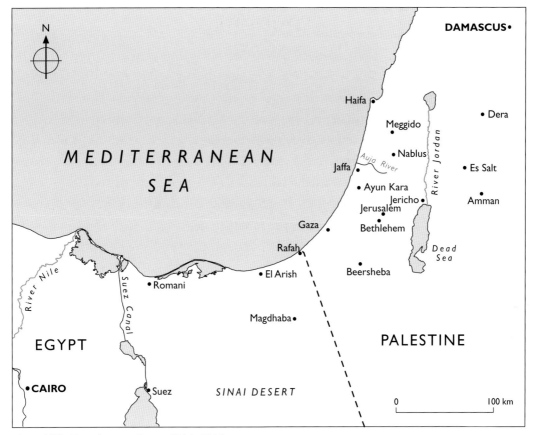

The Middle East theatre of war, 1916–1918.

and poor command decisions at critical times. In the finale at Bir el Abd, the Anzac Mounted Division was almost recklessly launched at a stronger-than-expected and very aggressive Turkish rearguard. The New Zealanders came close to being cut off and destroyed but escaped through the execution of a textbook fighting withdrawal, supported by covering fire from their horse artillery and machine guns.

By Christmas 1916 the EEF had advanced as far as the southern border of Syria (the province of Palestine). Near this border the NZMR Brigade played an important part in two small-scale battles at Magdhaba and Rafah that resulted in the capture of two Turkish infantry regiments. Rafah has been described as 'New Zealand's day'.[3] General Murray had abandoned the fight when the New Zealand mounteds made a final bayonet charge under intense enemy fire, covering 300 yards 'in two grand rushes' and captured a vital part of the enemy redoubt. An Australian light horse commander was reportedly heard to shout to his troopers to 'attack at once or those N.Z. b … s will take the lot!'[4]

In early 1917 the reinforced EEF invaded southern Palestine. At the first Battle of Gaza the New Zealand mounteds and the Australian light horsemen were close to capturing the town when General Murray ordered them back, fearing a Turkish counter-attack. Before they withdrew some enterprising Wellington troopers made good use of a captured German field gun to blast an enemy post in a house into submission, by sighting through the open breech. Not being experienced artillerymen, they were as dangerous to themselves as they were to the enemy. The first round ploughed up the ground in front of the muzzle, while the recoiling gun ran backwards over the amateur gun crew and tried to climb a tree.

In the reorganisation of the EEF that followed the failure of Murray's second attempt to take Gaza, Brigadier General Chaytor took over the Anzac Mounted Division, and the Commanding Officer of the WMR, William Meldrum, assumed command of the NZMR Brigade.

After these two false starts the Anzac mounted troops played a leading role in the eventual capture of Gaza and Beersheba, and in the pursuit of the defeated Turks across the coastal Plains of Philistine and up into the Judean Hills towards Jerusalem. In late October 1917 the New Zealanders captured the important redoubt of Tel el Saba near Beersheba, setting the scene for the 4th Australian Light Horse Brigade's now-famous charge into the town.

Two more stiff fights took place, at Ayun Kara, near Richon le Zion, and across the river Auja, near the modern city of Tel Aviv. The battle at Ayun Kara was the worst single day in the mounteds' war since Gallipoli: 44 men were killed and 141 more were wounded. The Auja fight, which took place 10 days later, was described by one officer as 'a very pretty little action'. As far as one veteran, Trooper O'Neill, was concerned, the greatest victory won at this time was the capture of the wine cellars at Jaffa 'which they held against all comers for over a week'.[5]

The Anzac Mounted Division moved down into the inhospitable Jordan Valley in early 1918. They captured Jericho and secured the western banks of the Jordan River. The New Zealand brigade then took part in two unsuccessful raids across the river against the Turks in the highlands around Amman and along the Hejaz Railway. The first raid in March 1918 was particularly costly: 44 New Zealanders were killed, 119 were wounded and 13 were missing.[6] In both raids the division was extracted from threatening situations by well-conducted fighting withdrawals and by the skill and tenacity of the troopers.

Finally, near the end of the First World War in the Middle East, the New Zealand

Canterbury mounted riflemen sitting on a Turkish shore battery gun at Gallipoli in December 1918.

Mounted Rifles Brigade crossed the Jordan River for the last time and played a major role in the capture of Amman and the entire Turkish 2nd Corps. With its armies in Egypt, Palestine and Syria soundly defeated, Turkey sued for peace at the end of October 1918. 'The Anzac Mounted Division here ended a very fine fighting record. It had taken a gallant part in practically every engagement since the E.E.F. had set out from the Canal two and a half years previously.'[7] In their hour of triumph, malaria and influenza swept through the ranks of the New Zealand brigade.

In December 1918 the Canterbury Mounted Rifles Regiment and the 7th Australian Light Horse Regiment returned to Gallipoli as temporary members of the occupation force. They spent several weeks there finding and tidying the graves of their fallen comrades, before rejoining the brigade in Egypt in late January 1919. Tragically, 11 Canterbury mounteds died of sickness while on Gallipoli.

The NZMR Brigade's return to New Zealand was delayed because of a lack of shipping, and most of the men of the brigade took part in the suppression of Egyptian riots in mid-1919 before finally returning home. At last, in July 1919, the men saw 'a wonderful sight on the starboard horizon, the Southern Cross. It made home seem so much nearer.'[8] The last mounted riflemen arrived back in New Zealand in August 1919.

From 1914 to 1919, 17,723 New Zealanders served in the ranks of the New Zealand Mounted Rifles Brigade. At least 1000 of them lost their lives, and 3000 others were wounded, some of them more than once. The survivors came home without their faithful mounts. During the war nearly 6000 horses were sent from New Zealand to serve with the NZMR Brigade. Three hundred and seventy were killed in action, out of a casualty total of 1402. Under New Zealand's strict quarantine regulations no horses could re-enter the country from the Middle East, so most of the surviving horses were passed on to British Army occupation forces. A few hundred New Zealand horses were sold to local Egyptians or shot. Only one horse with Middle East service, a mare named Bess, returned to New Zealand. 'So ended the career of the soldiers' best friends – the lovely horses. It was a sad parting for many of the lads who had had only the one horse throughout the campaign.'[9]

Notes

Introduction

1. Malthus, C., *Anzac: a Retrospect*, Whitcombe & Tombs, Christchurch, 1965, p.121.
2. Including the attached Otago regiment and the Maori Contingent.
3. The place names used in this book will be those that the Anzacs used in 1915. Similarly, the Anzacs always referred to their enemies as Turks, not Ottomans, and this book will follow that practice.
4. The true casualty rate is worse. Almost all these casualties took place before 1000 mounted rifles reinforcements joined the brigade in October. Thus, two thirds of the men on Gallipoli before this were killed or wounded.
5. Hamilton letter to Asquith dated 2 August 1915, PRO 30/57/63, The National Archives, London.
6. Pugsley, C., *The Anzac Experience: New Zealand, Australia and Empire in the First World War*, Reed Books, Auckland, 2004, p.147.
7. Harper, G., *The Spring Offensive: New Zealand and the Second Battle of the Somme*, HarperCollins, Wellington, 2003, p.14.

Prologue

1. Slater, Colonel H., 'Development of the New Zealand Mounted Rifles', *New Zealand Military Journal*, January 1912, p. 79.
2. The most notorious instance of such 'war crimes' took place in November 1868, when a detachment of Kai Iwi Cavalry rode down and killed six unarmed Maori children who were caught out gathering food for Titokowaru's nearby pa at Tauranga-Ika. Cowan, J., *The New Zealand Wars: a History of the Maori Campaigns and the Pioneering Period*, Volume 2, Government Printer, Wellington, 1922 (1983 reprint), p. 260, and Belich, J., *The New Zealand Wars and the Victorian Interpretation of Racial Conflict*, Penguin, Auckland, 1988, p. 274.
3. *New Zealand Volunteer Force Manual for Mounted Rifles 1895*, Government Printer, Wellington, 1900, p. 80.
4. Slater, p. 81.
5. *New Zealand Volunteer Force Manual for Mounted Rifles 1895*, p. 80. Picquets were security elements positioned between the parent force and an enemy, to provide early warning.
6. Crawford, J. & Ellis, E., *To Fight for the Empire: an Illustrated History of New Zealand and the South African War, 1899–1902*, Reed, Auckland, 1999, p. 66.
7. Crawford, J., 'The Best Mounted Troops in South Africa?', Crawford, J. and McGibbon, I. (eds), *One Flag, One Queen, One Tongue: New Zealand, the British Empire and the South African War 1899–1902*, Auckland University Press, Auckland, 2003, p.

73; McGibbon, I., *The Path to Gallipoli: Defending New Zealand 1840–1915*, GP Books, Wellington, 1991, p. 124.

8. McGibbon, *The Path to Gallipoli*, p. 155.

9. McGibbon, I., (ed.), *The Oxford Companion to New Zealand Military History*, Oxford University Press, Auckland, 2000, p. 235.

10. McGibbon, *The Oxford Companion to New Zealand Military History*, p. 236; McGibbon, *The Path to Gallipoli*, p. 134. Both these ideas came to nothing as the years passed, the likelihood of drawing on South African War veterans decreased and martial fervour waned.

11. In 1909 only 5000 members of the Volunteer Force completed any daylight field training. Godley, Major General A. J., 'The Making of the New Zealand Citizen Army', *The Army Review*, October 1913, p. 322.

12. Godley, Major General A. J., 'The New Zealand Mounted Rifles', *The Cavalry Journal*, Volume 8, 1913, p. 462.

13. McGibbon, *The Path to Gallipoli*, p. 136.

14. Godley, 'The Making of the New Zealand Citizen Army', pp. 319–20.

15. McGibbon, *The Path to Gallipoli*, p. 238.

16. Bauchop, Colonel A., 'The Mounted Man in New Zealand', *The Cavalry Journal*, Volume 3, January 1908, p. 59.

17. Godley, General Sir Alexander, *Life of an Irish Soldier*, John Murray, London, 1939, p. 137.

18. Godley, 'The Making of the New Zealand Citizen Army', p. 322.

19. Quoted in Pugsley, *On the Fringe of Hell: New Zealanders and Military Discipline in the First World War*, Hodder & Stoughton, Wellington, 1991, p. 12.

20. The importance of the far-flung countries of the British Empire as troop contributors should not be understated. In 1914 a quarter of the European population of the Empire lived in Canada, South Africa, Australia or New Zealand.

21. Godley, *Life of an Irish Soldier*, p. 151.

22. Godley, 'The New Zealand Mounted Rifles', p. 464.

23. Babington, Colonel J. M., 'The Mounted Men of New Zealand, Past & Present', *The Cavalry Journal*, Volume 2, July 1907, p. 285.

24. Bauchop, Colonel A., 'The Mounted Man in New Zealand', p. 56 ff.

25. 'Report by the Inspector-General of the Overseas Forces on the Military Forces of New Zealand dated 4 June, 1914', in Godley, Major General A. J., *Defence Forces of New Zealand: Report of the General Officer Commanding the Forces for the Period from 20th June 1913, to 25th June 1914*, Wellington, 1914, paragraphs 102–5.

26. New Zealand's response was to start to mobilise volunteers from the Territorial Force for Home Defence. All volunteers had to be prepared for overseas service if required. Army Department (AD) Series 1, Box 954, File 29/26, Archives New Zealand.

27. McGibbon, *The Path to Gallipoli*, p. 2.

Chapter 1 – War with Germany

1. New Zealand agreed, and added a divisional headquarters and an independent mounted rifles regiment (the Otago Mounted Rifles Regiment). London also accepted an Australian offer of 20,000 men. At the same time, the War Council asked New Zealand to send a force to capture German Samoa. This was successfully completed by the end of August.

2. Bean, C. E. W., *The Official History of Australia in the Great War of 1914–1918. Volume 1: The Story of Anzac: From the Outbreak of War to the End of the First Phase of the Gallipoli Campaign, May 4, 1915,* Angus & Robertson, Sydney, 1921, pp. 34–5.

3. Robertson, J., *Anzac and Empire: the Tragedy & Glory of Gallipoli,* Leo Cooper, London, 1990, p. 17.

4. *New Zealand Expeditionary Force (Europe) 1914 War Diary,* Government Printer, Wellington, 1915, p. 5.

5. The Otago regiment was intended to be part of the same British infantry division as the New Zealand Infantry Brigade. Its tasks would include patrolling, the provision of advance, rear and flank guards, and communications within the division, and between it and flanking forces. War Office, *Yeomanry & Mounted Rifle Training, Parts I and II,* His Majesty's Stationery Office, London, 1915 edition, p. 135.

6. Each regiment took another 53 men and 48 riding horses as its First Reinforcements.

7. Lightweight artillery guns firing a 13-pound (6-kilogram) projectile towed by teams of horses were needed to keep up with the brigade.

8. *NZEF War Diary,* Appendix 2.

9. Russell, Colonel A., letter dated 3 September 1914, in Gambrill, R. F. (compiler), 'The Russell Saga, Volume 3: World War 1', qMS 0822, Alexander Turnbull Library.

10. Godley letter to James Allen dated 16 December 1914, WA 252/1, Archives New Zealand.

11. Green, D., 'Mackesy, Charles Ernest Randolph 1861–1925', *Dictionary of New Zealand Biography,* updated 16 December 2003. URL: http://www.dnzdb.govt.nz/ and Nicol, Sergeant C. G, *The Story of Two Campaigns: Official War History of the Auckland Mounted Rifles Regiment, 1914–1919,* Wilson & Horton, Auckland, 1931, p. 4.

12. Grover, R., 'Meldrum, William 1865–1964', *Dictionary of New Zealand Biography,* updated 16 December 2003. URL: http://www.dnzdb.govt.nz/

13. Powles, Colonel C. G. (ed.), and Officers of the Regiment, *The History of the Canterbury Mounted Rifles 1914–1919,* Whitcombe & Tombs, Auckland, 1928, p. vii.

14. Stevens, K. M., *Maungatapere: A History and Reminiscence,* Whangarei Advocate, 1973, p. 83.

15. Peed, E. S., diary entry dated 22 September 1914, property of W. S. Peed and family, Taihape.

16. He sailed with the 2nd Reinforcements and joined his mates on Gallipoli. Andrews, T., *Kiwi Trooper: the Story of Queen Alexandra's Own,* Wanganui Chronicle, 1967, p. 102.

17. Pugsley, *Gallipoli: the New Zealand Story,* Hodder & Stoughton, Auckland, 1984, p. 54.

18. Nicol, p. 3.

19. *Ibid.*, p. 7.

20. Bauchop, Lieutenant Colonel A. 'The New Zealand Mounted Rifles', *The Cavalry Journal*, Volume 9, 1914, p. 95.

21. Only the Wellington Infantry Battalion wore the lemon-squeezer on Gallipoli. It was adopted by the NZEF in France in 1916.

22. They also wore the 1905 Pattern peaked forage cap or the Wolseley Pattern cork helmet on Gallipoli.

23. McMillan, J., 'Forty Thousand Horsemen: Being the Memoirs of 7/1322 Cpl Jim McMillan, Canterbury Mounted Rifles, First NZEF, on Service in Gallipoli and Palestine, WW1', unpublished manuscript, pp. 7–8.

24. Defence Council Report dated 14 October 1912, *Annual Reports on the Defence Forces of New Zealand*, Government Printer, Wellington, 1910–1922, p. 35.

25. A hand is 4 inches or 10 centimetres. A horse of 14.2 hands is 58 inches or 1.47 metres tall, measured at the shoulder. The ideal military horse was smaller than modern thoroughbred racehorses, which are usually over 16 hands tall. Robin, Colonel, memo to Minister of Defence dated 22 August 1914, quoted in Pugsley, *Gallipoli: the New Zealand Story*, pp. 47–8.

26. File 29/26, Mobilization, Mounted Rifles and Infantry Regiments, 1914, Archives New Zealand.

27. East, W., in Shadbolt, M., *Voices of Gallipoli*, Hodder & Stoughton, Auckland, 1988, p. 75.

28. File 40/76, Horses for NZEF, Box 1098, AD Series 1, Archives New Zealand.

29. Nicol, p. 6.

30. Powles, *The History of the Canterbury Mounted Rifles*, p. 2.

31. Nicol, pp. 6–7.

32. File dated 20 September 1914, in File 40/82, Saddlery, Box 1098, AD Series 1, Archives New Zealand.

33. File dated 20 September 1914, in File 40/96, Harness and Saddlery, Volume 1, Box 1095, AD Series 1, Archives New Zealand.

34. This equipment was probably for the NZMR Brigade. *NZEF War Diary*, p.8.

35. Russell letter dated 15 September 1914, 'The Russell Saga'.

36. Andrews, p. 103.

37. Mackenzie, C. N., *The Tale of a Trooper*, John Lane, London, 1921, pp. 12–13, 13–14.

38. Burton, O. E., *The Auckland Regiment: being an Account of the Doings on Active Service of the First, Second and Third Battalions of the Auckland Regiment*, Whitcombe & Tombs, Wellington, 1922, p. 3.

39. McKay, E. C. M., 'The Years Unfold: Memoirs', 1998.31, Kippenberger Military Archive, p. 54.

40. Wilkie, Major A.H., *Official War History of the Wellington Mounted Rifles Regiment, 1914–1919*, Whitcombe & Tombs, Auckland, 1924, p. 4.

41. Russell letter dated 15 September 1914, 'The Russell Saga'.

42. Nicol, p. 8.

43. Powles, *The History of the Canterbury Mounted Rifles*, p. 2; McMillan, p. 14.

44. Mackenzie, *Tale of a Trooper*, p.16. Clutha Mackenzie and some other Wellington men were sent south to Lyttelton, as they had been allocated to Canterbury ships for the journey to England.

45. *Ibid.*, pp. 14–15.

46. *Ibid.*, p. 17.

47. McGibbon, I., *Blue-Water Rationale: the Naval Defence of New Zealand 1914–1942*, Government Printer, Wellington, 1981, p. 24. In fact, most of the German squadron was near Tahiti and steaming away from New Zealand towards South America. However, the fast light cruiser *Emden* had been detached to operate in the Indian Ocean on a commerce-raiding mission, and it was well within range of the projected convoy route.

48. Bean, Volume 1, p. 93.

49. Carruthers, W. G., letter, undated, MS-Papers-1429, Alexander Turnbull Library.

50. Mackenzie, *Tale of a Trooper*, p. 17.

51. Mackenzie, *ibid.*

52. Russell letter dated 4 October 1914, 'The Russell Saga'.

53. Waite, Major F., *The New Zealanders at Gallipoli*, Whitcombe & Tombs, Auckland, 1919, p. 12.

54. Mackenzie, *Tale of a Trooper*, p. 18.

55. Doherty, P. G., diary entry dated 14 October 1914, 1989.943, Kippenberger Military Archive.

56. Mackenzie, *Tale of a Trooper*, p. 20.

57. Pyle, W. R., diary entry dated 16 October 1914, 1996.292, Kippenberger Military Archive; Doherty diary entry dated 14 October 1914; Grant, W., in Anonymous, *In Memoriam. Chaplain-Major William Grant: His Letters from the Front*, Herald Office, Gisborne, 1915, p. 8.

58. W. R. F., 'Retrospect', in *Amber & Black: The Journal of the Queen Alexandra's (Wellington West Coast) Mounted Rifles, New Zealand Military Forces*, Hawera, 1934–1938, p. 169; Doherty diary entry dated 16 October 1914.

59. By the end of the Gallipoli campaign, one man in every five who sailed with the NZEF in October 1914 was dead, another two had been wounded at least once, and most of the rest had suffered from debilitating sickness. By the time the war ended in 1918, fully one third of them were dead.

Chapter 2 – We might be a long time getting home

1. Mackenzie, *Tale of a Trooper*, pp. 21, 22–3.

2. Cunningham, W. H., Treadwell, C. A. L., and Hanna, J. S., *The Wellington Regiment N.Z.E.F. 1914–1919*, Ferguson & Osborn Ltd, Wellington, 1928, p. 6.

3. Baigent, E. J., undated diary entry in Townsend, C., *Gallipoli: From the Uttermost Ends of the Earth*, 2nd edition, Patricia Townsend, Paeroa, 2000, p. 5; Harper, letter dated 20 October 1914, in Harper, B. (ed.), *Letters from Gunner 7/516 and Gunner 7/517*, Anchor Communications Ltd, Wellington, 1978, p. 7.

4. Colbran, B. C., diary entry dated 6 November 1914, MS-Copy-Micro-0037, Alexander Turnbull Library.

5. Powles, *The History of the Canterbury Mounted Rifles*, p. 7; *NZEF War Diary*, Appendix 23.

6. *NZEF War Diary*, ibid.

7. Lynch, W. H., letter dated 20 October 1914, MS-Papers-4706, Alexander Turnbull Library.

8. Pocock, C., diary entry dated 6 November 1914, 1991.2136, Kippenberger Military Archive.

9. Mackenzie, *Tale of a Trooper*, p. 43; Lynch letter dated 23 September 1914; *In Memoriam. Chaplain-Major William Grant: His Letters from the Front*, p. 9.

10. 'History of the Otago Mounted Rifles (Independent Regiment)', WA 44/4, Archives New Zealand.

11. Doherty diary entry dated 29 October 1914; Baigent, undated diary entry in Townsend, p. 5.

12. 'History of the Otago Mounted Rifles'.

13. Mackenzie, *Tale of a Trooper*, p. 29. Note that Mackenzie wrote of himself in the third person as 'Mac'.

14. Cunningham *et al.*, p. 4; Bellis, C., 'The Role of the Horse in the Sinai and Palestine Campaign during the 1914–18 War', in Holden, D., *The New Zealand Horseman*, A. H. & A. W. Reed, Wellington, 1967, p. 52.

15. Mackenzie, *Tale of a Trooper*, p. 29.

16. Pyle diary entry dated 14 November 1914.

17. Nicol, p. 15.

18. Mackenzie, *Tale of a Trooper*, p. 36.

19. Hobson, F., diary entry dated 17 December 1914, MS 94/50, Auckland War Memorial Library.

20. Lynch letter dated 27 October 1914; Colbran diary entry dated 12 November 1914.

21. Pocock diary entries dated 19, 20 and 21 November 1914; Smith, L. E., diary entry dated 12 November, property of G. R. Smith and family, Wellington.

22. Cameron, A. E., diary entry dated 12 November 1914, MSX-2853, Alexander Turnbull Library; Pocock diary entry dated 22 November 1914.

23. McKay, *Memoirs*, p. 54; Pocock diary entry dated 25 November 1914.

24. Burton, p. 5; Ricketts, W., 'With Our Service Squadron in the Great War', *Amber & Black*, August 1935, p. 154; 'The Russell Saga'.

25. Mackenzie, *Tale of a Trooper*, p. 23.

26. Lynch letter dated 20 October 1914.

27. 'The Russell Saga'. The *Emden* was near Singapore, well within sailing range of the convoy, but unaware of its existence. The *Emden* sank or captured 23 merchant ships and sank two Allied warships during its brief wartime career.

28. The AIF consisted of the 1st Australian Division and the 1st Australian Light Horse Brigade, which was the Australian equivalent of the NZMR Brigade. In his autobiography, Godley states that the South African diversion was planned even before the convoy left New Zealand (Godley, *Life of an Irish Soldier*, p. 156). This

is unlikely, except perhaps as a contingency plan. Chris Pugsley notes that Major General Bridges, the AIF commander, wanted the New Zealanders to be sent to South Africa while his own division sailed on to England as planned. Pugsley, *The Anzac Experience*, p. 25. Bean, Volume 1, pp. 97–8.

29. *NZEF War Diary*, p.12. Two more Australian ships joined them from Fremantle in a few days.

30. Meldrum, Lieutenant Colonel W., 'Essay on the Handling of Mounted Rifles Independently and in Brigade', 14 November 1914, WA 42, Archives New Zealand; Godley letter to Allen dated 24 November 1914, WA 252/1, Archives New Zealand.

31. Peed diary entry dated 7 November 1914.

32. Stevens, p. 85; Powles, *The History of the Canterbury Mounted Rifles*, p. 7.

33. Godley letter to Allen dated 24 November 1914, WA 252/1, Archives New Zealand; Bean, Volume 1, p. 107.

34. Peed diary entry dated 8 November 1914; Nicol, p. 14.

35. Mackenzie, *Tale of a Trooper*, p. 30.

36. Pocock diary entry dated 11 November 1914.

37. *Ibid*.

38. Stevens, p. 85; Cameron diary entry dated 15 November 1914; Doherty diary entry dated 15 November 1914.

39. Mackenzie, *Tale of a Trooper*, p. 33; 'History of the Otago Mounted Rifles'; Stevens, p. 85.

40. Smith diary entry dated 15 November 1914; Fewster, K., *Gallipoli Correspondent: the Frontline Diary of C. E. W. Bean*, George Allen & Unwin, Sydney, 1983, p. 29; Pocock diary entry dated 18 November 1914.

41. Malthus, p. 19; Nicol, pp. 16–17.

42. Powles, *The History of the Canterbury Mounted Rifles*, p. 9.

43. Doherty diary entry dated 18 November 1914; Malthus, p. 18; Harper letter, dated 25 November 1914.

44. Maxwell, General Sir J., Introduction to Powles, Lieutenant Colonel C. G., *The New Zealanders in Sinai and Palestine*, Whitcombe & Tombs, Auckland, 1922, p. ix.

45. Bean, Volume 1, p. 111.

46. Peed diary entry dated 29 November 1914; Doherty diary entry dated 30 November 1914.

47. Doherty diary entry dated 1 December 1914; Powles, *The History of the Canterbury Mounted Rifles*, p. 9; Smith diary entry dated 1 December 1914.

48. Burton, p. 9.

49. Doherty diary entry dated 1 December 1914.

50. Doherty diary entry dated 29 November 1914; Stevens, p. 85; Cameron diary entry dated 1 December 1914.

51. Andrews, p. 104.

52. Peed diary entry dated 2 December 1914.

53. McGregor, D., letter dated 27 December 1914, 1998.331, Kippenberger Military Archive; Mackenzie, *Tale of a Trooper*, pp. 37–8.

54. *NZEF War Diary*, Appendix 35.

55. The stormy weather encountered by the Auckland ships in the Tasman Sea in September, in which 12 horses died in 24 hours, was fortunately never encountered again during the voyage. *NZEF War Diary*, p. 29.

56. Mackenzie, *Tale of a Trooper*, p. 39.

Chapter 3 – Egypt

1. The obvious weakness of his plan was that it placed 'the Empire's main line of communication as an obstacle in front of a fire trench,' but Maxwell had no choice. The Indian Army and British Territorial Army units that had already replaced the pre-war garrison in Egypt were not trained, equipped or acclimatised to fight in the arid deserts of Sinai.

2. Russell diary entry dated 3 December 1915, 'The Russell Saga'.

3. Nicol, p. 20.

4. Powles, *The History of the Canterbury Mounted Rifles*, p. 9; Mackenzie, *Tale of a Trooper*, pp. 42–3.

5. Nicol, p. 20; 'History of the Otago Mounted Rifles'.

6. Mackenzie, *Tale of a Trooper*, p. 44; Andrews, p. 105.

7. Thornton, G., *With the Anzacs in Cairo: the Tale of a Great Fight*, H. R. Allenson Ltd, London, 1916, pp. 15–16; Burton, p. 11.

8. The Australian infantry went to Mena next to the Giza pyramids, and the 1st Australian Light Horse Brigade went to Maadi, a little south of Cairo.

9. Powles, *The History of the Canterbury Mounted Rifles*, p. 10.

10. Pocock diary entry dated 4 December 1914.

11. Godley letter to Allen dated 7 December 1914, WA 252/1, Archives New Zealand; Waite, p. 33; Thornton, pp. 18–19.

12. Cameron diary entry dated 4 December 1914; Cunningham *et al.*, p. 15; Thornton, p. 20.

13. Mackenzie, *Tale of a Trooper*, p. 46; Pyle diary entry dated 4 December 1914.

14. Colbran diary entry dated 5 December 1914; Andrews, p. 105; Pocock diary entry dated 6 December 1914.

15. Pocock diary entry dated 14 December 1914; Lynch letter dated 16 December 1914.

16. Carbery, Lieutenant Colonel A. D., *The New Zealand Medical Service in the Great War 1914–1918*, Whitcombe & Tombs, Auckland, 1924, pp. 21–2.

17. McGregor letter dated 13 March 1915.

18. Thornton, pp. 22, 24, 21–2.

19. Doherty diary entry dated 11 December 1914.

20. *The Times History of the War*, Volume 13, p. 160; Godley letter to Allen dated 10 December 1914, WA 252/1, Archives New Zealand.

21. Powles, p. 10 and Andrews, p. 105; Thornton, p. 18.

22. Special Order dated 9 December 1914, WA 40/2, Archives New Zealand.

23. Cameron diary entry dated 18 March 1915; Lynch letter dated 16 December 1914.

24. Doherty diary entry dated 19 December 1914.

25. Colbran diary entry dated 10 March 1915; Lynch letter dated 27 April 1915.
26. Pocock diary entry dated 18 December 1914.
27. Pocock diary entry dated 5 December 1914; McKay memoirs, pp. 69–70.
28. 'History of the Otago Mounted Rifles'.
29. Lynch letter dated 18 March 1915.
30. Blackwell, F. and Douglas, D. R., *The Story of the 3rd Australian Light Horse Regiment*, NP, 1952, p. 15.
31. Pocock diary entry dated 16 January 1915.
32. Doherty diary entry dated 28 December 1914; Waite, p. 34.
33. Pocock diary entry dated 12 December 1914; Godley letter to Allen dated 16 December 1914, WA 252/1, Archives New Zealand; McKay memoirs, p. 70.
34. 'Anzac', *On the Anzac Trail: being Extracts from the Diary of a New Zealand sapper*, William Heinemann, London, 1916, pp. 50–1; Smith, N., *Men of Beersheba: A History of the 4th Light Horse Regiment 1914–1919*, Mostly Unsung Military Research & Publications, Melbourne, 1993, p. 44.
35. 'Anzac', p. 69.
36. Lynch letter dated 18 April 1915; McGregor letter dated 13 March 1915.
37. *The Times History of the War*, Volume 13, p. 160.
38. Buley, E. C., *Glorious Deeds of Australasians in the Great War*, Andrew Melrose Ltd, London, 1915, p. 48.
39. Tolerton, J., *Ettie: A life of Ettie Rout*, Penguin Books, Auckland, 1992, p. 123.
40. Waite, p. 38; Thornton, p. 29.
41. Waite, pp. 38, 40.
42. 'Anzac', p. 50.
43. Thornton, pp. 31, 32–3, 34.
44. *The Times History of the War*, Volume 13, p. 161; Burton, p. 13.
45. Andrews p. 107; Twisleton, F. M., undated letter, MS-Papers-1705, Alexander Turnbull Library.
46. Tolerton, p. 123.
47. Thornton, pp. 77, 67, 63, 61–2, 86–9.
48. Godley letter to Allen dated 10 December 1914, WA 252/1, Archives New Zealand.
49. Tolerton, pp. 124–5.
50. Pocock diary entry dated 19 December 1914; Colbran diary entries dated 4 and 7 December 1914.
51. Carruthers letter dated 6 January 1915; Pocock diary entry dated 25 March 1915; Bean, Volume 1, p. 129.
52. Lynch letter dated 16 December 1914.
53. Powles, *The History of the Canterbury Mounted Rifles*, pp. 20–1.
54. Cameron diary entry dated 2 April 1915.
55. Powles, *The History of the Canterbury Mounted Rifles*, p. 11; Thornton, p. 125.
56. Hobson diary entry dated 7 April 1915; 'Anzac', p. 70.
57. *NZEF War Diary*, p. 30; Pyle diary entry dated 20 December 1914.
58. Hill, A. J., *Chauvel of the Light Horse: A Biography of General Sir Harry Chauvel, G.C.M.G., K.C.B.*, Melbourne University Press, Melbourne, 1978, p. 66.

59. Doherty diary entry dated 23 December 1914; Harper, letter dated 4 January 1915, in Harper, *Letters from Gunner 7/516 and Gunner 7/517*, p. 12; Peed diary entry dated 1 January 1915.
60. Hobson diary entries dated 11, 15 December 1914.
61. 'Anzac', pp. 28–9.
62. Peed diary entry dated 5 January 1915. Captain James Bell and Trooper George Burlinson are buried in the Commonwealth War Graves Commission (CWGC) Cairo War Memorial Cemetery.
63. Buley, p. 49; Doherty diary entry dated 30 December 1914.
64. Carruthers letter dated 29 January 1915; Law, J., diary entry dated 1 January 1915, MS 90/20, Auckland War Memorial Library.

Chapter 4 – When will we fight?

1. *The Times History of the War*, Volume 13, pp. 158–9.
2. Pocock diary entry dated 8 December 1914.
3. Russell diary entry dated 14 December 1914, 'The Russell Saga'.
4. Bean, Volume 1, p. 139.
5. Bourne, p. 15; Doherty diary entry dated 28 December 1914.
6. Wilder, J. W., diary entry dated 9 April 1915, 1999.798, Kippenberger Military Archive.
7. Cameron diary entry dated 16 March 1915; Johns, W. H., letter dated 29 March 1915, MS 1392, Auckland War Memorial Library.
8. Doherty diary entry dated 14 December 1914.
9. Mackenzie, *Tale of a Trooper*, p. 53.
10. Doherty diary entry dated 25 February 1915.
11. Godley letter to Allen dated 10 January 1915, WA 252/1, Archives New Zealand.
12. Harper, letter dated 4 January 1915 in *Letters from Gunner 7/516 and Gunner 7/517*, p. 12.
13. McGregor letter dated 13 March 1915.
14. Mackenzie, *Tale of a Trooper*, pp. 77–8.
15. Doherty diary entry dated 13 January 1915.
16. Doherty diary entries dated 7, 11 January 1915.
17. Doherty diary entries dated 21, 12 January 1915.
18. Doherty diary entry dated 25 January 1915.
19. Doherty diary entry dated 5 February 1915; Pyle diary entry dated 25 January 1915.
20. Godley letter to Allen dated 28 January 1915, WA 252/1, Archives New Zealand.
21. Doherty diary entry dated 30 January 1915.
22. Johns letter dated 29 March 1915.
23. Powles, *The History of the Canterbury Mounted Rifles*, p. 19; 'Anzac', p. 35.
24. Mackenzie, *Tale of a Trooper*, p. 51; Doherty diary entry dated 1 February 1915.
25. Powles, *The History of the Canterbury Mounted Rifles*, p. 16.
26. Mackenzie, *Tale of a Trooper*, pp. 51–2.

27. Doherty diary entry dated 19 February 1915.

28. OMR War Diary entry dated 30 March 1915.

29. Allen letter to Godley dated 9 April 1915, WA 252/2, Archives New Zealand. The War Council declined the offer, asking instead for two more infantry battalions and an artillery battery.

30. 'Anzac', pp. 74, 106–07.

31. Charles Bean blamed New Zealanders for starting the riot. Fewster, p. 48.

32. 'Anzac', pp. 100–01; Pocock diary entry dated 3 April 1915, quoted in Pugsley, *On the Fringe of Hell: New Zealanders and Military Discipline in the First World War*, p. 32; 'Anzac', pp. 102–6; McMillan, pp. 292–3.

33. 'Anzac', pp. 102–6.

34. 'Anzac', *ibid.*; Andrews, p. 108; 'Anzac', pp. 102–6.

35. Burton, p. 20.

36. Bean, Volume 1, p. 218; Scott, D. C., diary entry dated 1 April 1915, in Townsend, p. 130; Pocock diary entry dated 3 April 1915, quoted in Pugsley, *On the Fringe of Hell*, p. 32; Godley to Robin dated 3 April 1915, quoted in Pugsley, *On the Fringe of Hell*, p. 31.

37. The New Zealand government was not consulted, in accordance with its agreement to leave decisions about the tactical disposition of the NZEF to the British authorities.

38. Chris Pugsley believes that this result was possible in March 1915. Pugsley, *The Anzac Experience*, p. 73.

39. Erickson, E. J., *Ordered to Die: A History of the Ottoman Army in the First World War*, Greenwood Press, London, 2001, pp. 78–9.

40. Hamilton had decades of operational command and staff experience behind him. A very intelligent man, he was known as a reformer in the British Army. He had studied amphibious warfare, and knew about its theoretical difficulties. He was also conscious of the effects of new weapons such as machine guns and heavy artillery. As Inspector General of Overseas Forces he had visited New Zealand to review the new Territorial Force.

41. Travers, T., 'Gallipoli: the Other Side of the Hill', in Cowley, R. (ed), *The Great War: Perspectives on the First World War*, Random House, New York, 2003, p. 182.

42. Aspinall-Oglander, Brigadier General C. F., *Military Operations: Gallipoli, Volume 2. May 1915 to the Evacuation*, Heinemann Ltd, London, 1932, p. 3.

43. Pugsley, *The Anzac Experience*, p. 78.

44. *NZEF War Diary*, p. 49.

45. Godley letter to Allen dated 2 April 1915, WA 252/2, Archives New Zealand; *NZEF War Diary*, 12 April 1915, p. 51.

46. Mackenzie, *Tale of a Trooper*, pp. 74, 77; Pocock diary entry dated 30 April 1915.

47. Doherty diary entries dated 7, 13 April 1915.

48. Pocock diary entries dated 25 March, 5 April 1915.

49. Doherty diary entry dated 21 April 1915.

50. Nicol, p. 27.

51. *NZEF War Diary*, 12 April 1915, p. 49; The OMR's Machine Gun Section went to

Gallipoli on 10 May, a squadron on 15 May, and the rest of the regiment on 20 May. The last squadrons did not actually land until 28 May.

52.   Mackenzie, *Tale of a Trooper*, pp. 75–6.
53.   Carruthers letter dated 25 April 1915.
54.   Hill, p. 50; Lynch letter dated 22 April 1915.
55.   Pugsley, *The Anzac Experience*, p. 88.
56.   Aspinall-Oglander, pp. 3–4.
57.   Nicol, p. 28; Carruthers letter dated 3 May 1915.
58.   Powles, *The History of the Canterbury Mounted Rifles*, p. 22.
59.   Bean, Volume 1, p. 599. Birdwood did not want them in their brigades, because he saw no use for the headquarters on the peninsula.
60.   Hill, p. 51.
61.   Hobson diary entry dated 5 May 1915; East, W. in Shadbolt, p. 75; Mackenzie, *Tale of a Trooper*, pp. 79–80.
62.   Pyle diary entry dated 17 May 1915; Hobson diary entry dated 7 May 1915.
63.   Andrews, p. 109.
64.   Nicol, p. 28.
65.   Mackenzie, *Tale of a Trooper*, p. 80.
66.   Doherty diary entry dated 7 May 1915.
67.   Wilkie, p. 14.
68.   Doherty diary entry dated 8 May 1915.
69.   Mackenzie, *Tale of a Trooper*, pp. 80–1.

Chapter 5 – At last, Gallipoli!

1.   Aspinall-Oglander, p. 14.
2.   Diary entry dated May 12, 1915, in Fenwick, Lieutenant Colonel Dr P. , *Gallipoli Diary 24 April to 27 June 1915*, David Ling Publishing/Auckland War Memorial Museum, ND, p. 31.
3.   Mackenzie, *Tale of a Trooper*, p. 84.
4.   Doherty diary entry dated 9 May 1915.
5.   Hobson diary entry dated 12 May 1915.
6.   'Peregrinations of a Trooper: VII – At Last', in Mackenzie, C.N. (ed.), *Chronicles of the N.Z.E.F., Volume 1,30 August 1916 to 14 February 1917*, NZ Contingent Association, London, 1917, p. 174.
7.   Andrews, p. 109.
8.   Powles, *The History of the Canterbury Mounted Rifles*, p. 25.
9.   Batchelor A. F., diary entry dated 12 May 1915, 1999.1088, Kippenberger Military Archive.
10.   Nicol, p. 32; Powles, *The History of the Canterbury Mounted Rifles*, p. 26.
11.   Mackenzie, *Tale of a Trooper*, pp. 89–90, 90–1.
12.   East, W., in Shadbolt, pp. 75–6.
13.   'Peregrinations of a Trooper: VIII – He Sets Foot in Europe', in *Chronicles of the N.Z.E.F.*, p. 199.

14. Harvey, J., letter dated 26 July 1915, in Harper, G. (ed.), *Letters from the Battlefield: New Zealand Soldiers Write Home 1914–18*, HarperCollins, Auckland, 2001, p. 41.
15. Waite, p. 134.
16. Nicol, p. 39.
17. Mackenzie, *Tale of a Trooper*, p. 91.
18. Nicol, p. 33.
19. Harper, letter dated 15 May 1915, in *Letters from Gunner 7/516 and Gunner 7/517*, pp. 17–18.
20. Stevens, p. 87; Mackenzie, *Tale of a Trooper*, p. 91.
21. Dawbin, W., diary entry dated 13 May 1915, Micro-MS-0004, Alexander Turnbull Library; Harper, G., letter dated 15 May 1915, in *Letters from Gunner 7/516 and Gunner 7/517*, p. 18; 'Peregrinations of a Trooper: IX – His First Week Ashore', *Chronicles of the N.Z.E.F.*, p. 246.
22. 'Peregrinations of a Trooper: IX – His First Week Ashore', *Chronicles of the N.Z.E.F.*, p. 246.
23. Wilkie, p. 17.
24. Harvey, J., letter dated 26 July 1915, in *Letters from the Battlefield*, p. 41; Wilkie, p. 18.
25. Waite, p. 136; Cameron diary entry dated 20 May 1915.
26. Smith diary entry dated 14 May 1915.
27. Stevens, pp. 139, 87.
28. Doherty diary entry dated 15 May 1915; Trooper William Hay is buried in the CWGC No. 2 Outpost Cemetery.
29. Quoted in Steel, N. and Hart, P., *Defeat at Gallipoli*, Papermac, London, 1995, p. 173; Hobson diary entry dated 14 May 1915; Fenwick diary entry dated 14 May 1915.
30. Twisleton letter; Doherty diary entry dated 20 May 1915.
31. Powles, *The History of the Canterbury Mounted Rifles*, p. 29.
32. Nicol, p. 36.
33. Bean, C. E. W., *The Official History of Australia in the War of 1914–1918, Volume 2, The Story of ANZAC from 4 May, 1915, to the Evacuation of the Gallipoli Peninsula*, Angus & Robertson, Sydney, 1924, p. 307.
34. Nicol, pp. 36, 35.
35. Catchpole, T., letter dated 23 May 1915, in Townsend, p. 165.
36. 'Peregrinations of a Trooper: IX – His First Week Ashore', *Chronicles of the N.Z.E.F.*, p. 247.
37. Stevens, p. 88; Mackenzie, *Tale of a Trooper*, p. 101; Doherty diary entry dated 19 May 1915. Captain Alfred Bluck and WO1 Joseph Marr are both buried in the CWGC Walker's Ridge Cemetery; Dawbin diary entry dated 17 May 1915. Trooper Alexander Bromley is buried in the CWGC Walker's Ridge Cemetery. Trooper William Dawbin died of wounds in England on 22 August 1915, aged 27. He is buried in the Compton Dundon (St Andrew) Churchyard in Somerset.

Chapter 6 – The Defence of Anzac

1. Kiazim Pasha, quoted in Bean, Volume 2, p. 133.
2. Aspinall-Oglander, p. 18.
3. Nicol, p. 43.
4. Bean, Volume 2, p. 135.
5. Stevens, p. 89; Hobson diary entry dated 20 May 1915.
6. Waite, p. 141.
7. Bean, Volume 2, p. 140.
8. NZMR Brigade War Diary entry dated 18/19 May 1915; Nicol, p. 43.
9. Hobson diary entry dated 19 May 1915; Nicol, p. 43.
10. Bean, Volume 2, pp. 151–2; Wilkie, p. 22.
11. Pugsley, *Gallipoli: the New Zealand Story*, p. 225.
12. Stevens, p. 89; Nicol, p. 44; Waite, p. 140; Nicol, p. 44.
13. Nicol, pp. 45–6; Lieutenant Cornelius James was killed. He is buried in the CWGC Walker's Ridge Cemetery under the name James Cornelius Nicholas.
14. 'Peregrinations of a Trooper: IX – His First Week Ashore', *Chronicles of the N.Z.E.F.*, p. 247; Bean, Volume 2, pp. 151–2.
15. Nicol, p. 43; Bean, Volume 2, p. 155.
16. Harper, G., letter begun on 15 May 1915, in Harper, *Letters from Gunner 7/516 and Gunner 7/517*, p. 18.
17. 'Anzac', p. 179.
18. Mackenzie, C. N., diary entry dated 20 May 1915, MS1078, Auckland War Memorial Museum Library.
19. Nicol, pp. 47–8.
20. Waite, pp. 141–2.
21. Bean, C. E. W., quoted in Fewster, *Gallipoli Correspondent*, p. 105.
22. Liddle, P. , *Men of Gallipoli: The Dardanelles and Gallipoli Experience August 1914 to January 1916*, Allen Lane, London, 1976, p. 149.
23. 'Peregrinations of a Trooper: X – A Weary Day', *Chronicles of the N.Z.E.F.*, pp. 270–1.
24. Wilkie, p. 23; Andrews, p. 111.
25. Andrews, *ibid*. Hardham had won New Zealand's only Victoria Cross awarded in the South African War.
26. 'Peregrinations of a Trooper: X – A Weary Day', pp. 270–1.
27. Honnor, H. W., quoted in Andrews, p. 111.
28. 'Peregrinations of a Trooper: X – A Weary Day', pp. 270–1.
29. Batchelor diary entry dated 19 May 1915; Stevens, p. 90; WMR War Diary entry dated 19 May 1915, WA 42/1, Archives New Zealand.
30. Stevens, p. 102.
31. NZ and Australian Division Memo to HQ NZMR Brigade dated 12 June 1915, WA 40/4, Archives New Zealand; Mackesy was actually 53 years old. Russell, Brigadier General A., letter dated 13 June 1915, 'The Russell Saga'.
32. NZMR Brigade War Diary entry dated 19 May 1915; Nicol, p. 47; Carbery, p. 55 and Bean, Volume 2, p. 161; Bean, C. E. W., *Anzac to Amiens*, Australian War Memorial, Canberra, 1946, p. 130.

33. According to CWGC records 27 mounted riflemen killed in the 19/20 May period are buried in the following CWGC cemeteries: No.2 Outpost (2), Ari Burnu (3), Canterbury (2), and Walker's Ridge (20). The names of two others with no known graves are inscribed on the Lone Pine Memorial.

34. Harper, G., letter dated 23 May 1915, in *Letters from Gunner 7/516 and Gunner 7/517*, p. 16.

35. Bean, Volume 2, p. 162.

36. *Ibid.*, p. 164.

37. Hobson diary entry dated 21 May 1915. Frank Hobson was killed in action on 24 May 1915. His body was lost, and his name is inscribed on the Lone Pine Memorial.

38. Smith diary entries dated 20, 23 May 1915; Malthus, pp. 76–7.

39. Had he attacked a week earlier, when the two Anzac infantry brigades were out of the line and before the NZMR and ALH brigades arrived, he might have succeeded in breaking through the line. Unfortunately for the Turks, the mounted brigades brought with them the machine gun sections of the 2nd and 3rd Light Horse Brigades, the 4th ALH Regiment and the OMR. Bean, Volume 2, p. 139.

40. Bean, *Anzac to Amiens*, p. 130; Bean, C. E. W., quoted in Fewster, *Gallipoli Correspondent*, pp. 110–11.

41. Stevens, p. 90.

42. Mackenzie diary entry dated 20 May 1915.

43. Stevens, p. 140.

44. Black, J., interview transcript, 1999.2881, Kippenberger Military Archive; Stevens, p. 89.

45. Fenwick diary entry dated 24 May 1915.

46. Wilkie, p. 25; Nicol, pp. 52–3.

47. Bean, *Gallipoli Mission*, p. 58; Liddle, p. 153.

48. Fenwick diary entry dated 24 May 1915.

49. Braithwaite, J. L., diary entry dated 24 May 1915, in possession of Meldrum family; Mackenzie diary entry dated 20 May 1915; Mackenzie, *Tale of a Trooper*, p. 117.

50. Nicol, p. 52; Mackenzie diary entry dated 24 May 1915.

51. East, W., in Shadbolt, p. 77; Martyn, J. L. Y., diary in Townsend, p. 91; 'Anzac', p. 192.

52. Waite, p. 146; Stevens, p. 91.

53. Waite, p. 146.

54. Mackenzie, *Tale of a Trooper*, p. 119; Stevens, p. 91.

55. Doherty diary entry dated 26 May 1915. Trooper Phillip Hunter and Sergeant Richard Boden are both buried in the CWGC Canterbury Cemetery. Lance Corporal Walter Johnston is buried in the CWGC No. 2 Outpost Cemetery. Trooper James Happer's body was lost, and his name is inscribed on the Lone Pine Memorial.

Chapter 7 – No. 3 Outpost

1. Meldrum, W., letter to 'Reveille' (Australia) dated 1932, in possession of Meldrum family.

2. Overton, P. J., letter dated 16 May 1915, quoted in Pugsley, *Gallipoli: the New Zealand Story*, p. 218.

3. Overton letter dated 30 May 1915, quoted in Pugsley, *Gallipoli: the New Zealand Story*, p. 218.

4. Pugsley, p. 221.

5. Smith diary entry dated 28 May 1915.

6. Waite, p. 149.

7. Twisleton letter.

8. Wilkie, pp. 29–30. Sgt. McDonald walked back to the regimental aid post without assistance. His arm was later amputated and he returned to New Zealand. Hardham never fully regained his health after this injury. Lieutenant Duncan McDonald died on a hospital ship on 6 June 1915 and was buried at sea. His name is inscribed on the Lone Pine Memorial.

9. Twisleton letter.

10. Andrews, p. 115, 114. Trooper James Moore survived Gallipoli. He was taken prisoner by the Turks in Egypt in 1916, but survived this experience too.

11. Twisleton letter; Wilder diary entry dated 30 May–2 June 1915.

12. Harvey letter dated 26 July 1915, in *Letters from the Battlefield*, p. 42. Lieutenant Norman Cameron's body was lost, and his name is inscribed on the Lone Pine Memorial.

13. Wilder diary, undated entry.

14. Wilkie, p. 30; Harvey letter dated 26 July 1915, in *Letters from the Battlefield*, p. 42.

15. Harvey letter dated 26 July 1915, in *Letters from the Battlefield*, p. 42. Sergeant Henry Smith's body was lost, and his name is inscribed on the Lone Pine Memorial.

16. Pyle diary entry dated 31 May 1915. Trooper Victor Christophers is buried in the CWGC No.2 Outpost Cemetery.

17. Wilkie, p. 30.

18. Wilkie, p. 31; Bean, Volume 2, p. 195.

19. Wilder diary, undated entry.

20. Bain, L., letter dated 12 August 1915, published in *Timaru Herald*, quoted in Tobin, C., *Gone to Gallipoli: Anzacs of Small Town New Zealand Go to War*, Boscoe Press, Timaru, 2001, p. 76.

21. *Ibid.*; Waite, p. 151.

22. Bean, Volume 2, pp. 195–6, and NZMR Brigade War Diary.

23. Mackenzie diary entry dated 31 May 1915; Mackenzie, *Tale of a Trooper*, p. 128.

24. *Ibid.*, p. 127.

25. Waite, p. 151.

26. Wilkie, p. 33. According to CWGC records, eight mounted riflemen killed in the period 30–31 May are buried in the CWGC No. 2 Outpost Cemetery and four in the CWGC Canterbury Cemetery. The names of 16 others from the same period with no known graves are inscribed on the Lone Pine Memorial.

27. Bean, Volume 2, p. 196.

28. Russell letter to wife dated May 1915, in 'The Russell Saga'.

29. Mackenzie, *Tale of a Trooper*, p. 127; Mackenzie diary entry dated 31 May 1915; Waite, p. 149.
30. Quoted in Bean, Volume 2, p. 197; Bean, Volume 2, p. 197.

Chapter 8 – Life and death on Gallipoli

1. Aspinall-Oglander, p. 72.
2. Doherty diary entry dated 25 May 1915.
3. Mackenzie, *Tale of a Trooper*, pp. 95–6.
4. Quoted in Bean, Volume 2, p. 365.
5. Christophers letter dated 23 May 1915, in *Letters from the Battlefield*, p. 39.
6. Martyn letter in Townsend, pp. 94–5; Stevens, pp. 92, 93; Ranstead letter dated 5 June 1915, MS-Papers-4139, Alexander Turnbull Library.
7. Bean, Volume 2, p. 378.
8. Twisleton letter; Stevens, p. 93; Ranstead letter dated 5 June 1915.
9. Mackenzie, *Tale of a Trooper*, p. 134; Ranstead letter dated 5 June 1915; Stevens, p. 95.
10. Waite, p. 164.
11. *Ibid.*, pp. 162–3.
12. Colbran diary entry dated 11 June 1915; Stevens, p. 97; Watson, W., diary entry dated 25 September 1915, 1999.3061, Kippenberger Military Archive. Watson believed that this food had been in the hold of the ship for five months.
13. Twisleton letter, quoted in Liddle, p. 159; 'Peregrinations of a Trooper: X – 'A Weary Day', *Chronicles of the N.Z.E.F.*, p. 271; Christophers letter dated 23 May 1915, in *Letters from the Battlefield*, p. 39.
14. Tuke, R., undated letter, MS-Papers-1547, Alexander Turnbull Library; Doherty diary entry dated 17 May 1915.
15. Mackenzie, *Tale of a Trooper*, p. 97.
16. OMR War Diary. The well provided water for 350 mules and 7000 litres per day for the men in the vicinity.
17. Masterman, J. W. V., 'Memoirs', 1998.1936, Kippenberger Military Archive.
18. Bean, Volume 2, p. 379; Stevens, p. 92.
19. Aspinall-Oglander, p. 73; Twisleton letter.
20. Carbery, p. 59.
21. Trolove, N., 'The Battle of Sari Bair 6th – 10th August 1915', 88-164, Alexander Turnbull Library; Fenwick diary entry dated June 8, 1915, *Gallipoli Diary*, p. 94.
22. Malthus, p. 97.
23. Aspinall-Oglander, p. 72; Harvey, J., letter dated 26 July 1915, in *Letters from the Battlefield*, p. 42; Nicol, p. 37.
24. Lynch letter dated 14 July 1915. Trooper William Lynch was killed in action on 9 August 1915. His body was lost, and his name is inscribed on the Chunuk Bair Memorial.
25. Mackenzie, *Tale of a Trooper*, p. 151; 'Anzac', pp. 157–8.
26. Powles, *The History of the Canterbury Mounted Rifles*, p. 42.

27. Trolove; Waite, p. 171.
28. Bean, Volume 2, p. 377.
29. Bowerbank, 'New Zealand Hospitals in Egypt', in Drew, H. T. B. (ed.), *The War Effort of New Zealand*, Whitcombe & Tombs, Auckland, 1923, pp. 113–4.
30. Bean, Volume 2, p. 378.
31. Braithwaite diary entry dated 30 May 1915.
32. Twisleton letter; Malthus, p. 78.
33. Wilkie, p. 38; Pocock diary entry dated 28 July 1915; NZMR Brigade War Diary.
34. Aspinall-Oglander, p. 122.
35. Twisleton letter; Mackenzie diary entry dated 12–20 June 1915; Barker letter dated 31 July 1915; Smith diary entry dated 14 June 1915.
36. Twisleton letter; Mackenzie, *Tale of a Trooper*, p. 139.
37. Black, J., interview transcript; Waite, p. 185.
38. Pugsley, *On the Fringe of Hell*, pp. 40–1.
39. Pyle diary entry dated 22 July 1915; Fenwick diary entry dated 14 May; Colbran diary dated 9 June 1915; Mackenzie, *Tale of a Trooper*, p. 130.
40. Wilder diary entry dated 5 August 1915.
41. Extract from General HQ Routine Orders dated 29 September 1915, WA 40/2, Archives New Zealand.
42. Mackenzie diary entry dated 12–20 June 1915.
43. Carruthers letter dated 11 November 1915; Cameron diary entry dated 19 May 1915; Fenwick diary entry dated May 27, 1915; Smith diary entry dated 18 July 1915.
44. Colbran diary entry dated 7 June 1915; Smith diary entries dated 18 June, 21 July 1915.
45. Waite, p. 184.
46. OMR War Diary.
47. Waite, p. 180.
48. Wilkie, p. 37.
49. Harvey letter dated 26 July 1915, in *Letters from the Battlefield*, p. 43.
50. Wilkie, p. 36.
51. Twisleton letter.
52. R. Stevens letter in Townsend, p. 139. Female Turkish snipers are mentioned in other sources, but their presence on Gallipoli has never been confirmed officially.
53. Bean, in Fewster, *Gallipoli Correspondent*, pp. 82–3.
54. Nicol, p. 12.
55. Hamilton, General Sir I., *Gallipoli Diary*, Edward Arnold, London, 1920, Volume 1, p. 370.
56. Twisleton letter; McRae, E., interview transcript, 1999.3002, Kippenberger Military Archive.
57. Powles, *The History of the Canterbury Mounted Rifles*, p. 41.
58. NZMR Brigade War Diary entry dated 21 June 1915.
59. Colbran diary entry dated 20 July 1915; OMR War Diary; Powles, *The History of the Canterbury Mounted Rifles*, p. 42.

60. Erickson, p. 88.
61. Smith diary entry dated 11 June 1915.
62. Stevens, p. 96.
63. Doherty diary entries dated 23 June, 4 November, 5 November 1915.
64. Doherty diary entries dated 6 November, 9 November, 3 December 1915.
65. Bellis, C., in *The New Zealand Horseman*, p. 53.
66. Special Order dated 5 August 1915, WA 40/2, Archives New Zealand.

Chapter 9 – Interlude

1. Hamilton, Volume 1, p. 304.
2. NZ&A Division Special Order dated 25 May 1915, WA 20/1, Archives New Zealand.
3. NZ&A Division order dated 1 June 1915, WA 20/1, Archives New Zealand.
4. Aspinall-Oglander, p. 114.
5. NZMR Brigade War Diary entry dated 2 June 1915, WA 40/1, Archives New Zealand; Pocock diary entry dated 2 July 1915.
6. Tuke letter, undated.
7. 'With our Service Squadron in the Great War', *Amber and Black*, July 1934, p. 24.
8. Harper, G., letter begun on 15 May 1915, in *Letters from Gunner 7/516 and Gunner 7/517*, p. 20.
9. Wilson, Brigadier General L.C., and Wetherell, Captain H., *History of the Fifth Light Horse Regiment (Australian Imperial Force), from 1914 to October 1917, and from October 1917 to June 1919*, Motor Press of Australia, Sydney, 1926, p. 22.
10. Powles, *The History of the Canterbury Mounted Rifles*, p. 38.
11. Colbran diary entry dated 6 June 1915.
12. Nicol, p. 54; Mackenzie, *Tale of a Trooper*, p. 129; Powles, *The History of the Canterbury Mounted Rifles*, p. 41.
13. Pyle diary entry dated 6 June 1915. Trooper Ernest Snow is buried in the CWGC No.2 Outpost Cemetery; Tuke letter, undated. Sergeant Frederick Overton is buried in the CWGC Ari Burnu Cemetery.
14. Aspinall-Oglander, p. 72; Pyle diary entry dated 18 July 1915.
15. Doherty diary entries dated 30 May, 28 June 1915.
16. Nicol, p. 59.
17. Waite, p. 178; Powles, *The History of the Canterbury Mounted Rifles*, p. 40.
18. Hamilton, Volume 1, p. 359.
19. Smith diary entry dated 30 June 1915. Trooper Leslie Smith was shot in the leg at Hill 60 on 27 August and evacuated to England. He did not return to Gallipoli.
20. Waite, p. 179; Carbery, p. 65.
21. Waite, pp. 159, 160.
22. Cowan, J., *The Maoris in the Great War: a History of the New Zealand Native Contingent and Pioneer Battalion*, Whitcombe & Tombs, Wellington, 1926, p. 30.
23. WMR War Diary entries dated 29, 30 July 1915, WA 42/1, Archives New Zealand.
24. Stevens, p. 98; Pocock diary entry dated 7 July 1915; Lynch letter dated 14 July 1915; Pyle diary entry dated 16 July 1915.

25. Powles, *The History of the Canterbury Mounted Rifles*, pp. 43–4.
26. Mackenzie, *Tale of a Trooper*, p. 138.
27. Bean, Volume 2, note to p. 463.
28. James, R. R., *Gallipoli*, Papermac edition, London, 1989, p. 237.
29. Bean, Volume 2, pp. 462–3.
30. *Ibid.*, pp. 464, 465.
31. *Ibid.*, p. 472.
32. Godley, Major General Sir A., 'Report on the Operations against the SARI BAIR Position 6th – 10th August', dated 16 August 1915, Kippenberger Military Archive.
33. James, p. 253.
34. Mackenzie, *Tale of a Trooper*, p. 153; Harvey letter dated 26 July 1915, in *Letters from the Battlefield*, p. 44.
35. Powles, *The History of the Canterbury Mounted Rifles*, p. 43; Carbery, p. 66.
36. Pocock diary entry dated 2 August 1915; Powles, *The History of the Canterbury Mounted Rifles*, p. 44; Twisleton letter.
37. Meldrum letter to 'Reveille' dated 1932; Bean, *Anzac to Amiens*, p. 143; Cunningham *et al.*, p. 62.
38. Aspinall-Oglander, p. 182.
39. Special Order from General Birdwood, WA 40/2, Archives New Zealand.

Chapter 10 – The Covering Force battle

1. Stevens, p. 99.
2. The effective strengths of the AMR, WMR, CMR and OMR were 401, 365, 331 and 401 men respectively, while the Maori contingent had 454 men. Adding Brigade HQ and the signal and engineer troops, the total strength was 2,003. NZMR Brigade War Diary entry dated 6 August.
3. Bean, *Gallipoli Mission*, p. 207.
4. Powles, *The History of the Canterbury Mounted Rifles*, p. 47; Browne diary.
5. Curry, A. A., letter dated 6 August 1915, 76–184, Alexander Turnbull Library; Harper, G., letter begun on 15 May 1915, in *Letters from Gunner 7/516 and Gunner 7/517*, p. 22.
6. Cowan, J., *The Maoris in the Great War*, p. 38.
7. Stevens, p. 100.
8. The fighting at Lone Pine raged for the next four days. Seven Victoria Crosses were won by the Australians there, and 2000 Australians and at least as many Turks were killed or wounded.
9. Browne diary, MS-Papers-3519, Alexander Turnbull Library.
10. Pyle diary entry dated 6 August 1915. Trooper William Pyle is buried in the CWGC No.2 Outpost Cemetery.
11. Mackenzie, *Tale of a Trooper*, p. 158; Doherty diary entry dated 6 August 1915; Waite, p. 206.
12. NZMR Brigade War Diary entry dated 6 August.
13. Nicol, p. 66.

14. Stevens, p. 100.
15. Nicol, p. 67.
16. Waite, p. 208.
17. Nicol, pp. 68, 67.
18. Nicol, *ibid.*; Cowan, *The Maoris in the Great War*, pp. 44–5, 39.
19. Bean, Volume 2, note to p. 569.
20. Bean, Volume 2, p. 569. Lieutenant Henry Mackesy was the son of the commanding officer of the regiment. He is buried in the CWGC NZ No. 2 Outpost Cemetery.
21. Mackenzie, *Tale of a Trooper*, p. 158.
22. Browne diary.
23. Browne diary. Trooper Robert Chamberlain is buried in the CWGC NZ No. 2 Outpost Cemetery.
24. Mackenzie, *Tale of a Trooper*, p. 160.
25. 'Reveille' letter by Meldrum.
26. Andrews, p. 121; 'Reveille' letter by Meldrum.
27. Godley, *Report on the Operations against the SARI BAIR Position 6th – 10th August.* According to Meldrum, Table Top was secure at 10.55 p.m. 'Reveille' letter by Meldrum. According to Bean, the brigade telephone logs show the capture of Table Top being reported at 12.30 a.m. Bean, Volume 2, p. 572.
28. Mackenzie, *Tale of a Trooper*, pp. 164, 167.
29. *Ibid.*, p. 163; Browne diary.
30. Hamilton's Despatch to the War Office dated 11 December 1915, as published in the *London Gazette* on 4 January 1916.
31. Regimental records have lower casualty figures. According to CWGC records eight Aucklanders, six Wellingtons and 13 Maoris were killed on 6 and 7 August. Those who died later from wounds received on 6 or 7 August are not included; 'Reveille' letter by Meldrum.
32. Bean, Volume 2, p. 572.
33. Hamilton's Despatch dated 11 December 1915.
34. Richards, M. A., quoted in Liddle, pp. 203–4.
35. Surprisingly, there is no mention of covering machine gun fire being provided from the nearby No. 3 Outpost.
36. Trolove.
37. Bean, Volume 2, p. 573.
38. Trolove. Trooper Robert Lusk is buried in the CWGC 7th Field Ambulance Cemetery. Trooper Frank Jarman is buried in the CWGC NZ No. 2 Outpost Cemetery.
39. Trolove. Sergeant Cotton appears to have survived; Harper, G., letter in *Letters from Gunner 7/516 and Gunner 7/517*, p. 23.
40. The regiment was then commanded by a succession of officers. Major George Hutton ran the unit until Lieutenant Colonel George Stewart (5th Reinforcements) took over the regiment on Lemnos in September. Stewart died of sickness on Lemnos (he is buried in the CWGC Portianos Cemetery) and was replaced in command by Major John Studholme, another reinforcement officer. Finally, Major Charles

Powles took over in December and commanded the regiment until its evacuation from Gallipoli.

41. Laurenson, D., letter published in *Timaru Herald*, 22 November 1915, quoted in Tobin, p. 94.

42. Trolove.

43. Harper, G., letter in *Letters from Gunner 7/516 and Gunner 7/517*, p. 23.

44. *Ibid.*, p. 23; Waite, pp. 211–12. Lieutenant Francis Davison is buried in the CWGC Embarkation Pier Cemetery.

45. Waite, p. 212; Fyfe, J., diary entry dated 7 August 1915, in Townsend, p. 150.

46. Bean, Volume 2, p. 575.

47. Trolove, this and following quotes.

48. Arthur Bauchop was 44 years old. His name is inscribed on the Lone Pine Memorial. Before he died, he told Godley, 'I hope we did what you wanted' and 'It was glorious while it lasted'. Godley letter to Allen dated 14 August 1915. WA 252/2, Archives New Zealand.

49. Trolove; Stevens, p. 101.

50. Waite, p. 212; Bean, Volume 2, pp. 574–5.

51. Powles, *The History of the Canterbury Mounted Rifles*, p. 49.

52. Francis Twisleton wrote that the Otagos lost 30 killed and 92 wounded on 6 and 7 August, while Bean states that 34 Otagos were killed and 65 wounded that night. Bean, Volume 2, p. 576. The CWGC records list the names of 80 mounteds and Maori killed on 6 and 7 August. Only 23 of them have known graves. The bodies of the others were buried at sea, lost or never identified. Others who died later from wounds received during that period are not included.

53. Bean, Volume 2, p. 576; Hamilton's Despatch dated 11 December 1915; Aspinall-Oglander, p. 188.

Chapter 11 – Chunuk Bair

1. Ferguson, D., *The History of the Canterbury Regiment N.Z.E.F. 1914–1919*, Whitcombe & Tombs, Auckland, 1921, p. 60.

2. According to Bean, this was further up the dere than the entanglement cleared by the mounteds in the mouth of the dere. Bean, Volume 2, p. 578; Burton, p. 58.

3. Kannengiesser was the commander of the two Turkish regiments that had been brought north to Anzac from Gaba Tepe the night before to help fight off the Australians at Lone Pine.

4. Bean, Volume 2, p. 613.

5. Stevens, p. 101; Bean, *Gallipoli Mission*, p. 109. After the war the bones of nearly 300 Australians were found on The Nek. Most of these men are buried in anonymous mass graves in the CWGC cemetery at The Nek.

6. Waite, p. 201; Handwritten comment on Waite's text, Meldrum papers, in possession of Meldrum family.

7. Browne diary. Major Selwyn Chambers' body was lost. His name is inscribed on the Chunuk Bair Memorial.

8. Stevens, p. 113.
9. Bean, Volume 2, p. 594. Major Percy Overton is buried in the CWGC 7th Field Ambulance Cemetery.
10. A Gurkha battalion from the 29th Indian Brigade turned up on Rhododendron Ridge in time to assault Chunuk Bair with the New Zealanders.
11. Mackenzie, *Tale of a Trooper*, p. 165.
12. According to Bean a few mounted riflemen from the Auckland regiment went up Chunuk Bair with the Wellington infantry. Note to Bean, Volume 2, p. 668.
13. Neither of these British battalions played a significant part in the defence of Chunuk Bair. They lost most of their officers to Turkish fire early on, and many of the soldiers lacked the training and the experience to fight on without them. Only about 100 of them fought with Malone's men. The rest took shelter below the crest line, where many of them were killed.
14. Had the Turks held them back until they had built a large counter-attack force, the New Zealand defence of Chunuk Bair would probably have been a much briefer affair.
15. Liddle, p. 207.
16. Cunningham *et al.*, p. 73.
17. Nicol, p. 74; Stevens, p. 140.
18. Bean, Volume 2, pp. 676–7. Major Frank Chapman's body was lost. His name is inscribed on the Chunuk Bair Memorial.
19. Bean, Volume 2, p. 677.
20. Law diary entry dated 8 August 1915.
21. The bodies of Ken and John McKinnon were lost. Their names are inscribed on the Chunuk Bair Memorial.
22. Bean, Volume 2, p. 678; Cunningham *et al.*, p. 74. The artillery fire that killed Malone was probably British.
23. Bean, Volume 2, p. 678.
24. Stevens, pp. 104–11.
25. Nicol, p. 73; Bean, Volume 2, p. 679.
26. Browne diary.
27. Mackenzie, *Tale of a Trooper*, pp. 173, 174.
28. Browne diary.
29. Bean, Volume 2, p. 679.
30. Browne diary.
31. Law diary entry dated 9 August 1915. Trooper Alfred Kent's body was lost. His name is inscribed on the Chunuk Bair Memorial.
32. Mackenzie, *Tale of a Trooper*, p. 172.

Chapter 12 – New Zealand's finest hour
1. Bean, Volume 2, pp. 679, 691–2.
2. Meldrum, W., quoted in Andrews, p. 123.
3. Bean, Volume 2, p. 705.

4. Meldrum, W., *Notes on Campaigns of NZMR,* Kippenberger Military Archive. The bodies of Troopers Michael and Richard Murphy were lost. Their names are inscribed on the Chunuk Bair Memorial.

5. Browne diary. The bodies of Troopers Hugh Pringle and Melville Bull were lost. Their names are inscribed on the Chunuk Bair Memorial.

6. Mackenzie, *Tale of a Trooper,* pp. 180–1; Clutha Mackenzie was a Member of Parliament in 1921–2, and was knighted for his work with the blind in New Zealand in 1935.

7. Bean, Volume 2, pp. 692–3. Major Jim Elmslie and Captain Victor Kelsall were both veterans of the South African War. Their bodies were lost, and their names are inscribed on the Chunuk Bair Memorial.

8. Allison, C., quoted in Andrews, p. 127.

9. According to Bean, 27 Aucklanders went back down the hill, to be joined later by another 25 men. Bean, Volume 2, p. 691.

10. Mackenzie, *Tale of a Trooper,* p. 178; Browne diary.

11. Malthus, p. 121.

12. Browne diary.

13. Bean, Volume 2, p. 705.

14. Browne diary.

15. According to Meldrum most of these reinforcements immediately took cover and did not fire a shot. Bean, Review, AWM 38, 3 DRL 1722, quoted in Pugsley, *The Anzac Experience,* p. 111.

16. Travers, T., 'Gallipoli: the Other Side of the Hill', in Cowley, R., *The Great War: Perspectives on the First World War,* Random House, New York, 2003, p. 193.

17. Travers, p. 134.

18. Trolove. Noel Trolove survived the war.

19. Travers, p. 136.

20. Laurenson letter, published in *Timaru Herald* 22 November 1915, quoted in Tobin, p. 112.

21. Losses by regiment were: AMR 57 killed, 144 wounded and 27 missing; WMR 26 killed, 105 wounded and 15 missing; CMR 24 killed and 63 wounded; OMR 28 killed, 84 wounded and 7 missing; Maori Contingent 16 killed, 84 wounded and 4 missing. Brigade HQ and the Signal Troop had 5 men wounded. Most of those listed as missing were dead. NZMR Brigade War Diary.

22. Travers, p. 136, and Erickson, p. 91. Missing and prisoners are not included.

23. Aspinall-Oglander, p. 309.

24. *Ibid.*

25. Waite, p. 243.

26. Nicol, pp. 77–8.

27. Colbran diary entry dated 19 October 1915.

28. Godley, *Life of an Irish Soldier,* pp. 187–8.

29. Stevens, p. 112.

30. O'Carroll, J. N., quoted in Stevens, p. 111; Contrast this with the Australians, who won seven VCs at Lone Pine; McKay memoirs, p. 94.

31.   East, W., in Shadbolt, p. 78; Hamilton, General Sir I., *Gallipoli Diary*, Volume 2, p. 118.

Chapter 13 – Anyone's mutton
1.   Martyn letter in Townsend, pp. 96–7.
2.   Bean, Volume 2, p. 726. Hill 60 was known to the Turks as Kaiajik Aghala (Sheepfold of the Little Rock) and, after the August fighting, as Bomba Tepe (Bomb Hill). It is 60 metres above sea level, hence its name.
3.   Aspinall-Oglander, p. 355.
4.   Pugsley, *Gallipoli: the New Zealand Story*, p. 318; Holmes diary entry dated 19 September 1915. Alan Holmes survived the war.
5.   Waite, pp. 251–2.
6.   Twisleton letter; NZMR Brigade War Diary.
7.   Harper letter dated 1 March 1916 in *Letters from Gunner 7/516 and Gunner 7/517*, p. 38. Sergeant George Ferguson is buried in the CWGC Hill 60 Cemetery. This is Gordon Harper's last contribution to the story of the mounteds on Gallipoli. After being shot in the neck on 21 August he was evacuated to England. Harper returned to the brigade in Egypt and died of wounds after the Battle of Romani on 12 August 1916. He is buried in the CWGC Cairo War Memorial Cemetery.
8.   OMR War Diary entry dated 21 August 1915.
9.   Waite, pp. 251–2; Powles, *The History of the Canterbury Mounted Rifles*, pp. 56–7.
10.   Twisleton letter.
11.   Powles, *The History of the Canterbury Mounted Rifles*, p. 57; Waite, p. 252.
12.   Quoted in Bean, Volume 2, p. 736.
13.   Twisleton letter.
14.   Waite, p. 253.
15.   Bean, Volume 2, p. 746; Waite, p. 253, and NZMR Brigade War Diary entry dated 22 August 1915.
16.   Twisleton letter.
17.   Powles, *The History of the Canterbury Mounted Rifles*, note to p. 57.
18.   *Ibid.*, p. 59.
19.   Aspinall-Oglander, p. 358.
20.   Bean, *Anzac to Amiens*, p. 167.
21.   Bean, Volume 2, p. 744. Davy and Margaret Sustins of Christchurch lost their sons Leon (aged 21) and Nolan (aged 25) at Hill 60 on 21 August. Their bodies were lost, and their names are inscribed on the Hill 60 Memorial.
22.   Nicol, p. 81.
23.   According to Bean the NZ&A Division issued orders to stop lightly wounded or sick men from being evacuated. Anyone who was able to hold a rifle and stand in a trench was kept on the peninsula. Bean, Volume 2, p. 746.
24.   Waite, p. 255.
25.   Pocock diary entry dated 25 August 1915; Wilder diary entry dated 26 August 1915. Sergeant John Wilder was killed the next day. His body was lost, and his name is inscribed on the Hill 60 Memorial; East, W., in Shadbolt, p. 79.

26. Rudd, J. F., quoted in Liddle, p. 210. Trooper John Bindon is buried in the CWGC Hill 60 Cemetery.

27. East, W., in Shadbolt, p. 79. Captain Henry Taylor's body was lost. His name is inscribed on the Hill 60 Memorial.

28. Twisleton letter.

29. Waite, p. 255; Powles, *The History of the Canterbury Mounted Rifles*, p. 60.

30. Bean, Volume 2, p. 751.

31. Quoted in Robertson, *Anzac & Empire*, p. 139.

32. Watson diary entry dated 29 August 1915; Two-thirds of the Australians were killed or wounded. Bean, Volume 2, p. 750; Powles, *The History of the Canterbury Mounted Rifles*, p. 61.

33. *Ibid.*

34. Wilkie, p. 66; Andrews, p. 130. Grant's body was lost, and his name is inscribed on the Hill 60 Memorial.

35. Twisleton letter; Andrews, p. 130.

36. Powles, p. 61; Waite, p. 256; Twisleton letter.

37. Twisleton letter. Francis Twisleton later collapsed from exhaustion. After later serving on the Western Front, in Egypt and Palestine, he died of wounds on 15 November 1917. He is buried in the CWGC Ramleh Cemetery in Israel.

38. Keenan letter dated 16 December 1915, quoted in Robertson, *Anzac & Empire*, p. 187. This was one of the regiments that had taken part on the charge at The Nek on 7 August.

39. Russell letter to father dated 30 August 1915, in 'The Russell Saga'.

40. Brigade HQ and 100 men stayed at Hill 60 for another six days until their replacements were thoroughly broken into trench work; Powles, *The History of the Canterbury Mounted Rifles*, p. 65.

41. Powles, *The History of the Canterbury Mounted Rifles*, p. 62; Bean, Volume 2, p. 761.

42. Waite, p. 258; Watson diary entry dated 30 August 1915.

43. Bean, Volume 2, p. 761. There are 27 mounted riflemen buried in named graves in the CWGC Hill 60 Cemetery, and the names of another 174 whose bodies were lost or unidentifiable are inscribed on the Hill 60 Memorial (a total of 712 men lie in unmarked mass graves at Hill 60). Another 35 mounted riflemen who were killed or who died of wounds in the period 21–30 August are buried or commemorated elsewhere on Gallipoli. Others died in hospitals in Egypt and elsewhere from wounds received at Hill 60. At least eight Maoris and one New Zealand engineer also died at Hill 60. The Hill 60 Memorial today marks the approximate forward edge of the trenches captured in August 1915.

44. Bean, Volume 2, note to p. 761.

45. Godley letter to Allen dated 3 September 1915, WA 252/2, Archives New Zealand; Ferens, O. L., *The History and Tradition of the Queen Alexandra's (Wellington-West Coast) Mounted Rifles Regiment 1860 to 1931*, manuscript in preparation, Wanganui District Library, 1935.

46. The bodies of Henry and Edward Brittan and the bodies of David and Robert Watson

were lost. Their names are inscribed on the Hill 60 Memorial. Frank Clark's body was also lost, and his name is inscribed on the Hill 60 Memorial.

47. Doherty diary entry dated 31 August 1915; Pocock diary entry dated 29 August 1915.
48. Powles, *The History of the Canterbury Mounted Rifles*, p. 63.
49. Waite, p. 258. *Maheno* returned to Anzac five more times to pick up sick and wounded men before sailing for New Zealand with 319 convalescent patients on New Year's Day 1916. Elliott, J.S., 'The New Zealand Hospital Ships', in Drew, *The War Effort of New Zealand*, pp. 127–30.
50. Braithwaite diary entry dated 28 August 1915; Ricketts, W., 'With our Service Squadron in the Great War', *Amber & Black*, August 1935, p. 156.
51. James, p. 309.
52. Aspinall-Oglander, p. 362.

Chapter 14 – So long Johnnie …
1. Carbery, p. 108.
2. Waite, p. 259.
3. By October 1915 2500 New Zealanders were dead, 2233 had been invalided home to New Zealand and thousands more were in hospital. Pugsley, *Gallipoli: the New Zealand Story*, p. 333.
4. Russell, 'The Russell Saga'.
5. NZMR Brigade War Diary entry dated 13 September 1915; Powles, *The History of the Canterbury Mounted Rifles*, pp. 65–6.
6. Watson diary entry dated 29 September 1915.
7. NZMR Brigade War Diary entry dated 18 September 1915; NZ Mounted Field Ambulance War Diary entry dated October 1915.
8. Nicol, p. 85.
9. Powles, *The History of the Canterbury Mounted Rifles*, p. 67.
10. In recognition of the very high casualties in the mounted rifles brigade on Gallipoli, the New Zealand Government had agreed on 19 June to increase the size of future reinforcement drafts by 50 per cent, and to 'back-date' the increase in numbers to the 2nd Reinforcements. The first of these large contingents of reinforcements left New Zealand in August and were amalgamated into the NZMR Brigade on Lemnos. Branch of the Chief of the General Staff, *New Zealand Expeditionary Force: its Provision and Maintenance*, Government Printer, Wellington, 1919, p. 7.
11. Nicol, p. 85; Andrews, p. 131.
12. Bean, Volume 2, note to p. 802; Powles, *The History of the Canterbury Mounted Rifles*, p. 68.
13. Doherty diary entry dated 21 September 1915.
14. Waite, p. 262.
15. Unit strengths on 13 November were HQ and Signal Troop 41, AMR 342, WMR 406, CMR 403, OMR 367. NZMR Brigade War Diary entry dated 13 November 1915.
16. Fewster *et al.*, *Gallipoli: the Turkish Story*, 2nd edition, Allen & Unwin, Crows Nest, 2003, pp. 124–5.

17. Altay, in Liddle, p. 211.
18. Aspinall-Oglander, pp. 401–2.
19. Powles, *The History of the Canterbury Mounted Rifles*, pp. 68, 69.
20. McMillan, pp. 27, 33.
21. Cunningham *et al.*, p. 82; Carbery, p. 109; Liddle, p. 244.
22. Pugsley, *Gallipoli: the New Zealand Story*, p. 336. Some of those who died had been wounded or fallen sick during the August fighting.
23. Wilkie, p. 70.
24. Carbery, p. 130; Waite, pp. 273, 274.
25. Ferens, *The History and Tradition of the Queen Alexandra's (Wellingon-West Coast) Mounted Rifles Regiment 1860 to 1931*.
26. Martyn, J. L. Y., letter, in Townsend, p. 99; Powles, *The History of the Canterbury Mounted Rifles*, p. 70; Waite, p. 276.
27. Bean, *Anzac to Amiens*, p. 174.
28. Waite, p. 276.
29. Godley letters to Allen dated 20 October, 9 December 1915. WA 252/2, Archives New Zealand.
30. Aspinall-Oglander, p. 440.
31. Powles, p. 72.
32. Waite, p. 277.
33. Bean, *Anzac to Amiens*, p. 176.
34. Doherty diary entry dated 6 December 1915.
35. McMillan, p. 36.
36. Waite, pp. 282–3.
37. McKay memoirs, p. 91; Waite, p. 279.
38. Masterman; Unknown mounted rifleman quoted in McKay memoirs, p. 93.
39. Carruthers letter dated 16 December 1915; Martyn, letter, quoted in Waite, p. 281.
40. Bean, Volume 2, p. 882.
41. Powles, *The History of the Canterbury Mounted Rifles*, p. 73.
42. Bean, *Anzac to Amiens*, p. 179.
43. Waite, p. 288.
44. Rudd letter; Cox, A. O., interview transcript, 1999.2887, Kippenberger Military Archive.
45. Waite, p. 288.
46. Davis, Colonel J. B., quoted in Andrews, p. 134. Sergeant Thomas Fawcett's body was left behind and lost. His name is inscribed on the Chunuk Bair Memorial.
47. Godley letter to Allen dated 18 December 1915. WA 252/2, Archives New Zealand.
48. Andrews, p. 134.
49. NZMR Brigade War Diary entry dated 20 December 1915.
50. Waite, p. 292.
51. Ferens, *The History and Tradition of the Queen Alexandra's (Wellington-West Coast) Mounted Rifles Regiment 1860 to 1931*; McMillan, pp. 37–8; Martyn letter, in Townsend, p. 100.

52. Aspinall-Oglander, p. 460; Travers, in Cowley, *The Great War: Perspectives on the First World War.*
53. These numbers are based on Turkish records for the period 4 April–19 December 1915. Erickson, p. 94.
54. Pugsley, Gallipoli: *the New Zealand Story*, p. 346.
55. Between May and December 1915, 390 mounted riflemen were killed in action and 83 were listed as missing (almost all of whom were later included in the lists of fatalities). Between May 1915 and May 1916, 160 others died of wounds, 68 died of disease and 26 died of other causes. Casualties in the supporting units of the NZMR Brigade are not included, as the casualty records do not list them as belonging to the brigade. *New Zealand Expeditionary Force, Alphabetical List of Casualties, Books 1–14*, Government Printer, Wellington, 1916–1919. Two thousand mounted riflemen landed in May 1915, and 920 reinforcements joined them before the end of August. However, some of those reinforcements were men who were returning to their regiments after recovering from wounds or sickness. Casualties in each regiment were: AMR: 207 dead, 326 wounded; WMR: 203 dead, 311 wounded; CMR: 189 dead, 333 wounded; OMR: 128 killed, 269 wounded. *New Zealand Expeditionary Force, Alphabetical List of Casualties.*
56. CWGC fact sheets dated 2001, URL: http://www.cwgc.org/cwgc/task.html
57. He is one of three New Zealanders buried in the CWGC Haidar Pasha Cemetery in Istanbul.
58. The fighting strengths for 28 May and 22–30 August 1915 are missing from the War Diaries, so strengths for these dates are estimated from other sources. Any slight inaccuracies in the daily records do not affect the overall impression.
59. Meldrum, W, 'Notes on Campaigns of NZMR', undated, property of Meldrum family.

Epilogue

1. The other three brigades, later reduced to two, were Australian light horse brigades.
2. Through no real fault of their own, the infantry divisions of the EEF played a relatively small part in these battles.
3. Powles, p. 75.
4. Nicol, pp. 132–3; Andrews, p. 147.
5. Wilkie, p. 170. Francis Twisleton was mortally wounded in the Ayun Kara fight; Powles, p. 161; O'Neill quoted in Andrews, p. 160.
6. Nicol, p. 210.
7. Wavell, Lieutenant General Sir A. P., *The Palestine Campaigns*, 3rd edition, Constable, London, 1941, p. 222.
8. Andrews, p. 198.
9. Bellis, p. 56.

Bibliography

Unpublished Sources
Archives & Manuscripts
Archives New Zealand/Te Whare Tohu Tuhituhihinga O Aotearoa, Head Office, Wellington
AD Series 1, Box 954, File 29/26, Mobilization, Mounted Rifles and Infantry Regiments, 1914.
AD Series 1, Box 1095, File 40/76, Horses for NZEF, 1914.
AD Series 1, Box 1098, File 40/82, Saddlery, file dated 20 September 1914.
AD Series 1, Box 1095, File 40/26, Harness and Saddlery, Volume 1, file dated 18 September 1914.
WA 20/1, New Zealand & Australian Division General Staff War Diary.
WA 40/1, NZMR Brigade War Diary, 1915.
WA 40/2, NZMR Brigade Routine Orders.
WA 40/4, NZMR Brigade Miscellaneous Files.
WA 41/1, AMR War Diary, 1915.
WA 42, Meldrum, W., 'Essay on the Handling of Mounted Rifles Independently and in Brigade', dated 14 November 1914.
WA 42/1, WMR War Diary, 1915.
WA 44/1, OMR War Diary, 1915.
WA 44/4, 'History of the Otago Mounted Rifles (Independent) Regiment', not dated.
WA 47/1, NZ Mounted Field Ambulance War Diary.
WA 252/1, Letters of Colonel Allen and General Godley, 1912–March 1915.
WA 252/2, Letters of Colonel Allen and General Godley, April – December 1915.

Wanganui District Library
Ferens, O. L., *The History and Tradition of the Queen Alexandra's (Wellington–West Coast) Mounted Rifles Regiment 1860 to 1931*, manuscript in preparation, 1935.

The National Archives, United Kingdom
PRO 30/57/63, letter Hamilton/Asquith dated 2 August 1915.

Personal Papers, Letters, Diaries & Interview Transcripts
Kippenberger Military Archive, Army Museum Waiouru
Batchelor, A. F., diary, 1999.1088.
Black, J., interview transcript, 1999.2881.
Cox, A. O., interview transcript, 1999.2887.
Doherty, P. G., diary, 13 October 1914 to 24 November 1915, 1989.943.
Godley, Major General Sir A.J., 'Report on the Operations against the SARI BAIR Position 6th – 10th August', dated 16 August 1915.

Masterman, J. W. V., 'Memoirs', 1998.1936.

McGregor, D., letters, 1998.331.

McKay, E. C. M., 'The Years Unfold: Memoirs', 1998.31.

McRae, E., interview transcript, 1999.3002.

Pocock, C., diary, 1991.2136.

Pyle, W. R., diary, 1996.292.

Watson, W., diary 14 August 1915 – 9 April 1916, 1999.3061.

Wilder, J. W., diary, 1999.798.

Alexander Turnbull Library, National Library of New Zealand, Wellington

Browne, H. E., diary, MS-Papers-3519.

Cameron, A. E., diary, MSX-2853.

Carruthers, W. G, letters & associated papers, MS-Papers-1429.

Colbran, B. C., diaries, MS-Copy-Micro-0037.

Curry, A. A., letters and diary, 76-184.

Dawbin, W., diary, Micro-MS-0004.

Judge, H., papers relating to service in Palestine, MS-Papers-4312.

Holmes, A., diary, MS-Papers-1447.

Lynch, W. H., letters, MS-Papers-4706.

Ranstead, G., letters, MS-Papers-4139.

Trolove, N., 'The Battle of Sari Bair, 6th – 10th August', 1915, 88-164.

Tuke, R., letters, MS-Papers-1547.

Twisleton, F. M., letters, MS-Papers-1705.

Gambrill, R. F. (compiler), 'The Russell Saga Volume 3: World War 1', qMS 0822.

Auckland War Memorial Museum Library

Hobson, F. E., diary, MS 94/50.

Johns, W. H., letters, MS 1392.

Law, J. O., papers 1914–1917, MS 90/20.

Mackenzie, C. N., diary 1914–1916, MS 1078.

Meldrum family

Braithwaite, J. L., diary.

Meldrum, W., draft letter to 'Reveille', NSW Branch of Returned Sailors and Soldiers Imperial League of Australia, in reply to a request for information about the fighting of the NZMR Brigade on Sari Bair, dated 19 May 1932.

Meldrum, W., 'Notes on Campaigns of NZMR', undated.

Other

McMillan, J., 'Forty Thousand Horsemen: Being the Memoirs of 7/1322 Cpl Jim McMillan, Canterbury Mounted Rifles, First NZEF, on Service in Gallipoli and Palestine, WW1', property of C. B. McMillan and family, Whangarei.

Peed, E. S., diaries, property of W.S. Peed and family, Taihape.

Smith, L. J., diaries, property of G.R. Smith and family, Wellington.

Published Sources
Official Publications

Annual Reports on the Defence Forces of New Zealand, Government Printer, Wellington, 1910–1922.

Aspinall-Oglander, Brigadier General C. F., *History of the Great War. Military Operations: Gallipoli, Volume 2: May 1915 to the Evacuation*, William Heinemann Ltd, London, 1932.

Bean, C. E. W., *The Official History of Australia in the War of 1914–1918, Volume 1, The Story of ANZAC from the Outbreak of War to the End of the First Phase of the Gallipoli Campaign, May 4, 1915*, Angus & Robertson, Sydney, 1921.

Bean, C. E. W., *The Official History of Australia in the War of 1914–1918, Volume 2, The Story of ANZAC from 4 May, 1915, to the Evacuation of the Gallipoli Peninsula*, Angus & Robertson, Sydney, 1924.

Branch of the Chief of the General Staff, *New Zealand Expeditionary Force, Its Provision & Maintenance*, Government Printer, Wellington, 1919.

Godley, Major General A. J., Defence Forces of New Zealand: Report of the General Officer Commanding the Forces for the Period from 20th June 1913, to 25th June 1914, Wellington, 1914.

Government of New Zealand, *The New Zealand Official Year Book*, Government Printer, Wellington, 1913.

Hamilton's Despatch to the War Office dated 11 December 1915, as published in the *London Gazette* on 4 January 1916.

Macmunn, Lieutenant General Sir G. & Falls, Captain C., *Military Operations – Egypt & Palestine: From the Outbreak of War with Germany to June 1917*, HMSO, London, 1928.

New Zealand Expeditionary Force, Alphabetical List of Casualties, Books 1–14, Government Printer, Wellington, 1916–1919.

New Zealand Expeditionary Force (Europe) 1914 War Diary, Government Printer, Wellington, 1915.

New Zealand Volunteer Force Manual for Mounted Rifles 1895, Government Printer, Wellington, 1900.

Studholme, Lieutenant Colonel J., *Records of Personnel Services During the War of Officers, Nurses and First-Class Warrant Officers; and Other Facts Relating to the N.Z.E.F, Unofficial but Compiled from Official Sources*, Government Printer, Wellington, 1928.

The Great War, 1914–1918, New Zealand Expeditionary Force, Roll of Honour, Government Printer, Wellington, 1924.

War Office, *Yeomanry & Mounted Rifle Training, Parts I and II*, His Majesty's Stationery Office, London, 1915 edition.

Books

Amber & Black: The Journal of the Queen Alexandra's (Wellington West Coast) Mounted Rifles, New Zealand Military Forces, Hawera, 1934–1938.

Andrews, T., *Kiwi Trooper: the Story of Queen Alexandra's Own*, Wanganui Chronicle, Wanganui, 1967.

Annabel, Major N., *Official History of the New Zealand Engineers during the Great War, 1914-1919*, Evans, Cobb & Sharpe, Wanganui, 1927.

Anonymous, *In Memoriam. Chaplain-Major William Grant: his Letters from the Front*, Herald Office, Gisborne, 1915.

'Anzac', *On the Anzac Trail: being Extracts from the Diary of a New Zealand Sapper*, William Heinemann, London, 1916.

Bean, C. E. W., *Anzac to Amiens: a Shorter History of the Australian Fighting Services in the First World War*, Australian War Memorial, Canberra, 1946.

Bean, C. E. W., *Gallipoli Mission*, Australian War Memorial, Canberra, 1948.

Belich, J., *The New Zealand Wars and the Victorian Interpretation of Racial Conflict*, Penguin, Auckland, 1988.

Blackwell, F. and Douglas, D. R., *The Story of the 3rd Australian Light Horse Regiment*, NP, 1952.

Buley, E. C., *Glorious Deeds of Australasians in the Great War*, Andrew Melrose Ltd., London, 1915.

Burton, O. E., *The Auckland Regiment: being an Account of the Doings on Active Service of the First, Second and Third Battalions of the Auckland Regiment*, Whitcombe & Tombs, Wellington, 1922.

Butler, Colonel A.G., 'The Gallipoli Campaign,' in *The Official History of the Australian Army Medical Services in the War of 1914–1918, Volume 1: Gallipoli, Palestine and New Guinea*, Australian War Memorial, Canberra, 1930.

Carbery, Lieutenant Colonel A. D., *The New Zealand Medical Service in the Great War 1914–1918*, Whitcombe & Tombs, Auckland, 1924.

Carlyon, L., *Gallipoli*, Macmillan, Sydney, 2001.

Cowan, J., *The New Zealand Wars: a History of the Maori Campaigns and the Pioneering Period*, Volume 2, Government Printer, Wellington, 1922 (1983 reprint).

Cowan, J., *The Maoris in the Great War: a History of the New Zealand Native Contingent and Pioneer Battalion*, Whitcombe & Tombs, Wellington, 1926.

Cowley, R. (ed.), *The Great War: Perspectives on the First World War*, Random House, New York, 2003.

Crawford, J. & Ellis, E., *To Fight for the Empire: an Illustrated History of New Zealand and the South African War 1899–1902*, Reed, Auckland, 1999.

Crawford, J. & McGibbon, I. (eds), *One Flag, One Queen, One Tongue: New Zealand, the British Empire and the South African War 1899–1902*, Auckland University Press, Auckland, 2003.

Cunningham, W. H., Treadwell, C. A. L., and Hanna, J. S., *The Wellington Regiment N.Z.E.F. 1914–1919*, Ferguson & Osborn Ltd., Wellington, 1928.

Drew, Lieutenant H. T. B (ed.), *The War Effort of New Zealand: a Popular History*, Whitcombe & Tombs, Auckland, 1923.

Erickson, E. J., *Ordered to Die: a History of the Ottoman Army in the First World War*, Greenwood Press, London, 2001.

Fenwick, Lieutenant Colonel Dr P., *Gallipoli Diary 24 April to 27 June 1915*, David Ling Publishing/Auckland War Memorial Museum, ND.

Ferguson, D., *The History of the Canterbury Regiment, N.Z.E.F., 1914–1919*, Whitcombe & Tombs, Auckland, 1921.

Fewster, K. (ed.), *Gallipoli Correspondent: the Frontline Diaries of C. E. W. Bean*, George Allen & Unwin, Sydney, 1983.

Fewster, K., Basarin, V. & H. H., *Gallipoli: the Turkish Story*, 2nd edition, Allen & Unwin, Crows Nest, 2003.

Godley, General Sir A., *Life of an Irish Soldier*, John Murray, London, 1939.

Hamilton, General Sir I., *Gallipoli Diary*, Volumes 1 and 2, Edward Arnold, London, 1920.

Harper, B. (ed.), *Letters from Gunner 7/516 and Gunner 7/517*, Anchor Communications Ltd, Wellington, 1978.

Harper, G., *Spring Offensive: New Zealand and the Second Battle of the Somme*, HarperCollins, Wellington, 2003.

Harper, G. (ed.), *Letters from the Battlefield: New Zealand Soldiers Write Home 1914–18*, HarperCollins, Auckland, 2001.

Hill, A. J., *Chauvel of the Light Horse: a Biography of General Sir Harry Chauvel, G.C.M.G., K.C.B.*, Melbourne University Press, Melbourne, 1978.

Holden, D., *The New Zealand Horseman*, A.H. & A.W. Reed, Wellington, 1967.

Idriess, I., *The Desert Column: Leaves from the Diary of an Australian Trooper in Gallipoli, Sinai & Palestine*, Angus & Robertson, Sydney, 2nd edition, 1951.

James, R.R., *Gallipoli*, Papermac edition, London, 1989.

Laffin, J., *Damn the Dardanelles! the Story of Gallipoli*, Doubleday, Sydney, 1980.

Lee, J., *A Soldier's Life: General Sir Ian Hamilton 1853–1947*, Macmillan, London, 2000.

Liddle, P., *Men of Gallipoli: the Dardanelles and Gallipoli Experience August 1914 to January 1916*, Allen Lane, London, 1976.

Malthus, C., *Anzac: a Retrospect*, Whitcombe & Tombs Ltd, Christchurch, 1965.

Mackenzie, C. N. (ed.), *Chronicles of the NZEF, Volume 1, 30 August 1916 to 14 February 1917*, NZ Contingent Association, London, 1917.

Mackenzie, C. N., *The Tale of a Trooper*, John Lane, London, 1921.

McGibbon, I., *Blue-Water Rationale: the Naval Defence of New Zealand 1914–1942*, Government Printer, Wellington, 1981.

McGibbon, I., *The Path to Gallipoli: Defending New Zealand 1840–1915*, GP Books, Wellington, 1991.

McGibbon, I. (ed.), *The Oxford Companion to New Zealand Military History*, Oxford University Press, Auckland, 2000.

Moorehead, A., *Gallipoli*, Andre Deutsch, London, 1989.

New Zealand at the Dardanelles, Christchurch Press, 1915.

New Zealand's Roll of Honour 1915: the Auckland Weekly News Illustrated List, Wilson & Horton, Auckland, 1915.

Nicol, Sergeant C. G, *The Story of Two Campaigns: Official War History of the Auckland Mounted Rifles Regiment, 1914–1919*, Wilson & Horton, Auckland, 1931.

Phillips, J., Boyack, N., & Malone, E. P. (eds), *The Great Adventure: New Zealand Soldiers Describe the First World War*, Allen & Unwin, Wellington, 1988.

Powles, Lieutenant Colonel C. G., *The New Zealanders in Sinai and Palestine*, Whitcombe & Tombs, Auckland, 1922.

Powles, Colonel C.G. (ed.), and Officers of the Regiment, *The History of the Canterbury Mounted Rifles 1914–1919*, Whitcombe & Tombs, Auckland, 1928.

Pugsley, C., *Gallipoli: the New Zealand Story*, Hodder & Stoughton, Auckland, 1984.

Pugsley, C., *On the Fringe of Hell: New Zealanders and Military Discipline in the First World War*, Hodder & Stoughton, Auckland, 1991.

Pugsley, C., Barber, L., Mikaere, B., Prickett. N., and Young, R., *Scars on the Heart: Two Centuries of New Zealanders at War*, Auckland Museum/David Bateman Ltd., Auckland, 1996.

Pugsley, C., *The Anzac Experience: New Zealand, Australia and Empire in the First World War*, Reed Books, Auckland, 2004.

Robertson, J., *Anzac and Empire: the Tragedy & Glory of Gallipoli*, Leo Cooper, London, 1990.

Rodenbeck, M., *Cairo: the City Victorious*, Alfred A. Knopf, New York, 1999.

Shadbolt, M., *Voices of Gallipoli*, Hodder & Stoughton, Auckland, 1988.

Smith, Lieutenant Colonel N., *Men of Beersheba: a History of the 4th Light Horse Regiment 1914–1919*, Mostly Unsung Military Research & Publications, Melbourne, 1993.

Steel, N. & Hart, P., *Defeat at Gallipoli*, Papermac, London, 1995.

Stevens, K.M., *Maungatapere: a History and Reminiscence*, Whangarei Advocate, 1973.

Strachan, H., *The First World War: Volume 1, To Arms*, Oxford University Press, Oxford, 2001.

The Times History of the War, Volume 13, The Times, London, 1917.

Thornton, G., *With the Anzacs in Cairo: the Tale of a Great Fight*, H. R. Allenson Ltd, London, 1916.

Tobin, C., *Gone to Gallipoli: Anzacs of Small Town New Zealand go to War*, Boscoe Press, Timaru, 2001.

Tolerton, J., *Ettie: a Life of Ettie Rout*, Penguin Books, Auckland, 1992.

Townsend, C., *Gallipoli 1915: From the Uttermost Ends of the Earth*, 2nd edition, Patricia Townsend, Paeroa, 2000.

Travers, T., *Gallipoli 1915*, Tempus Publishing, Stroud, 2002.

Waite, Major F., *The New Zealanders at Gallipoli*, Whitcombe & Tombs, Auckland, 1919.

Wavell, Lieutenant General Sir A. P., *The Palestine Campaigns*, Constable, London, 3rd edition, 1941.

Wilkie, Major A.H., *Official War History of the Wellington Mounted Rifles Regiment, 1914–1919*, Whitcombe & Tombs, Auckland, 1924.

Williams. P., *A New Zealander's Diary: Gallipoli and France 1915–1917*, 2nd edition, Cadsonbury Publications, Christchurch, 1998.

Wilson, Brigadier General L. C., and Wetherell, Captain H., *History of the Fifth Light Horse Regiment (Australian Imperial Force), from 1914 to October 1917, and from October 1917 to June 1919*, Motor Press of Australia, Sydney, 1926.

Articles

Babington, Colonel J. M., 'The Mounted Men of New Zealand, Past and Present', *The Cavalry Journal*, Volume 2, July 1907, pp. 281–6.

Bauchop, Colonel A., 'The Mounted Man in New Zealand', *The Cavalry Journal*, Volume 3, January 1908, pp. 56–9.

Bauchop, Lieutenant Colonel A., 'The New Zealand Mounted Rifles', *The Cavalry Journal*, Volume 9, January 1914, pp. 93–6.

Godley, Major General A. J., 'The Making of the New Zealand Citizen Army', *The Army Review*, October 1913, pp. 319–28.

Godley, Major General A. J., 'The New Zealand Mounted Rifles', *The Cavalry Journal*, Volume 8, 1913, pp. 464–6.

Pugsley, C., 'Russell: Commander of Genius', *New Zealand Defence Quarterly*, Summer 1998, pp. 25–9.

Slater, Colonel H., 'Development of the New Zealand Mounted Rifles', *New Zealand Military Journal*, January 1912, pp. 78–85.

Non-Written Material

Commonwealth War Graves Commission (CWGC) fact sheets dated 2001, URL: http://www.cwgc.org/cwgc/task.htm

Grover, R., 'Meldrum, William 1865–1964', *Dictionary of New Zealand Biography*, updated 16 December 2003, URL: http://www.dnzdb.govt.nz/

Green, D., 'Mackesy, Charles Ernest Randolph 1861–1925', *Dictionary of New Zealand Biography*, updated 16 December 2003, URL: http://www.dnzdb.govt.nz/

Acknowledgements: photographs and maps

Photographs and maps in this book have been obtained from the following sources:

Photographs

Alexander Turnbull Library: pp. 33 (Mackesy), 49, 139, 164, 184, 262; S.P. Andrew Collection: p. 33 (Meldrum); R.W. Crofter Collection: p. 117; Gill Denniston Collection: pp. 225, 238; *Evening Post* Collection: p. 33 (Russell); Field-Dodgson Collection: p. 214; W.A. Hampton Collection: p. 228; Powles Family Collection: pp. 144, 253; *The Press* (Christchurch) Collection: p. 54; J.C. Read Collection: pp. 124-5 (montage courtesy of Andrew Caldwell, *New Zealand Geographic*), 154, 197 (and front cover), 241, 246; Schmidt Collection: p. 23; Strand Collection, Kapiti Public Library: p. 43; H.N. Whitehead Collection: p. 45; C. Athol Williams Collection: pp. 158, 167, 192, 235.

Australian War Memorial: pp. 40, 58, 60, 87, 88, 104, 122, 126, 127, 169, 171, 191, 193, 199, 237, 250, 254, 257, 261, 266.

Author: pp. 119, 138, 153, 155, 196, 209, 231, 249.

Kippenberger Military Archive, Army Museum, Waiouru: pp. 33 (Bauchop), 62, 65, 66, 67, 70, 76, 91, 92, 123, 132, 142, 179, 195, 204, 205, 226, 227, 277.

New Zealand Herald: pp. 48, 81.

New Zealand's Roll of Honour 1915; The Auckland Weekly News Illustrated List: pp. 75, 121, 134, 150, 151, 162, 176, 177, 190, 202, 211, 216, 223, 243, 245, 248.

C.G. Nicol, *The Story of Two Campaigns: Official War History of the Auckland Mounted Rifles Regiment 1914-1919*: pp. 247, 270.

C.G. Powles, *The History of the Canterbury Mounted Rifles 1914-1919*: pp. 33 (Findlay), 115, 147.

Lynda Young: p. 36.

Maps

C.E.W. Bean, *The Official History of Australia in the War of 1914-1918, Volume 2*: pp. 133, 152, 194, 242 (adapted with permission of Australian War Memorial).

Andrew Caldwell / *New Zealand Geographic*: pp. 102, 108, 183.

Ian McGibbon, *The Oxford Companion to New Zealand Military History*, Oxford University Press, Australia: pp. 56, 275 (adapted with permission).

F. Waite, *The New Zealanders at Gallipoli*: pp. 71, 114, 234 (adapted).

Index

Note: Page numbers in *italics* refer to photographs.

1st (Canterbury Yeomanry Cavalry)
Mounted Rifles

Queen Alexandra's 2nd (Wellington West Coast)
Mounted Rifles

5th (Otago Hussars) Mounted Rifles

6th (Manawatu) Mounted Rifles

9th (Wellington East Coast) Mounted Rifles

10th (Nelson) Mounted Rifles